THE NATURE

OF THE

ATONEMENT

J. McLeod Campbell

WITH A NEW INTRODUCTION BY

JAMES B. TORRANCE

Wipf & Stock
PUBLISHERS
Eugene, Oregon

The original work was published in 1856 by MacMillan at Cambridge with no
introduction. A copy of that edition, and subsequent ones, is in the National
Library of Scotland, Edinburgh (I.I.3/2 and 4/2). This new edition includes
McLeod Campbell's introduction to the second edition, and is published in 1996
in the U.K. by
The Handsel Press Ltd,
The Stables, Carberry, EH21 8PY, Scotland

[Nature of the atonement and its relation to remission of sins and eternal life]
The nature of the Atonement / J. McLeod Campbell;
with a new introduction by James B. Torrance.

Wipf and Stock Publishers
199 West 8th Avenue, Suite 3
Eugene, Oregon 97401

The Nature of The Atonement
By Campbell, J. McLeod
Copyright©1996 Eerdmans Publishing Co.
ISBN: 1-57910-320-0
Publication date 12/16/1999
Previously published by Eerdmans Publishing Co., 1996

Thanks are expressed to Linda Elston for her skilled and sensitive typing of the whole
text and introduction; to Agnes Llano for other secretarial assistance; to David Wright
and Michael Jinkins for advice on text and sources of quotations; and to the National
Library of Scotland.

CONTENTS

The Atonement presupposes the incarnation of which it is the development,
yet some believe in the incarnation who do not believe in the Atonement.
Two hindrances to faith in the Atonement --
    (1) Views of human progress
    (2) Views of the Reign of Law
Two regions of divine self-manifestation --
    (1) The Reign of Law (2) The kingdom of God
The place which prayer has in the kingdom of God
Theism and religion
The kingdom of God seen in Christ
Miracles considered
The Atonement belongs to the kingdom of God

THE ENDS CONTEMPLATED IN THE ATONEMENT
AWAKEN THE EXPECTATION THAT WE ARE
TO UNDERSTAND ITS NATURE --
Three aspects of the Atonement: its extent, object and nature
The third aspect now to be considered
Reasonableness of the demand for light on this subject
Twofold aspect of the Gospel, retrospective and prospective
Importance of the internal evidence of the Atonement
Conscience testifies to a need be for an Atonement
Further, there is in conscience --
    (1) A response to the testimony of Scripture as to the evil of *sin*
    (2) A capacity of apprehending the excellence of *Eternal Life*
Difficulty of habitually realising these two opposite states
Importance of doing so in studying this subject
Belief that there is forgiveness with God, the first demand of the Gospel
This belief found difficult by the awakened conscience
The doctrine of the Atonement alone meets this difficulty
This doctrine, however, involves difficulties of another kind
Due prominence has not been given to the prospective aspect of the
        Atonement
The righteousness as well as the love of God a ground of hope

True meaning of being "washed in the blood of Christ"
A moral and spiritual atonement, when understood, is seen
       to be a perfect expiation for man's sin
It is also the light of life to us

(2) Our reconciliation to God *must* have this origin
True significance of the words, "The Father sent the Son"
The faith that God is the Father of our spirits has as deep a root in us as
    the faith that there is a God
A similar faith belongs to the two great results of the Atonement,
    Sonship and Brotherhood
1.   *Sonship towards God*
Examination of the view that "adoption" rests upon a legal justification
"Have I a right to call God Father?" this question considered
As faith excludes boasting so does the confidence of sonship exclude
    self-righteousness
Luther's teaching as to faith superior to that of the Calvinists
But, as to sonship, he falls short of the Apostles' teaching
Possible objections to the present teaching
Progress of mind often experienced in reference to this subject
Bearing of these thoughts on the doctrine of Baptismal Regeneration
2.   *Brotherhood towards men*
Brotherhood fulfils the second commandment
We cannot be in Christ the sons of God if we refuse to be in Christ
    the brothers of men
It is in the death of self that the life of God is quickened

SOME NOTES ON THIS EDITION

There is considerable confusion over the number of editions of *The Nature of the Atonement and its Relation to Remission of Sins and Eternal Life* - as the full title originally was. I am indebted to David F. Wright of New College, Edinburgh, for much of the following information.

The first edition, published by Macmillan and Co. at Cambridge, is dated 1856. It contains no introductory material of any kind.* The 'Contents' list only the main chapter titles, without synopsis. The pagination is 1-382, followed by two unnumbered pages for the 'List of Books...'. The print run was 1000 copies.

The 'Second Edition with an Introduction and Notes' was published in 1867 by Macmillan, now in London. The list of contents is unchanged except for including the Introduction (occupying pp.ix-xl) and four Notes (pp.387-410). The text occupies pp.1-385, and the List of Books pp.411-412. Campbell said of this second edition, on Nov. 9th 1867: "The book itself is almost a simple reprint, but I hope that the introduction and notes add to the value of the volume." (*Memorials*, vol. II, p.182) There appears to be no change in the text itself, the difference in pagination being the result of resetting the type.

The 'third edition' of 1869 was again published by Macmillan in London., but printed (as was the 'second edition') by Robert Maclehose of Ayr. Campbell referred once to its good sales (*Memorials* vol.II, p.269). The List of Contents now provides the detailed breakdown retained by all subsequent printings. The Introduction consequently shifts to pp.xiii-xliv, but the pagination of the rest is identical with 1867. Campbell died on Feb. 27th 1872, and so had nothing to do with any subsequent printings.

The 'fourth edition' of 1873 reset the book entirely, without the List of Books. The 'fifth edition' of 1878 introduced the format and pagination that survived through the sixth edition of 1886 and its reprintings of 1895, 1906 and 1915. The Introduction is pp.xvi-xl, the text pp.1-329, the Notes pp.330-355, and there is again a List of Books. All these are by Macmillan, London.

The so-called 'Fourth Edition' of 1959 with an Introduction by E.P. Dickie (London, James Clarke) reproduces the 'third edition' of 1869, with Dickie's Introduction on pp.xiii-xx and Campbell's Introduction on pp.xxi-lii.

There are therefore, strictly speaking, only two editions of the work, that of 1856 and 1867. This present book is likewise more of a reprint than a new edition, apart from the new Introduction by Professor James Torrance, and the indices. The only change I have made to the text, apart from minor grammatical updating, is to break up some of the dense paragraphs to make them more readable. The footnotes in chapters 3 and 4 are from research by Michael Jinkins of Austin Presbyterian Seminary in Texas, and David Wright.

Jock Stein

---

* Campbell returned "the last sheet of the proof" on Christmas Day, 1855 - *Memorials of John McLeod Campbell*, London 1877, vol. I p.268. "I have also given up the attempt to do anything in the way of preparing my reader's mind by a preface", *ibid.*

INTRODUCTION

From the history of Christian thought we can see that our doctrine of God determines our understanding both of the doctrine of atonement and of the nature of Christian assurance. If our basic concept of God is primarily that of the Lawgiver (interpreted in terms of the Latin concept of *Lex*, law of contract, as in Western jurisprudence) then our doctrine of atonement will imply that God has to be conditioned into being gracious, either by human merit, or by Christ satisfying the conditions of such a law that the Father might be gracious to the elect, as in certain forms of scholastic Calvinism. This can also lead to a stress on the conditions we must fulfil or the evidences of repentance we must show if we are to enjoy any assurance of salvation.

Conversely, however, if our basic concept of God is that of the Triune God of grace who has being in communion as Father, Son and Holy Spirit, and who has created us to share that life of communion, then our doctrine of atonement will be seen rather as God in grace bringing these loving purposes to fulfilment in redemption. In love God created us for 'sonship', to find our true being-in-communion, and in Jesus Christ gives us that gift of communion, through the Spirit, of being daughters and sons of the Father. God in grace in the person of the Son, comes to stand in for us, to bring to fulfilment those loving filial purposes by fulfilling the promises and the law for us, and in love submitting to the condemnation of the law for us. Law is then seen, not as some impersonal law of contract, but rather (as in Torah in the Bible) as spelling out the unconditional obligations of grace as the Father's loving heart coming out to us in the form of commandments, and Christ is then seen as the Father's loving heart coming out to us in the fulfilling of that law. On such a view we see the priority of grace over law, the filial over the judicial, and that God is a covenant-God of faithfulness, not a contract-God. Then Christian assurance, on this second, Trinitarian, view is God's gift to God's children where we look away from ourselves to what we are in the loving heart of the Father and what we are by grace in the gift of Christ the Son, through the Spirit of adoption.

No Scottish theologian saw this more clearly than John McLeod Campbell (1800-1872), who from his earliest days in the parish ministry and throughout all his writings was so passionately concerned to call the Church back to the Triune God of grace in a land where he felt so much 'religion' was moulded by concepts of God which owed more to some 'light of nature' where God is conceived primarily as Lawgiver and Judge, than to the 'light of revelation', where the Father makes himself known in the Son, and lifts us by the Spirit into a life of shared communion.

He is most widely known because of the General Assembly proceedings against him on the charge of heresy, which led to his deposition from the ministry of the Church of Scotland in 1831, and because of his book *The Nature of the Atonement* (1856), which, with Athanasius' *De Incarnatione* and Anselm's *Cur Deus Homo*, is one of the classics of all time on this doctrine.

He was born in 1800 in Argyllshire, the son of a minister, educated in Glasgow University and Divinity Hall, and in May 1825 was presented by the Duke of Argyll to the Parish of Rhu (Row) in Dumbartonshire, where he spent the next five years as devoted pastor and preacher. It was while he was there that objections were made to his teaching on assurance, leading to charges being brought against him, and found proven, first by the Presbytery of Dumbarton in March 1831, then by the Synod of Glasgow and Ayr in April 1831, and finally by the General Assembly in May 1831 - resulting in his deposition from the holy ministry.

The charges against him declared that:

> ...*the doctrine of universal atonement* and pardon through the death of Christ, as also the doctrine that *assurance is of the essence of faith* and necessary for salvation are contrary to the Holy Scripture and to the Confession of Faith approven by the General Assemblies of the Church of Scotland, and ratified by law in the year sixteen hundred and ninety: and were moreover condemned by the fifth act of the General Assembly held in seventeen hundred and twenty, as being directly opposed to the Word of God, and to the Confession of Faith and Catechisms of the Church of Scotland... (*Proceedings* I, p. 1)

That is, he was charged with teaching two doctrines, 'universal atonement' and 'assurance of faith' - doctrines which were said to be contrary to Holy Scripture, the Westminster Confession of Faith, and the Act of the General Assembly of 1720 (condemning the teaching of the book *The Marrow of Modern Divinity*).

What was it that led him to assert these two doctrines? In his *Reminiscences and Reflections* he tells us that it was in the first instance the **pastoral situation** in which he found himself, the attitudes of his people, and their understanding of the Christian Gospel.

Secondly, it was certain aspects of scholastic or so-called federal Calvinism, which had come to be the orthodox view of the Church, but which he felt were a departure from **the teaching of the New Testament**. It was the first (the religious attitude of the people) which led him to scrutinise the kind of Calvinism that had moulded their thinking. We cannot read Campbell's writings without being aware that here is a godly man with the heart of a pastor and an evangelical concern to instruct his flock in the Gospel of grace. His theology is one hammered out on the anvil of the parish ministry.

One of the first things he discovered in Rhu was his people's lack of any kind of Christian assurance. Whereas the New Testament rings with the note of assurance, and the imperatives of the Gospel flow from the Apostles' understanding of the indicatives of the Gospel, among his people he found little evidence of peace and joy and confidence in God. The more he thought about this, the more he became convinced it was due to a 'legal strain' in their thinking that led to a want of true religion in the land. Although his people professed belief in the Gospel, in fact he says:

> I came to see that, in reality, whatever I preached, they were only hearing a *demand on them to be* - not hearing the Divine Secret of the Gospel as to how to be — *that which they were called to be*. Of this they themselves had no suspicions; they said, and honestly, that they did not question Christ's power to save, neither did they doubt the freeness of the Gospel or Christ's willingness to save them: *all their doubts were as to themselves. (Reminiscences and Reflections*, p. 132)

In other words, deep in their thinking was a **doctrine of conditional grace** - 'only if we do this, and don't do that, can we come to the enjoyment of salvation'.

> This meant, it was clear, that between them and the comfort of the consciousness of a personal possession of Christ as Saviour they were vaguely conscious of a something by which they were to make Christ their own - a *condition* proposed to them, the consciousness of compliance with which, would introduce them to the enjoyment of salvation. This something they attempted to speak of as *repentance, faith or love*, or 'being good enough', which last expression gave really the secret of their difficulty. Christ was to be the reward of some goodness - not 'perfect' goodness but, some goodness that would sustain a personal hope of acceptance in drawing near to him. In this mind, the Gospel was practically a law, and the call to trust in Christ only an addition to the demand that the law makes - an additional duty added to the obligation to love God and to love man, not the secret of the power to love God and to love man. Seeing this clearly, my labour was to fix their attention on the love of God revealed in Christ, and to get them into the mental attitude of looking at God to learn his feelings towards them, not at themselves, to consider their feelings towards him. (*op. cit.* pp.132-133)

That is, he made it his concern to summon them to look away from themselves - to the love of God, that they might know him as Father and discover there is forgiveness in God, and that God's grace, which certainly lays costly unconditional claims upon us, is not conditioned by considerations of worth and merit. Repentance, faith and love, are not conditions of grace, but our *response* to grace, and the way to evoke that response is to hold out to people the love of the Father, the grace of the Lord Jesus Christ, and the promises of the Spirit - and this is the road to *assurance*.

The other thing that led to his people's lack of assurance and joy, was **the high Calvinist doctrine of election,** the concept of a double decree - the doctrine that Christ did not die for all humanity, but only for some, the elect. Deep down, his people were tortured by the question, 'Yes, Christ died on the cross to bring forgiveness, but did he die for me? Am I one of the elect? Have I any grounds for believing that God loves me?' Consequently, they looked inward to their own subjective experience to see if they could discern the fruits of faith - 'evidences' of the work of the Spirit. Hadn't Jesus said, 'By their fruits ye shall know them?' The Calvinist preachers had taught them to *repent* of their sins, and that only if they came under deep conviction of sin, and renounced them, could they have grounds for claiming the blessings of the Gospel, and believing they were among the elect.

In other words, the doctrine of a limited atonement ploughed into a legalism and an inward looking attitude which cut away the possibility of finding the 'assurance of faith':

> This led [me] directly to the closer consideration of the *extent of the atonement*, and the circumstances in which mankind had been placed in the shedding of the blood of Christ; and it soon appeared to me manifest that unless Christ had died *for all*, and unless the Gospel announced him as the *gift of God to every human being*, so that there remained nothing to be done to give the individual a title to rejoice in Christ as his own Saviour, there was no foundation in the record of God for the Assurance which I demanded, and which I saw to be essential to true holiness. The next step, therefore, was my teaching (as the subject matter of the Gospel) Universal Atonement and pardon through the blood of Christ. (*op. cit.* p.24)

Campbell saw that fundamental to the whole issue was the doctrine of God. Instead of thinking of God as the Father, who loves all humanity, and who in Christ gives us the gift of sonship and who freely forgives us through Jesus Christ, they thought of God as One whose love is conditioned by human repentance and faith, and whose forgiveness had to be purchased by the payment of the sufferings of Christ on behalf of the elect.

> Instead of resting in the character of God as revealed in Christ, they looked upon the death of Christ as so much suffering - the purchase money of heaven to a certain number, to whom it infallibly secured heaven. (*op. cit.* p.25)

They saw God as a contract-god who needs to be conditioned into being gracious.

McLeod Campbell was disturbed at the fierce opposition to this teaching, and the false misrepresentation of his view as universalism, antinomianism, etc.... 'Such opposition made more and more apparent to me the want of true religion in the land.' There was a loss of the Gospel of Grace.

His teaching about assurance, and universal atonement, led him consequently into conflict with federal Calvinism - as expounded in a mild form in the Westminster Confession of Faith, and as widely preached and taught in Scotland.

What then is Federal Calvinism, and what are the features in it which, for Campbell, obscure the New Testament meaning of Grace?*

Federal Calvinism developed at the end of the sixteenth and particularly in the seventeenth century in England and Scotland - as well as in Holland and New England. It is that form of theology which gave central place to the concept of *covenant*, and which distinguished different covenants in God's relation to the world, and made out of them a framework within which all theology is cast. In particular, it made a hard and fast distinction between the so-called *Covenant of Works* or *Covenant of Nature* and the *Covenant of Grace*.

According to this scheme, God made Adam the child of nature, who could discern the laws of nature by the light of reason. On the basis of this, he entered into a covenant or contract with him (the so-called Covenant of Works) that if he obeyed the laws of nature (which are the laws of God) and fulfilled the conditions of the Covenant, he would find eternal life. This is the *foedus naturale* - the contract of nature upon which all society is based. Adam as such is not a private individual but the federal head of the race. Thus when he disobeyed, he brought the curse not only on himself, but all for whom he contracted. But God in his sovereign grace does not destroy the human race, but elects out of the mass of fallen humanity a number for himself and makes a covenant of grace for them in Christ. God then calls the elect by his Spirit and brings them to saving faith by the instrumentality of Word and Sacrament, the signs and seals of the Covenant of Grace.

This distinction between a Covenant of Works and a Covenant of Grace was unknown to Calvin and the Reformers - nor indeed would Calvin have ever taught it. For Calvin there has been only *one eternal Covenant of Grace* promised in the Old Testament and fulfilled in Christ. 'Old' and 'New' do not mean two covenants, but two forms of the one eternal covenant:

> God has never made any other covenant than that which he made formerly with Abraham. (Calvin on Jeremiah 31.31-35)

---

* See *The Concept of Federal Theology - Was Calvin a Federal Theologian?* in *Calvinus Sacrae Scripturae. Calvin as Confessor Holy Scripture* (ed. W.H.Neuser) - paper by James B.Torrance to the International Congress of Calvin Research 1990 (Eerdmans, Grand Rapids 1994). Also Michael Jinkins, *A Comparative Study in the Theology of Atonement* in *Jonathan Edwards and John McLeod Campbell, Atonement and the Character of God* (Mellen Research University Press, San Francisco 1993).

The first person to use the phrase 'Covenant of Works' in Scotland was
Robert Rollock, the first Principal of Edinburgh University, in a work
published in 1596. It had already been used in England by the English
Puritan, Dudley Fenner, about 1585, and William Perkins in 1590. The
Westminster Confession of Faith (with the Larger and Shorter Catechism)
was the first reformed Confession to embody the federal scheme.

It is beyond the scope of this *Introduction* to expand on the theme of the
rise and development of federal theology - but we can single out those
features of it which led McLeod Campbell to break with the scheme.

(1) The whole federal scheme is built upon the deep-seated confusion
between a *covenant* and a *contract*. Whereas a covenant (theologically
speaking) is a promise in which two people or two parties bind themselves
to *love* one another *unconditionally* (as in the marriage covenant), a contract
is a *legal* relationship in which two people or two parties bind themselves
together on mutual *conditions* - as in business and political contracts. No
doubt a covenant and a contract mean the same thing in Scots law (e.g. 'deed
of covenant') and in political philosophy (e.g. 'social contract') but in
theology they must be carefully distinguished. The God of the Bible, the
God and Father of our Lord Jesus Christ is a covenant-God, and not a
contract-God. God's covenant brings its promises, its obligations and its
warnings. But the obligations of grace are *not* conditions of grace, and it is
false in Christian theology to articulate moral obligation in contractual
terms. It is no accident that with the rise of federal theology the *question of
assurance* became a highly problematic one, as in the Marrow controversy in
the early eighteenth century, when Thomas Boston wrote in his diary:

> I perceived I had no fondness for the doctrine of the conditionality of
> the covenant of grace.

Indeed Boston set out to reinterpret the federal scheme to show that the
Covenant of Grace is an unconditional covenant of love made for the elect
in Christ. But he still held to the doctrine of the Covenant of Works made
with Adam.

(2) The federal scheme made a *radical dichotomy between the sphere of nature
and the scheme of grace*, of natural law and Gospel. All people by nature stand
related to God, the contracting sovereign, as to a *judge*, under natural law and
exposed to the sanctions of law. Only the elect are related to God by grace
through Christ the Mediator. The relationship between Church and the
world, Church and state, is no longer understood Christologically as by
Calvin and Knox, but in terms of Gospel and natural law. This separation
between nature and grace amounts to a reversion to the pre-Reformation
medieval view that grace presupposes nature - and *grace perfects nature* - a
departure from the great emphasis of the Reformation that nothing is prior
to grace.

(3) As a result the federal scheme, with the doctrine of a double decree, thrust up the doctrine of a *limited atonement*, that Christ only died for the elect - a doctrine or a conclusion unknown to Calvin. The consequence of this doctrine is twofold:

(a) The doctrine implies a loss of the notion of Christ's headship over all creation as Mediator, his solidarity with all humanity as the Head of the race, as in the theology of Ephesians and Colossians or as expounded by Irenaeus, Athanasius and the Cappadocian divines as well as by Calvin. The emphasis in doctrine is no longer on the Incarnation, on Christ's solidarity with all humanity, but almost exclusively on Christ's *work* on behalf of the elect, his passive obedience on the cross and satisfaction for the sins of believers, with whom he stands related, not in terms of incarnational oneness - but of *foedus*, contract. As a consequence, the older doctrine which interpreted faith in terms of 'Union with Christ the Head' and 'Participation in Christ' is replaced by a more judicial interpretation of faith, as Thomas Boston saw.

(b) Limited atonement also means that you cannot say to all people unequivocally, 'Christ died for you'. But what you can say to all people is, 'You are all under the law. You are all guilty and under judgment.' What you can then say to all people without exception is 'Repent!' (an imperative). Then, if in fact they do repent, we can take that as *evidence* of election and grace, and hold out the comforts of the Gospel! It was in these terms that Principal Hadow of St Andrews attacked the Marrowmen who held that Christ should be offered freely to all, even if Christ did not die for all. Christ is 'God's deed of gift to all mankind'. But as the Marrowmen saw this approach made forgiveness conditional on repentance, and gave priority to the preaching of the Law over the preaching of the Gospel, and bred a deep lack of assurance. When the Marrowmen said that, they were condemned in 1720, and in 1831 the General Assembly interpreted McLeod Campbell's views as a reassertion of those condemned in 1720.

(4) In the federal scheme, the focus of attention moves away from *what Christ has done for us* and for all humanity to *what we have to do* IF we would be (or know that we are) in covenant with God. For preaching, this means that the emphasis falls less on the indicatives of grace and more on the imperatives of repentance, obedience and faith. Baptism and the Lord's Supper are seen, not so much as seals of the Gospel (as evangelical or 'converting ordinances' - as in the older Scottish tradition, an interpretation rejected by George Gillespie) - but rather as seals of our *faith*, or seals of our *repentance*. Where this shift of emphasis occurs, then sacraments become badges of *our* personal covenant and the Lord's Table becomes a feast of the converted, of the penitent. With the emergence of this changed emphasis, the fencing of the table and catechising assume a different significance in the discipline of the Church, as stressing the need for repentance and faith as *conditions* for coming to the Lord's Table, which had become such a hallmark of Scottish Calvinism.

In each of these four negative evaluations of the federal scheme, we can see **an impoverishment and restriction of the concept of grace** - a shift of emphasis from what God has so freely and unconditionally done for all humanity in Christ, to a more *subjective* interest in what *we* have to do - to our need for repentance, personal covenanting, obedience, subjective grounds for assurance - a preoccupation with election and the *evidences* of election.

We can begin to see something of McLeod Campbell's concern to reinterpret in more biblical and New Testament terms the meaning of grace as the Father's gift of his Son to the world, who on behalf of all humanity in our humanity has fulfilled for us all God's holy requirements, and in whose vicarious life and intercession we are freely given to participate through the Holy Spirit.

We can also see how McLeod Campbell was led to see that here was one of the *root* causes of the lack of joy and assurance in Scottish religion. Already by 1827, after only two years in the parish ministry, Campbell, in his concern to be faithful to the Gospel of grace, felt the need to preach less on the imperatives of the Gospel, and the need for repentance in the decision of faith - on 'experience' - and more on the Person and atoning Work of Jesus Christ in order to bring his people to authentic faith and assurance. He sees that more important than our experience of Christ is the Christ of our personal experience, the Christ in whom we are lifted up by the Spirit, out of ourselves into a life of sonship and joy, in communion with the Father.

We can summarise his critique of federal Calvinism on this score:

(1) He saw that the doctrine of a 'limited atonement' destroyed the Gospel offer to all humanity, and undermined the basis of the assurance of faith. The Marrowmen a century before in their concern to recover the doctrine of the assurance of faith, had seen that the New Testament gives us a warrant to offer the Gospel to all people - to preach grace to all. But they still held to the doctrine of a limited atonement in the federal scheme. McLeod Campbell came to see, that you can only offer the Gospel to all people if indeed it *is* good news for all people - that Christ died for all. Only then can we have an adequate ground for rejoicing in God and calling on others to rejoice in God.

(2) The doctrine of election - as so expounded - turns our attention away from God the Father and Jesus Christ the Son to *ourselves*, to the question of 'evidences' and the consideration of our own repentance and faith and holiness as grounds for inference that we might be among the elect.

(3) McLeod Campbell saw - as in his discussion of the views of John Owen and Jonathan Edwards in *The Nature of the Atonement* - that the doctrine of God was at stake. In the federal scheme, the justice of God *is* the essential attribute, and the love of God (or mercy of God) is an arbitrary attribute. All people are necessarily related to God as Judge in the framework of law, but only the elect are related to God by his love and mercy. The demands of

justice must be met before God can be merciful and this he does by providing One in Jesus who satisfies the demands of justice on behalf of the elect, in virtue of which there is forgiveness and salvation for these in whose stead Christ died.

This McLeod Campbell rejected. God is love as truly as he is just, and God is related to all humanity as Father in holy love as well as in justice. Indeed there is no divorce between holy love and justice in God. His justice is his holy love in action - his righteousness. Campbell saw that the doctrine of a limited atonement cuts away the basis of our assertion that *God is love* in his innermost Being. It is a fundamental axiom in Christian theology, that what God is towards us, He is eternally and antecedently in himself. So the early Church rejected Sabellianism. Because God reveals himself to humanity as Father, Son and Holy Spirit, he is Father, Son and Holy Spirit in himself.

The doctrine of limited atonement runs into the same problems. God is loving towards some people but not towards other people. If so, there is an arbitrariness in God and we have no warrant for believing that God is love in *himself*. We are left asking, 'Yes, the Bible says God loves the world - but doesn't that mean the elect of all nations? Does he love me? Perhaps, God in himself in the secret counsels of eternity is different to me from what He appears to be towards the elect.' Consequently, we have no grounds in the Fatherly heart of God for peace and assurance and for rejoicing in God. But this Campbell was convinced we do have in the teaching of the New Testament. Jesus, the true Son of the Father, in his 'oneness of mind with the Father', has declared to *all* humanity, the love of the Father.

(4) The federal scheme, in its doctrine of atonement and penal substitution (as expounded there) inverts the biblical order of the relationship between forgiveness and atonement. In the teaching of the Bible, *there is forgiveness in God our Father* who loves his world, and because there is forgiveness, he offers us a way of atonement and propitiation in Christ to cover our sins. In the federal scheme, that order is inverted. There can only be forgiveness of sins for the elect when atonement has been first made - and, because of the priority of retributive justice, there must be an equivalence of sufferings in Christ to the sufferings due as the just penalty for the sins of the elect, before forgiveness can be held out to the elect as the *reward* for the sufferings of Christ.

In other words, the Father has to be conditioned into being gracious by the obedience and the satisfaction of the Son - a view which Calvin in the *Institutes*, following St Augustine, had explicitly rejected. Atonement, Calvin argued, flows from the loving, forgiving heart of the Father (*Inst.* 2.xvi.4). (The extreme form of this kind of Calvinism comes in the three-fold federal scheme - covenant of works, covenant of redemption, and covenant of grace - taught by Samuel Rutherford, David Dickson and James Durham, and expounded in *The Sum of Saving Knowledge*.)

(5) The federal scheme, with its priority of justice over love, consequently (McLeod Campbell argued) gives priority to the *judicial* over the *filial*. It comes to the New Testament, to the study of theology, with a prior framework - a set of doctrines about the nature of God, the nature of justice, the need for the penalties of the law being met as a condition of forgiveness - with the result that the *filial* categories, the filial purposes of the Father for humanity, are, if not eclipsed, pushed into the background, in a way that is not true to the New Testament.

In the Bible, God is the Father who created all to be 'sons', and in order to fulfil his filial purposes for humanity, sends his Son to become our brother, to make the Father known to humanity, to lead us to the Father, and to give us the Spirit of adoption, the Spirit of his Son, whereby we cry, 'Abba Father'. God's end for humanity is that through the Holy Spirit we might participate in the Son's communion with the Father (which worship is) but to secure that end - to accomplish it - he provides a way of atonement. So in theology, Campbell argues, we must not think of Incarnation as simply the necessary means toward atonement (for the sins of the elect, as in the federal scheme); but rather think of the atonement as securing the ends of the Incarnation - the Father's filial purposes for humanity.

Traditional doctrines of atonement, McLeod Campbell argues, have limited themselves to the retrospective aspect of atonement (dealing with our guilty past) and have not given adequate consideration to the *prospective* aspect - 'bringing many sons to glory'. He often quotes Galatians 4.4:

> In the fulness of time, God sent forth his Son, born of a woman, made under the law, that he might redeem those who are under the law *that we might receive the adoption of sons*. And because you are sons, God has sent forth the Spirit of his Son into your hearts, crying 'Abba Father'.

Consequently in *The Nature of the Atonement*, he takes care to balance both the retrospective and the prospective. Christ takes away our past sins in order that he might fulfil his purpose of sharing his sonship.

What then is the nature of the Atonement which God has provided for us in the Person of his Son to secure his filial purposes for humankind?

Campbell sees that the question of the *extent* of the atonement is bound up with the question of the *nature* of the atonement. The doctrine of a limited atonement unfolded from certain views of its nature. So universal atonement, as he understands it, unfolds from a view of its nature and in turn from our view of *the nature of God*.

The *twin* categories in terms of which he expounded its nature are:

(1) the *Father-Son relationship*, which we see in Jesus Christ, in whom the Eternal Son of God has become incarnate in time, and into whose communion

with the Father we are called to participate by the Spirit in receiving eternal life; and

(2) the *Vicarious Humanity of Jesus Christ*, in whom and through whom we come to know the Father and who in our name and on our behalf, in leading us to the Father, made the One True Response to the Father in his whole life of filial obedience as well as in his sufferings and death upon the Cross.

The coming of Jesus Christ is at once the coming of *God as God* and at the same time, the coming of *God as Man* in our humanity. We do not know God as God apart from the humanity of Jesus Christ - by some 'light of nature'. But in the humanity of Jesus Christ, we come to know God by the 'light of revelation'. We come to know the Father, in the person of the incarnate Son.

So McLeod Campbell focuses our attention, in a decidedly devotional and moving way on the whole history of the human Jesus. Jesus Christ has a double ministry of representing God to humanity and representing humanity to God. There is a God-humanward movement in Jesus Christ. God (and the Kingdom of God) came in Jesus Christ. But there is also a human-Godward movement (in worship, communion, prayer, loving trust, obedience, and in the self-offering of Jesus on behalf of the sins of the world in the priestly intercessions of Christ). In Campbell's language, Christ deals with humanity on behalf of the Father, in making the Father and his loving judgments known to humanity, and Christ deals with the Father on behalf of humanity in a life of perfect acknowledgment and obedient submission to the loving judgment of God.

It is in this latter context that McLeod Campbell made his famous statement about Jesus making 'a perfect Amen in humanity to the judgment of God on the sin of man' and expounds what has come to be known (and which has been so often misunderstood) as the doctrine of *vicarious penitence*. (*Nature of the Atonement*, chapter VI)

What was his teaching about Vicarious Penitence?

To understand it aright, we must see it:

(a) In the total context of his understanding of the *Vicarious Humanity* of Jesus Christ - of the Son's oneness of mind with the Father's holy yet loving condemnation of our sins; in the light of the Priesthood of Christ, which is so central in Campbell's theology - the thought of the High Priest vicariously confessing the sins of all Israel on the day of atonement, foreshadowing Christ.

(b) Against the background of Scottish theology and federal Calvinism, John Calvin, in the *Institute* (Book III, chapter 3) in his critique of the medieval sacrament of penance drew a distinction between *legal* repentance and *evangelical* repentance. *Legal* repentance said, 'Repent, and if you repent, you will be forgiven!' This made the imperative prior to the indicative, and made forgiveness conditional upon an adequate repentance. So the medieval world said that *if* the sinner is truly contrite, *if* he confesses his sins and makes due amends (*contritio, confessio, satisfactio*) then he may be forgiven and restored. This was the root of much of the medieval doctrine of merit. Calvin argued that this inverted the evangelical order of grace, and made repentance prior to forgiveness, whereas in the New Testament *forgiveness is logically prior to repentance. Evangelical repentance*, consequently takes the form 'Christ has borne your sins on the Cross, therefore repent!' Repentance, Calvin argued, is our response to grace, not a condition of grace.

This same question became a living issue in Scotland 150 years after the Reformation, in the so-called 'Marrow controversy' which is most illuminating because it highlights some of the consequences of the rise of federal theology.

During the seventeenth century, a change began to take place in Scottish preaching, where a subtle kind of legalism began to creep in. The Scottish preacher preached the law in such a way that his concern was to produce a conviction of sin and a fear of judgment, so that he could call upon the sinner to repent and renounce his sin that he might receive the word of forgiveness and hear the comforts of the Gospel. This pattern became so widespread that many divines (Thomas Boston, Ralph and Ebenezer Erskine, Hog of Carnock and others) began to see that it was producing a doctrine of conditional grace which was foreign to the Gospel. But when they sought to bring the matter out into the open - appealing to this very distinction between legal and evangelical repentance as expounded in a Puritan work called *The Marrow of Modern Divinity* (Edward Fisher, 1645), they ended by being condemned by the General Assembly of 1720 - for teaching on these grounds, that *assurance is of the essence of faith*.

What did Calvin and the Marrowmen mean by saying that 'forgiveness is logically prior to repentance'? Let me use an illustration. Suppose I had the misfortune to have a quarrel with someone, and the result was that we became estranged from one another. Then suppose after some time I came to my friend sincerely seeking reconciliation and said to him, 'I forgive you!', it would be clear that this would be not only a word of *love*, it would also be a word of *condemnation* for I would be clearly implying that he was the guilty party! How would he react? His immediate reaction would probably be one of indignation, for, sensing the element of judgment in my words, he might reject my word of forgiveness, by refusing *to submit to the verdict of guilt implied in it.* He would be impenitent - there would be no 'change of heart' toward me. But suppose on subsequent reflection, he comes back and says 'I am sorry. I was quite wrong.' That would mean, in accepting my approach of love and forgiveness, he would in the very act be submitting to the verdict of guilty. There would be a change of mind - an act of penitence on his part.

The good news of the Gospel is that there is forgiveness with God our Father and he has spoken his word of forgiveness in Christ on the Cross - a word of love to humanity, and yet also a word of judgment. But that word summons from us a response of faith and penitence. In accepting the forgiveness of the Cross, we not only accept the gift of love, but in the very act know we are submitting to the verdict of guilty - acknowledging that it was our sins which put Christ on the Cross. Before the Cross, we know we are unconditionally summoned to renounce the sins for which Christ died. That is, God's forgiveness is logically prior to our repentance. It is the goodness of God which leads us to repentance. We might symbolise this in the following way:

(1) God's word to humankind in Christ   (2) Our human response

John McLeod Campbell grasped very vividly the significance of this understanding of forgiveness for his pastoral situation but carried it further than the Marrowmen, working it out in terms of Christ's vicarious humanity.

(1) On the one hand, God *has spoken* this word of forgiveness (of love and judgment) to the world in Jesus Christ. So Jesus lived a life of real *oneness of mind with the Father*, when in the course of his whole life on earth, he made the Father's love and the Father's holy condemnation of sin known. That in itself meant suffering, and in the sufferings of Jesus we see the sufferings of the Father, in *his dealings with humanity on behalf of the Father*.

(2) But Jesus Christ does not merely represent God to humanity in bringing God's word of forgiveness to humanity (dealing with humanity on behalf of the Father). He also represents *humanity go God*, and *deals with the Father on behalf of humanity* - as our great High Priest, our Intercessor. So as man, his whole life of sonship is a perfect *Response on our behalf to the Father*, as the well-beloved Son in whom the Father is well pleased - a response which is at once one of perfect trust in the Father's love and at the same time one of *perfect submission on our behalf to the verdict of guilty* (yet 'without any personal consciousness of sin').

That oneness with the Father, which towards man took the form of condemnation of sin, would in the Son's dealing with the Father in relation to our sins, take the form of a perfect confession of our sins. This confession as to its own nature, must have been *a perfect Amen in humanity to the judgment of God on the sin of men*. . . . He responds (to the divine wrath) with a perfect response - a response from the depths of that divine humanity - and *in that perfect response He absorbs it.* For that response has all the elements of a perfect repentance in humanity for all the sins of man - a perfect sorrow - a perfect contrition - all the elements of such a repentance, and that in absolute perfection, all - *excepting the personal consciousness of sin*; and by that perfect response in Amen to the mind of God in relation to sin is the wrath of God rightly met, and that is accorded to divine justice which is its due, and could alone satisfy it. (*This edition*, p.118)

Very movingly, McLeod Campbell interprets the once and for all vicarious humanity of Christ and the continuing vicarious humanity of Christ under the category of *prayer and of Christ's Priesthood*, seeing the whole ministry of Jesus in dealing with the Father on behalf of humanity in these terms, presenting us to the Father as God's dear children.

Does the vicarious Response of Jesus Christ offered to the Father on our behalf then eliminate the need for a response on our part? Not at all. Conversely, it gives us a basis for a joyful response of praise and gratitude and trust and love - a basis for worship, where our response is the gift of participating by the Spirit in the Son's self-offering on our behalf to the Father. When we realise that Christ bore our sins in his own body on the tree and submitted *for us once and for all* to the verdict of guilty, *then* we know we are unconditionally summoned to personal repentance and faith.

Participation is consequently a key word in McLeod Campbell's theology. The Son of God has participated in our humanity, that through the Spirit we might participate in his Sonship and communion with the Father. Participation is what *we* do - we pray, we repent, we believe, we worship - but only in the sense of participating in what *Christ* has done and is doing. In this way, faith and repentance and prayer are *not conditions* of grace, but the gift of the Spirit of sonship who so unites us with Christ in his communion with the Father that we might have a ground for rejoicing in God.

We can see therefore how McLeod Campbell develops the concept of 'evangelical repentance' as expounded by Calvin and the Marrowmen, and interprets it in terms of Christ's vicarious humanity and priesthood - of his twofold mission of representing God to humanity and humanity to God as Mediator - in order to eliminate any notion of conditional grace, and interpret the Gospel in New Testament terms as good news for all in the gift of Jesus Christ to the world. One of his favourite texts is, 'God has given to us eternal life, and this life is in his Son. He who has the Son has life; and he who has not the Son has not life'. (1 John 5.11-12)

We might therefore expand the above model to summarise McLeod Campbell's understanding of atonement and vicarious penitence, in these terms:

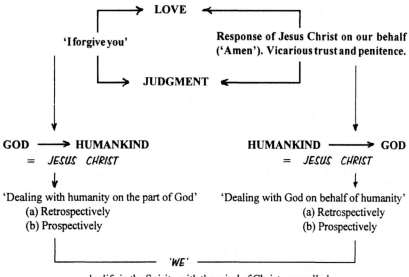

Thus if, following Calvin and the Marrowmen, he interprets 'evangelical repentance' to mean - 'forgiveness, therefore repentance'; and NOT 'repentance, therefore forgiveness', in terms of his doctrine of atonement he sees with Augustine and Calvin that the order is - 'love, therefore atonement'; and NOT 'atonement, therefore love' (as in certain types of Western penal satisfaction theories). In his own language, the filial is prior to the judicial; NOT the judicial prior to the filial.

McLeod Campbell was not rejecting the doctrine of substitutionary atonement, as is too often said. Far from it. He had a profound view of Christ standing in our place but he did reject any notion that God the Father has to be conditioned into being gracious by Christ satisfying the law and bearing the penalty of the law. It is the other way round. Christ, the incarnate Son, in grace fulfils the holy requirements of the law, takes its condemnation to himself, that by standing in for us we might be forgiven and given the gift of sharing by the Spirit in his Sonship and communion with the Father. Substitution so understood is the heart of a true doctrine of atonement where it is seen in terms of the Triune God of Grace in the Person of his Son coming to do for us what we cannot do for ourselves and calling us by the Spirit to participate as sons and daughters in his Sonship, in what he has done for us and is still doing for us today. This is the concept of 'the wonderful exchange' (*mirifica commutatio*) so dear to Luther and Calvin, that Christ takes to himself what is ours (our sin, enmity, death) to give us what is his in exchange (his righteousness, love and eternal life).

It is highly significant that in our century, so many leading theologians have been calling the Church back to the centrality of the Trinity - Barth, Rahner, T.F. Torrance, Moltmann, Jüngel, Zizioulas, Gunton and others. More and more theologians are becoming aware of the extent to which our Western concepts of God in Roman Catholic and Protestant thought owe more to Aristotle, Stoic concepts of natural law, Western jurisprudence, post-Enlightenment thought, than to the God of the New Testament, who in the person of the Son is revealed as our Father, drawing us by the Spirit of adoption into a life of communion and of participation, in worship, prayer and mission in the very Triune life of God. Dietrich Bonhoeffer used to make the plea that in theology we give priority to the Who question over the How question and seek to interpret What Christ has done and How we apply the Gospel in the light of Who God is. This was Campbell's insight and plea a hundred and fifty years ago, when he anticipated so many twentieth century insights. This is why McLeod Campbell's call to return to the Triune God of Grace, to a better and more biblical doctrine of atonement, is so important and relevant for our own time if we are to recover a proper understanding of the unconditional freeness of grace and have grounds for rejoicing in God.

James B. Torrance
Edinburgh, Scotland

McLEOD CAMPBELL'S INTRODUCTION
(to the Second Edition)

I avail myself of a second edition to ask attention to some thoughts in relation to the Atonement which may be a needed help to some of my readers, but which I was not led to notice in writing this book.

That is an abiding obligation which the Apostle expresses when he says, "Be ready always to give an answer to every man that asketh you a reason of the hope that is in you with meekness and fear." The freedom of thought which so strongly characterises our time, and the liberty taken to regard all questions on the subject of Religion as open questions, render due obedience to this charge of the Apostle's peculiarly difficult: the range of the questions which may be put to us is so wide, and our answers are so likely to suggest previous questions. At the same time the field in which we are to look for our answer may be regarded as narrowed by the words "a reason of the hope that is in you." The Apostle's "becoming all things to all men!" suggests a wide range, which yet is narrowed by the words, "by manifestation of the truth commending ourselves to every man's conscience in the sight of God."

The free controversy of the present day would be regarded with less anxiety and with more hope than it often is, if this were clearly seen to be the course to which that controversy shuts us up. We believe that God is, that God is light, that it is His will that in His light we should see light. We, therefore, cannot recognise, in the questioning and controversy which abound, a reason for suspended faith or universal doubt on the one hand, or for an unreasoning and blind faith on the other.

It has been said - and some have received it as at this time a word in season, ministering comfort which many have needed - that "there lives more faith in honest doubt... than in half the creeds". The creeds may, we know, be held without faith, that living faith which alone God accepts and doubt, if honest, may be assumed to have some true faith underlying it. The very freedom and strength to question is often traceable to the firm hold of something true. The faith of righteousness sustains the spirit in asking, "Is this righteous?" so long as the righteousness of what is presented to us is not yet discerned. The faith that God is love is often the root of questionings which have not yet issued in the apprehension of the divine love present in that concerning which the questions arise; while on the other hand, many things are received in a way of blind submission to authority which, in the light of righteousness and love, would be seen to be unbelievable. It is also true that at the present time the expression of doubt is often connected with an undeniable earnestness of spirit which contrasts strongly with the levity of the scepticism of a former age: and we cannot be too thankful for the tenderness and respect with which many deep thinkers, themselves strong in faith, deal with the earnest and anxious doubting to which I refer.

Yet two considerations seem here to ask our attention:

First, the jealousy for God as never asking for any but "a reasonable service," while "without faith it is impossible to please Him," which should always be present in our dealing with unbelief. However tenderly it becomes us to deal with difficulties of other minds, however much we should guard against measuring their responsibility by our own light, we should never feel, or appear to feel, as if we admitted that God had left Himself without a witness, or that unbelief was more reasonable than faith.

Secondly, the danger to which undue concessions as to the reasonableness of doubt may expose those with whose doubts we are dealing; for by such concessions we may help them to a self-complacency on the ground of their doubts - to the feeling that doubting pertains to a higher order of mind than simple faith, and thus to a self-righteous trust in their doubting; a form of self-righteousness not worse, it may be, than the self-congratulations of a blind orthodoxy which knows not the living God; yet surely not better, but equally remote from that living dealing with God which gives its preciousness to faith as a grain of mustard seed.

I have in this volume approached the subject of the atonement from the side of faith; in some sense writing for those who believe that they may believe. Yet I have sought to have present in my mind whatever I felt most reasonable or deserving of consideration in the difficulties of those who doubt: and I may here beg readers of this latter class not to be deterred by the title which indicates my subject because I seem to *take for granted* points as to which they would ask a proof. An atonement, remission of sins, the gift of eternal life, and a relation of the two last to the first, all are in one view assumed; yet my hope has been that the manner of considering them will be in effect a successful argument for their reality. For I believe that Christianity has its highest and ultimate evidence in what it is; that therefore to illustrate any element of Christianity successfully is to establish its claim on faith.

But I have approached my subject, not only from the side of faith, but also through an examination of the forms which faith in the atonement presents in the systems which I have assumed to be most in possession of the religious mind of our land. It has been suggested to me that it might have been better to have limited myself to the exposition of my own faith, and this would have had some advantages; but the experience of many has justified the choice I made, as they have found the attempt to separate the elements of truth in received systems from the error present in them profitable. I have not gone further back than the Reformation. A recent writer on the *Catholic Doctrine of the Atonement* [Henry Nutcombe Oxenham MA - ed.] traces its development in the Church from the beginning "historically," not "controversially," though indicating clearly some of the grounds on which he objects to the teaching of the Reformers as that teaching presents itself to his mind. His book gives the impression of fairness, though the writer may not have altogether overcome the difficulty of seeing a subject from the point of view of an antagonist. Two things must strike one, first, the great diversity of views on the subject of the atonement before the Reformation, as well as then and since, and secondly, the "anxious hope" with which the writer looks to the "Catholic thinkers of Germany" in closing the record of the past; for he thus leaves us under the impression that his introduction "On the principle of Theological developments" has been intended, in reference to the subject of his book, to prepare us to accept something which the Church has yet to speak, rather than to rest in what she has spoken.

The faith of atonement presupposes the faith of the incarnation. It may be also said historically that the faith of the incarnation has usually had conjoined with it the faith of the atonement. The great question which has divided men as to these fundamental doctrines of the Faith has been the relation in which they stand to each other - which was to be regarded as primary, which secondary? - was an atonement the great necessity in reference to man's salvation, out of which the necessity for the incarnation arose, because a divine Saviour alone could make an adequate atonement for sin? - or, is the incarnation to be regarded as the primary and highest fact in the history of God's relation to man, in the light of which God's interest in man and purpose for man can alone be truly seen? - and is the atonement to be contemplated as taking place in order to the fulfilment of the divine purpose for man which the incarnation reveals.

I feel it impossible in any measure to realise what I believe in believing in the incarnation without giving a preference to the latter view; and accordingly my attempt to understand and illustrate the nature of the atonement has been made in the way of taking the subject to the light of incarnation. Assuming the incarnation, I have sought to realise the divine mind in Christ as perfect Sonship towards God and perfect Brotherhood towards men, and, doing so, the incarnation has appeared developing itself naturally and necessarily as the atonement.

This attempt to see the atonement by the light of the incarnation is so far an attempt to answer Anselm's question, "*Cur Deus homo*" by the light of the divine fact itself as to which the question is put; instead of seeking an answer, as he has done, in considerations exterior to that fact. If, as has been my endeavour and is my hope, I have kept within the limits of self-evidencing light, it will be felt by those who accompany me to that light that I have set down nothing as having a place in the life of Christ which has not really had such a place; although long cherished thoughts as to the nature of the atonement may, in the case of some, make it specially difficult for them to regard the divine facts traced as filling with their true meaning such expressions as propitiation, sacrifice for sin; while others, hitherto not believing in an atonement at all, may hesitate to ascribe that character to these facts, although seeing them to be facts. But whether the results at which I have arrived be or be not accepted, I trust the path in which I lead the mind will be felt to be one of deep interest; and also one which it is not presumption to attempt to tread, seeing that the life of Christ is the light of life to us, and that the divine mind in Him is presented to our faith as human, while divine, and what therefore humanity sustained in its faith by the divine Spirit may understand. That this light is human while divine saves from the charge of presumption the attempt to see by it; yet doubtless that it is divine while human may well fill us with awe while making this attempt: rendering our hope in engaging in it, not merely a reverent use of the intelligence with which God has endowed us, but also trust in our Heavenly Father's willingness to give His Holy Spirit to them that ask Him. An intellectual form our spiritual apprehensions must receive, that the demand of our intellectual nature may be met; but that which is spiritual must be spiritually discerned, and, while I hope to carry the understanding of my readers along with me, I am not to be regarded as seeking to recommend the doctrine of the atonement by what might be called a bringing it down to the level of the human understanding. I seek rather to raise the understanding to that which is above it, and to that exercise of thought on that which is spiritual in which we feel ourselves brought near to what is divine and infinite, and made partakers in the knowledge of the love which passeth knowledge.

If the atonement is rightly conceived of as a development of the incarnation, the relation of the atonement to the incarnation is indissoluble; and in a clear apprehension of the incarnation must be felt to be so. Further, if the eternal life given to us in Christ is that divine life in humanity in which Christ made atonement for our sins, then the connection between the atonement and our participation in the life of Christ is not arbitrary, but natural: and thus the incarnation, the atonement, and man's participation in the divine nature, offer to our faith one purpose of divine love, reaching its fulfilment by a path which is determined by what God is and what He wills that man should be. This unity and simplicity in the grace of God to man, and natural relation subsisting among the elements of our faith, is "the simplicity that is in Christ," - a harmony in the gracious whole the apprehension of which must strengthen faith.

Yet I cannot forget that there are earnest and deep-thinking minds in whose case the faith of the incarnation and their acceptance of it as the fundamental grace of God to man to the light of which all that concerns God's relation to man is to be taken, has issued, not in the recognition of the atonement as a development of the incarnation, but on the contrary, in regarding the atonement as in the light of the incarnation alike uncalled for and inconceivable.

So soon as the incarnation, no longer regarded only as a mystery of condescending love - love which took this form because of the need-be for an atonement, is accepted as itself the light to which the subject of the atonement must be taken, we are prepared to find that all conceptions of the atonement which accord not with the love of the Father of Spirits to men His offspring manifested in the incarnation, will be rejected. But we expect true conceptions on this great subject to take the place of the errors rejected. For, if the atonement be the development of the incarnation, how can we stop short with the fact of the incarnation itself as if it were the whole of the Gospel? One reason for stopping short with the incarnation may be the overwhelming sense of the deep root of man's relation to God, of man's inconceivable preciousness in the sight of God, which fills the mind in realising the incarnation - fills the mind apart from and antecedent to all tracing of the course of the incarnate Saviour, in His working out of our salvation. As divine love fitted to subdue man's enmity, as divine power entering into humanity and equal to the task of regenerating all humanity, the incarnation may seem a Gospel sufficient to meet all the need of man.

Yet our "need" is to be measured, not by our own sense of need, but by what God has done to meet our need. How little may meet our *sense* of need, the inadequate and superficial views of the gospel which so often gives peace, even to minds considerably awakened on the subject of religion, may warn us. The faith of what the Scriptures teach of the development of the incarnation is not less essential to an enlightened peace of mind than the faith of the incarnation itself. And if the greatness of the grace of God to man in the incarnation is enough to ensure us of the hope that is for man in God, is not the unanticipated and marvellous character of that divine mystery what should constrain us to the attitude of reverently learning from the course of its development in the work of our redemption all that concerns the manner of the love which the Father hath bestowed on us? It seems to me a contradiction to believe in the incarnation, and to expect to understand its relation to us otherwise than through the faith of the divine facts which are the form which divine wisdom has taken in accomplishing the results which, in the incarnation, divine love has contemplated.

The incarnation may itself be traced back to the love which has taken that form, and we may propose to ourselves to set out from the axiom that God is love, and think that we can deduce from it creation, incarnation, and the ultimate participation of individual men in the divine nature. But we cannot, in contradiction to the history of human thought, assert that we could have anticipated the course of the divine self-manifestation; while we may and must thankfully rejoice that God gives us the capacity of recognising His glory in all these manifestations of Himself. But to be thus *in the light of revelation* children of the light and of the day is very different from stopping short at any divine fact, however high and ultimate, and substituting our own deductions from it for the facts of the gospel. It is natural and right to ascend from the facts of historical Christianity to the principles and laws of the kingdom of God which these facts make known to us. But, if this has been a sound process of thought, to descend again in order to rest in these facts with a confirmed faith must also be natural, and what we shall rejoice to do. And so it is with the

Apostles. St Paul says, "God commendeth His love toward us, in that, while we were yet sinners, Christ died for us," and the language of St John is, "Herein is love, not that we loved God, but that He loved us, and sent His Son to be the propitiation for our sins". Both Apostles see the love of God not in the incarnation simply, but in the incarnation as developed in the atonement.

Those who in former times gave the first place to the incarnation, subordinating the atonement to it, while still believing in the atonement, sometimes speculated on the probable history of man if he had not sinned, as what would still have implied the incarnation in order to the fulfilment of the divine purpose in man. Such speculations are recalled to us when we now see faith in the incarnation combined with the rejection of the atonement. What is left out of Christianity is just that part of revealed truth in which the love of God is connected with the need of man as a sinner; all, in a word, which gives the Gospel a *remedial* character, representing the Son of God as having come "to seek and to save that which was lost," -- representing man as having destroyed himself, while revealing the hope that remained for him in God. Redemption only *reveals* the deep love of the Father of our spirits; and hence an Apostle, in the full light of redeeming love, speaks of "Committing ourselves unto God as unto a faithful Creator." But to trace redemption to its ultimate root in the divine Fatherliness, and to regard that Fatherliness as leaving no room for the need of redemption, are altogether opposite apprehensions of the grace of God.

Two tendencies of philosophic thought which strongly characterise our time, favour their resting in the faith of the incarnation, while rejecting that of the atonement.

1.   We can hear as an echo of Christianity, such words as

> Yet I doubt not thro' the ages one increasing purpose runs

in reference to the race, and

> Men may rise on stepping stones
> Of their dead selves to higher things

in reference to the individual man. For in the light of revelation we see the "increasing purpose" that runs through the ages, and through Christ we rise from our "dead selves to higher things". But speculation on man as a subject of progress has sometimes assumed what we feel to be an anti-Christian character; as when sin is regarded as only one form of ignorance, deliverance from which is a gain, like every other advance in knowledge, but not as what can be rationally regarded with self-blame, penitence, remorse. It is not too much to say that the real ignorance which is present in sin is what that man has not yet been delivered from who is not looking back on sin with genuine self-blame. To judge otherwise is to treat the light of conscience, surely, at lowest co-ordinate with that of pure reason, as on a level with what we have been called delusions of sense, from which philosophy delivers us.

But far short of this denying, as we may say, that sin is sin, there is room for thoughts excusing and palliating sin whose operation is to hinder the sense of a need-be for an atonement. We believe that through the redemption man is raised to a level higher than that on which he stood at the first, while we see the God of creation in the God of redemption, and accept the unsearchable riches which we have in Christ, as the divine purpose from the beginning; but to philosophic thought not accepting the utterances of conscience as axiomatic, redemption and the atonement which it implies do not harmonise with development and progress, while incarnation may.

2.   Another tendency of thought strongly characteristic of our time, to which I refer as hindering faith in the atonement, is that which has its extreme evil development when a personal God is lost to the human spirit in the uniformity of the course of nature or the reign of law.

The reign of law, making experience possible, and all those results of experience which we call Science, has necessarily the deepest practical interest to us; while, apart from practice, it is full of intellectual interest, and an ever inviting theme of speculative thought; but its highest and purest interest is that which belongs to it as the form which the will of God has taken in ordering this fair universe, and in respect of which it is to faith a revelation of God.

There are indeed minds, and some even of a high order intellectually, to which the scientific interest of the reign of law is its highest, and seems its only rational interest. They are satisfied to take the facts of existence as they present themselves as facts; regarding the contemplation of them as manifestations and revelations of a divine mind as an exercise of speculative thought in which we have no sure footing, into which we are tempted by our own human consciousness, which, they say, suggests to us the conception but does not justify the faith of God.

But it is not too much to say that what is thus rejected as an unwarranted exercise of thought, leading to no sure results, is what the laws of thought necessitate. We are so constituted that the appearance of design suggests to us a designing mind; and, in proportion as this appearance is varied, wide spread, and abiding, our sense of the necessity of the recognition of design deepens. So truly is this the case, that the realisation of the reign of law, which the ordered universe on which we find ourselves a part presents to us, renders the possibility of accepting that reign simply as a fact, and without being constrained to rise from the fact to the faith of mind and thought as manifested in the fact, inexplicable. Thus to stop short of God is, we feel, to do violence to a deep instinct of our being.

Further, as the manifestation of design in the ordering of the universe as we know it raises our faith to a divine purpose and plan, as what we see being realised, so does the same necessity of thought which we are thus obeying constrain the further stop of tracing all the laws and powers, which we see acting together in obedience to One Will, to that Will as the source of their existence. Here we are come to the point at which our own experience no longer accompanies us as light, and we pass from that in God of which there is an image in man, to that which is distinctive of God as God -- which the Apostle names as His "eternal power and Godhead". For here we pass from the relation of a reign of law to thought and design using law, to the relation of that reign to thought and design manifested in giving laws their existence. There is a certain likeness in human action to divine action as employing means to accomplish ends; but there is no likeness in any human consciousness to what we must ascribe to God when we contemplate Him as giving to means their existence and their fitness to accomplish ends. Intelligent beings as we are, we find ourselves encompassed by a reign of law of the stability and fixedness of which we avail ourselves, finding the knowledge of laws to be to us power. But we cannot for a moment conceive of the *original* relation of this universe to God as that of an infinite multitude of laws to an infinite mind, having perfect knowledge of them, and using this knowledge in turning them to account in accomplishing designs of infinite wisdom. We cannot conceive of infinite wisdom thus, as it were, finding infinite resources already existing. A capacity to be used for ends of wisdom could not be fortuitous. That capacity as well as the use made of it must be traced to wisdom, to designing thought. It is quite essential that our consideration of the reign of law, while it begins with our human consciousness of forming designs and employing means, should thus pass beyond and rise above any consciousness possible to us, in order that the invisible things of God may be revealed to our faith by the things that are made, even His eternal power and Godhead.

We cannot lose the living God in the reign of law, if we freely yield ourselves to the necessary relations of thought in our meditation on that reign even as seen in the physical universe, still less I may say is this possible in regard to the moral world: although the tendency to rest in law without ascending to God is manifested in relation to moral law also. There is this difference between the laws of the moral universe and those of the physical universe, that we do not trace the existence of the former to an act of will in God, as we do that of the latter. I know that to some it has appeared otherwise; but to my mind, to say that God has given existence to goodness, as He has given existence to Himself. The Being of God implies goodness. But what we refer to the divine will here is the existence of beings such as we know ourselves, to whom God has given goodness as the law of their being. And so the differences between the physical universe and the moral universe in respect of law is, that the former we trace to the will of God, that latter to what God is.

But we are called to ascend to a higher region than pure Theism. As it appears due obedience to a voice of reason and to necessities of thought to rise from Science to Theism, so do I believe is there a corresponding necessity in reason and the constitution of our being, for rising from Theism to Religion, from the faith of God as God, to the faith of God as the Father of our spirits.

For, for us as God's offspring there is intended a nearer approach to God than even the apprehension and faith of His eternal power and Godhead.

Theism raises us into a higher light of truth than that to which Science attains, and in seeking the reign of law in its relation to God we may be said to ascend from what we possess in God's works to a certain possession in God Himself. The power, goodness and wisdom, of God become riches to us - the goodness of God especially, both as putting the highest seal upon the excellence of moral law, and as enabling us in our own conscious weakness to realise that excellence with a peaceful hope, while meditation on the moral universe and its yet undeveloped future. Praise also, though it be but silent, will be added to our joy in God as God. I do not know that pure Theism can be regarded as going beyond this.

In passing from Theism to Religion, or rather in adding Religion to Theism, we are changing a contemplative position in God's universe, for the active occupation of our own special place as God's offspring. We are welcoming the privileges, and accepting the responsibilities which pertain to this our personal relation to God, in the faith of the feelings with which God is regarding us, and in the apprehension of the response to these feelings which is due from us. We are welcoming a life in communion with God, a life in His favour, a life the lights and shadows, the joys and sorrows of which, have exclusive reference to the aspect of our God towards us; the aspect towards us of that divine love which, while as love it is unchanging, yet must, because of its very nature, ever change in the look with which it regards us according to our changing selves. Such a life, the interest and aim of which is to occupy aright a filial relation to God, is at least conceivable, if only it be the will of God concerning us, and that He has made provision for it; and to such a life it is that the Gospel calls us, and it is in relation to it that it is said that God has given to us all that pertains to life and Godliness.

Here then are two regions of the divine self-manifestation to which we are related; the one the reign of law, as seen in the light of Theism, the other the kingdom of God proclaimed in the Gospel and the light of which is the Son revealing the Father.

As our connection with both these regions is of God, what practical obligations our relations to them severally may imply, cannot be contradictory. But they are two, and distinct, though the former is subordinated to the latter, and it is important that we discern clearly their distinctness; because though we cannot live in the latter and forget the former, we may give place in our thoughts to the former while not knowing the latter. I mean, that while Religion presupposes Theism, Theism may exist without Religion: although in truth Religion is, as well as Theism, contemplated in the most elemental statement of the faith without which it is impossible to please God, that it is the faith that God is, and that He is the rewarder of them that diligently seek Him.

To the practical demands made upon us as related to these two several regions, this is common, that in both we have to do with fixed and determinate laws, which we are capable of knowing, and to which we have to conform ourselves. The difference between these regions lies in this, that in our relation to the former we have to do with a work of God - a system of things to which He has given existence; while in our relation to the latter we have to do directly with the will of God; that is to say, His will as His mind and character - that in respect of which we say, God is love. To know the system of things of which we find ourselves a part, and to conform ourselves to it, as practical wisdom in relation to the reign of law. To know the mind of God, and conform ourselves to it, is practical wisdom in our relation to the kingdom of God.

And here we mark this difference, that the practical wisdom which the reign of law demands, may exist apart from faith in God, while that which the kingdom of God demands cannot. Thus, two men may cultivate Science with equal success, of whom the one never thinks of God - may even be an atheist, while the other acknowledges God in that stability of the laws of nature on which they both alike are calculating. But any corresponding absence of faith in God, in the exercise of wisdom proper to the kingdom of God, is manifestly impossible. For, while Theism may be said to crown science, ennobling and exalting it by the relation to God in which it contemplates it, it in no way affects Science viewed simply in itself; but of Religion Theism is the foundation, underlying it as that on which it must rest or not be at all.

The distinction between the will of God as what has taken a fixed form in the constitution of things around us, and the will of God as the divine mind or character is what we must endeavour clearly to apprehend and realise, in seeking to understand our own place - our responsibilities and our privileges - in the kingdom of God. What God is in that He is love is what God wills us to be. His choice for us He desires may be our choice for ourselves. In making that choice known to us He speaks at once with authority and in love, expecting the response of obedience and love from us; the authority and love on His part being blended in the claim to be known as the Father of our Spirits, the obedience and the love expected from us being blended also in the Spirit of Sonship.

Further, what He reveals Himself as desiring that we should be, He authorises us to seek in prayerful trust, expecting His strength to be perfected in our weakness. Therefore the inner aspects of our relation to the kingdom of God, to which as God's offspring we belong, are, God's favour as our life, oneness of mind with God, as the condition of that favour, help of God and strengthening of His Spirit as our felt need, in order to being in that condition; while the aspects of our spirits in the measure in which we are occupying aright our place in the kingdom of God, are faith, hope and love - "faith", as the fellowship of the mind of the Son towards the Father in the life of the Sonship which is being quickened in us; "hope" in God according to the words "If children then heirs, heirs of God and joint heirs with Jesus Christ"; and "love", faith and hope resulting in our dwelling in love, being dwelling in God. Thus we are receiving that kingdom of God which cannot be moved, for the coming of which we pray, the light of which is the Divine Will, not yet done on earth as it is done in heaven, and which is the deepest interest of existence to us as God's offspring, on which the light of the Divine name "our Father" is dawning, and in whom the desire for the hallowing of that name is being quickened.

What most fixes our attention, in the practical aspect of the kingdom of God, is the place which prayer has in it. God is the hearer and answerer of prayer: our aspect towards Him is in its spirit prayer without ceasing. We see a place of free action occupied by God as the Father of our Spirits, and a liberty in relation to Him conceded to us as His offspring, which permit direct personal dealing on His part and on ours: so that we are free to ask directly from God what, in the light of His will, we see to be good; and He is free to grant with simple and direct reference to us, and in response to our trust, that which we ask.

That place which the fixedness of law, as what we may always assume, has in our practical relation to the reign of law, the character of God, as the hearer and answerer to our prayer, has in our practical relation to the kingdom of God; and, as Science in the largest sense of the word is our practical light under the reign of law, so is Christ the light of the kingdom of God. Accordingly we see rejection of Christianity taking the form of a denial of the existence of the kingdom of God, as distinct from the reign of law.

The circle of those is not large, who, looking around them on the reign of law under which we find ourselves, feel it enough to see that reign as a subject of scientific interest, not rising from it to God. There is, however, a larger circle who ascend from Science to Theism, and feel the *Divine* interests of the works of God, who yet do not advance from Theism to Religion. These are those who seem to themselves to have come as near to God as they are warranted in doing, when from a distance they admire and adore Him as He is revealed to their faith in His works; holding the due expression of reverence on their part to be the grateful use of this universe which He has made, in the exercise of the powers by which He has fitted them for their place in it, and feeling any personal approach to God, any seeking of communion with Him, still more any exercise of trust toward Him for a putting forth of His power in response to such trust, that is, anything strictly of the nature of prayer, as an unwarranted stepping out of man's proper place.

This stopping short in Theism, not rising to Religion, has always had much charm for philosophic minds; while the instinct in man which gives attraction to Religion has ever in some way or other influenced the ordinary thought and feeling of humanity. How blindly the religious instinct has wrought, how unworthy of the true God have so often been the approaches made to Him, in which ignorance of that in which He delights men have sought His favour - *this* we know: and how far philosophic thought of old has been excused in its shrinking from the confines of religion, by which the popular religions of heathendom have been, we may not judge; while surely we may give thanks for what has been pure and high in its Theism. But, doubtless, philosophers as well as their unreflecting brethren have both needed and shared the forbearance extended to a time, at the ignorance of which God is said by the Apostle to have winked; excusing in some sense what yet He condemned as disobedience to a light men's possession of which was evidenced in that one of their own poets had spoken of men as God's offspring.

But to us the claim, which a kingdom of God in which He makes Himself known as the Father of our spirits, asking for a filial response from us, has on our faith, goes beyond that which has existed always in proportion as our relation to God in Christ goes beyond that germ of religion which the words express, "In God we live and move and have our being" and "He appoints the bounds of our habitation that we should seek after Him."

The kingdom of God as it asks our faith is seen in Christ. The conception of God as a Father, and of a relation to Him which is sonship, is seen realised in Christ. The Son of God is seen revealing the Father as the Father, by being in our sight the beloved Son in whom the Father is well pleased. What therefore we are called to judge is whether this is a reality. As we look on Him who has thus come to us in the Father's name, hear His words, trace His path, do we find ourselves in a condition to accept His claim, to believe that God is a Father, that Christ is His Son, and that the life seen in Him is the life of Sonship? In so high a matter, the warrant for faith must be as high as the demand for faith. It is recorded that, when Jesus was on earth, a voice from heaven was heard saying, "This is my beloved Son.". This voice was received as the voice of God. It was accepted as the Father's testimony to the Son - the Father's seal to the claim on man's faith which the Son made in coming in the Father's name.

Is there at all times in the spirit this testimony of the Father to the Son? Is there such a drawing of us to the Son by the Father as this? And is this drawing what our Lord referred to in saying "It is written in the prophets, and they shall be all taught of God. Every man therefore that hath heard, and hath learned of the Father, cometh unto me?" And is this testimony of the Father to the Son in humanity addressed to us with a personal reference to ourselves? Is it now added in the spirit as then outwardly, "Hear ye Him?" And do we understand that we are thus taught that the Son has come to reveal the Father to us, and to quicken in us the life of sonship towards the Father? If it be so, if the living God thus teach us that He has given to us eternal life, and that this life is in His Son, then is this the highest and ultimate claim which the kingdom of God revealed in Christ has on our faith. On this turns our responsibility in reading the New Testament record, and our responsibility in reading the history of Christianity also; for though Christianity may not have realised the promise of its early dawn, yet have Christians, being living branches in Christ the true vine, and abiding in Him borne fruit which helps our faith in the purpose of God for man, in the measure in which it has been a fulfilling of that purpose.

No doubt veils, in the form of corruptions of Christianity, have from time to time during these eighteen hundred years been thrown over the face of Christ. Human systems also, identifying themselves with Christianity, while diverse one from another, have caused Christianity to appear to superficial thought not one, but many, and conflicting religions; and we are not to forget how much all this has tended to hinder man's passing on from Theism to Religion. ("Ye have taken away the key of knowledge: ye enter not in yourselves, and them that were entering in ye hindered," St Luke xi. 52). But, at the worst, Christianity has never been that difficulty to philosophic thought which heathenism was formerly.

In our inability to know what has come between even earnest and thoughtful minds and the clear vision of that which has claimed their faith, we must abstain from individual judgement. But believing in the abiding testimony of the Father to the Son in the Spirit, we believe in a corresponding abiding responsibility for the due response of faith on men's part. This is a responsibility which men cannot put from them in considering the claim which the kingdom of God has on their faith. Is Divine Fatherhood, and Divine Sonship, and the love of God as contemplating for us, God's offspring, participation in the Divine Sonship, a conception which commands faith - a faith harmonizing with while transcending the elements of our previous faith in God? Our affirmative answer to this question is, however, rightly given only if given in the light of God; and we must be careful not to plead with others on lower ground than that on which we stand ourselves; viz. the ground on which we feel that our Lord stood, when He came to men in the Father's name, and complained that so coming he had not been received by them. While He was come to make known the Father by being in men's sight the Son in whom the Father was well pleased, He constantly assumed that His commending of the Father ought to have a response in their spirits - that the footing of fatherliness in God on which He rested the demand for faith toward God should at once justify that demand to the conscience of those to whom He addressed it. "Not a sparrow shall fall on the ground without your Father." "Your Father knoweth that he have need of these things."

For we may say that the one postulate in all His teaching of faith, and reproof for the want of faith, was that those to whom He was speaking, were, and ought to know themselves, God's offspring. Is it not thus that we are to understand the words "Whosoever shall not receive the kingdom of God as a little child shall in no wise enter therein," and "I thank thee, O Father, Lord of heaven and earth, that thou hast hid these things from the wise and prudent, and hast revealed them unto babes?" The receiving as little children God's kingdom, His being revealed to babes, contemplates not a blind credulity, nor even teachableness in any merely general sense, but the welcome to a Father's voice which is the germ of the life of Sonship, a spiritual instinct belonging to our relation to the Father of our spirits. We must therefore be careful in claiming faith for the kingdom of God, to occupy, as I have said, the ground which our Lord occupied, to assume the reasonableness in the demand we make which He assumed, and that, in respect of the divine dealing with men's spirits in the Spirit, we in our pleading for faith are not alone, for the Father is with us. In following this course we are only doing as to the highest obligation which rests on the human spirit what is done in all sound and healthful teaching of morality, viz. looking for and seeking to awaken an inward response in the taught. And in truth no other course is compatible with the assumption that men ought to know God, and trust God as a Father.

This however is no reason for not attempting to meet, in so far as our understanding of their mental position may enable us to do so, difficulties of other minds whose habits of pure scientific investigation are to them a temptation to approach the claim of the kingdom of God on our faith by a wrong path, causing them to ask for a kind of evidence not proper to the subject, and so hindering their weighing fairly what belongs to it. No scientific study of the phenomena which imply a reign of law could ever have issued in the discovery of the kingdom of God. But neither can it issue in any discovery that contradicts the existence of that kingdom; nor can any mind in the light of the kingdom of God hesitate to conclude that if such seeming contradiction arise there is implied the presence of error, either as to facts or as to conclusions from facts.

Considering the universality of the obligations to be in the light of the kingdom of God, and the consequent universality of the divine provision for meeting this obligation, while Science is the calling of the few, and ability to weigh its evidence aright the endowment of exceptional men, it seems to me altogether reasonable to ask from scientific men that they should first deal with the claim which the kingdom of God makes on their faith, as what is addressed to them in common with all other men, and, as men, judge of that claim, and feel no liberty to recall their acceptance of it once given on its own proper evidence because of difficulties met in another region where there is no corresponding responsibility for knowledge, nor universality of provision for attaining it. This we are entitled, I think, to urge, irrespective of the fact that the difficulties here felt by some men of science are not felt by all, not by some having the highest place in science, nor by some taking the subject of the reign of law to the light of large philosophic thought on that subject viewed in itself.

Nevertheless it is the part of brotherhood, and due from those who, believing in God as the hearer and answerer of prayer, feel themselves in a light which harmonizes this faith with the faith of the reign of law, to seek to make others partakers with them in that light. Such harmonizing light must be welcome even to those who most feel that it would be disobedience to the highest light to suspend their faith in the kingdom of God on the success of any thing attempted in this direction.

The attempt to solve difficulties in this region of thought by dividing the divine action in relation to the universe into departments, not mutually related nor strictly one whole, must fail to satisfy, though some in their perplexity have had recourse to it. Apart from the faith of the kingdom of God as revealed in Christ, the faith of God as a moral governor is not satisfied, if, in the name of science, the concession of self-executing moral laws is offered as parallel to self-executing physical laws, in order to reconcile the mind to the emptying the events which touch us through our physical nature of all moral purpose on God's part. And so also the shutting out of the reign of law, physical and moral, from the Father's personal dealing with us in the kingdom of God is what no marking out of a distinct region for the kingdom of God can reconcile us to as God's offspring. No doubt the kingdom of God in its internal aspect may seem to be, so to speak, self-contained; and in proportion as we seek first the kingdom of God and His righteousness - that kingdom which is neither meat nor drink, but righteousness and peace and joy in the Holy Ghost - the words "Ask and ye shall receive, seek and ye shall find, knock and it shall be opened unto you" are felt to have their supreme interest in their relation to the words with which they seem more immediately connected, viz. "If ye then, being evil, know how to give good gifts unto your children, how much more shall your Father which is in heaven give His Holy Spirit to them that ask Him?" But the spirit of sonship in us forbids our recognising any limitation to the freedom of God in the directness of His dealing with us in all things as our Father, or restriction of our freedom in that direct dealing with God and trust in Him, in respect of which we are authorised to "be careful for nothing, but in every thing by prayer and supplication with thanksgiving" to let "our requests be made known unto God."

In regard to miracles as included in what we know historically of the kingdom of God, what I can believe as to the subordination of the reign of law to the kingdom of God in so far as the reign of law is within my mental horizon, I must believe as to its expansion beyond that horizon, whatever that may be. But whether miracles are to be regarded as belonging to such an extension, and to be traced to a higher law in the reign of law than the laws which they seem to put aside, or to be conceived of as altogether differently related to God, is a question which may receive different answers without affecting our faith either in the reign of law or in the kingdom of God.

Our faith in the reign of law has, as we have seen, two aspects: first, as seen realising divine thoughts and fulfilling divine purposes; and secondly, as deriving its existence from God. In the first view, God is seen using means to ends; in the second, giving existence to means. This latter view brings us direct to the will of God, as acting not mediately but immediately, and all observation of God's acting mediately thus takes us up ultimately to His acting immediately. It appears to me that we do not know enough to say as to anything that transcends our knowledge of the reign of law, in which way we are to view it, whether as belonging to the system of law, but to a region of it out of our sight, or as outside of it and having the same immediate relation to God which the system of law itself ultimately has. There is no doubt that the ordinary feeling with regard to miracles is one that claims for them the latter character; but to me it appears that to decide on this claim transcends our powers; while, at the same time, our ultimate faith in God's "eternal power and Godhead" leaves room for the question. But whether we are to conceive of miracles as only a special and unusual use of the powers embraced in a reign of law or not, this is common to them with our ordinary experience in the kingdom of God, that they imply a direct dealing with God on man's part - an accomplishing of something through asking and trusting God to do it.

All human acting that makes this claim, and is a reality, belongs to the kingdom of God. And here I would notice in relation to miracles, that their place as elements in our faith is much more closely connected with our confidence in what I may call the testimony regarding them of those who have performed them, than with any intrinsic authority to command belief which we can recognise as inherent in the miracle itself. A miracle has been defined "a manifestation of superhuman power", and to sight it is, and can be, no more. But the manifestation of superhuman power gives no claim on our faith. It may be superhuman power in appearance only, as that was which Cortez claimed when he made use of his knowledge of a coming eclipse to impose on the Mexicans. But, assuming it to be superhuman, it is not therefore divine. It is only in reality a faith in him who performs it, and who claims to do it by "the finger of God" to believe that it is of God. That faith may be justified by what we know otherwise of the performer of miracle, or by the divine character of the teaching in connection with which it is performed; while there is also an instinctive faith in God which prepares us to believe that superhuman power put forth by one coming to us in His name would not be permitted to be without His presence. But the instance just referred to of imposture by Cortez proves that God does not authorise such blind confidence in mere manifestation of power.

We must therefore hold that the miracle divides with the teaching of a joint claim on our faith. To say this is by no means to admit that the miracle hangs as a dead weight on the teaching once supposed to hang on it. They are part of one divine manifestation, whose claim on our faith is to be weighed in its totality, and whose value to us in relation to our place in the kingdom of God is its fitness to help and strengthen the faith by which we believe and move in that kingdom. When I read the 11th chapter of the Epistle to the Hebrews, my faith as to the facts is that certain men, my brethren, did certain things wearing the aspect of superhuman power, and that they professed to do them through direct trust in God. Thus these men are to me witnesses for God that He invites and acknowledges such trust. ("Seeing we also are compassed about with so great a cloud of witnesses," Heb. xii. 1.)

In being taken to the faith of our Lord, "The author and finisher of our faith" - in whom it has its root and perfect development - we are only taken to the highest form of the same thing which we have been already contemplating; viz. direct trust in God and the acknowledgement of that trust on God's part. What is here immediately referred to is the faith in which our Lord "endured the cross despising the shame"; but the teaching of the whole record of His faith and of His mighty works is one and the same.

> And Jesus lifted up His eyes, and said, Father I thank Thee that thou hast heard me, and I know that thou hearest me always: but because of the people which stand by I said it, that they may believe that thou has sent me. And when He thus had spoken, He cried with a loud voice, Lazarus, come forth.

We are permitted to know that our Lord's part in the mighty work here recorded was faith in the Father, prayer and trust. It was thus an act of the Son revealing the Father - light shed on the kingdom of God; but which light it could not have been to us apart from our knowledge of the faith by which this miracle was performed. It is in truth as the history of acts of faith and of the divine acknowledgement of faith, that the record of miracles preserved for us in the Scriptures has its essential value to us. It is so receiving them that I find them no clog on Christianity, but indeed one element in is power. Whatever philosophic attraction has been found in the work of trying to extract from Christianity as presented to us in the Scriptures a pure essence of light (eliminating all that claims a miraculous character as, if not altogether to be rejected, only causing difficulty and embarrassment) to one seeking to walk by faith, the record of human faith and of the Divine acknowledgement of that faith is intended to be, and should be, a most welcome help, a part of the experience of humanity for which to feel ourselves debtors to God and man.

How painfully does the suggestion that our Lord's raising Lazarus might be the putting forth of a power within the reign of law emanating from Himself strike at the very life of the faith, which, read as the record of power put forth through God, the narrative of the raising of Lazarus cherishes in us. So also when I read that "God raised Christ from the dead and gave Him glory that our faith and hope might be in God", and connect the Son's part in the divine transaction with the prayer in dying "Father into thy hands I commend my spirit", I understand my own calling as a child of God to live by direct faith in God as God, and am made deeply conscious of the distance which separates such naked faith in God, triumphing over death in the knowledge that the fountain of life remains with Him, from man's ordinary walking by sight with an unreflecting trust in the stability of things that are, and in that promise for the future which man seems to himself to hear as the voice of the experience of the past; feeling the earth firm under him, and that it will be so tomorrow, because it is so today.

In the present state of men's minds on the subject of miracles, it is impossible to enter at all into the region of thought in which we now are without suggesting the question, how are miracles to be regarded? But I am anxious that it should be clearly understood, that in pleading for faith in the kingdom of God, what I am immediately concerned with is *this* aspect of that kingdom, that in it God presents Himself to our faith as the hearer and answerer of prayer. What lies between the Divine Will, *willing* an answer to prayer, and that answer as realised, faith as faith in God considers not. "Abraham was strong in faith, giving glory to God; and being fully persuaded that, what He had promised, He was able to perform."

Our highest teaching here is the life of Christ as Sonship towards the Father. The claim of the kingdom of God on our faith is one with the claim of Christ on our faith. What I have now been attempting to do is to fix attention on this claim, *as made by our Lord in coming to men in the Father's name.* To us every word He spoke comes with authority because He spoke it. But we shall suffer loss if we forget that it was otherwise with those who originally heard His words of truth from His own lips. If we rightly consider the record of His personal ministry, we shall see Him ever taking His hearers to a light already given in the Spirit, and in every man; to which light it is that He appeals in claiming to be received because coming to them in the Father's name. Consider that one word already quoted, "If ye then, being evil, know how to give good gifts unto your children: how much more shall your heavenly Father give His Holy Spirit to them that ask Him?" No higher faith could be asked for God, no faith so connected with the deepest need of man, as the faith that He gives His Holy Spirit to them that ask Him. Yet the form in which it is taught is a question which assumes preparedness to concede whatever is implied in God's relation to them as the Father of their spirits.

It is as having a place in the kingdom of God that we understand the atonement; for it is to our personal relation to God as the Father of our spirits that the atonement belongs; out of disorder in that relation has the need for it arisen; to bring that relation into harmony with its divine ideal is the end which it has contemplated. The reign of law as such offers no place for an atonement, even as it offers no place for prayer. The incarnation is the foundation of the kingdom of God, and faith in it prepares us for the faith of whatever nearness to God in love has been contemplated for those into whose nature the Son of God has come. But the incarnation not seen in its development as the Son revealing the Father may come, and has come, to be thought of only as a higher region of the reign of law. Christ has come to be contemplated simply as the mind of God become visible in humanity; the words "He that hath seen me hath seen the Father" being received as claiming nothing but this visibility. So understood, they would shed no light on the Divine Fatherhood, and the Divine Sonship to which it is the grace of God in Christ to raise us. But the words "He that hath seen me hath seen the Father" are explained by the words, "I am the way and the truth and the life, no man cometh unto the Father but by me." We see the Father when we see the Son, not merely because of identify of will and character in the Father and Son, but because a father as such is known only in his relation to a son.

CHAPTER 1

THE ENDS CONTEMPLATED IN THE ATONEMENT AWAKEN THE EXPECTATION THAT WE ARE TO UNDERSTAND ITS NATURE

The fundamental place which the atonement occupies in Christianity, gives importance to every aspect in which it can be contemplated. Of these aspects the chief are, its reference, its object, and its nature. For whom was it made? what was it intended to accomplish? what has it been in itself?

These are distinct questions, though the discussion of any one of them has generally more or less involved that of the other two. Certainly to be in possession of the true answer to any one of them must be a help in seeking the answers of the others; as also a misconception as to the answer of one must tend to mislead us in our consideration of the others. This is true, whichever aspect of the subject we may regard as the most important, or as having in it most light.

The question between the Reformers and the Church of Rome - the question of justification by faith alone - was most closely connected with the second aspect of the atonement viz., what it has accomplished. The discussions which subsequently divided the Reformers among themselves turned on the first; being as to whether the atonement had been made for all men, or for an election only. Much recent advocacy of the atonement has dealt freely with the third point, *i.e.*, what the atonement is in itself, as to which there was no question raised in the earlier discussions, but as to which it has been latterly felt, that the other questions could not be rightly taken up until this one was more closely considered; and as to which the advocates of the universality of the atonement have begun to feel, that the received conceptions of its nature have given to the advocates of an atonement referring to an election only, an advantage in argument which a true apprehension of what the atonement has been would do away with.

It is this third aspect of the atonement - *i.e.*, its nature - that I now propose to consider; which I propose to do with more immediate reference to the second aspect of the atonement, what it has accomplished *i.e.*, its relation to the remission of sins, and the gift of eternal life. The first point, viz., the extent of the reference of the atonement, it is no part of my immediate purpose to discuss. I believe that the atonement has been an atonement for sin, having reference to all mankind; I believe this to be distinctly revealed; I believe it to be also implied in what the atonement is in itself. But it is the illustration of the nature of the atonement which I have immediately in view; for it is in the prevailing state of men's minds on this subject that I feel a call to write.

I have just noticed that the exigencies of controversy, and the natural desire to give a philosophical harmony to theological system, has recently led to a reconsideration of the subject of the nature of the atonement. I shall subsequently have occasion to notice particularly what the result has been: and why I am not satisfied with that result: which had I been, I should gladly have felt this volume superseded. But the intellectual exigencies of systems are, if real, closely connected with the spiritual exigencies of the living man; and something higher than an intellectual demand, though that is not to be slighted as if it were not of God also, is felt to call for light on the nature of the atonement, when previously received conceptions no longer satisfy conscience, developed, and spiritually enlightened. The internal evidence of Christianity all prize, and anything felt to be a real addition to it all must welcome, though the freedom with which men seek such increase in the internal light of the gospel, is various. Some, indeed, may give too much ground for the charge of intellectual arrogance, in the demand they make for internal evidence at every step; while others, while thankfully receiving such evidence, fall into the error of treating it as something over and above what was needed for faith. I believe the former little realise how much more they believe than they understand; and I believe the latter as little realise how much their reception of what they believe depends ultimately upon what of it they do understand, and spiritually discern to be to the glory of God. I am not now to write on the nature of the atonement as one whose first faith in the atonement rested on a clear understanding of its nature; and yet I do not look back on that first faith as unwarranted and unreal. Our first faith may have in it elements which are true and abiding, although mingled with much darkness, which, in the low undeveloped condition of conscience, causes us no pain or uneasiness. As the divine life is developed in us, these two things proceed happily together, viz., a growing capacity of judging what the conditions are of a peace with God in full harmony with his name and character; and the apprehension of these conditions as all present in the atonement. But it would be altogether in contradiction to the nature of that love, which, while we were yet sinners, gave Christ to die for us, to suppose that true yieldings to the drawings of that love, however dimly and imperfectly apprehended, ever deceive the heart; or that the hope towards God, which accompanies them, can ever disappoint. To come to see more of the glory of God in the face of Jesus Christ is not to come to see reason to conclude that my hope was vain while I saw less. Yet surely, on the other hand, that God acknowledged me while I saw least, yet seeing something truly, is no reason why I should not seek to see more - yea as much as God may give me to see.

The kindness and love of God our Saviour towards man - the grace of God which hath appeared bringing salvation to all men - has a two-fold aspect; the one retrospective, referring to the evil from which that grace brings deliverance; the other prospective, referring to the good which it bestows. Of that evil men have the varied and sad experience, as they have also feelings that may be interpreted as longings after that good; but that experience is unintelligent, and these longings are vague, and the grace which brings salvation is itself the light which reveals both our need of salvation, and what the salvation is which we need; explaining to us the mystery of our dark experience, and directing our aimless longings to the unknown hope which was for us in God.

The light which reveals to us the evil of our condition as sinners, and the good of which God saw the capacity still to remain with us, reveals to us, at the same time, the greatness of the gulf which separated these two conditions of humanity; and the way in which the desire which arose in God, as the Father of spirits, to bridge over that gulf, has been accomplished. That way is the atonement; as to which it is certain that, if we were so far from seeing the evil of our own evil state as God saw it, and, I may say, so much farther still from being conscious to the measure of our own capacity of good, the way in which God was to accomplish the desire of his love for us we could not have of ourselves anticipated, but God himself must make it known to us.

But we know that, though the gospel alone sheds clear and perfect light on the evil of man's condition as a sinner, conscience fully recognises the truth of that revelation of ourselves which the gospel makes to us. Were it otherwise, assuredly its light would be no light to us. So also as to the gift of eternal life. When that gift is revealed to our faith, its suitableness to us, and fitness to fill all our capacities of well-being as God's offspring, is discerned by us in proportion as we are awakened to true self-consciousness, and learn to separate between what God made us, and what we have become through sin. And, in like manner, I believe that the atonement, related as it must needs be, retrospectively to the condition of evil from which it is the purpose of God to save us, and prospectively to the condition of good to which it is his purpose to raise us, will commend itself to our faith by the inherent light of its divine adaptation to accomplish all which it has been intended to accomplish.

Nor can I doubt that the high prerogative which belongs to us of discerning, and, in our measure, appreciating the divine wisdom, as well as the divine goodness, in other regions of God's acting, extends to this region also; which doubtless is the highest region of all, but which, while the highest, is also the region in which our human consciousness, and the teaching of the Spirit of God in conscience, should help our understandings most. When the apostle represents himself as by manifestation of the truth commending himself to every man's conscience in the sight of God, we are not to doubt that he so speaks with reference, no less to the atonement itself, than to the high ends which it contemplates.

In this view the internal evidence of the atonement ought to be the securest stronghold of Christianity: whereas we find many who profess to rest all their hope of acceptance with God upon the atonement, receiving it as a mystery which they do not feel it needful to understand; so that to them it is no part of the evidence of revelation, being commended to their faith only by the authority of a revelation itself received upon other grounds; while there are others to whom the presence of that doctrine in revelation is a strong objection to revelation itself. In this state of things it is natural to ask, "Can it be *that* conception of the atonement which the apostle expected would commend itself to every man's conscience in the sight of God which some thus treat as an argument against revelation, and which others, while receiving it, hold only as mystery?" and the latter part of the question is the more difficult: for a rebellious spirit may reject revelation for the very reason for which it has most claim to be received: while a meek, obedient spirit may be expected at once to receive and to understand. For "the secret of the Lord is with them that fear him, and he will shew them his covenant."

The lowest measure of internal evidence claimed for the doctrine of the atonement is, that conscience testifies to a need-be for an atonement. It has been usual, in arguing with those who refuse to concede even this much, to urge the fact that in all nations, in every age, men have sought to atone for sin by sacrifice. Whether this practice be referable to the universal tradition of an original institution of sacrifice, or be regarded as a consentaneous utterance of humanity, expressing its thoughts independently at all successive periods, and in places the most remote from each other, it is unquestionably an arresting fact. But, not to found a sweeping rejection of all the elements of the worship of the heathen on the testimony that they sacrificed to devils and not to God, even in the highest view that can be taken, their worship was that of "the unknown God" and, when brought by us to a higher light, must be judged by that higher light. If, in attempting so to judge, one man says - "I see here sacrifices offered to propitiate the divine favour. They are offered in manifest ignorance, for some of them are monstrous and revolting, and the least objectionable are manifestly inadequate to the end contemplated; but still we must respect the feelings that suggested sacrifice;" another may reply, "To me the feeling and its expression are alike referable to radical ignorance of God." Clearly the determination of this controversy must be sought elsewhere than in the historical fact which is its subject.

As to the use that has been made of the recorded instances of heroic self-sacrifice connected with assumed divine requirements - in reference to which it has been lately beautifully said that the love of Christ was "foreshadowed in these weaker acts of love" (Thomson,* p. 35) - however much we must admire the self-devotion manifested, it is not very clear how far the moral

---

* *The Atoning Work of Christ*, by William Thomson (Oxford)

element in the sacrifice, by which the person sacrificing himself was endeared to those for whose sakes he so devoted himself, was that which was supposed to give its value to the sacrifice in the eyes of the angry deities whom it was sought to propitiate. All that the demand implied was the high value of the offering to those from whom it was required, and the offended gods may have been thought of only as accepting what cost the people dearly; as Moloch received the children cast into the fire. But if indeed we are to conclude that the spirit of self-sacrifice in the victim was recognised as constituting the virtue of the sacrifice, there is here unquestionably a marvellous ray of light, from the midst of that gross darkness, shed upon the nature of atonement.

But if the testimony of conscience on the subject of the need-be for an atonement, is sought in the history of religion, let it be sought in the history of Christianity: and let not this seem a begging of the question. No man is entitled to put aside the assertion of a true man, declaring what the testimony of his conscience is, because that testimony coincides with the man's faith. And to those who say that they find in themselves no internal testimony to the doctrine of the atonement, we present a face which no serious mind will lightly put aside, when we refer, not to the dark and blind endeavours of the heathen to propitiate an unknown God, but to the experience, recorded by themselves, of those who, in all ages of the Church, have seemed to have attained to the highest knowledge of God, and closest communion with Him, and who have professed that they have seen a glory of God in the cross of Christ; that is, in the atonement as the channel through which sinful man receives the pardon of sin and eternal life. No one, indeed, is called upon to constrain his conscience to adopt the testimony of the conscience of others, whoever they may be. But if a man understand the nature of conscience, and realise how imperfect its development usually is, and how much the more matured Christian mind of one man may, without dictating, aid the faith of another man, he can never make little account of the conclusions on this great subject at which men characterised by holiness, and love to God and man, have arrived.

But the question is not to be decided by authority. Nor would I seem to be insensible - for I am not - to the force of what may be urged, even in reference to the recorded experience of the better portion of the Church, as to the extent to which theological systems, and traditional habits of thought, may affect, and have affected, religious experiences. I have, indeed, seen, in cases of deep awakening of spirit on the subject of religion, an identity of experience in reference to this matter under teachings so very different as to form of thought, as to preclude the idea that these experiences were an echo of the teaching; while, most certainly, they were not traceable to any previous habits of thought in the taught. But I dwell not on the argument from this source, as no man will or should accept the doctrine of the atonement because it has commended itself to the consciences of others while it does not as yet commend itself to his own.

But a response in conscience as contemplated by the apostle, implies much more than a recognition of a need be for an atonement; nor can it be regarded as accomplished, unless the atonement revealed be felt to commend itself by its own internal light, and its divine fitness to accomplish the high ends of God in it. And as this presupposes that these ends are themselves seen in the light of God, it is necessary, before proceeding further, to fix attention for a little, on the amount of the assertion, that there is a response in conscience to the testimony of the gospel regarding the evil condition in which the grace of God finds us, and the excellence of the salvation which it brings.

When it is said that the representations of revelation on the subject of our sin and guilt, and need of forgiveness, have a response in conscience, this is not asserted on the ground of the ordinary habit of thought of men's minds on these subjects, or of the feeling with which they usually treat the statements of the word of God regarding them. Men, indeed, readily enough confess that they are sinners, and that they need forgiveness; but this does not at all imply that they understand the charge of guilt which the Scriptures contain, far less respond to it; or that they have any conception of the forgiveness which they need while they speak about it so easily. How far it is otherwise becomes very manifest when the reality of sin is steadily contemplated, and the charge of guilt is weighed, and the testimony of conscience in reference to that charge is calmly listened to, and its solemn import is considered. All the experience that now ensues, shews how much the fact of sin is a discovery to the awakened sinner. Seeing what it amounts to, he now shrinks from the admission which he had previously made so easily; - though he may not now dare to recall it; while, as to forgiveness, in proportion as he comes to understand that he really needs it, he finds it difficult to believe that he himself, and his own sins, can be the subject of it. As long as to confess that I am a sinner is felt to be nothing more than to confess that my moral state is an imperfect one, that it presents a mixture of good and evil - that much in me needs forgiveness - I cannot say how much; while I trust that there is also good in me which God accepts, and which may so far counterbalance the evil, I can easily say, "I know I am a sinner; but I trust in God's mercy." But when the light of that word, "Thou shalt love the Lord thy God with all thy heart, and with all thy soul, and with all thy strength, and with all thy mind, and thy neighbour as thyself," shines in upon me, and with the clear, calm, solemn testimony within, is heard responding, "It is true - so it ought to be;" and in proportion as I am honest with myself, I feel constrained to reply, "But it is not so with me, I do not so love God, I do not so love my neighbour;" then the case is altogether changed. I am tempted to turn away, alike from the testimony of Scripture, and the testimony of conscience - shrinking from the confession which, if I listen and reply honestly, I must make. Or, if I am too much awakened, and too much in earnest, so to tamper with the light that is dawning on me - if I feel that I must look this terrible fact of sin full in the face, and do look at it; then does the forgiveness, of which I spoke easily while I knew not what it was to be forgiven, becomes to me most difficult of faith.

Now it is not strange, or, in one sense, wrong, that we should shrink from the feeling of simple unqualified guilt. It would not be well that it should be otherwise than both painful and terrible to conclude that, in the sight of God, I am guilty of not loving God, and not loving men. Things would be worse than they are with us, if such a discovery could be without causing both self-loathing and fear. Nor, as to forgiveness, is it to be wondered at, that, when we really come to understand that we need it, we find it most difficult to believe in it. God has been to us too much an unknown God, and our thoughts of him too far removed from the apprehension that there is forgiveness with God that he may be feared, to permit it to be otherwise. But, however painful the discovery of our sin, and however unprepared we may be to bear it by the knowledge of the help that is for us in God, the thoroughly awakened conscience, or rather conscience when we are thoroughly awakened to hear its voice, forces upon us the conviction, that the testimony of the Scriptures as to our sin and guilt before God and our need of forgiveness - of a forgiveness that shall be *purely* and *simply* such - the forgiving of a debt to one who has nothing to pay, is just and true.

If any will not concede this much - if any will extenuate the guilt of sin by referring what man is to his circumstances - or by treating his moral condition as a low state of development, corresponding to that in which intellectually he is found in savage life, and if the forgiveness needed be thus reduced to the lowest possible amount, until, indeed, it ceases to be *forgiveness*, and there is room left only for a benevolent pity at the most; from persons in this mind I cannot expect that they will take the next step with me in this path, seeing they do not take the first. But, although I can concede much qualification of the apprehension of sin which we find uttered by newly awakened sinners, and admit that their language is very much affected by their ignorance of God, and the perturbing effect of the awful discovery as to their own moral and spiritual state which they have made, I cannot qualify the assertion, that the testimony of Scripture as to the reality and guilt of sin, and the sinner's dependence upon free grace for pardon, has a clear and unequivocal response in conscience; the recognition of which response on the sinner's part, is the proper attitude for his mind to assume, in listening to and weighing the doctrine of the atonement.

Nay more, looking at sin in reference to a still deeper weighing of a man's own state as a sinner, I believe that the experience which the apostle Paul speaks of, in the close of the seventh chapter of his Epistle to the Romans, must be recognised as the completeness of that development of conscience, which fitly prepares the mind for understanding and welcoming the atonement. I refer to that condition of the human spirit in which a man has so seen the claims of the law of God in the light of conscience, that he can say, "I delight in the law of God after the inner man," while by that same light, he judges what his own flesh is, and what its power over him makes him to be; so that he says, "I find a law in my members warring against the law of my mind, and bringing me into captivity to the law of sin that is in my members," and his heart's cry is, "O wretched man that I am! who shall deliver me from the body of this death?" Until, not only the contrariety that is between sin and the law of God, and the position of guilt in which it places the sinner, are seen in the light of conscience; but, beyond this, the inward contradiction with the law of his own well-being, and with that which he must recognise as the true ideal of excellence for humanity, is also seen in that light, and painfully felt, a man is not truly having the full testimony of conscience on the subject of sin, or conscious in himself to that full response which is in man to the teaching of revelation on this subject. And until a man has come to stand at this point, he is not fully prepared to consider the atonement *retrospectively*, that is, in its relation to the evil condition from which it is our deliverance.

As to the testimony of conscience to the discovery of revelation on the subject of the gift of eternal life, to which the atonement has *prospective* reference, the fact of this testimony is not alleged on the ground of men's ordinary habits of thought and feeling, in this case any more than in the former. The intelligent apprehension of that which is said, when it is said, that "God has given to us eternal life," and the enlightened self-consciousness in which that gift is welcomed as altogether suited to man, and the highest good of which he is capable, imply a development of conscience, and a clearness of inward light, beyond even what the fullest reception of the teaching of the Bible on the subject of sin, and guilt, and spiritual death, supposes.

But conscience is capable of such development; and eternal life may be apprehended by us as a manner of existence - a kind of life, the elements of which we understand, the excellence of which commends itself to us, and our own capacity for participation in which as originally created in God's image, and apart from our bondage to sin, we can discern in ourselves.

I speak of eternal life - that life which was with the Father before the world was, and which is manifested in the Son - of his own acquaintance with which as a life lived in humanity, through his acquaintance with Him in whom it was manifested, the apostle John speaks with such fulness of expression in the beginning of his first epistle. I do not speak of an unknown future blessedness, in a future state of being, of which conscience can understand nothing; but I speak of life which in itself is one and the same here and hereafter - however it may be developed in us hereafter beyond its development here. Of this life conscience can take cognisance, its elements it can understand and consider - comparing them with the elements of that other perishing life of which man has experience; and, taking both to the light of what man as God's offspring, it can, in that light, decide on the excellence of eternal life, and on the great grace of God in bestowing it, and the perfect salvation in which man partakes in receiving it. How little men's consciences address themselves to this high task, is too manifest; inasmuch as ordinary religion is so much a struggle to secure an unknown *future happiness*, instead of being the meditation on, and the welcoming of the *present gift* of *eternal life*. But to this high task conscience is equal, and to engage in it is the imperative demand which the preaching of the gospel makes on it, that preaching which seeks to commend itself to every man's conscience in the sight of God.

This, then, is the second part of the due preparation for considering the nature of the atonement, with the purpose of coming to know what response that doctrine has in the heart of man, viz., that the gift of eternal life, revealed as bestowed on us through the atonement, be taken to the light of conscience; and what that gift is, be there seen; and the high result that is accomplished in man in his coming to live that life, be truly conceived of. For thus having before the mind what God has proposed to do through the atonement, now prospectively, as formerly retrospectively, there is the likelihood that its nature, and its suitableness for accomplishing the divine end, shall become visible to us; if that may be at all.

These two extreme points being clearly conceived of, and together present to the mind; and the evil condition of man which the gospel reveals, and the blessed condition to which it raises our hopes, being seen in the light of conscience, developed to this degree under the teaching of God; the gulf which separates them is seen to be very great. We are contemplating extreme opposites, in the highest and most solemn region of things: - spiritual darkness and death, sin and guilt, the righteous condemnation and wrath of God, inward disorder and strife between man and the law of his own well-being; - from these our thoughts pass to divine light filling humanity, eternal life partaken in, righteousness and holiness, the acceptance and favour of God, inward harmony experienced in the fulfilment in man of that ideal for him which was in the divine mind from the beginning.

It is difficult for us to realise the opposite states, which, by such words, we attempt to describe. The very words we use, though we know them to be the right words, we use with the consciousness, that they have, in our lips, but a small part of their meaning. If we set ourselves steadfastly to study their use in the Scriptures, and listen with open ear and heart to the interpretation of them, which conscience, under the teaching of the Holy Spirit, accepts, we find these awful realities of evil and good, becoming gradually more and more palpable and real to us; so that they come to be felt as the only realities, and existence comes to have its interest entirely in relation to them. But the wings of our faith do not long sustain this flight. Not that we come to doubt the conclusions at which in such seasons we have arrived; but that, so to speak, we descend from this high region of light and truth, and come down to the earth, and to ordinary human life, and the conditions of humanity that present themselves around us; and, looking at men and women as they are, and at the mixture of good and evil which they exhibit - seeing also ourselves in others - we practically reconcile ourselves to them, and to ourselves; and the vision of unmixed evil, and of perfect good, fades from our remembrance, or, at best, from having been felt as that which was most real, becomes but as an ideal.

One cause of the practical difficulty that is experienced in keeping our habitual thoughts and feelings in harmony with the perceptions of our most far-seeing moments, is this, that the world in which we are is actually a mixture of good and evil; that it presents neither the unmixed evil of which the Scriptures speak, and to which conscience testifies as man's sinful state, nor the unmixed good, which the Scriptures reveal, and which, in the light of conscience, we recognise as eternal life. We are not in a world yet unvisited by the grace of God; on the contrary, we are encompassed by fruits of that very atonement in which we are called to believe. Nay, the appearances presented in man's condition as we know it, which have furnished the objectors to the atonement with their most specious arguments, are actually to be traced to that atonement itself; while, at the same time, the power for good which belongs to the atonement, and its true working, have no perfect realisation in what men are seen to be; for none are, simply and absolutely, what the atonement would make them; so that, on the one side, none are seen so far from God as, but for the atonement, they would have been; - while, on the other hand, none are seen so near to God as it has been the end of the atonement to bring them. The light shining in the darkness modifies the darkness, even while the darkness comprehends it not; - and, even where it is comprehended, the darkness is not yet seen altogether destroyed by it.

Therefore we must, in studying the subject of the atonement, exercise our minds to abide in that sense and perception of things to which we attain, when the teaching of the Bible, as to the sinful state from which the atonement delivers us, and the eternal life which through it we receive, is having a full response in conscience. So shall we see the work of God in Christ in the light of a true apprehension of what that work had to accomplish; and shall not fall into the error of allowing the partial effects of that work itself to be to us arguments for doubting its necessity and reality.

The first demand which the gospel makes upon us in relation to the atonement is, that we believe that *there is forgiveness with God*. Forgiveness

- that is, love to an enemy surviving his enmity, and which, notwithstanding his enmity, can act towards him for his good; this we must be able to believe to be in God towards us, in order that we may be able to believe in the atonement.

This is a faith which, in the order of things, must precede the faith of an atonement. If we could ourselves make an atonement for our sins, as by sacrifice the heathen attempted to do, and as, in their self-righteous endeavours to make their peace with God, men are, in fact, daily attempting, then such an atonement might be thought of as preceding forgiveness, and the cause of it. But if God provides the atonement, then forgiveness must precede atonement; and the atonement must be the form of the manifestation of the forgiving love of God, not its cause.

But surely the demand for the faith that there is forgiveness in God has a response in conscience; and doubtless it is, in part at least, ignorance of God that causes the difficulty in believing in forgiveness, which is felt when an actual need of forgiveness that shall be purely such, is realised. For it ought not to be difficult to believe that, though we have sinned against God, God still regards us with a love which has survived our sins. Nay more, we cannot realise the two ideas with reference to man which we have just been considering, viz. the evil state into which sin has brought him, and the opposite good state of which the capacity has remained in him, as together present to the mind of the Father of the spirits of all flesh, without feeling that he must desire to bridge over the gulf that separates these two conceived conditions of humanity; - that if it can be bridged over He will bridge it over; that, if that conceivable good for man is a possible good for man, it will be put within man's reach. Therefore, the first tone that catches the ear of the heart in hearing the gospel being that "there is forgiveness with God," it ought not to be felt difficult to believe this joyful sound. It ought to have, and doubtless it has, an answer in conscience.

The expression once familiar to the lips of ministers of Christ in our land, and which the greater awakenedness of their people's minds on the subject of sin, caused them to feel the need of practically, viz. "that it is the greatest sin to despair of God's mercy," surely is a record of the inward sense of mercy as entering into our original and fundamental apprehension of God: "Unto us belong shame and confusion of face: unto the Lord our God belongeth mercy," is an instinctive utterance of the human heart. Accordingly, when our Lord teaches us to "love our enemies that we may be the children of our Father in heaven, who makes his sun to shine on the evil and on the good," he assumes, that the witness without which God has never from the beginning left himself, in that he has given rain from heaven and fruitful seasons, has addressed something in man which could interpret the acting of love to enemies.

The atonement, I say, presupposes that there is forgiveness with God; and in doing so has a response in conscience. But this is not the question which the doctrine of the atonement raises, neither is it because it implies such forgiveness that it has been objected to: on the contrary, the objection has been made - but an objection that could apply only to a false view of the atonement - that that doctrine did not recognise the mercy that is essentially in God, inasmuch as it represented God as needing to be propitiated - to be made gracious. An atonement to make God gracious, to move him to compassion, to turn his heart toward those from whom sin had alienated his love, it would, indeed, be difficult to believe in; for, if it were needed it would be impossible. To awaken to the sense of the need of such an atonement, would certainly be to awaken to utter and absolute despair. But the Scriptures do not speak of such an atonement; for they do not represent the love of God to man as the effect, and the atonement of Christ as the cause, but - just as the contrary - they represent the love of God as the cause, and the atonement as the effect. "God so loved the world, that he gave his only begotten Son, that whosoever believeth in him, might not perish, but have everlasting life."

Those, therefore, who object to the doctrine of the atonement on the assumption that the atonement is presented to them as the cause of God's forgiving love, are placed under a great disadvantage by this misapprehension of the demand that is made on their faith. What they are asked to believe has its difficulties - and I do not wish to understate these: but they are as nothing in comparison; and let them learn with thankfulness, that that is not the true conception of the atonement which has so repelled them. That which they are really asked to consider as what it is expected, being truly apprehended, will commend itself to conscience in the sight of God, is the way in which the forgiving love of God has manifested itself for the salvation of sinful men.

Those, who, being under no misapprehension on this point, still draw back from the faith of the atonement, do so as feeling a difficulty which may be thus expressed: Seeing that there is forgiveness with God that he may be feared, and that his love not only survives men's transgressions, but can confer new gifts on those who have transgressed, why should not this love be manifested without an atonement? Why should not the pardon of sin as an act of Divine Clemency be simply intimated? Why should not this new and great gift of eternal life be simply bestowed, and presented to men as the rich bounty of God?

I have referred to the difficulty which a thoroughly awakened sinner feels in believing that God will pardon his sins, and grant to him eternal life; and such an objector would say, "Why should he feel any such difficulty? Is it not the evidence of a morbid moral state so to feel?" Now I have admitted that the feeling in question, arises in part from the extent to which God has been previously an unknown God. But only in part. There are other elements in that difficulty which are connected with the dawn of a true knowledge of God. God's mercy has not been previously apprehended, otherwise it would be felt wrong to despair of it; but neither have God's holiness and righteousness, and his wrath against sin been previously apprehended, and the fears, represented as indications of a morbid moral state, are, I believe, in reality the effect of light visiting the spirit of the man - light as to the real sinfulness of sin, and its contrariety to the mind of God. Admitting that there is much perturbation of mind - admitting that the light that is shed upon the truth of man's moral and spiritual condition, is but partial, and that the name of God and its glory have not yet shone in upon his soul and conscience full orbed - still it is light that is visiting the man who uses language as to his own sinfulness, and the deserts of his sin, with the expression of fears as to the wrath of God, which the objector would refer to a morbid state of mind; fears which may, indeed, seem extravagant, and almost madness to others who have not yet taken themselves and what they are in themselves, to that light of God in which he sees himself, and who can therefore speak to him of trusting in God's mercy, and rebuke his fears, so easily; not because they know more of God's mercy and forgiveness than he does, but because they have such different apprehensions of that, sin, as to which forgiveness is needed.

Nor is the distress experienced connected with the forgiveness of past sin alone. That grace for the time to come - the gift of eternal life - which appears to the objector to the atonement what may easily be believed in is not found to be so. It may be so far conceived of by the awakened sinner, and may so commend itself to him, that he can say, "I delight in the law of God after the inward man;" and yet, to believe that the good he apprehends is freely granted to him, may prove so far from an easy act of faith in God's goodness, that the ideal which has dawned upon him, is felt to be the ideal of a hopeless good. He finds "a law in his members warring against the law of his mind, and bringing him into captivity to the law of sin that is in his members;" - so that he cries out - "O wretched man that I am! who shall deliver me from the body of this death?"

Now, we know that where, in such cases, all general urging of God's mercy and clemency, and willingness to pardon and to save, fail to give peace, or quicken hope; the presenting of the atonement for the acceptance of faith does both. Awakened sinners (and I use the expression simply as to my own mind the most accurate, while also it is the echo of the word "Awake, thou that sleepest,") who are finding themselves unable to believe that God - not because He is not merciful and gracious but though merciful and gracious, and however merciful and gracious He is - can pardon their sins and bestow on them eternal life, are found able to believe in such pardon, and to receive the hope of eternal life, when these are presented to them in connection with the sacrifice of Himself by which Christ put away sin, becoming the propitiation for the sins of the whole world.

This fact is surely deserving of the serious consideration of those whose objection to the atonement is, that it should be enough for man's peace and hope to be told, that the Lord God is merciful and gracious and ready to forgive, and to relieve all who call upon him. Here there is manifested an inability to believe in God's forgiveness as meeting man's need, when presented simply as clemency and mercy: - but, presented in the form of the atonement, it is believed in. Not surely because less credit for love and mercy is given to God now; for on the contrary the conception of love simply forgiving, and of love forgiving at such a cost to itself, differ just in this, that in the latter, the love is infinitely enhanced.

An objector may reply that doubtless this is a remarkable mental phenomenon, and that he does not deny that what are called religious memoirs abound in illustrations of it; but that he cannot assume that those who have had this history were in the light, and that he himself is in the dark; - and that to his mind, to preach forgiveness, and the gift of eternal life, in connection with an atonement, is only to increase the difficulty of faith - for that, while he sees in both these, contemplated simply in themselves, what he receives as worthy of the goodness of God, the addition of the doctrine of the atonement introduces other, and to him, mysterious elements into the question, complicating what should be a simple matter, and, in fact, representing the love of God as not at liberty freely to express itself, but, having difficulties and hindrances to encounter - the removal and overcoming of which involved such mysteries as the incarnation, and the self-sacrifice of the Son of God.

It is even so: and, this, doubtless, is the difficulty - the great and ultimate difficulty; and let its amount be distinctly recognised. That God should do anything that is loving and gracious - which implies only an act of will - putting forth power guided by wisdom, this seems easy of faith. But, either that any object should appear desirable to God's love, which infinite power, guided by infinite wisdom, cannot accomplish by a simple act of the divine will, or that, if there be an object not to be thus attained, God will proceed to seek that object by a process which implies a great cost to God, and self-sacrifice - either of these positions is difficult of faith. But the doctrine of the atonement involves them both: and this we must realize, and bear in mind, if we would deal wisely, nay justly, with objectors.

Yet, doubtless, the elements in the atonement which cause difficulty are the very elements which give it its power to be that peace and hope for man which the gospel contemplates, and which a simple intimation of the divine clemency and goodness could not quicken in him. It is that God is contemplated as manifesting clemency and goodness at a great cost, and not by a simple act of will that costs nothing, that gives the atonement its great power over the heart of man. For that is a deep, yea, the deepest spiritual instinct in man which affirms, that in proportion as any act manifests love it is to be believed as ascribed to God who is love. No manifestation of power meeting me can so assure me that I am meeting God as the manifestation of love does. Therefore they greatly err who seek an external evidence of power, instead of an internal evidence of love, in considering the claim of anything to be received as from God.

Accordingly, a high argument in favour of Christianity, and which has awakened a deep response in many a heart, has been founded upon this very aspect of the doctrine of the atonement, viz. that it represents God as manifesting self-sacrificing love; and so reveals the depth, not to say the reality, of love, as creation and providence could not do. And as a final cause for the permission of a condition of things, giving opportunity to the divine love to shew the self-sacrificing nature of love, and to bless with the blessedness of being the objects of such love, and, as the fruit of this, the blessedness of so loving - in this view this argument is both true and deep.

But the internal evidence which at the point at which we stand in our inquiry we need, must be something different from this. The evil condition to which sin had reduced man, the good of which nevertheless man still continued capable; these ideas in relation to man being conceived of as together present to the divine mind, it appeared to us that we could believe, that the desire would arise in the heart of the Father of the spirits of all flesh to bridge over this gulf if that could be: nay, it seemed impossible to believe that that desire should not arise. Now the gospel declares, that the love of God has, not only desired to bridge over this gulf, but has actually bridged it over, and the atonement is presented to us as that in which this is accomplished. What we seek is internal evidence - a response in our own spirits, as to the divine wisdom manifested in what is thus represented as the means by which divine love attains the object of its desire.

But in this view it is not enough to say that this way is that in which the greatest proof of love is afforded. Love cannot be conceived of as doing anything gratuitously, merely to shew its own depth, for which thing there was no call in the circumstances of the case viewed in themselves. A man may love another so as to be willing to die for him; - but he will not actually lay down his life merely to shew his love, and without there being anything to render his doing so necessary in order to save the life for which he yields up his own.

Therefore the question remains, "How was so costly an expression of love as the atonement necessary?" - and how costly this expression of divine love has been to God we must fully recognise. For there is no doubt that a chief source of the difficulty which is felt in receiving the doctrine of the atonement is, that the atonement presupposes the incarnation. "God commendeth his love toward us, in that, while we were yet sinners Christ died for us." A man who is contented to die for another manifests his love

at the greatest cost to himself. By such an illustration, therefore, the Apostle
teaches that the love that is manifested in Christ's dying for us is manifested
at a great cost to God. Of course this assumes that Christ is God. That God
should sacrifice one creature for another - subject one of His offspring to
death that others of His offspring might live - would have nothing in it
parallel to a man's laying down his own life for another. To say that Christ
was not after all sacrificed in this transaction; - that what he endured was on
his part voluntary, and endured in the contemplation of a reward - for that,
"for the joy set before him he endured the cross, despising the shame," is no
answer: for that *God* takes credit to *Himself* for the love that *Christ* manifests
in dying for us - *this* is the point of the Apostle's argument. As to the reward
set before Christ, it is that fruit of His self-sacrifice which must be presupposed in order that the self-sacrifice should be a reasonable transaction. Self-
sacrificing love does not sacrifice itself but for an end of gain to its object;
otherwise it would be folly. Does its esteeming as a reward that gain to those
for whom it suffers, destroy its claim to being self-sacrifice? Nay, that which
seals its character as self-sacrificing love is, that this to it is a satisfying reward.
"He shall see of the travail of his soul, and be satisfied."

In considering why our redemption has been at such a cost, and the whole
subject of the nature of the atonement, we shall be greatly helped by keeping
distinctly before our minds, these two extreme points to which the atonement is related in that it refers to the one retrospectively, to the other
prospectively, viz. the condition in which the grace of God finds us, and the
condition to which it raises us.

   Christ has "redeemed us who were under the law, *that* we might receive
the adoption of sons" - Christ "suffered for us, the just for the unjust, *that* he
might bring us to God." Both that we were "under the law" and "unjust" and
that we were "to receive the adoption of sons" and to be "brought to God"
may be expected to have affected the nature of the atonement as determining
what it must be adequate to: more especially the latter, as the great result
contemplated. Accordingly, in the writings of the Apostles, we find the
necessity for the atonement being what it was, connected with both - but
more especially with the latter.

   Yet in our systems of theology the former, and not the latter, has been
chiefly the foundation of the arguments employed. Not that the latter has
not also been taken into account, and provision made for it; but it has not
been regarded as shedding light on the *nature* of the atonement. This is
certain. For however our "receiving the adoption of sons" and our being
"brought to God" enter into the *scheme of salvation* as represented in these
systems, it is in the fact that we "were under the law" and "unjust" - that is
to say, that we were sinners, under the condemnation of a broken law, that
the *necessity for the atonement* has been recognised.

The important consequences that have followed from this, as seems to me, departure from the example of the Apostles will appear as we proceed. But with the conclusions arrived at as to the necessity for an atonement, as arising from the fact, that we, whom the grace of God has visited, were sinners under the condemnation of a broken law, I fully accord. I believe that "by the deeds of the law could no flesh living be justified" - understanding by the law, not the Mosaic ritual, but that law of which the Apostle speaks when he says, "I delight in the law of God after the inward man" - that is to say, the law, "Thou shalt love the Lord thy God with all thine heart and mind and soul and strength, and thy neighbour as thyself." I believe that no modification of the law *as a law*, in accommodation to man's condition as a sinner, is conceivable that could either give the assurance of the pardon of sin, or quicken us with a new life; and that all idea of bridging over, by a modified law, the gulf which we have been contemplating is untenable. I believe that, if this was to be accomplished, it could only be by some moral and spiritual constitution quite other than the law: while, at the same time, such other constitution cannot be conceived of as introduced in any way that does not duly honour the law; or that delivers from the consequences of transgressing it, without vindicating the righteousness of the law, and the consistency of the law-giver. Finally, I believe that this requirement is recognised in the gospel, being fully met in the atonement.

But I must guard against seeming to give to the reasonings by which these conclusions have been arrived at, an unqualified assent. When it is argued that the justice or righteousness of God and his holiness, and also his truth and faithfulness, presented difficulties in the way of our salvation, which rendered for their removal an atonement necessary, I fully assent to this; - and, when it is added, as I have seen it lately urged, that the goodness, the love of God as the moral ruler and governor of the universe, also demanded an atonement, that our salvation might be consistent with the well being of the moral universe - I freely concede this also: - nay, more, I would say, not the love of God having respect to the interests of the moral universe only, but the love of God having respect to the interests of the subjects of the salvation themselves. For indeed to me salvation otherwise than through the atonement is a contradiction.

But while in reference to the not uncommon way of regarding this subject which represents righteousness and holiness as opposed to the sinner's salvation, and mercy and love as on his side, I freely concede that all the divine attributes were, in one view, against the sinner in that they called for the due expression of God's wrath against sin in the history of redemption; I believe, on the other hand, that the justice, the righteousness, the holiness of God have an aspect according to which they, as well as his mercy, appear as intercessors for man, and crave his salvation. Justice may be contemplated as according to sin its due; and there is in righteousness, as we are conscious to it, what testifies that sin should be miserable. But *justice* looking at the sinner, not simply as the fit subject of punishment, but as existing in a moral condition of unrighteousness, and so its own opposite, must desire that the sinner should cease to be in that condition; should cease to be unrighteous - should become righteousness: righteousness in God craving for righteousness in man, with a craving which the realisation of righteousness in man alone can satisfy. So also of holiness. In one view it repels the sinner, and would banish him to outer darkness, because of its repugnance to sin. In another it is pained by the continued existence of sin and unholiness, and must desire that the sinner should cease to be sinful. So that the sinner, conceived of as awakening to the consciousness of his own evil state, and saying to himself, "By sin I have destroyed myself. Is there yet hope for me in God?" should hear an encouraging answer, not only from the love and mercy of God, but also from his very righteousness and holiness. We must not forget, in considering the response that is in conscience to the charge of sin and guilt, that, though the fears which accompany that response are partly the effect of a dawning of light, they also in part arise from remaining darkness. He who is able to interpret the voice of God within him truly, and with full spiritual intelligence, will be found saying, not only, "There is to me cause for fear in the righteousness and holiness of God" - but also, "There is room for hope for me in the divine righteousness and holiness." And when gathering consolation from the meditation of the name of the Lord, that consolation will be not only, "Surely the divine mercy desires to see me happy rather than miserable" - but also, "Surely the divine righteousness desires to see me righteous - the divine holiness desires to see me holy - my continuing unrighteous and unholy is as grieving to God's righteousness and holiness as my misery through sin is to His pity and love." "Good and righteous is the Lord; therefore will He teach sinners the way which they should choose." "A just God and a Saviour," not as the harmony of a seeming opposition, but "a Saviour," *because* "a just God."

If this thought commends itself to my reader's mind as it does to mine, he will feel it to be important; and he will see, in reference to the atonement, not that it tends to make an atonement appear less necessary, but that it may greatly affect the nature of the atonement required: for it implies that the prospective aspect of the atonement - its reference to the life of sonship given to us in Christ, has been its most important aspect as respects the demands of righteousness and holiness, as it confessedly is as respects those of mercy and love. This is so - while, assuredly, it is also true that the retrospective aspect of the atonement as connecting the pardon of sin with the vindicating of the honour of the divine law, is not less a meeting of a demand of divine love than of the demands of righteousness and holiness. How could it be otherwise, seeing that the law is love?

CHAPTER II

TEACHING OF LUTHER

The evil of the condition in respect of which we needed salvation, and the excellence of the salvation given to us in Christ; and the reality and exceeding greatness of the difficulties which stood in the way of our salvation, and which the Saviour had to encounter in accomplishing our redemption, have perhaps never been more vividly realised than by the great reformer Luther. And, though he does not afford much help to one seeking a clear intellectual apprehension of the nature and essence of the atonement, or of that might by which Christ prevailed; yet that his spiritual insight into these things has been great, is implied in the depth of his understanding of justification by faith, and of the relation in which peace in believing stands to that which our Lord asserted concerning himself when He said, "He that hath seen me hath seen the Father." I believe it will be of much advantage to us subsequently to occupy a little space here with the consideration of his teaching in relation to the atonement, and what it has accomplished.

I have referred more than may meet the indulgence of some readers, though less than my own feeling of its value as a source of light would have inclined me to do, to the experience of deeply awakened sinners. The great reformer was such an one: and this part of his history has impressed a special character on his teaching more than anything else that went to make him what he was. To any who read his words, not as extravagance and fanaticism, but - as I believe they are entitled to be read - words of truth and soberness, his commendation of his great doctrine of "Justification by faith alone" from his own experience of its preciousness, is deeply interesting, and, I may say, most affecting. For, when Luther speaks of the law and the Gospel - of the righteousness of works, and of the righteousness of faith, it is not as a speculative theologian, reasoning out principles to their conclusions, and arranging the parts of a system in their due relations. He speaks of the law as what wrought with his spirit until it had brought him to the brink of despair. He speaks of the gospel as what had spoken peace and life to him, and, by its revelation of Christ to his faith, had raised him as from hell to heaven. Seeking to be justified by works is to him no mere theological error, as to which he can conclusively reason. The very thought of it moves him to the depths of his being; renewing to him, with all its horrors, the past in which he had himself so sought justification, and stirring him to a vehement indignation against those who direct men's steps into that path of death. On the other hand, the righteousness of faith seems to be to him that of which he cannot speak without the renewed sense of his first peace and joy in believing, and of the excellent glory of that "new world" into which "faith mounts up, where is no law, no sin, no remorse or sting of conscience, no death, but perfect, joy, righteousness, grace, peace, life, salvation, glory" (p.84).* The law and the gospel in their relation to the human spirit, are to Luther as two spiritual regions which his spirit knows, having trembled and agonised in the one, and rejoiced and triumphed in the other; - but the former of which has no claim upon his presence in it, and ought to be to him as if it were not; being, indeed, done away by Christ, and having no existence now but through unbelief; while in the latter it is the will of God that he should dwell by faith; to do which is to give God glory and be righteous in His sight. The vividness and picturing form of his speech is quite startling: yet is it in no sense figurative or rhetorical; for he is manifestly keeping as close to the simple expression of his mental and spiritual perceptions as he can. Reading his pleadings against the law, and for the gospel, it is impossible not to feel that he who gave such a fundamental place to justification by faith, was himself the preacher of it in an altogether distinctive and preeminent sense.

I shall endeavour briefly to express the conception of Luther's mind on the subject of the atonement which I have received from a careful study of his full commentary on the Epistle of the Apostle Paul to the Galatians.

This epistle has had a special interest to Luther, because he recognised Paul's controversy with the judaising teachers, by whom the Galatian converts to Christianity had been seduced, as substantially the same with that in which he himself was engaged with the church of Rome; and, as is common to him with the other Reformers, his arguing on the subject of the atonement has a special character impressed upon it, by the relation to certain errors in the church of Rome in which he was contemplating it. Luther had not to contend with persons denying the doctrine of the atonement: what he had to contend against was human additions to the provision for peace of conscience and hope towards God, revealed in the gospel; and what we learn of his mind on the subject of the atonement is what he is led to utter in pleading for justification by faith alone.

I have said that no man ever more realised than Luther did, that there were actual difficulties in the nature of things to be dealt with in accomplishing our redemption - difficulties which a simple act of the Divine will could not do away with; but which have been successfully and triumphantly dealt with in the atonement for the sins of men, made by the Son of God. His deep feeling of the dishonour done to Christ by combining any other element with our vision of Him by faith, in our peace and confidence towards God,

---

* Page references in this chapter seem to be from the 'Middleton' edition of Luther's Commentary on Galatians - first published in 1807 by the Revd Erasmus Middleton of Turvey in Bedfordshire. There is an 1810 edition in New College Library, Edinburgh.

may have, in part, moved him to the use of the strong language which he employs, both in setting forth what Christ had to accomplish, and how he has accomplished it. But it is manifest that he could not speak of these subjects without feeling it difficult to find language strong enough for his convictions. And the law, and sin, an death, and the devil who had the power of death, are set before us as awful realities against man; and as to be encountered and overcome by Him who had undertaken to save man: and Christ's victory over them is seen in Luther's words, not as a simple act of divine, resistless, power, but as a moral and spiritual victory - the triumph of good as good over evil as evil, of righteousness and life, over sin and death; bringing with it all secondary external results in its train.

Not that on these difficult and mysterious subjects, he does not - as well as those who do not give the same impression of having approached them nearly - leave us disposed to ask many questions. He, as well as others, speaks of our sins as laid upon Christ, without helping us to understand what this means; - while he is distinguished from others by the anxiety he shews to select the strongest words to express the identification of Christ with our sins; refusing (p. 300) to understand "was made sin for us," in 2 Cor. v. 21, as meaning a sacrifice for sin (while he admits that the word used will bear that meaning), choosing rather to insist that He was made sin for us in some more absolute way of identifying Himself with us and our sin, in order that we, with whose sin He had so identified Himself, might be identified with Him in respect of His righteousness; and that sin and righteousness meeting in Him, and righteousness triumphing over sin, we might partake in the triumph and all its fruits.

> Because in the self-same person which is the highest, the greatest and the only sinner, there is also an everlasting and invincible righteousness; therefore these two do encounter together the highest, the greatest and the only sin, and the highest, the greatest and the only righteousness. Here one of them must needs be overcome and give place to the other . . . righteousness is everlasting, immortal, invincible . . . therefore in this context sin must needs be vanquished and killed, and righteousness must overcome and reign. So in Christ all sin is vanquished, killed and buried, and righteousness remaineth a conqueror and reigneth for ever. (pp. 294, 295)

This conception of Christ as the one man, having present together in Himself the sin of all other men, and His own righteousness, Luther endeavours in all possible forms of speech to present as an *actual fact*, and as what justifies, and underlies such statements as that, "the Lord laid on Him the iniquity of us all," and that, "He bore our sins in His own body on the tree." And, whatever difficulties the matter may have presented to Luther's own mind, or whatever difficulties his words may cause to us, attempting to attach to them a definite and consistent meaning, he leaves no room to doubt that what he sought to set forth he conceived of as a reality, and not as a legal fiction. For he thus illustrates the identifying of Christ with men:

> For when a sinner cometh to the knowledge of himself indeed, he feeleth not only that he is miserable, but misery itself; not only that he is a sinner, and is accursed, but even sin and malediction itself. For it is a terrible thing to bear sin, the wrath of God, malediction and death. *Wherefore that man which hath a true feeling of these things as Christ did truly and effectually feel them for all mankind*, is made even sin, death, malediction. (p.300)

But to think of Luther as really having any unworthy conceptions of Christ would be altogether erroneous. It was, doubtless, because of his great realisation of the divine and perfect righteousness which were in Christ, and which in the *deepest*, and doubtless, he must have felt *only absolute* sense were *alone* His, that he was able to use that which he thus calls an "apostolic liberty of speech" in setting forth the reality of His bearing our sins.

Such is Luther's teaching as to the retrospective aspect of the atonement. His teaching as to its prospective bearing - the positive fruits of benefit to us through Christ's victory, the gift of eternal life itself - is the following out of that root conception of Christ's identifying of Himself with us. In virtue of this identification, the freedom and righteousness and life which are in Christ, being His own proper endowments, and of which His coming under our sins did not despoil Him, but which proved themselves mightier than all that power of darkness - coming forth triumphant from the conflict - these all are ours. As ours we are called to recognise them. As endowed with them we are called to conceive of ourselves. As the provisions of the salvation granted to us we are to use them. As the elements of our new divine life we are to live in them and by them. They are all ours as Christ is ours - "He is made of God unto us wisdom and righteousness and sanctification and redemption."

Christ our life is presented to our faith, that believing in Him we may live - yet not we, but Christ in us. Faith does not make these high endowments, the elements of the gift of Christ, ours: they are ours by the gift of God. Faith apprehends them, accepts them - gives God glory in accepting them; and thus faith saves by bringing us into living harmony with the divine constitution of things in Christ; - and, come into this harmony, God pronounces us righteous - and abiding in this faith, light and life, and joy in God abound in us, and the end of God in Christ is being fulfilled in us; - partially now and here - to be completely so hereafter.

I do not feel that I can more pointedly express Luther's conception of faith than in saying, that it lifts us into Christ and makes us one with Him, both in our own consciousness, and in God's judgment of us; - as we were, before faith, one with Him in God's gracious desire and purpose.

Luther's conception of how God is justified in "justifying the ungodly who believe," we may learn from what he says, first of Faith's own nature;

and then of the results of the living relation to Christ into which it brings us. First of Faith's own nature he says,

> Paul by these words "Abraham believed," of faith in God maketh the chiefest sonship, the chiefest duty, the chiefest obedience, and the chiefest sacrifice. Let him that is a rhetorician amplify this place, and he shall see that faith is an almighty thing; and that the power thereof is infinite and inestimable; for it giveth glory unto God, which is the highest service that can be given unto Him. Now to give glory unto God, is to believe in Him, to count Him true, wise, righteous, merciful, almighty; briefly, to acknowledge Him to be the author and giver of all goodness. This reason doth not, but faith. That is it which maketh us divine people, and, as a man would say, it is the Creator of (a) certain divinity, not in the substance of God, but in us. For without faith God loseth in us His glory, wisdom, righteousness, truth, and mercy. To conclude: no majesty or divinity remaineth unto God, where faith is not. And the chiefest thing that God requireth of man is that he give unto Him His glory and His divinity; that is to say that he taketh Him not for an idol, but for God, who regardeth him, heareth him, sheweth mercy unto him and helpeth him. This being done, God hath His full and perfect divinity, that is, He hath whatsoever a faithful heart can attribute unto Him. To be able therefore to give that glory unto God it is the wisdom of wisdoms, the righteousness of righteousness, the religion of religions, and sacrifice of sacrifices. Hereby we may perceive what an high and excellent righteousness faith is, and so, by the contrary, what an horrible and grievous sin infidelity is. Whosoever then believeth God, as Abraham did, is righteous before God, because he hath faith, which giveth glory unto God; that is, he giveth God that which is due to Him. (pp.250, 251)

But, secondly, because this excellent condition of faith is in us but as a germ - a grain of mustard-seed - a feeble dawn, God, in imputing it as righteousness, has respect unto that of which it is the dawn - of which, as the beginning of the life of Christ in us, it is the promise, and in which it shall issue, even the noontide brightness of that day in which the righteous shall shine as the stars in the kingdom of their Father. So he adds in reference to the words "it was imputed to him for righteousness":

> For Christian righteousness consisteth in two things, that is to say, in faith in the heart, and in God's imputation. Faith is indeed a formal righteousness, and yet this righteousness is not enough; for after faith there remain yet certain remnants of sin in our flesh. This sacrifice of faith began in Abraham, but at last it was finished in death. Wherefore the other part of righteousness must needs be added also, to finish the same in us, that is to say God's imputation. For faith giveth not enough to God, being imperfect; yea our faith is but a little spark of faith, which

beginneth only to render unto God His true divinity. We have received the firstfruits of the Spirit, but not yet the tenths. . . . Wherefore faith beginneth righteousness, but imputation maketh it perfect unto the day of Christ (p. 252)... Wherefore let those which give themselves to the study of the Holy Scripture, learn out of this saying, "Abraham believed God, and it was counted to him for righteousness," to set forth truly and rightly this true Christian righteousness after this manner; - that it is a faith and confidence in the Son of God - *or rather a confidence of the heart in God through Jesus Christ*; and let them add this clause as a difference; which faith and confidence is counted righteousness for Christ's sake... For as long as I live in the flesh sin is truly in me. But because I am covered under the shadow of Christ's wings, as is the chicken under the wings of the hen, and dwell without fear under that most ample and large heaven of the forgiveness of sins, which is spread over me, God covereth and pardoneth the remnant of sin in me: that is to say, because of that *faith wherewith I began to lay hold upon Christ, He accepteth my imperfect righteousness even for perfect righteousness*, and counteth my sin for no sin, which notwithstanding is sin indeed. (p.254)

The essence of the difference between the law and the gospel, as conceived of by Luther, seems to be shortly this:- that the law reveals man himself to man - that the gospel reveals God to man:- that the law brings man to self-despair, in order that the gospel may teach him faith and hope in God. Therefore, in the gospel, and not in the law, is God to be seen and known.

And this is substantially true. For, though the law, being love, may seem to reveal God who is love, yet is it rather a demand for love than a revelation of love; and, though it might have been, in the light of high intelligence, and where there was no darkening of sin, concluded that love alone could demand love, yet does the mere demand never so speak to sinners; - but "by the law is the knowledge of sin:" wherefore "the law worketh wrath." But the first front and aspect of the gospel is, the revelation of love; then follows the end contemplated, the quickening of love in us, in fact the fulfilment of the righteousness of the law in us - (Rom. viii. 4) but its instrument of working is, not the law, but grace. "Herein is love, not that we loved God, but that He loved us, and sent His Son to be the propitiation for our sins;" "We love Him because He first loved us" - "If God so loved us we ought also to love one another." (1 John iv. 11)

Therefore, the gospel being the revelation of what God is, rather than of what He calls for - though therein implying what He calls for, and providing for its accomplishment - Luther, understanding this, rests, not in the scheme of redemption as a plan, or in the work of Christ as a work, the parts of which he is careful to analyse, that he may turn them to their several uses in his intercourse with God; but, in the scheme and the work, and shining through all the details of the work, he sees God appearing to him as He is in Himself, as He eternally is; and he yields his heart and his whole being to the attraction of the heavenly vision. Thus he learns that

> God is the God of the humble, the miserable, the afflicted, the oppressed and the desperate, and of those that are brought even to nothing; and His *nature is* to exalt the humble, to feed the hungry, to give sight to the blind, to comfort the miserable, the afflicted, the bruised, the broken-hearted, to justify sinners, to quicken the dead, and to save the very desperate and damned. For he is an almighty Creator, and maketh all things of nothing. (p.321)

Not that the law had not spoken truly of God, not only when it declared the will of God as to what man should be, but also when its terrors were revealed in the conscience, through its testimony of God's wrath against sin; - but it left untold - it was not its function to tell - what deeper thing than wrath against sin was in God - even mercy towards the sinner.

So Luther, as one whom "the gospel hath led beyond and above the light of law and reason into the deep secrets of faith" (p.168), and to a knowledge of God to which reason had not attained, connecting upon the words - "Seeing the world by wisdom knew not God in the wisdom of God, it pleased God by the foolishness of preaching to save them that believe," applies them a teaching "that men ought to abstain from the curious searching of God's majesty" (p. 100). For:

> True Christian divinity setteth not God forth unto us in His majesty, as Moses and other doctors do. It commandeth us not to search out the nature of God; but to know His will set out to us in Christ. (*Ibid.*) ... Therefore begin thou there where Christ began, viz. in the womb of the virgin, in the manger, and at His mother's breast, &c. For to this end He came down, was born, was conversant among men, suffered, was crucified, and died, that by all means He might set forth Himself plainly before our eyes, and fasten the eyes of our hearts upon Himself; that thereby He might keep us from climbing up into heaven, and from the curious searching of the divine majesty. Whensoever thou hast to do, therefore, in the matter of justification, and disputest with thyself how God is to be found that justifieth and accepteth sinners; where and in what sort He is to be sought; then know thou that there is no other God besides this man Christ Jesus. Embrace Him and cleave to Him with thy whole heart, setting aside all curious speculations of the divine majesty. For he that is a searcher of God's majesty shall be overwhelmed of His glory. I know by experience what I say. But these vain spirits, which so deal with God that they exclude the Mediator, do not believe me. Christ Himself hath said, 'I am the way, the truth and the life; no man cometh unto the Father but by me,' - John xiv. 6. Therefore, besides this way,

Christ, thou shalt find no way to the Father, but wandering, no verity, but hypocrisy and lying, no life, but eternal death. Wherefore mark this well in the matter of justification, that when any of us wrestle with the law, sin, and death, and all other evils, we must look upon no other God but this God incarnate and clothed with man's nature . . . Look on this man Jesus Christ who setteth Himself forth to us to be a mediator, and saith "Come unto me all ye that labour and are heavy laden, and I will refresh you," - Matt. xi. 28. Thus doing, thou shall perceive the love, goodness and sweetness of God; thou shalt see His wisdom, power, and majesty, sweetened and tempered to thy capacity. Yea thou shalt find in this mirror and pleasant contemplation all things according to that saying of Paul to the Colossians: "In Christ are hid all the treasures of wisdom and knowledge".... The world is ignorant of this, and therefore it searcheth out the will of God, setting aside the promise in Christ to his (its) great destruction, "For no man knoweth the Father but the Son, and he to whom the Son will reveal him". Matt. xi. 27 (p.101)

Philip saith unto him, Lord, shew us the Father, and it sufficeth us. Jesus saith unto him, Have I been so long with you, and yet hast thou not known me, Philip? he that hath seen me hath seen the Father. John xiv. 8, 9

I add two more quotations to the same effect:

For in Christ we see that God is not a cruel exactor or a judge, but a most favourable, loving and merciful Father, who to the end He might bless us, that is to say, deliver us from the law, sin, death, and all other evils, and might endue us with grace, righteousness and everlasting life, spared not His own Son, but gave Him for us all. This is a true knowledge of God and a divine persuasion which deceiveth us not, but painteth God unto us lively (living). (p.389)

For the true God speaketh thus; No righteousness, wisdom, nor religion pleaseth me but that only whereby the Father is glorified through the Son. Whosoever apprehendeth this Son, and me, and my promise in Him by faith, to him I am a God, to him I am a Father, him do I accept, justify and save. All others abide under wrath because they worship that thing which by nature is no God. (p.390)

How does this language recall that of the Apostle John:

And we know that the Son of God is come, and hath given us an understanding, that we may know Him that is true; and we are in him that is true, even in his son Jesus Christ. This is the true God and eternal life. Little children, keep yourselves from idols. Amen. 1 John v. 20, 21

One other point remains to be noticed that we may have distinctly before us Luther's teaching on the subject of the atonement - I mean the weight which he lays on the personal appropriation of the atonement as of the very essence of faith.

Of course, teaching as the result of the victory of Christ over all our spiritual enemies, that Christ was made of God unto us wisdom, and righteousness, and sanctification, and redemption, and setting forth this as a constitution of things established by God in His love to man, and revealed to be known and received by faith, he could not teach merely that men *might* appropriate Christ and His work - that they were at liberty so to do, and invited so to do, and that Christ was freely offered to them, and would become theirs by such appropriation. He must needs teach that such appropriation was of the very essence of faith; being implied in the most simple reception of that which was revealed. But he has a further reason for insisting on this, viz. that in this personal appropriation he recognised at once the power and the difficulty of faith.

The teaching I refer to is in his comment on the words, "who gave Himself for our sins," in which, after insisting on the power of these words to destroy all false religions, "For if our sins be taken away by our own works, merits, and satisfactions, what needed the Son of God to be given for them? But seeing He was given for them, it followeth that we cannot put them away by our own works," (p. 104) - he adds:

> But weigh diligently every word of Paul, and especially mark well this pronoun "*our*," for the effect together consisteth in the well applying of the pronouns, which we find very often in the Scriptures, wherein also there is ever some vehemency and power . . . Generally and without the pronoun it is an easy matter to magnify and amplify the benefit of Christ, viz. that Christ was given for sins, but for other men's sins which are worthy. But when it cometh to the putting to of this pronoun *our*, there our weak nature and reason starteth back, and dare not come nigh unto God, nor promise to herself that so great a treasure shall be freely given unto her. (p. 105)

This is said in reference to the difficulty in believing in forgiveness noticed above as what comes to be felt as soon as the need of forgiveness begins to be realised. Of this Luther was fully aware, as well as of the unmeaning, and, indeed, self-righteous nature of those general confessions of sin which unawakened sinners so easily make; combining with them as easily expressed a trust in Christ:- in reference to which he says,

> Men's reason would fain bring and present unto God a feigned and counterfeit sinner, which is nothing afraid, nor hath any feeling of sin. It would bring that is whole, and not him that hath need of a physician, and when it feeleth no sin, then would it believe that Christ was given for our sins.

"But," says he,

> Learn here of Paul, to believe that Christ was given, not for feigned
> or counterfeit sins, nor yet for small sins, but for great and large sins;
> not for one or two, but for all; not for vanquished sins (for no man,
> no, nor angel, is able to subdue the least sin that is), but for invincible
> sins. And except thou be found among those that say "our sins," that
> is which have this doctrine of faith, and both hear, love, and believe
> the same, there is no salvation for thee (p. 106)... I speak not this
> without cause, for I know what moveth me to be so earnest that we
> should learn to define Christ out of the words of Paul. For indeed
> Christ is no cruel exactor, but a forgiver of the sins of the whole
> world... Learn this definition diligently, and especially so to exercise
> the pronoun *our*, that this one syllable being believed may swallow up
> all thy sins. (p.108)

I have reluctantly curtailed these quotations from Luther's commentary
on the Apostle Paul's Epistle to the Galatians - into the spirit of which the
great Reformer has so truly entered. The deep insight into our redemption,
as it has taken its character from our being "under the law" and "unjust,"
which he manifests; - his vivid realisation of "the grace wherein we stand,"
being redeemed; - his true appreciation of the glory which God has in our
faith; - his discernment of the relation in which the peace and confidence
towards God, which are present in faith, stand to the perfection of the
revelation of the Father in the Son; the personal interest in Christ, which he
recognises as possessed by all men, and revealed to faith in the gospel; and the
importance which he attaches to an appropriating response on our part:
these all are aspects of truth which I am thankful should now be present to
the mind of my reader in Luther's strong and vivid form of speech.

As to my immediate subject - the nature of the atonement - I have
admitted that he does not offer much help towards a clear intellectual
apprehension of it. Christ's identifying of Himself with us, "joining Himself
to the company of the accursed, taking unto Him their flesh and blood," in
order that in humanity He might encounter "our sin," and "our death," and
"our curse" (p.301); and the consequent conflict between these and Christ's
own eternal righteousness, as meeting together in Him - and the triumph of
that divine righteousness, issuing in our redemption; - these are conceptions
which he may have been content to hold as matters of revealed fact, but still
mysteries which precluded clear intellectual apprehension.

Yet the earnestness with which he insists upon the presence together of
these opposites in Christ, and on the reality of their conflict as matter of
consciousness to Christ - taken along with his true understanding of our
participation in Christ and His righteousness - give me the conviction that
Luther was indeed contemplating spiritual realities which had a place in the
work of redemption when using language as to the nearness of the relation

to us, and to our sin, into which Christ came, which has, and not without cause, given so much offence. In Luther's apprehensions, Christ's bearing of our sins was not a mere imputation in the mind of another; it was a deep and painful reality in his own mind; and the victory of righteousness in Him was not such in respect of the award to righteousness itself as a living divine might in Him. A legal fiction would be no explanation. The assumption of a delusive consciousness Luther would reject.

What the truth of the case has been, (and which, as having taken place in humanity, may be expected to be utterable to men), Luther's words, as he has written, do not make us to know; whatever spiritual truth these words have had in his own mind:- for interpreted according to their plain grammatical meaning, the words by which he expresses Christ's relation to our sins cannot be true. His use of them is, therefore, not to be defended. Yet shall we suffer loss if we allow ourselves to suppose that as used by a man of so much spiritual insight as Luther they had not a meaning at once true and important. Indeed, if there be not a true sense in which Christ did bear on his spirit the weight of our sins, and all our evils, and did deal with the law of God as so bearing them, seeking redemption for us - and did triumph in so doing by the might of righteousness, Luther's marvellous teaching of justification by faith alone is left a superstructure without a foundation.

CHAPTER III

CALVINISM, AS TAUGHT BY DR OWEN AND PRESIDENT EDWARDS

If the great Reformer's teaching had obtained and kept possession of the faith of the reformed Church, and that I could calculate on the presence in the minds of my readers of his preaching of Christ, I might now proceed to consider the nature of the atonement, without further preface or preparation. But I need not say how far the fact is otherwise. And as I am anxious to carry along with me the minds of those who not only believe in the atonement, but give it that very prominent place which it has in the teaching usually designed "evangelical" - though my appeal is not to what is specially distinctive of any, but is to the consciences of all - I shall now detain my readers for a little with the teaching on the subject of the atonement associated with the name of Calvin.

Calvinism, as now living in our generation of men, presents to our attention two very distinctly marked forms. The one, that which I believe those who hold it would recognise as best expounded by Dr Owen and President Edwards;* to whom I may add Dr Chalmers, (whose recognition of Edwards as his theological teacher is known, and is abundantly manifest in his *Institutes of Theology*); the other is that recent modification of Calvinism which is presented to us in the writings of Dr Pye Smith, Dr Payne and Dr Jenkyn, in England; and Dr Wardlaw, in Scotland. I name these writers only - while I am aware that there are others - because my knowledge of the system is derived from them.

Two centuries separate us from Dr Owen, and one from President Edwards; but their theology, which is one, still lives in the present generation - of the Presbyterian section at least - of the Church of Scotland; and, I presume, has much hold on men's minds also in England and in America. No man can accord with these two men in their faith without rejoicing in them as bulwarks of that faith. Owen's clear intellect, and Edwards' no less unquestionable power of distinct and discriminating thought, combined

---

* There was a ten volume edition of Edwards' Works, ed. by Sereno E. Dwight (New York, G. & C. & H. Carvill 1830). However, Michael Jinkins of Austin Seminary, Texas, believes that the edition Campbell used was the four volume reprint of the Worcester edition of *The Works of President Edwards* (New York, Leavitt, Trow & Co., London, Wiley & Putnam, 1843-44).

with a calmer, and more weighty, and more solemn tone of spirit; - the former writing as a man whose life was much one of theological controversy, the latter more as living among religious awakenings of which he was at once a subject and the instrument; - justify our regarding them as having set forth the modification of the doctrine of the atonement which they teach to the greatest advantage of which it is capable: - while, wherein any may think it dark and repulsive, they hide nothing, gloss over nothing, soften nothing; for they were true men, and not ashamed of the Christ in whom they believed.

Luther's anxiety to warn men "to abstain from the curious searching of God's majesty," has been noticed above. Not by such searching, but by becoming acquainted with Jesus Christ, would he teach us to expect the true knowledge of God; and this counsel is altogether in the spirit of the words, "In Him was life, and the life was the light of men." "He that hath seen me hath seen the Father."

How sound Luther's judgment was in sending us to Jesus, that in Him we might see and embrace God manifested in the flesh; and how much was thus to be learned which systematic theology cannot teach, and yet which we must learn if our systematic thought is to be safe, may well be suggested to us by the history of the preparation for their high calling which the disciples received. Only after their Lord's resurrection were their minds open to understand that "it behoved Christ to suffer, and afterwards to enter into His glory."

Yet were they, in that ignorance, already far advanced in the true knowledge of God, because in the true knowledge of Christ - not of his work, and of its bearing, but of Himself. Luther in telling us "to go straight to the manger, and embrace the Virgin's little babe in our arms," expresses a sense of God's approachableness, as divested of all terrors and revealed in the simple confiding attraction of love, which we feel full of instruction. We can conceive the long self-tortured monk, who had sought God earnestly but ignorantly, thinking, as he tells us, of Christ as an exactor and judge, as now, in the light of love, contemplating the infant Jesus, and saying to himself, "This is God, thus does God come among men;" - and, while the whole life in the flesh of which that is the dawn, passes before him in thought, and he traces the Lord's path from the manger to the cross, and then on to glory, we can conceive of him as repeating to himself - "This is my God, in this God am I to put my trust;" and we can understand how, while contrasting what he is thus consciously learning of "the true God and eternal life" with all the results of men's "curious searching of God's majesty" with which he was not unacquainted, he would treasure up his own conscious experience, - to minister it to others for warning and guidance.

Now, what, in passing from the record of Luther's thoughts on the atonement to that of the thinking of Owen and Edwards, has come vividly home to my mind, is, that it would be well that they had proceeded more in harmony with the spirit of Luther's warning now referred to. Not that I would presume to speak of their solemn weighing of the question "what is divine justice? and to what conclusions does it lead on the subject of the atonement?" as "curious searching;" but that it seems to me that it would have been well that they had used the *life* of Christ more as their *light*.

That I say not this self-confidently, or on slight grounds, will, I trust, be made clear to my readers as we proceed. I do not make little account of philosophy, nor would I be contented to see it sharing in the Apostle's condemnation of "philosophy falsely so called." I believe that a true philosophy has often done much service to religion; - neither can I under-stand how a philosophical mind can, without submitting to fetters which I believe are not of God, be contented to hold a religion which is not to it also a philosophy, and the highest philosophy. But no one will doubt that the beloved disciple John, who attained to such high apprehensions of God, and to whom we listen, telling us that "God is love," as to one speaking himself in the light of the eternal love, had his high - and the only adequate - training for this divine philosophy when following the footsteps of Jesus, listening to His words, seeing His deeds, and, from time to time, favoured to lean upon His breast.

> That which was from the beginning, which we have heard, which we have seen with our eyes, which we have looked upon, and our hands have handled of the Word of life; (For the life was manifested, and we have seen and bear witness, and shew unto you that eternal life which was with the Father, and was manifested unto us); That which we have seen and heard declare we unto you, that ye also may have fellowship with us: and truly our fellowship is with the Father and with His Son Jesus Christ. (1 John i. 1-3)

I am not going to analyse the reasoning on the Divine Attributes by Dr Owen and President Edwards to which I refer, and as to which I feel as if the recorded work of Christ were contemplated in their system in the light of that reasoning - rather than that reasoning engaged in after the due study of the life of Christ. It has been said that Calvinism is a philosophy in its essence; and I do not object to it on that account, but, because it is not to me a true philosophy. If what I have already said of the hope for sinful man that should be found in the righteousness and holiness of God, no less than in His love - contemplating these divine attributes, as much as may be, in their distinctness - be present to the mind of my readers, it will be felt by those of them that are familiar with the theological writings of Owen and Edwards, that, however clear their reasonings are as reasonings, they must appear to me open to this fundamental objection, that they leave out of account certain important first principles. But not to engage in the analysis of what in the pages of Edwards especially I have read with so solemn and deep an interest as listening to a great and holy man, while, at the same time, feeling the axiomatic defect to which I have referred, it will be enough for my present purpose to notice the results arrived at.

1. The most palpable of these results, and that which first attracts attention, is the **limitation of the atonement**; - I mean the conceiving of it as having reference only to a certain elected portion of the human family.

This result arose naturally, and, it seems to me, most logically, from the first principles from which these clear and acute thinkers have reasoned. The divine justice is conceived of by them as, by a necessity of the divine nature, awarding eternal misery to sin, and eternal blessedness to righteousness. That the sinner may be saved from this misery, and partake in this blessedness, he must, in the person of Christ, endure the misery thus due to sin, and fulfil the righteousness of which this blessedness is the due reward. But the co-relative position is, that, having thus, in the person of Christ, endured the punishment of sin, he cannot in justice be eventually punished himself; and that, having, in like manner, fulfilled all righteousness, he must in justice receive the reward of that righteousness. "The sum of all is, the death and blood-shedding of Jesus Christ hath wrought, and doth effectually procure for all those that are concerned in it, eternal redemption, consisting in grace here and glory hereafter." (Vol. x. 159)*

All that is of the nature of pain and suffering in the history of our Lord, from what the cries of feeble infancy tell, with what aggravation may have been in the circumstances of the manger and the stable, and the lowly lot of Mary and Joseph, on to the mysterious agony of Gethsemane, and that which seems to them indicated, if not revealed in the cry on the cross, "My God, my God, why hast thou forsaken me?" - all this is set down as penal suffering - the punishment of the sins of the elect. On the other hand, all that is of the nature of holiness, goodness, obedience, fulfilling of all righteousness, from the same dawn to the solemn close, and the submission of will uttered in the words, "the cup which my Father gives me to drink, shall I not drink it?" - "Father, into thy hands I commend my spirit" - all this is set down as accomplishing that perfect righteousness which is to endow the elect with a title to eternal blessedness.

The grace of God according to this conception - that is his grace to the elect - is, properly speaking, manifested in the original gift of Christ; all the subsequent history is the just and faithful acting out of the details of a covenant thus graciously entered into with Christ for the elect. But, of course, the original grace underlies all the subsequent history; so that, while, in one sense, the pardon of the sins of the elect is a matter of simple justice,

---

* Campbell is here referring to Owen's book, *The Death of Death in the Death of Christ*, Book 1, Chapter 1, section III; this book is vol. X in *The Works of John Owen*, ed. by William H. Goold, T. & T. Clark, Edinburgh 1862 - though Campbell would have used the 1852 edition. (Note by Michael Jinkins)

Christ having borne the punishment of their sins; and the bestowal of eternal blessedness upon them is, also, a matter of simple justice, Christ's righteousness having endowed them with a right to that blessedness - still the whole dispensation is one grace.

Adhering strictly to his conception of the fixed relation between sin, and its due punishment, Owen anxiously insists upon the identity of that punishment which Christ endured for the elect, with what they would have endured themselves, and what the non-elect do eventually endure. "Now from all this, thus much (to clear up the nature of the satisfaction made by Christ) appeareth, viz. - It was a full, valuable compensation made to the justice of God for all the sins of those for whom He made satisfaction, by undergoing that same punishment which, by reason of the obligation that was upon them, they themselves were bound to undergo. When I say the same I mean essentially the same in weight and pressure, though not in all accidents of duration and the like; for it was impossible that He should be detained by death." (p.269)* His language everywhere is in harmony with this conception; as to which I do not feel that it is justly liable to the treatment which it has received when objected to as a mercenary, and so an unworthy view of the subject. The mere language of commerce, viz. "purchase, ransom," &c. is not Owen's, but that of the Scriptures; and as to the substance of his meaning it is simply, that the justice of God punishes sin as it deserves, and that, having in the exercise of an unerring judgment once determined what is deserved, God cannot be conceived of as acting in any way that would imply a change of mind.

As to the difficulties that present themselves, the moment the attempt is made to form clear conceptions of what has thus been asserted - that is to say, to conceive to ourselves, on the one hand, what the punishment was which the elect were bound to undergo; and, then, on the other hand, how Christ can have endured the punishment so conceived of; - with these difficulties Owen does not really grapple.

Edwards, indeed, approaches this solemn subject more nearly; and there is no passage in his exposition of "The Satisfaction for Sin"** made by Christ of deeper interest than the one in which he does so. After premising that "Christ suffered the wrath of God for men's sins in such a way as He was capable of, being an infinitely holy person who knew that God was not angry with Him personally - knew that God did not hate Him but infinitely loved Him," he goes on to specify two ways in which he conceives that Christ could endure the wrath of God. But the elements of suffering which he specifies, however connected with the sin of those for whom Christ died, cannot be recognised as the punishment which they themselves were bound

---

* *The Works of John Owen*, vol. X p.269-70

** Edwards' essay, *On Satisfaction for Sin* appears in vol. 1 of the four volume edition.

to undergo - if such sufferings can rightly be represented as punishment at all.

But, not to enter here on the nature of the sufferings specified, when explanations are offered as to how Christ endured the punishment of the sins of those for whom He died, the important point is, that His sufferings are regarded as implying, that it would be unjust that those should themselves eventually suffer punishment for whom He had suffered, as in the same way it was held, that it would be unjust that those should not eventually inherit eternal blessedness for whom Christ had merited eternal blessedness.

We are not to wonder that, having come to such conclusions as these from such axioms as that "God is just" and that "God is immutable," texts of Scripture such as those who believe that the atonement was for all men, quote in proof of that doctrine, were, however large their sound, urged with little effect. Some of these might seem difficult of explanation on their system - others might be more easily disposed of. No one ever took more ingenuity to such a task than Owen did; as no one ever urged more perplexingly the dilemmas in which those were involved, who, agreeing with him as to the nature of the atonement, differed from him as to its reference.

> To which I may add this dilemma to our universalists (i.e. those who held that Christ had died for all), God imposed His wrath due unto, and Christ underwent the pains of hell for, either all the sins of all men, or all the sins of some men, or some sins of all men. If the last, some sins of all men, then have all men some sins to answer for, and so shall no man be saved; for if God enter into judgment with us, though it were with all mankind for one sin, no flesh should be justified in His sight. "If the Lord should mark iniquities who should stand?".... If the second, that is it which we affirm, that Christ in their stead and room suffered for all the sins of all the elect in the world. If the first, why then are not all freed from the punishment of all their sins? You will say 'Because of their unbelief; they will not believe.' But this unbelief, is it a sin, or not? If not, why should they be punished for it? If it be, then Christ underwent the punishment due to it, or not. If so, then why must that hinder them more than their other sins for which He died from partaking of the fruit of His death? If he did not, then did He not die for all their sins. Let them choose which part they will. (p.173)*

I add his winding up of a striking argument on Mark x. 45: "I shall add no more but this, that to affirm Christ to die for all men is the readiest way to prove that He died for no man in the sense Christians have hitherto understood." (p.290)* As addressed to those who agreed with him as to the

---

* These references also are from *The Death of Death in the Death of Christ*. The first is actually pp.173-74, and in the second, Owen has 'believed' not 'understood'.

nature of the atonement, while differing with him as to the extent of its reference, this seems unanswerable.

To those who approach the subject of the atonement with the conviction that Christ died for all men, and who see this to be clearly revealed in the Scriptures, it must be an insuperable objection to any view taken of the nature of the atonement that it is inconsistent with this faith; and I have already alluded to the fact, that the force felt to be in such reasonings as those just quoted, assuming the truth of that conception of the atonement on which they proceed, has latterly led those who contend that Christ died for all to reconsider the nature of the atonement. I am thankful for this result. *That cannot be the true conception of the nature of the atonement which implies that Christ died only for an election from among men.*

But, besides the scripture argument against the limitation of the atonement, on which I do not enter, I would notice two important further conclusions which that limitation involves, and which are very weighty objections to the doctrine to which they are ultimately traceable.

(1) The limitation of the atonement, and therefore the conception of the nature of the atonement which implies that limitation, abstracts from the faith of the gospel that element on which Luther lays so much stress in what he says of the use of the pronoun "our". This it does because it takes away the warrant which the universality of the atonement gives to every man that hears the gospel to contemplate Christ with the personal appropriation of the words of the apostle, "who loved me, and gave himself for me."

This Owen fully admits, but he denies that any man is asked to believe, as the first act of faith, that Christ died for him in particular, or to believe anything but what he recognises as actually revealed. He then proceeds to state successive acts or steps of faith; in each one of which the believer has a clear scripture warrant for his faith; but the taking each successive step of which narrows the circle of those who come to be dealt with; some taking the first step who will not take the second; some taking both who will not take the third; some taking the first three who will not take the fourth:- while as to those who take the *whole four, their having taken them* has become a ground for that personal appropriation of Christ, as their own Saviour in particular, which was not afforded by the revelation made in the gospel messages, but which has thus been added by that work of grace which has proceeded so far in them, and has individualised them as persons for whom Christ died; "for certainly Christ died for every one in whose heart the Lord by His almighty power works effectually faith to lay hold on Him, and assent unto Him according to the orderly proposal that is held forth in the gospel" (p. 315).

But the difficulty of dealing with awakened sinners on this system has been practically felt to be very great. And the importance, with reference to all fruit of that faith whose nature it is to work by love, of being able to realise that relation to Christ which the words "who loved me, and gave himself for me," express, has pressed so upon such men as Boston and others, in the days of our fathers, that, in order to facilitate that "appropriating act of faith" on which so much depended, they introduced that doctrine of "a deed of gift of Christ to all men," which they combined with the faith, still adhered to, that He died only for the elect; - shewing what a response Luther's teaching as to the use of the pronoun "*our*" has had, even when that broad basis of an atonement for all on which Luther stood has not been seen to be the truth of God.

Another indication of the same response is presented in Dr Chalmers' *Institutes*, in the chapter on "the universality of the gospel." I refer to the tone of the whole chapter, but quote only these words:- "The particular redemption of all who are saved, is made good by their right entertainment of those texts which are alleged in behalf of universal redemption; *and it is the very entertainment which the advocates of this doctrine would have all men to bestow upon them. And so I am sure would we.* We should like each individual of the world's population *to assume specially for himself* every passage in the Bible where Christ is held forth generally to men or generally to sinners, and would assure him that, did he only proceed upon these, he would infallibly be saved."*

I am not sure to what the concession that seems to be made in the words which I have marked by italics really amounts, and am fearful of even seeming to strain his words. I know indeed that "that entertainment which the advocates of universal redemption would have all men to bestow" upon "the texts which they allege in behalf of that doctrine" includes this, that each man should assume, on the authority of these texts that Christ died for him - that Christ is made of God unto him, wisdom, and righteousness, and sanctification, and redemption. How far Dr Chalmers means that any man, *assuming this*, and trusting Christ accordingly, is justified in so doing, and is saved by so doing, I am not quite certain, considering that he insists so much on the word "offer;" but this much is, I think, abundantly clear, that he recognises the importance of the appropriating act of faith, while adhering to the doctrine of a limited atonement.

But thus to use the expressions of Scripture in a vague largeness in connection with the faith of an atonement for the elect only, affords no real basis for that personal appropriation of Christ which is recognised as so needful to the practical working of Christianity. And those who see clearly

---

* Campbell here refers to Chapter 7 of Chalmers' essay, *On the Extent of the Gospel Remedy*, in which he deals with the subject of the human will, the doctrine of predestination and the universality of the gospel. This essay is to be found in volume 2, from p.418, in Thomas Chalmers, *Institutes of Theology*; these two volumes appear in the larger edition, *Posthumous Works of the Rev. Thomas Chalmers*, ed. Hanna, as vols. 7 and 8 (New York, Harper and Brothers 1855) - there Campbell quotes from p.421. (Jinkins)

that the Apostle could not have said, "I am crucified with Christ; nevertheless I live; yet not I, but Christ liveth in me," unless he had first known that Christ "had loved him, and given Himself for him," must see that such previous knowledge in the Apostle implied *that the gospel in which he had believed had imparted that knowledge.*

However much Owen's four steps of faith without this personal appropriation, followed by a fifth, in which, through the help of these previous four, that appropriation is attained, must repel us as a departure from the simplicity of faith, his teaching is consistent with the doctrine of a limited atonement; but how, without the element of an indication in the inner man of the individual that he is of the elect, the certainty of a personal interest in Christ can be reached by one believing that Christ died for the elect only, I cannot conceive.

(2) But a more solemn result of limiting the atonement remains to be noticed, viz. that, as appears to me, it makes the work of Christ to be no longer a revelation of the name of God, no longer a work revealing that God is love.

The conception of the nature of the atonement on which the system of Owen and Edwards proceeds, and the reasonings in relation to the Divine Attributes by which they attempt to lay a deep foundation for it in the verity of what God is, present this - I may surely say startling - result, that, while they set forth justice as a necessary attribute of the divine nature, so that God must deal with *all men* according to its requirements, they represent mercy and love as not necessary, but arbitrary, and what, therefore, may find their expression in the history of *only some* men. For according to their system justice alone is expressed in the history of all men, that is to say, in the history of the non-elect, in their endurance of punishment; in the history of the elect, in Christ's enduring it for them. Mercy and love are expressed in the history of the elect alone. Surely, not to enter into the question of the absolute distinctness of the Divine Attributes, or their central and essential unity, if any one attribute might be expected to shine full-orbed in the revelation which testifies that "God is love," that attribute is love; and, feeling this strongly, I have ventured to say, that it would be well that these deep reasoners had "used the life of Christ more as their light."

But, not only do I object that in this system the illustration of the divine love by the atonement is presented in the history of the election alone; what I feel is, that *so presented* the atonement *ceases to reveal* that *God is love.*

However little the thought may have received the consideration which its importance deserves, nothing can be clearer to me than that *an arbitrary act cannot reveal character.* We may be reconciled to an act of which we see not the reasons, by what we know otherwise of the character of him whose act it is: but an act which is strictly arbitrary, or at least so far as we are informed arbitrary - an act of which he that performs it gives us no other account than that he wills it because he wills it - can never, by any light in it, make the character of him whose act it is known to us. Now the doctrine that the work of Christ has had reference only to the elect, and that the grace which it embodies was only grace to them, and that they were elected, and the non-elect passed over arbitrarily, or at the least on no principle of choice that can be made known to us, or at all events, that is made known to us - this doctrine makes the work of Christ as presented to the faith of human beings strictly an arbitrary act.

To say that God does not authorise us to expect an explanation of the reasons of His acting - that He gives not account of His matters - is not to the point. Be it so. But if *it be so*, it does not the less follow, that what He has done has left us ignorant of Himself - that *so far as the acting of which He gives us no account is concerned*, He is to us the *unknown God*.

That the transaction has such an aspect of grace to those to whom it has reference - that to the elect it is free unmerited kindness - yea kindness to enemies - this is not to the purpose, our inquiry being as to the name and character of God. For, if we allow our minds due freedom in the contemplation of this high and solemn object, it is impossible for us not to feel, that however great the personal obligations conferred upon the elect, and however the sense of these may attach them to God, even they cannot intelligently venture to say that their experience of God - the way in which God has dealt with them - proves what God is - in Himself is - essentially is - when the way in which He has dealt with others - the experience of others related to Him exactly as they were, and whose position was, by *assumption* of the *system itself*, in every point identically the same as theirs - has been so different. That other treatment is assumed to be God's acting as much as this. By which are we to judge of him? From which are we to conclude what God is?

I am unable to see any way out here, or any escape from the conclusion, that the doctrine of an atonement for the elect only, destroys the claim of the work of Christ to be what fully reveals and illustrates the great foundation of all religion, that God is love. I may still cling to that spiritual instinct in me which responds to the assertion that God is love, apart from all revealed justification of that assertion. But, instead of being helped by God's gift of Christ to the elect to cherish this instinctive faith, all deep consideration of that gift can only embarrass me; so that, if I believe in it, I must be contented to receive it as a mystery, not a revelation of God; - a mystery of the explanation of which I must endeavour, in the strength of my instinctive faith that God is love, patiently to wait for.

I know that when the doctrine of free grace as meaning absolute unconditional election, is presented to those who have not yet come under the power of God's love, it is usual to treat the repulsion they feel as a manifestation of carnal pride, and their objections as the suggestions of a self-sufficient reason, which refuses to submit itself to the authority of revelation. But is it fair to ask men to put their trust in that God of whom we cannot tell them whether He loves them or does not? in that Saviour of whom we cannot tell them whether He died for them or did not? And when they find their difficulties so treated by those who not only are, as it will naturally appear to them, reconciled to an unconditional election by having come to believe that that election has included themselves, but who have this strong inducement to limit the atonement, that they believe that to assert that Christ died for all men, is, in effect, to assert that He died for no man in the sense in which His death for themselves is their hope towards God - is it strange that some degree of irritation, and even indignation, should be manifested? May not the appearance of such a special interest in limiting the atonement excusably recall the words - "A bribe blinds the eyes of a judge?"

What practically goes far to neutralise all this, and to disarm the feeling of irritation which it awakens, even appearing an argument in reply, is, the loving spirit often manifested by those who urge such views as these - a spirit the very opposite of what we should expect in the holders of a system which veils the love that is in God to every man.

The fact that much of this seeming contradiction meets us is certain. How does it arise? Although, as I have said, their personal experience of God cannot warrant those, who, living in the faith of God's love in Christ as love to themselves, cherish that faith in connection with the faith of an arbitrary election and limited atonement in concluding as to what God is - that He is love; yet they may so conclude - they may think of God exclusively as He appears in His acting towards themselves; leaving out of view the different history of others: or, if they think of it, regarding it rather as a mystery, with which they may not meddle, and which, with their convictions, they would feel it irreverent to trace out to logical conclusions.

Thus they will be found extolling the love which is the plain meaning of what they are experiencing at the hand of God, viewed simply in itself; and, feeling it as love, they will respond to it with love; and living in an atmosphere of love, their spiritual state will have its character determined accordingly. And so dealing with God as a living God, and receiving from him day by day forgiving love - alive to God, and drawing daily for their own need out of the fulness that is in Christ, it comes to pass, that the living love quickened in their hearts is, if I may so speak, glad to find in the darkness that veils the subject of election an excuse for going forth freely to men, even while it is not doctrinally held that God's love itself, the fountain love, goes thus freely forth. And thus a contradiction is allowed to exist between the faith of the head and the love of the heart; and, in spite of their theology, the men "who love God much because much is forgiven them" love men much also, and are thankful to devote themselves, under the power of that love, to bringing others into the fellowship of that love.

In all this conscience, testifying that love is the fulfilling of the law, helps them greatly; and also the bearing and general impression of the Scriptures, which even the misunderstanding of many important texts does not neutral-ise: and thus a Brainerd, holding as his creed that Christ died only for an unknown few, is seen yearning over every human being he meets, desiring that individual human being's salvation with an intenseness of love that we feel would be content to die for him that he should live: for no man ever laboured for the salvation of others, the record of whose labours impress us more deeply with this conviction.

In Brainerd's case, indeed, as also in the case of his master Edwards, this contradiction between the faith of the head and the love of the heart, is the more remarkable, in that, that faith was not taken up blindly, or without much reasoning and weighing of all that it involved. How marvellous it appears that such reasoners did not give to their understandings the help that they might have found in their own spiritual consciousness, and make, so to speak, an axiom of the love to man that was in their own hearts, and reason from it, as a simple uneducated man did, who, when the doctrine of the universality of the atonement was first introduced to the attention of a prayer and fellowship meeting of which he was a member, when others were arguing against it, said, "I cannot refuse it, for I feel that when I have most of the spirit of Christ in me I feel most love to all men; and I cannot believe that the spirit of Christ would move me to love all men if Christ did not love all men Himself."

2. The limitation of the reference of the atonement to an election from among men, and the consequences involved in that limitation, must be regarded as bringing into question that conception of the nature of the atonement, which, being consistently followed out, has such results. An-other result of that conception of the nature of the atonement, not less conclusive as an argument against it, is **the substitution of a legal standing for a filial standing** as the gift of God to men in Christ.

"When the fulness of the time was come, God sent forth His Son, made of a woman, made under the law, to redeem them that were under the law, *that we might receive the adoption of sons.*" (Gal. iv. 4, 5) Therefore, when we contemplate the Son of God, in our nature, dealing on our behalf with the condemnation of sin, and the demand for righteousness, which are in the law, we are to understand that He is not thus honouring in humanity the Law of God for the purpose of giving us a perfect legal standing as under the law, but for the purpose of taking us from under the law, and placing us under grace - redeeming us that we may receive the adoption of sons. So that not a legal standing, however high or perfect, but a filial standing, is that which is given to us in Christ.

But the purpose of *giving a title* to a *legal* confidence, and that of *quickening* with a *filial* confidence, are manifestly different; and, the latter being recognised as that in the contemplation of which the Father sent the Son to be the Saviour of the world, we must conclude that that conception of the nature of the atonement which has led to the substitution of the former in men's thoughts, cannot be the true conception.

President Edwards represents the righteousness of Christ as a perfect obedience - yet not perfected until rendered as obedience unto death; and he enters into a full detail of all the forms or aspects of law under which Christ came, and the demand of which He fully met; and God's acceptance of this perfect obedience he calls, the Father's justification of Christ; and this he says was in the Father's raising Him from the dead; and in this justification is it that the elect are interested, and into the communion of which they enter by faith; and this perfect obedience it is that is imputed to them, and to the reward of which they are entitled. In all this attention is fixed upon the obedience of Christ as the *fulfilling of a law*, and the *life of sonship* in which this fulfilment has taken place, *is left out of view*. But that life of sonship is, in reality, what ought to be prominent; and the proper value of that fulfilment of the law, besides the honour which it accords to the law, is, that it is a demonstration of the virtue and power which is in sonship. For the prospective relation of men to that fulfilment, is, not that they are to receive eternal blessedness as the reward due to it, but that God's acceptance of it as a perfect righteousness in humanity is a justification of humanity in the person of Christ, on the ground of which that life of sonship, in which this glory has been given to God in humanity, may be given to men in the Son of God.

A work of infinite excellence performed by Christ as the representative of men, and men invested with its excellence, and clothed with its worthiness in God's eyes, and rewarded accordingly, is a thought that has had much acceptance. Surely to bestow on us in Christ the life that has taken outward form in that work, is at once a more natural, and a far higher result of that work; - a far higher reward to Christ, and a far higher gift to us: as it is also a higher glory to God in us and so a higher glory to God in Christ, through whom there is that glory to God in us. "For what the law could not do, in that it was weak through the flesh, God sending His Son in the likeness of sinful flesh, and as a sacrifice for sin, condemned sin in the flesh; that the righteousness of the law might be fulfilled in us, who walk not after the flesh, but after the spirit," - that is, the spirit of the Son, for the root idea here is that conveyed by the word "Son." For the law of the spirit of the life that is in Christ Jesus - viz. sonship - makes us "free from the law of sin and death."

Dr Chalmers dwells much on the legal standing given in Christ, as meeting, by its retrospective and prospective bearing, all the need of the awakened sinner; and, in connection with this, has some very striking remarks on what he calls "natural legalism," as a source of difficulty to men in receiving the Gospel, in addition to natural pride, and one which he thinks ministers of the Gospel have not sufficiently considered, or recognised, in dealing with the consciences of men. These remarks are, I believe, just. I believe that difficulties have often their root in conscience, which are ignorantly and rashly referred to pride; and I also believe that Dr Chalmers is historically justified in saying, that such a stand as he conceives we are called to take, in virtue of the imputation of our sins to Christ, and of His righteousness to us, will meet the demands of conscience to a certain extent awakened only: *not* of conscience *fully awakened*. This is true, inasmuch as conscience fully awakened may be expected to demand, in relation to the righteousness of the law, that which God has contemplated; which we have just seen has been "that the righteousness of the law might be fulfilled in us;" - but I say this rather in reference to that other aspect of the fulfilment of God's purpose; viz. "that we should receive the adoption of sons;" - in relation to which I believe there is such a response in conscience that one is justified in saying, that conscience is not fully awakened in us who are God's offspring, until the orphan condition to which sin has reduced us is revealed in us, and the cry arises in spirit, if not in form of words, "Shew us the Father, and it sufficeth us."

In the chapter of Dr Chalmers' *Institutes*, to which I am now referring, that "on the satisfaction that had to be rendered to the truth and justice of God, ere that sinners could be readmitted into favour," there is much important elucidation of the fact, that it is not as a Father, but as a Judge, that God is thought of by awakened sinners; - from which he justly argues, that there is both a departure from the truth of things, and an embarrassing result to the awakened sinner in not duly acknowledging that voice of conscience which causes so much terror, and in, as he says, "keeping the divine jurisprudence out of sight," and "contemplating the relation between God and man simply as a family relation." Those who do so, he designates as "the advocates of a meagre and sentimental piety."

When any thus sink the Lawgiver in the Father, they surely err. But, on the other hand, if any think the idea of the Lawgiver the higher and more root idea they also err. Let us take the warning given, not "to keep the divine jurisprudence out of sight;" but let us guard also against awakenings which do not reach to the depths of man's being; neither prepare for that Gospel which comes from the depths of the heart of the Father. It must ever be remembered, that, while the Gospel recognises the law, and honours the law, it raises us above the law; while, as to the very point of these two characters of God, viz. the Lawgiver and the Father, we know that it is only by the *revelation* of the *Father* that God succeeds in realising the *will* of the *Lawgiver* in men. How much more can He thus alone realise the *longings* of the *Father's heart!*

And let us weigh well this question, "How much more could God thus alone realise in us the longings of His heart as our Father?" For that the atonement really contemplated the realizing of these longings, and should be seen by us in its relation to these longings, this is what is not understood when the legal perfection of Christ's righteousness is thus abstracted from the law of the spirit of the life of sonship in Christ Jesus, which took outward form in that righteousness, and from the revelation of the Father, which in being perfect sonship, it presents to faith. If that obedience were not, in its inner aspect, and in its nature, sonship - if it were not a revelation of the Father, its legal perfection, had such perfection been in that case possible, would have availed little to us, who were to be redeemed from under the law that we might receive the adoption of sons.

Therefore was our Lord ever careful to keep before the minds of the disciples, that, in that perfect obedience to the will of God which they saw in Him, they were contemplating the doing of the will of the Father by the Son. For in His Father's name was he come to them. Had it been otherwise, Christ could not have said, "He that hath seen me hath seen the Father." A servant may make us acquainted with his master; a subject may make us to know the lawgiver and king to whom he owes allegiance; the Son alone could reveal the Father. "No man knoweth the Father save the Son, and he to whom the Son revealeth Him."

I have urged above, that the limitation of the atonement, renders the grace of God in the gift of Christ no longer a revelation of the name of God - that He is love. I say now, that the righteousness of Christ being contemplated as what was intended to give us a legal standing as righteous through its imputation to us, has, if not as a necessary consequence, at all events as a matter of fact, marred the efficiency of the work of Christ as *in itself* a revelation of the Father by the Son. I mean, that those who, in looking at Christ as fulfilling all righteousness, have contemplated Him as employed in providing a legal righteousness for us, have not been in the way of receiving that knowledge of God which they would have received, if their contemplation of Christ had been determined by the faith of that word, "He that hath seen me hath seen the Father."

Thus it has come to pass, that our Lord has been contemplated by them as fulfilling the law of love towards all men, and yet that they have not recognised His doing so as the revelation of God's love to all men. Edwards, in his enumeration of the elements of Christ's righteousness, mentions those virtues which more immediately respect other men, and these under the two heads of meekness and love; and, in illustration of the love of men which He manifested, he says, "Christ's love to men that He shewed when upon earth, and especially in going through His last sufferings, and offering up His life and soul under these sufferings, which was His greatest act of love, was far beyond all parallel." This as a part of Christ's righteousness, is clearly here love to men as men; not love to the elect as the elect.

The specifying, as illustrating His love to men, those sufferings of Christ, and that offering up of His life and soul, which the system assumes had reference to the elect only, is indeed a manifest contradiction; but it seems to have arisen from his looking at the righteousness of Christ as the meeting of the demand for righteousness which the law makes on man, and not as the revelation of the heart of the Father by the Son. For Edwards did not doubt that the righteousness which Christ fulfilled, and with which, by imputation, believers are clothed, included love to all men; - any more than that the example which He left for the guidance of His followers, was that of love to all men. But the legal reference to man in which alone the atonement has been viewed, has caused that neither Christ's sufferings for our sins, nor His own righteousness, reveal anything of God by what they are in themselves beyond what the law testifies; - being, simply, the meeting of the demands of the law; the former an awful, the latter a glorious seal put to the law by the Son of God, and no more.

Justification by faith is so closely related to that work of Christ which the faith that justifies apprehends, that an error in regard to the nature of the atonement must affect that doctrine. But there will be some advantage in postponing the consideration of the teaching of the earlier Calvinists on this subject, so far as the object of this volume calls for the consideration of it, until I have first directed attention to the great modification which Calvinism, as taught by the theological school to which I have referred above, has recently undergone.

CHAPTER IV

CALVINISM, AS RECENTLY MODIFIED

Calvinism, as recently modified, differs from the earlier Calvinism in these points. First, as to the reference of the atonement, which is held to have been for all men and not for the elect only.

Secondly, as to the need-be for an atonement, which is not regarded as arising out of the demands of distributive and individual justice, requiring that each man should receive his due desert, according to an eternal necessity in the divine nature, according to an eternal necessity in the divine nature, as maintained by Owen and Edwards: but is held to arise out of the demands of rectoral and public justice, which necessitate God, as the moral governor of the universe, if He extend mercy to sinners, to do so only in a way that will preserve inviolate the interests of His moral government.

Thirdly, as to the nature of the atonement - Christ's suffering for our sins not being held to be the endurance, on the part of the Saviour, of the same punishment, or of punishment equivalent in amount of suffering, with that to which those for whom He suffered were exposed, but to be the substitution of other sufferings for the threatened punishment, which substituted sufferings were equivalent in reference to the result in relation to God's moral government; - and Christ's meritorious obedience not being held to be the fulfilling of the law in our room and stead, so as to provide us with a righteousness to be imputed to us, investing us with a right to the reward of righteousness - but a moral excellence giving a moral virtue to the atonement whereby it is made a fit ground on which may be rested all acts of grace and clemency towards sinners, and all bestowal of favours upon them.

Fourthly, as to the results of the atonement, that it does not of itself, and by its own nature, secure salvation to any, but only is an adequate provision for the salvation of all, free to all, effectual to salvation in the case of those who are disposed by the sovereign grace of God to avail themselves of it.

These points of difference involve others as implied in them. Thus the idea of imputation of guilt and righteousness, viz. of our guilt to Christ, and of Christ's righteousness to us, as this imputation was held by Owen and Edwards, is rejected as untenable; - "Guilt and merit not being transferable - but only their consequences." (Payne, 254) The idea of a legal claim to salvation, which we have just seen commended as the full meeting of the instinctive legalism of the human heart, is rejected as destroying the gracious character of the gospel dispensation; - and, most important of all - the relation of the atonement to the divinity of Christ, is altogether differently conceived of; for whereas, in the earlier Calvinism the divinity of the Saviour is contemplated as making possible infinitely great sufferings endured in time - the needed substitute for sufferings that would have been infinite in that they would have been eternal - on this system the divinity of Christ is regarded as giving infinite value to any suffering of His; so that the value of the sufferings would be infinitely great though its amount were infinitely small.

The assumed advantages of this system as a modification of the earlier Calvinism are chiefly these. First, as to the extent of the atonement. To teach that Christ died for all is consonant with the most obvious meaning of the language of the inspired writers - which cannot be brought to utter a limited atonement without much forcing. While, besides, an universal atonement is an adequate, and the only adequate foundation for the preaching of the Gospel as good news of salvation to all; and they dwell with much force on the kind of mental reservation which to older system ascribes to God in inviting all to partake in what is only prepared for some, because the some only will accept the invitation.

Secondly, as to the need-be for atonement. A necessity for an atonement arising out of rectoral or public justice, is felt less repulsive than one that implies a demand in the divine nature for a certain amount of suffering as the punishment of a certain amount of sin.

Thirdly, as to the nature of the atonement. All the men have revolted from in the idea of the Son of God being actually in His Father's eyes as a criminal through imputation of man's sin, and being punished accordingly, is thought to be avoided; as well as all that is of the nature of legal fiction in imputation of guilt to an innocent being, or of righteousness to a guilty being.

Fourthly, as to the results of the atonement. They dwell largely on the manifestation of the divine character, and on the vindication of the divine judgment on sin, as well as of the divine sovereignty in the salvation of those who are saved - seeing that those who perish, perish, not because a salvation was not provided for them, but because they would not accept of it. Owen had said in a passage already quoted, that "to affirm Christ to die for all men, is the readiest way to prove that He died for no man in the sense Christians have hitherto believed, and to hurry poor souls into the bottom of Socinian blasphemies." Here, that Christ died for all men is maintained; but, at the same time, "the objections of the Socinian" to "redemption through the merits of Christ," are held to be "all silenced."

> If he is not allowed for his weapons the wrath of a God of love - the transfer of moral character - the infliction of legal punishment on the innocent, his gauntlet can grasp no other. The doctrine of a substitutionary atonement not only blunts but breaks and shivers these favourite and long used lances of Socinianism.*

---

* Thomas W. Jenkyn, *On the Extent of the Atonement in its Relation to God and the Universe*, p.317.

But doubtless, Owen would regard this as a victory obtained only by concessions; - for Owen would say, that the doctrine that Christ died for all men is combined with the distinct concession, "that He died for no man in the sense Christians have hitherto believed;" - and he would be entitled so to reply, at least in reference to the sense attached to the word atonement in the discussions between himself and Arminians.

With much in what seems to be the mental history of this modified Calvinism I have full sympathy. The constraint felt in preaching Christ to all, while believing that He only died for some, is easily understood; while, doubtless, Owen's arguments for a limited atonement, if the atonement had been what, in the controversies between him and Arminians it was on both sides assumed to be, were unanswerable as arguments whatever scriptural difficulties they might involve. Again, in the concession which seems made to Socinians, on the subject of the untransferable nature of guilt and merit, and the difficulty of assuming that by a legal fiction God sees things other than as they really are, I concur with them; although I feel that there are important principles in Edwards' argument on the substitution of Christ for us, to which they do not seem to me to give due weight; and although the even stronger language of Luther as to Christ's identification of Himself with us, instead of repelling me, as it does them, is to my mind a very near approach to truth; and I am disposed to think was spiritually, though not intellectually, truth in him.

But I have much more sympathy in their difficulties than satisfaction in the way in which they have dealt with them. Believing that Christ died for all, and perceiving that the conceptions of the nature of the atonement from which the earlier Calvinists reasoned, did indeed imply, if logically followed out, that He only died for some, the teachers of this modified Calvinism have seemed to themselves to have found a solution of the difficulty, in their conception of rectoral or public justice as what called for an atonement for sin. But, surely, rectoral or public justice, if it is to have any moral basis - any basis other than expediency - must rest upon, and refer to, distributive or absolute justice.

In other words, unless there be a righteousness with blessedness, looking at individual cases simply in themselves, I cannot see that there is a rightness in connecting them as a rule of moral government. "An English judge once said to a criminal before him, 'You are condemned to be transported, not because you have stolen these goods, but that goods may not be stolen'." (Jenkyn, pp.175-6) This is quoted in illustration of the position, that "the death of Christ is an honourable ground for remitting punishment," because "His sufferings answer the same ends as the punishment of the sinner." I do not recognise any harmony between this sentiment of the English judge and the voice of an awakened conscience on the subject of sin. It is just because he has sinned and deserves punishment, and not because he says to himself that God is a moral governor and must punish him to deter others, that the wrath of God against sin seems so terrible - and as just as terrible. As little is this sentiment in harmony with what the words teach, "The wages of sin is death."

Owen and Edwards do not err in believing, that the righteousness of God connects sin with misery, as by a righteous reward, irrespective of state reasons. Their error is, I believe, twofold - concluding as to that award beyond what they had light for their guidance - and - and this chiefly - not seeing any hope for the sinner in the very righteousness of God - as if the righteousness of God would have full satisfaction in reference to the unrighteous, in their being miserable. "Good and *righteous* is the Lord, *therefore* will he teach sinners the way which they should choose."

Rectoral justice so presupposes absolute justice, and so throws the mind back on that absolute justice, that the idea of an atonement that will satisfy the one, though it might not the other, must be a delusion.

The recommendation of the distinction sought to be drawn has been, that it seemed to harmonise an atonement for all, with the ultimate punishment of those who do not accept of that atonement; - that is to say, as Calvinists pressed the point on Arminians - the punishment of many whose punishment Christ had previously endured: this stronghold of Calvinism it seemed to overturn. But as long as Christ's sufferings are held to be *penal*, which, even when the old form of words is most departed from, is the expression still used, I cannot see what difference it makes, whether they be held as by Owen, to have been the same that those for whom he suffered were obnoxious to; - or as Baxter, with Grotius, held - equivalent; - or as Dr Jenkyn holds, "different in nature, and kind - in quantity and degree." If they were penal then, that those for whom He suffered should be punished themselves, must still suggest the idea sought to be avoided, of sin twice punished.

Nor is the difficulty less because, not regarding our sins as imputed to Christ in the sense of the elder Calvinists, objection is made to speaking of Christ as punished for our sins; the expression being substituted, that what he suffered was the punishment of our sins. This distinction, introduced by Andrew Fuller, is adopted by Dr Payne, who would press it further than Fuller; and I suppose that it is contemplated by Dr Jenkyn when he says "Christ's sufferings were not a punishment." (p.292) But Dr Payne recognises our sins as imputed to Christ in the sense of "inflicting upon Him the punishment due to them"; (p.260) and while Dr Jenkyn at as much pains to bring out the difference between what Christ suffered and what those for whom He suffered were exposed to suffer, as Dr Owen is to bring out, if he could, an identity, (being indeed quite successful in this, while Owen is altogether unsuccessful), still he regards "made a sin offering for us" (in 2 Cor. v. and 21) as equivalent to "made liable to punishment for us" (p.287) - and he enlarges on Christ's "suffering as if He had been a sinner." (p.284) If Christ was "made liable to punishment," if He was "treated as if He were a sinner," that is, if God so treated Him - for the misapprehensions of men are nothing - then to say that He was not punished though the punishment of our sins was endured by Him, however it is a softening of expressions, is not to any real effect so to modify the idea of atonement as to do away with the difficulty of a double punishment for sin.

This distinction between being punished, and enduring sufferings which are a punishment, is adopted in connection with the denial of the imputation of our guilt to Christ, and in this view is held to remove the difficulties of one class of objectors - although to call sufferings a punishment while the sufferer is not regarded as punished, involves new difficulties. But, the change of which most weight is laid, is in the view taken of the relation in which the sufferings endured are represented as standing to the divinity of the sufferer. That the personal dignity of the Saviour is the important aspect of the incarnation in relation to the atonement, is much insisted on. Divinity as a capacity for enduring infinite penal infliction, is an idea which is recognised as rightly offending. Divinity as giving infinite value to any measure of humiliation or suffering condescended to, is urged as what should recommend itself as a far more worthy conception. How far removed from either conception the truth of the case has been - how far different from a capacity of enduring infinite penal infliction, or a giving infinite value to penal suffering, however small its amount has been the relation of the divinity of Christ to His sufferings in making propitiation for our sins will, I trust, be made clear in the sequel.

But there are two points in relation to the sufferings of Christ, as spoken of in these two forms of Calvinism severally, which appear to me deserving of our special attention, viz. that the language employed in speaking of the part of the Father in relation to these sufferings, is much the same; - and that, the details specified when details of the elements of suffering are ventured, are much the same, or at least are of the same nature.

(1) The language of the latter Calvinists in speaking of the part of the Father in relation to the sufferings of Christ, is not essentially different from that of those whose system they feel it necessary to modify.

President Edwards is quoted by Dr Stroud (who dedicates his book to Dr Pye Smith) as representing Christ as "suffering a positive infliction of divine wrath," which to teach, he esteems chargeable with error - "not to say absurdity". (p.209)* These are some of the sentences which he quotes.

Revenging justice then spent all its force upon Him on account of our guilt... and this was the way and means by which Christ stood up for

* William Stroud, *A Treatise on the Physical Cause of the Death of Christ and Its Relation to the Principles and Practice of Christianity* (London, 1847). The reference should probably be to p.203.

the honour of God's justice, viz. by thus suffering its terrible executions: for when He had undertaken for sinners, and had substituted Himself in their room, divine justice could have its due honour no other way than by His suffering its revenges.

Yet Dr Stroud himself says,

A transition more sudden or violent than that which took place from the seraphic discourses and devotions of Christ after the paschal supper, to the horrors of Gethsemane, can scarcely be conceived. That He was about to suffer from the immediate hand of God is implied by His prediction to the apostles on the way. In the absence of all external infliction, the cup of trembling which was then presented to Him by the Father, and which He so earnestly petitioned might if possible be withdrawn, could have been no other than the cup of the wrath of God, 'the poison whereof drinketh up the spirit'. (p.215)*

and he quotes with approbation from Rambach, a passage in which he speaks of our Lord as having "to suffer all the floods of the divine wrath to pass over Him, which would have overwhelmed our Saviour's human nature, had not the divinity within Him supported it in this terrible trial." Dr Pye Smith says,

Jesus Christ voluntarily sustained that which was the marked punishment of sin (p.35)... The tremendous manifestations of God's displeasure against sin, He endured, though in Him was no sin: and He endured them in a manner of which those unhappy spirits who shall drink the fierceness of wrath of Almighty God will never be able to form an adequate idea. (p.42) **

Dr Jenkyn says, "The most amazing circumstance connected with His death was, that He suffered as one disowned, and reprobated, and forsaken of God," &c. (p.284). "The just is treated as if He had been unjust, the Son of God suffered as if He had been a transgressor" (p.285). ***

Dr Payne **** concludes, that the sufferings of our Lord were "dreadful beyond conception," and resulted from "intense mental suffering, from the burden of our guilt which rested upon Him, from that light of His Father's countenance which then suffered a total eclipse," in relation to which he quotes Psalm lxxxviii. 4-7, concluding with the words, "thy wrath lieth hard upon me, and thou hast afflicted me with all thy waves."

---

*   Stroud, op.cit.

**   John Pye Smith, *Four Discourses on the Sacrifice and Priesthood of Jesus Christ, and the Atonement and Redemption Thence Accruing*, third edition (London, 1847).

***   Jenkyn, op.cit.

****Payne: *On the Reality of the Atonement*, part of his *Lectures in Divine Sovereignty;* the ref. is on pp.185-7 of the 1st edition (1836).

(2) But the other point to which I would direct attention, is more striking still; viz. the oneness of character in the elements of suffering which they specify.

What are the "revenges of divine justice," and "its terrible executions," which were in Edwards' contemplations when he employed those general expressions which have exposed him to the charge of error, nay, absurdity? The only direct dealing of God with Christ which he specifies, is purely negative; - "God forsook Christ and hid Himself from Him, and withheld comfortable influences, or the clear ideas of pleasant objects." This negative wrath, if the expression is not a contradiction, is indeed represented as being in order that the positive elements of suffering present should act with unmitigated power; and what were these?

First, God hid Himself from Christ "that He might feel the *full burden of our sins that was laid upon Him*." But *how laid upon Him?* "His having so clear an actual view of sin and its hatefulness, was an idea infinitely disagreeable to the holy nature of Christ; and therefore, unless balanced with an equal sight of good that comes by that evil, must have been an immensely disagreeable sensation in Christ's soul, or, which is the same thing, immense suffering... Thus Christ bore our sins; God laid on Him the iniquities of us all, and he bare the burden of them."

Secondly, God thus dealt with Christ, that "He might suffer God's wrath." But again, *how?* - "His suffering wrath consisted more in the sense He had of the other thing; viz. the dreadfulness of the punishment of sin, or the dreadfulness of God's wrath inflicted for it;" viz. on those on whom it is inflicted. "Thus Christ was tormented, not only in the fire of God's wrath, but in the fire of our sins; and our sins were His tormentors; the evil and malignant nature of sin was what Christ endured immediately," *i.e.* in being realised by Him as an object of mental contemplation - as well as more remotely, in bearing the consequences of it," *i.e.* the sense of these consequences as endured by others.

> Thus Christ suffered what the damned in hell do not suffer. For they do not see the hateful nature of sin... and as the clear view of sin in its hatefulness necessarily brought great suffering on the holy soul of Christ, so also did the view of its punishment. For both the evil of sin and the evil of punishment are infinite evils, and both infinitely disagreeable to Christ's nature: the former to His holy nature, or His nature as God; - the latter to His human nature, or His nature as man. ... Christ's love brought His elect infinitely near to Him in that great act and suffering wherein He specially stood for them, and was substituted in their stead; and His love and pity fixed the idea of them in His mind, as if He had really been they; and fixed their calamity in His mind, as though it really was His. A very strong and lively pity towards the miserable, tends to make their case ours; as in other

respects, so in this in particular, as it doth in our idea place us in their stead, under their misery... as it were feeling it for them, actually suffering it in their stead by strong sympathy. *On Satisfaction for Sin,* § 9, 1 *

I am quite sensible of the justice done to the remarkable passage from which I quote, by thus curtailing it. But I have given enough of it for my purpose in quoting it; viz. to shew that, however strong and startling Edwards' general expressions as to Christ's being, in consequence of the imputation of our guilt, subjected to "the revenge of divine justice," there is, when he explains himself, nothing of the nature of legal fiction in his conception of *the way in which Christ bore the burden of our sins*; as neither is there anything of the nature of the *actual going forth of divine wrath against the holy one*, because of his standing in the room of sinners, in what is called "His endurance of wrath;" but that the whole suffering conceived of, is resolved into a vivid perception and realisation of the hatefulness of sin, and of the greatness of the wrath to which it has exposed sinners; these two ideas affecting our Lord in the measure of His infinite holiness and love.

So strictly has Edwards, in endeavouring to imagine ingredients to fill a full cup of suffering, adhered to the limits which he recognises in saying that "Christ suffered the wrath of God for men's sins in such a way as He was capable of, being an infinitely holy person, who knew that God was not angry with Him personally, knew that God did not hate Him, but infinitely loved Him." It is, indeed, a great relief, to see this great and good man, while dealing so much in the language of what seems legal fiction in that high region in which fiction can have no place, when he comes to explain the facts of Christ's actual experience, as they were conceived of by him, saying nothing that implied, either that God looked on Christ in wrath, or that Christ felt as if He did. And, when I use the word "explain," I am very far indeed from intending to suggest any attempt to soften, or explain away. Edwards is in no way attempting to make his doctrine less obnoxious: on the contrary, as in the choice of general expressions he selects the most extreme, so in setting forth the elements of the Saviour's sufferings, he is making out the strongest case that he can, within the limit which he has recognised.

The teaching that substitutes, "enduring the punishment of our sins," for, "being punished for our sins," has still to seek for elements of penal suffering; - and the same relief which is felt in interpreting the general expressions of Edwards in reference to the divine wrath which Christ suffered, by the details of Christ's actual sufferings which he specifies, is again experienced in passing from the general expressions of the modified Calvinism to the illustrations of these which are offered. The "wrath" or "malediction,"

---

* Edwards, *On Satisfaction from Sin*, vol. 1 of the four volume edition, pp.603-605.

as he more frequently expresses it, which Dr Stroud contemplates, is "the loss for a time of all sense of God's friendship, all enjoyment of His communion", (p.192)* - which, the *consciousness of sinlessness remaining*, and their being no *misconception assumed as to the Father's true estimate of Him as the holy one of God*, although it would be suffering, could with no propriety be called malediction and wrath.

Dr Pye Smith's specification of the elements of suffering, is strikingly like that of President Edwards, both in the limit recognised, "He suffered in such a manner as a being perfectly holy could suffer", (p.41)** and in the moral nature assigned to the suffering, as arising from holiness and love realising the evil of sin, and intensely interested in those who were its victims. (p.42) The elements which Dr Payne finds in our Lord's sufferings, are also intense views of the evil of sin, combined with the withholding of counter-balancing support. (p.181)*** He speaks indeed of the "penal elements" in our Lord's cup of suffering, and recognises the withholding of those manifestations of supreme complacency in His character and conduct which He had previously enjoyed, as in itself a most distressing testimony of the divine anger against sin, and probably implied in the language of the prophet, "It pleased the Lord to bruise Him." This thought he adopts from Dr Dwight, but he proceeds to object to Dr Dwight's representing the hidings of God's face as implying "the suffering of His hatred and contempt," saying, "No sober minded man can admit this.

The fact of the case most unquestionably is, that the Father did not despise Him, - was not angry with Him when He hung on the cross. Never, indeed, did He regard Him with such ineffable complacency. How then could He manifest that displeasure which did not exist?" (p.182). Dr Jenkyn, intending to indicate a mitigation of Christ's sufferings, and speaking rather of what they were not than of what they were, says - "His sufferings were not a punishment. His consciousness of personal rectitude, and his confidence in His Father, never forsook Him. In the darkest hour of His anguish, His assurance of God's approbation and acceptance was in the highest exercise, - 'Father,' He said, 'into thy hands I commend my spirit'." (p.292)****

My quotations are necessarily brief, but the references will guide those who may be disposed to verify the correctness of the impressions which these quotations convey. What remains with me, after fully weighing all that either school of Calvinists have felt warranted to present to our faith in picturing the actual elements of the sufferings of Christ, is the conviction,

---

*   Stroud, *op.cit.*, quotation imprecise.

**   John Pye Smith, *op.cit.*

*** Payne, *op. cit.*

****Jenkyn, *op.cit.*

that they have not ventured to assume anything as to the actual consciousness of Christ in suffering, or as to the actual mind of the Father towards Him, while it pleased the Father so to bruise Him, or as to His own apprehension of the light in which His Father saw Him, in His dealing with the Father, and the Father's dealing with Him in reference to our sins, which at all accords, either with the older idea of guilt being imputed to Him, and therefore wrath going forth upon Him - the wrath due to guilt - or, with the new idea of His being treated as if He were guilty, as if He were a transgressor.

Elements of great sufferings are specified - by some with more definiteness than by others; the former writers also giving more prominence to the Saviour's sense of the eternal misery to which sin had subjected sinners; - the latter, more to His sense of the sin itself; - elements of suffering are specified, all of them at least conceivable, - of suffering which some call infinitely, others, indefinitely great. But however these accord, and they do, so far as they go, accord with the idea of sacrificial atoning suffering, they do not accord with the penal character ascribed to them. Yet this penal character ascribed to these sufferings, without necessity as respects their own nature - I believe in contradiction to their own nature - is that very thing which had originated the difficulty as to the universality of the atonement; and, as appears to me, leaves it a difficulty on the system of the modern, as much as of the elder Calvinists.

But, my objection to the conception of rectoral or public justice, as that in which the necessity for the atonement has originated, is much more serious than its inadequacy to remove difficulties as to the universality of the atonement. My great objection is that, equally with the view for which it is offered as a substitute, it takes a limited, and - in respect of the important elements which it leaves out of account - an erroneous view of that which the atonement was intended to accomplish.

If my readers have entered into my objections to the mere legal character of the atonement, as we see it in the system of the elder Calvinists, they will see that in respect of these objections, the modified Calvinism has no advantage. An atonement which has conferred on those with reference to whom it was made a legal standing of innocence, as having had their guilt already punished, and of righteousness as having a righteousness already wrought out for them; and an atonement whose result is merely to lay a foundation on which God may proceed to pardon sin, and to treat as righteous, are likely purely *legal* atonements, that is, atonements, the whole character of which is determined by man's relation to the divine law. Dr Wardlaw asks:

Man having sinned, what is to be done? The unconditional absolution of the transgressor would be a flagrant outrage on the claims of retributive justice; - his annihilation would be a tacit evasion of these claims; - while, if the law has its course, and the demands of justice are satisfied by the infliction of its penalty, he is lost for ever - eternal life forfeited, and eternal death endured. Here, then, is the place for ATONEMENT - what is it? (p.10)*

He then, quoting from Dr Alexander, says - "In its simplest form the problem of a religion may be expressed thus: Given a Supreme Deity, the Creator and Governor of all things, and an intelligent creature in a state of alienation and estrangement from his Creator; to determine the means whereby a reconciliation may be effected, and the creature restored to the favour and service of God." This statement of the question he adopts - adding, "The problem to be solved is this, How may this be accomplished honourably to the character and government of Supreme Ruler?" He then quotes several definitions of atonement, among them, this from Dr Jenkyn, "Atonement is an expedient substituted in the place of the literal infliction of the penalty, so as to supply the government just and good grounds for dispensing favours to an offender;" - and this is from Andrew Fuller, "that a way was opened by the mediation of Christ, for the free and consistent exercise of mercy in all the ways which sovereign wisdom saw fit to adopt."

The definitions are all to the same effect, and all accord with what I have said of the legal character ascribed to the atonement; so that, retrospectively, it but meets a demand that pertains to the character of God as a Lawgiver, and prospectively, it is related to the mercy He may manifest, only in the way of making such manifestation of mercy consistent with the interests of His moral government, and promotive of them.

But the problem which the work of God in Christ solves, while it includes, goes far beyond that stated by Dr Alexander, or recognised in these definitions. In the light of the Gospel we see, that our need of salvation, and our capacity of salvation as contemplated by the Father of our spirits, involved the problem - not "how we sinners could be pardoned and reconciled, and mercy be extended to us;" but "how it could come to pass, that we, God's offspring, being dead, should be alive again, being lost, should be found." "God sent forth His Son, made of a woman, made under the law, that He might redeem us who were under the law, that we might receive the adoption of sons." It was as employed "in bringing many sons to glory, that it became Him, of whom are all things, and by whom are all things, to make the Captain of their salvation perfect through sufferings."

Nothing can illustrate the way in which this purely legal view of the atonement works, and what is its development, better than the conclusions at which Dr Wardlaw has arrived, and which he expresses in commenting upon the words "to put away sin."

---

* Ralph Wardlaw, *Discourses on the Nature and Extent of the Atonement of Christ*, second edition (Glasgow 1844). The quotation actually begins with "What is to be...". The quotations in the next paragraph are from pp.11-12.

The expression is significantly general. And, for my own part, I am unable to discover any valid objection to our stating the design of the atonement in this form: That it was an atonement FOR SIN, an atonement whose value was so unlimited, so strictly and properly infinite, that on the ground of its merits, had God willed it, fallen angels might have been saved as well as fallen men: nay, had there been a thousand rebel worlds, the inhabitants of them all. (p.107)*

Thus he concludes - contemplating the atonement as simply a grand moral display, illustrative of God's condemnation of sin and delight in holiness. And such a display it undoubtedly is; but it is much more than this. *Nor is it even this* healthfully and truly, *apart from* those specialities in man's condition, and from that divine purpose concerning man, by which its nature and character have been determined. How different from this abstract atonement for sin, is the specific reference to the condition of human spirits in the words, "For what the law could not do, in that it was *weak through the flesh*, God sending *His own Son* in the likeness of sinful flesh, and for sin, *condemned sin in the flesh*: that the *righteousness* of the law might be *fulfilled in us*, who walk *not after the flesh, but after the spirit*."

The objection to both forms of Calvinism on the ground of the narrow and exclusively legal basis on which the necessity for atonement is placed, is instructively illustrated by the relation in which the atonement is represented as standing to justification by faith. We may here take President Edwards as the representative of the earlier Calvinism, and Dr Payne as the representative of the modified Calvinism.

Both Edwards and Payne regard the work of Christ as the meritorious ground of justification. Both regard faith as that by which the individual is so connected with that work as to be justified on the ground of it: both are alike solicitous to exclude the faith present in justification from being itself in any measure included in the ground of that justification: while at the same time, both regard this faith as that which has a rightness in itself, and as that which is due from man as the right reception of the gospel. Payne, indeed, treats faith more as an intellectual act than Edwards does. But, still, he objects to putting it on a footing with the ordinary case of belief under the power of evidence; in doing which he thinks some others have erred.

The difference between their several systems is connected with the idea of imputation. As Edwards holds man's guilt to have been imputed to Christ when He suffered for sin, so he holds Christ's righteousness to be imputed to believers, making them personally righteous in God's sight; which imputation he holds, not only to clothe their persons, determining the complacency with which God regards them, but also, all their virtues and

---

* Wardlaw, *op. cit.*, pp.107-108.

graces, giving them a value beyond their intrinsic value. Payne on the other hand, as he rejects the conception of imputation of guilt, rejects also that of imputation of righteousness, and holds

> that to be in a justified state, is not either to be pronounced just, or to be made actually just - for both are impossible in the case of a sinner - but it is to be treated as if we were just; or rather, perhaps, to be in the state of those whom God declares that He will treat as if they were just, *i.e.* it is to be in the faith of Christ; for the divine declaration is, that believers are the persons who shall be treated as if they were just".
> (p. 333)*

Whatever difficulty attaches to the idea of imputation, this way of escaping from it is to me very unsatisfactory. The idea "that guilt and innocence or sin and righteousness are transferable in their effects but untransferable in themselves,"** which underlies the whole system of modern Calvinism on this subject, and is the ground on which Dr Payne, while rejecting the word "imputation," continues to use the expression "treated as if,"*** seems to be tenable, if tenable at all, only if we exclude from our consideration all the more important effects of sin and righteousness.

As respects the sinner's relation to God, the effect of sin which is most important is the displeasure awakened in the divine mind. But, Christ is not held to have been really the object of the divine displeasure through the relation in which He stood to us and our sins, although expressions have been used which, apart from the details offered in explanation, might seem to contain that assertion; and Dr Payne has not only asserted the very opposite to have been the case, but has asked, and the question is unanswerable - "How could God manifest that displeasure which did not exist?" Neither God's displeasure, nor, therefore, anything expressing God's displeasure, are we to conceive of as included in the alleged transferred effects of sin. But what in all our Lord's sufferings can be rightly spoken of as "transferred effects of sin"? were not these sufferings in their nature altogether determined by what He was who suffered? and is not the fact that Christ's sufferings were in reality the effects of holiness and love, and not transferred effects of sin, discernible in all the attempts which we have seen made to specify the elements of his sufferings?

But, are the effects of righteousness more transferable? It is, indeed, far less repulsive to think of these as transferred to us than to think of the effects of sin as transferred to Christ; as it is also far less repulsive to think of Christ's righteousness as imputed to us than to think of our sin as imputed to Christ

---

*   Payne, *op. cit.*, p.233 (Campbell cited p.333 in error).

**   Payne, *op. cit.*, p.254 from Fuller.

***   Payne, *op. cit.*, e.g. pp.260-261.

- to think of God as well pleased with us for Christ's sake than to think of God as contemplating Christ with displeasure for our sake. But *are* the effects of righteousness transferable any more than the effects of sin?

The root matter here is God's favour, as there it was His displeasure. Is the favour of God - that favour which is life - thus transferable? nay, is any real fruit of righteousness as respects the experience of the human spirit in its relation to God, and intercourse with Him; or in its relation to man, and what man is to man through love; or in the mind's self-consciousness, and inward peace and harmony - is any real fruit of righteousness in any of these aspects of the subject - and these are the fundamental and alone important aspects of it - transferable any more than righteousness itself? or, are any of these at all separable from righteousness? If, indeed, we descend to a lower region, it is at least intelligible how certain benefits may be conceived of as conferred for Christ's sake - though it would be far from correct to speak of these as "effects of righteousness transferred," or, of their bestowal upon us as a treating us as if we were righteous. But is there place for anything so outward as this in the matter of justification? Surely, a justification which does not introduce into the divine favour, into the light of the divine countenance, is no justification at all.

The strict maintenance of the idea of imputation enables Edwards to give to the expression, "for Christ's sake," an amplitude of meaning that, as respects justification, may seem to meet all the exigencies of the subject. If God sees us as clothed with the righteousness of Christ, He may be conceived of as smiling on us with the smile of favour proper to that righteousness: and to this the faith of the elder Calvinists rose. But, if this idea of imputation is given up, then, whatever else may be supposed to be given for Christ's sake, nothing that is suggested by the words "the favour of God which rests upon Christ," can be conceived of as so given.

Dr Payne* quotes Mr Bennet as "having happily and satisfactorily shewn, that 'the practice of conferring favours upon many, from regard to, and as an expression of approbation of, some eminently distinguished individual,' may be regarded as a law of the divine government: while, on the other hand, the procedure supposed, VIZ. CONSIDERING a person what he really is not, and then TREATING *him as if he* HAD *been what he is not*, has no analogy in any part of the divine conduct." (p.263)

No doubt this is true. But we must not forget the high region in which we now are, and that not of *secondary* gifts, but of *that life which lies in God's favour*, are we speaking. This we receive through Christ, or we receive nothing; and in reference to this, any correct use of the expression, "for Christ's sake," must have a far higher meaning than these analogies furnish. Abraham believed God, and was called the friend of God, and his descend-

---

* Payne, *op. cit.*, pp.263-264.

ants received many favours for his sake; - but were they for his sake "friends of God," or "treated as friends of God," *apart from their participation in that reality* in respect of which he was the friend of God? "They who are of faith are blessed with faithful Abraham."

Edwards ascribes the place which faith has in justification simply to this, that it connects the individual with Christ. Payne says,

> If we are justified solely on the ground of the perfect work of Christ, there is nothing to prevent the justification of all men, without a single thought or act on their part, but the rectoral character and relation of Jehovah, which renders it necessary that some rule of justification should be enacted, that the justice of the Divine Being may be rendered apparent by His bestowing it upon those, and those only, who comply with that rule. Now, it is manifest that any requisition (and it must be a requisition on account of the rectoral character of God) would secure this object; it might be love, for instance.*

But to this, *i.e.* making it love, the objection, he says, would be that this justification might appear to be by works, but faith is not liable to this objection, because it "cannot be confounded with fulfilling the law."* Yet Dr Payne has just been employed in objecting, and not without reason, to the idea that faith is as it were a new law. Now certainly there is no conception of the relation of faith to justification which seems so fitted to suggest that objectionable idea as the conception which Dr Payne has expressed in the words just quoted:- for if faith is a *requisition*, compliance with which is required that the *justice of the Divine Being* may be *rendered apparent in His distinguishing of individuals* in the bestowal of justification, then what is more natural than to feel that the new law of faith is that under which we are, compliance with which is righteously acknowledged by including us in the number who shall be treated for Christ's sake as if they were righteous, and non-compliance with which shall infer condemnation? That it seems to Dr Payne that the moral Governor of the Universe was "free to adopt any rule - only it must be some fixed and declared rule," indicates a greater departure from the consideration of the nature of the case than I can well understand. Surely the conception of Edwards, that faith is connected with justification, because it connects with Christ, commends itself much more - as it also is, in my apprehension, more fitted to secure the end which both seek to attain, viz. that the meritorious work of Christ should be really the believer's felt ground of confidence towards God, and not his own faith.

It may seem, indeed, as if this were secured on Dr Payne's system by its being a part of the gospel believed, that the work of Christ was the meritorious ground of justification - as well as on President Edwards' system, by its being a part of the gospel believed, that we are made righteous and are

---

* Payne, *op. cit.*, p.309.

accepted because of the imputation of Christ's righteousness; and, no doubt, in strictness of thought it is a contradiction to say, that I am trusting to Christ's work as the ground on which God treats me as if I were righteous, and, at the same time, that I esteem my own faith that ground, as truly as it is a contradiction to say, that I am trusting to the imputation of Christ's righteousness, and, at the same time, to my own faith.

But I cannot in either case forget that my faith is that which has individualised me; and the remembrance of this is, as it seems to me, less likely to produce a self-righteous feeling, if I am thinking of myself as clothed with the righteousness of Christ, and in the mind of the Father identified with Christ, than if I am thinking of myself as by my faith introduced into the circle of those with whom, according to the rule of government which He has revealed, God will, for Christ's sake, deal as if they were righteous. For, in proportion as *faith* is contemplated as a requisition made in order that it may be the basis of *a judgment,* and is not felt to be simply the natural and necessary link connecting us with Christ, there is an opening afforded for the coming in of self-righteousness.

But the fear about self-righteousness arises entirely from not seeing, that the true protection from self-righteousness is found in the very nature of faith. The true faith precludes self-righteousness, because that which it apprehends is the Father revealed by the Son. He who beholds the glory of God in the face of Jesus Christ, is saved from self-righteousness by the native power on his spirit of the glory which he beholds. He is in the presence of the true God, truly known, and "no flesh shall glory in His presence."

It is an error to hold the connection between faith and justification to be arbitrary, but it is a deeper error not to see, that faith excludes boasting, not by the arrangements of a scheme, but by its being the knowledge of the true God. To take precautions that the confidence towards God which arises in faith shall not be self-righteous, is to me as monstrous as it would be to take precautions that light should not be darkness. Indeed this is the very thing which, in taking such precautions, is done - done in reference to the highest, the absolute light - the light of eternal life.

This serious error would never have been fallen into, if the atonement had been seen in its prospective relation to the gift of eternal life in Christ, and as that by which God has bridged over the gulf between what we were through sin, and what, in the yearnings of His Father's heart over us, He desired to make us. "This is the record, that God has given to us eternal life, and this life is in His Son."

Less than our being alive in that eternal life which is sonship, could not satisfy the Father of our spirits; nor as orphan spirits, as in our alienation from God we are, would less than the gift of that life have met our need. And the faith which apprehends this gift as given, excludes boasting, because it occupies the spirit, not with itself, but with the gift which it apprehends. For the gift is given; and he that understands what it is, and apprehends it as given, is altogether filled with the excellent grace wherein he stands, rejoicing in it, and conforming himself to it; and thus, seeing the Father as He is revealed by the Son, and apprehending the Son as the living way to the Father, and as the Lord of his spirit, he welcomes the Son to reign in his heart, and in the spirit of the Son cries, "Abba, Father." And the confidence towards the Father in which he so worships, is not only sustained by the faith of the Father's delight in the perfection of sonship as it is in Christ, but also belongs to the very nature of the spirit of sonship, as it is a response to the Fatherliness that is in God; for the feeblest cry of faith is a cry in Christ, and one with and a part of that which is in its absolute perfection in Christ; sharing in His preciousness to the heart of the Father. So sharing, not through any process of fiction or imputation - as men have spoken - but through a process strictly natural, and which commends itself to us as inevitable.

Now, because of the very near approach to this which is in the conception of Edwards, though the legal light in which he has so exclusively seen the atonement has kept him intellectually (though I do not think spiritually) away from it, I would prefer the language of Edwards, notwithstanding the tone of legal fiction which it has, to what, in seeking to avoid fiction, Dr Payne and others have substituted. It is really true, that he that comes to God in Christ, comes invested with the interest to the Father's heart of that sonship in which he comes, and finds that sonship a living way to the Father - an actual getting near to God.

Therefore, rightly in his own thoughts, because truly in the Father's thoughts, is such a worshipper as one on whom that very favour rests, which rests upon Christ. So that I cannot help feeling, in reading President Edwards' representations of the way in which Christ's righteousness invests with its own dignity and worth, not only the persons, but the feeblest graces of those who are in Christ by faith, that what he says is *substantially true, must be true*, although not in the way of the fiction of an imputation: and I am persuaded that, if he had seen the atonement as that by which the Father of spirits bridges over the gulf between the condition of rebellious, alienated children, and the condition of reconciled children trusting in the Father's heart, and reposing on His love, instead of seeing it in the legal aspect in which he has so exclusively viewed it, he would have conceived truly, and spoken unobjectionably, of God's imputation of righteousness, and of our acceptance for Christ's sake - as we have seen Luther does.

Dr Payne may feel that this standing of sonship given in Christ, and revealed for faith to apprehend and enter upon, is liable to the objection that he urges against the idea that the atonement confers legal rights; which idea, while it has had acceptance with others, appears to him destructive of the grace of the gospel. And, no doubt, if the absoluteness with which God bestows a gift, leaving it for him on whom it is bestowed simply that he should receive it and use it according to its nature - if this takes from the free grace of God in bestowing, the objection lies equally against anything *actually given*, and as to which it is not merely the fact that God has put it in His own power to give it if it should please Him.

But Dr Payne himself is not able so to order his words as to escape all the objectionableness that he finds in the language of others. As the most guarded and unexceptionable statement he can offer of the relation of Faith to Justification, he says, "Faith justifies by bringing an individual into that body, to every individual of which the blessing of justification is secured by the promise, and covenant, and oath of God." (p.322)*

But wherein does the having a thing through faith "secured to me by the promise, and covenant, and oath of God," differ from having through faith *a legal right conferred on me?* He quotes Bishop Hopkins** as using the language of *right* in pleading with God on the ground of the work of Christ, and contrasts his expressions with those of David, "Have mercy on me, O God, according to Thy lovingkindness;" and no doubt the contrast is striking and instructive. But the oath of God, that if we comply with the required condition of faith He will treat us as if we were righteous, might justify, in the believer, the language of which Dr Payne complains, as well as the doctrine of legal right objected to. David's language - the language of true faith - the language of the spirit of Christ in man - is, and ever must be, free from all legal taint, simply because it is the language of truth, expressing in him who is led by the spirit of truth, a confidence in harmony with the truth of things - a confidence in which *confession of sin* is *combined with filial trust in the Father's heart.*

No part of this system presents a more instructive development of the working of this conception of rectoral justice - and of rectoral justice, not only as distinct from fatherly love, but also from absolute justice as contemplated by Edwards - than the arbitrary character already noticed as ascribed by Dr Payne to the relation of faith to justification. For while the relation of faith to sanctification is recognised as a relation in the nature of things, its relation to justification is held to be arbitrary; and, in connection with this distinction, Dr Payne objects to Dr Russell's saying that, "the whole efficacy of faith in the matter of justification arises from its object." To this Dr Payne objects, as embodying "the error of forgetting that man needs a change of state as well as a change of character," *i.e.* justification as well as sanctification. I would quite object to regarding such a change of state as amounts only to the "being treated as if we were righteous," had such a thing been possible, as at all filling up the words "from being unjust becoming just."

---

*   Payne, *op. cit.*
** Payne, *op. cit.*, pp.267-268.

But the truth is, that the relation of faith to justification is as absolutely one in the nature of things as its relation to sanctification. The purpose of God that He might be just, and the justifier of him that believeth in Christ, has a far deeper and more perfect fulfilment than this scheme recognises: and to understand that fulfilment, we must learn with Luther to conceive aright of that glory for Himself in man which God contemplated when He proposed to justify the ungodly by faith. We must discern the relation in which the human spirit has come to stand to the Father of Spirits, when man is apprehending and believing the testimony of God, that He has given to us eternal life in His Son, we must see the glory that God has in his faith - how, where it exists, God is in His true place in the heart of man, and man is in his true place in relation to God - how man has come to be nothing - how God is now all in all - how all trust in the flesh, all self-righteousness has ceased to be - how trust in the Father's heart has come into being, and is the commenced breathing of the breath of eternal life.

Of this which in faith is accomplishing in the human spirit, of this which is the glory which God has in our having faith in His Son, we must have some discernment, that we may understand how God is just, and the justifier of him that believeth in Jesus. If the weakness and scanty measure of this faith, as it is found in those that believe, render what Luther calls God's imputation necessary - if, in order that the righteousness of God in our acceptance may be fully discerned, the nature and development of faith, as these are seen in Christ, must be considered rather than the measure of our faith - this we can understand. For we may say that the dawn of the life of Christ in us is to the heart of the Father but a hope and promise, as the infant is to the parent the promise of the future man.

The illustration is indeed perfect, because this dawning life is Christ in us, of whose fulness we are receiving. But, the important point is, that the joy of the heart of the Father over those who are alive to Him through faith in the Son, is simply and purely joy in the reality of the life of sonship quickened in them, and is not sustained by anything of the nature of fiction or imputation; and that it is in this view of what in faith is accomplished as to the real living relation of man to God, that we are to see the justification of God in man's justification by faith. For do we not feel that, if the Eternal Father is satisfied, then must the Judge of all the earth be satisfied - that the provision which secures the fulfilment of the longings of the Father's heart, must secure the highest ends of rectoral government? "My son was dead, and is alive again; he was lost, and is found" - answers all things.

Dr Payne teaches that "the judicial sentence is not revealed to the conscience, but contained in the Scriptures,"* that sentence being, "that all who believe in the Son of God are justified." And this he teaches both in opposition to the doctrine of the eternal justification of the elect, and to that of an act of God in reference to the individual taking place in time, according to the definition of the Assembly's Catechism. (p.234-239)

It accords with his conception of the relation between faith and justification as being arbitrary, that the justified should have no other knowledge of their being justified than as an inference from their having complied with the arbitrary condition revealed. But if the faith that justifies be the faith that apprehends the gift of sonship, and cries, Abba, Father, then must justification be revealed in the conscience - even there where condemnation had been revealed, and where need of justification had been revealed. "If any man have not the Spirit of Christ he is none of His." "As many as are led by the Spirit of God they are the sons of God," and, "the Spirit itself beareth witness with our spirit that we are the children of God."

This is equally remote from the assumption of a special personal revelation of the fact of justification, and from, resting in an inference from the declarations of Scripture, that those who believe are justified; for what it amounts to is simply this - that in "counting faith for righteousness" God recognises it as what it truly is - and therefore, that He not only in His own mind pronounces this condition of faith our right condition, but also by His Spirit utters this judgment in our own hearts.

Let us trace one step further the different developments of the faith of an atonement which merely meets the demands of divine justice, either absolute, or rectoral; and of the faith of an atonement through which we have the adoption of sons.

The faith that apprehends the gift of eternal life, is eternal life commenced. The faith that apprehends the gift of the Son, utters itself in the cry, Abba, Father. Therefore, in the deepest sense, the Son of God has left us an example that we should walk in His steps. In the highest path that our spirits are called to tread, that is to say, in our intercourse with the Father of spirits, the foot-prints of Jesus are to guide us; our confidence is to be the fellowship of His confidence; our worship, the fellowship of His worship:- for sonship is that worship, in spirit and in truth, which the Father seeketh.

But if, according to the system of the earlier Calvinists, we draw near to God in the confidence of the legal standing given to us in Christ, and not as drawn to God and emboldened by the Fatherliness of the Father's heart revealed by the Son; or if, according to the system of the later Calvinists, we draw near, having mental reference to an atonement which has furnished a ground on which God *may shew us mercy*, and not in the light of an atonement by which we *see ourselves redeemed from the law, that we might receive the adoption of sons*, then is our walk with God - if such it can be called - no longer a being

---

* Payne, op. cit., p.239.

** Payne, op. cit., not an exact quotation, but from pp.235-8.

led by the spirit of Christ, neither are our spiritual steps in His foot-prints; - for our experience is no repetition of, no fellowship in His experience, nor the breathing of our new life the free breathing of the life of sonship.

I have given to this modified Calvinism a large space, but not larger than the acceptance which it has met with may justify. It has necessarily arisen from the purpose with which I have noticed it, that I have dwelt on that in it to which I object, rather than on that in it with which I agree; - but I cannot pass on without bearing testimony to the clearness and power with which its teachers expose much of that which is untenable in the earlier Calvinism, especially on the subject of the extent of the atonement. But, as I have endeavoured to shew, what is negative is more satisfactory than what is positive - their breaking down, than their building up. They have shed no light on the nature of the atonement that renders their faith in the universality of the atonement more consistent than that of the Arminians, with whom Dr Owen contended; still less have they done anything towards freeing the doctrine of the atonement from its exclusively legal character, or that has connected it more intelligently with the purpose of God in redeeming us who were under the law, that we might receive the adoption of sons.

So that whatever foundation for a trust in God's mercy this system may offer, it may be said as truly of it as of the earlier Calvinism, that *strictly adhered to*, and all consciousness that does not exactly accord with it being rejected, our walking in the footsteps of the Son in His intercourse with the Father - in other words, our participation in the life of sonship, and all direct dealing on our part with the Father's heart as the Father's heart - in other words, all experimental knowledge of God, would become impossible.

I say "strictly adhered to." But in truth, in men's actual, living dealing with God, neither form of Calvinism, however it may have possession of the intellect, affects the spirit of Christ; whose identify as in the head and in the members abide - whose cry, Abba, Father, is one and the same as to the nature of the confidence which that cry expresses, being alike faith in the heart of the Father, whether as that is perfect in the eternal Son who ever dwells in the bosom of the Father, or as it is quickened by Him in those to whom He reveals the Father, giving them power to be the sons of God.

But a true conception of the work of Christ must be in perfect harmony with the nature of that eternal life - the life of sonship - which is given to us in Christ. The atonement by which the way into the holiest is opened to us, must accord with what that living way is and with what it is to draw near to God in that way. The sacrifice for sin by which the worshippers are sanctified, must accord with the nature of the worship - that worship which is the response of the Spirit of the Son to the Father; - God is a Spirit; and they that worship Him must worship Him in spirit and in truth - the Father seeketh such to worship Him.

The persuasion of being in some measure in that light as to the nature of the atonement in which this unity is seen; the desire to teach what I seem to myself to have been taught; the hope to be enabled of God so to do; - these are the feelings under the influence of which I am now writing. - I have dwelt so long on what others have taught, believing that it would appear that they have not made my present endeavour superfluous, and hoping so far to secure the interest of my readers, that they will at least feel that further light is desirable, whether a ray of such further light be in these pages or not.

But that no misconception may be entertained as to the sense in which I use the word "desirable," I may state here first, what light I recognise the atonement to have shed on men's minds, even while it has been, as appears to me, so imperfectly understood; and further, what there has been in the means of grace which men have been enjoying, to make up for the shortcoming that has been in their apprehension of the atonement, and even to neutralise practically elements of error.

As to the first point, it is clear that these two rays of divine light have been shed on the spirits of all who have believed in the atonement, in whichever of the forms of thought which we have been considering, or in whatever kindred form of thought it has been present to their minds - viz. 1st, the exceeding evil and terrible nature of sin; and 2nd, the pure and free nature, as well as infinite greatness of the love of God. I mean that the human spirit that saw the atonement in relation to itself, has, of necessity, been filled with an awful sense of the evil of sin, and with an overwhelming sense of the love of God.

That the atonement should tell with its full power as to the latter of these, (and indeed as to both), the use of the pronoun "our," which Luther so insists on, must be known. But with some of this power, and that power increasing as the approach to personal appropriation has been nearer, must the atonement ever have been realised by human spirits. Of the cords of love by which God is felt to draw us when the atonement is believed, Gambold* has said,

> When we learn, that God, the very Maker of heaven and earth, in compassion to us fallen and wretched creatures, (who did no more answer the law of our creation), and to make propitiation for our sins, came down, conversed, suffered, and died as a real meek man in this world; that by the merit of this act we might be everlastingly relieved, pardoned, and exalted to greater privileges than we had lost: what must be the effect, but an overwhelming admiration, an agony of insolvent gratitude, and prostration of our spirit in the dust before our Benefactor?

---

* From John Gambold, *The Reasonableness and Extent of Religious Reverence: A Sermon*, in *Works*, with introductory Essay by Thomas Erskine, second edition (Glasgow, Chalmers & Collins 1823) p.250.

Nor is the power of the atonement to impart an awful sense of the evil of sin less certain, and that, not only as testifying to the divine judgment on sin, but also as by the excellence of pure unselfish love which it vindicates for God, awakening in the human spirit the sense of the exceeding sinfulness of sin as rebellion against God.

But further, not only have these rays of the light that is in the atonement been reaching men's spirits even when that doctrine has been most clouded; much also of that light of life which is in the atonement, which men from their limited or erroneous views of its nature have failed to receive from it directly, they have still, so to speak, had refracted to them from the writings of those inspired teachers, who themselves were in its full light. In this way, though not seen in the atonement itself, perceptions of God's purpose for man as revealed in Christ have been attained, which men have proceeded to add to their system, and even to connect with the atonement, though not as its due development and what its very nature implied.

Thus, with the earlier Calvinists, while that legalism which was in their views of the work of Christ, hindered, as we have seen, their perceptions of the relation between the atonement and the law of the spirit of the life that is in Christ, viz. sonship, still, the purpose of God that we should be sons of God, was recognised as taught in the Scriptures, and adoption was both added to justification in the system formed, and also connected with the atonement as a part of what Christ's work had purchased for those for whom He had given Himself. So also of sanctification, and of all things, in short, pertaining to life, and to godliness; they were all recognised as entering into God's gracious purpose in Christ, and as received through Christ - and were also connected with the atonement as purchased by it, though this connection was in an arbitrary way; the real connection between the atonement and the eternal life given in Christ not being understood. So also in the modern Calvinism, although the necessity for, and nature of the atonement, are exclusively referred to the character of God as a moral governor, bound by the obligations of rectoral justice, a large benevolence, not to say a Fatherly heart, is recognised as availing itself of the removal of the legal obstacle to its outflowing.

The history of Christianity affords many illustrations of the divine life that abides in the *disjecta membra* - the fragmentary portions of divine truth, and which so vindicates its divine character in spite, not only of men's misarrangements, but even of the admixture of error. This power, which is seen to belong to portions of truth put out of the place they have in the divine counsel, and even mixed with error, is mainly to be referred to conscience, and the light that is from God in every man; for great as are the obligations of conscience to the Scriptures, not less assuredly are those of the Scriptures to conscience, by which men's power to pervert the Scriptures has been partly limited and partly neutralised.

But this comforting fact is also partly to be referred to the awe with which the Scriptures are regarded, and which forbids the practical contradiction of them in those who use them reverently as a lamp for their feet and a light for their path; and this even where practical conformity with the Scriptures is practical contradiction to men's own systems. Thus, however conclusive the arguments of Dr Payne or Dr Jenkyn appear, when exposing the wrong footing before God on which sinners are made to stand, when taught to think of all they ask as what they have a legal vested right to obtain, the serious and devout among those who hold the doctrine objected to, are not found to be in consequence less lowly, or humble, or less frequent in the use of the most heart-broken pleadings of the psalms in their actual intercourse with God.

Thus also are the conclusions we would draw, as to the results of believing that Christ died only for some, seemingly practically contradicted by the love to all men by which many are seen animated who have adopted that error.

Thus again are antinomian systems seen combined with tenderness of conscience, and the anxious desire for entire conformity with the will of God. These facts arise, I say, partly from the power of conscience, and partly from this divine excellence in the Scriptures, that, being pervaded by the truth of the will of God, in all variety of form, as doctrine, precept, example, that truth, though excluded by a wrong system from portions of the word, meets the human spirit at other points; and, so, the practical teaching of an apostle may neutralise a misconception on our part as to his doctrines, or an error as to one doctrine be counteracted by the full reception of another: - a misapprehension, for example, of that which is taught when it is said, that "God justifies the ungodly who believe," by the apprehension that "without holiness no man may see God."

Yet are we not on this account the less earnestly to labour to attain to the apprehension of the unity and simplicity of truth. Therefore, while we should be thankful for the power which the atonement has over men's spirits, even when only partially understood and in part misconceived of, and thankful that justification, adoption, and sanctification are recognised in men's systems, though the relation in which these stand to the atonement be artificial rather than natural, yet should we feel it desirable to attain, if it may be, to that fuller apprehension of the great work of God in Christ which will render it to us a full-orbed revelation of God, and a manifestation, not of the rectitude of the moral Governor of the universe merely, but of the heart of the Eternal Father - connecting itself naturally with our justification, adoption, and sanctification, and all that pertains to our participation in the eternal life which is the gift of the Father in the Son.

CHAPTER V

REASON FOR NOT RESTING IN THE CONCEPTION OF THE NATURE OF THE ATONEMENT ON WHICH THESE SYSTEMS PROCEED - THE ATONEMENT TO BE SEEN BY ITS OWN LIGHT.

The idea that the Divinity of our Lord was a prerequisite to the atonement, because it rendered possible the endurance in time of infinite penal sufferings - sufferings therefore commensurate with the eternal sufferings which were the doom of sin - has, as we have seen, been felt repulsive; and it has been thought a worthier conception to regard the personal dignity of Christ as giving infinite value to His sufferings, without relation at all to their amount.

Yet the immeasurably great, if not infinite amount of Christ's sufferings is still dwelt upon; nor is any attempt made on the ground of the dignity of the sufferer to weaken the impression which the sacred narrative had hitherto been felt to give of what was endured by the man of sorrows, and more especially of the awful and mysterious agony of the garden and on the cross.

Faithfulness to the inspired record is not alone the explanation of this. The awful conceptions of the Saviour's sufferings which have from the beginning entered into men's thoughts of the atonement, have been so manifestly at the foundation of the apprehensions of the divine wrath against sin, and the divine mercy towards sinners, which the faith of the atonement has quickened in men, that it could not but be felt, that to lower these conceptions would be to lessen the power of the atonement on human spirits. But - however much it may be felt that the dignity of the sufferer gave infinite value to any sufferings to which He submitted, and however true it is - and it is most true - that infinitely less than we believe our Saviour to have suffered for us would, *being believingly apprehended by us as expressing our preciousness to the heart of God*, inspire in us hope towards God; and however much, on the other hand, we may feel repelled by that weighing in scales of the sufferings of the Son of God, and the sufferings of the damned, in which their conceptions of divine justice and of the atonement which it demanded, engaged the earlier Calvinists; - the truth is that the sufferings of Christ arose so naturally out of what He was, and the relation in which He stood to those for whose sins He suffered, that though His divine nature might be conceived of as giving them weight, however small in themselves, yet to that very divine nature must be refer their awful intensity, and, to us, immeasurable amount. The necessity which has, as we have seen, been felt alike by earlier and later Calvinists, in attempting to specify the elements of the Saviour's sufferings, to keep within the limits indicated by who and what He was that suffered, has obliged them to recognise *holiness* and *love* as what in Christ made the sources of pain specified, sources of pain to Him; and if the sinfulness of sin, and the misery to which it exposed sinners, were painful to Christ because of His holiness and love, then must they have been painful in proportion to His holiness and love.

But there is a further and a still more important thought which seems fitly suggested by these details, on which these men of God have ventured in much reverence of spirit, I believe, and love to Him who was their hope. What I have felt - and the more I consider it, feel the more - is, surprise that the atoning element in the sufferings pictured, has been to their minds *sufferings as sufferings*, the pain and agony *as pain and agony*. It no doubt arose out of the conception that the sufferings endured were the punishment of our sin - endured for us by our substitute - that the pain present should as pain become the prominent object of attention. But my surprise is, *not* that, to men believing the sufferings contemplated to be strictly penal, the pain as pain should be the chief object of attention, being indeed that for which alone, on this view, a necessity existed; but my surprise is, that these sufferings being contemplated as an atonement for sin, the holiness and love seen taking the form of suffering should not be recognised as the atoning elements - the very essence and adequacy of the sacrifice for sin presented to our faith.

President Edwards seems to have put this question to himself, "Christ being what He was, how could God, when imputing the sins of the elect to Him, lay the weight of these sins upon Him and punish Him for them, subjecting Him to the infinite suffering which was their due?" And he has answered thus:* Christ being infinitely holy, God was able to cause Him to feel the awful weight of the sins of the elect by revealing their sins to Him in the spirit - so bringing Him under a weight and pressure of these sins to be measured by His holiness; - thus God laid the sins of the elect on Christ: - and again, Christ loving the elect with a perfect love, God was able - by bearing in upon Christ's spirit the perfect realisation of what these objects of His love were exposed to suffer - to make, through His love to them, their conceived-of suffering, real, infinite suffering to Him.

In this way God is represented, not only as punishing the innocent for the guilty, but as, in doing so, availing Himself of a capacity of enduring pain which consisted in the perfection of holiness and love - pain endured by holiness through being holiness, and by love through being love, being represented as the punishment inflicted.

---

* Not, it seems, an actual quotation, but Campbell's summary of Edwards' argument in *Concerning the Necessity and Reasonableness of the Christian Doctrine of Satisfaction for Sin.*

Now, while it is easy to realise that the sin of those whom He came to save, and the misery to which through sin they were obnoxious, being present to the spirit of Christ, these would press upon Him with a weight and affect Him with an intensity of suffering, proportioned to His hatred to sin and love to sinners; and while in respect of the suffering thus arising, the sufferer is seen to be a sacrifice - and a sacrifice in which if we meditate upon it, it seems to me that we may see atoning virtue; - yet it seems to me impossible to contemplate the agony of holiness and love in the realisation of the evil of sin and of the misery of sinners, as penal suffering. Let my reader endeavour to realise the thought:- The *sufferer suffers* what he suffers *just through seeing sin and sinners with God's eyes, and feeling in reference to them with God's heart.* Is *such* suffering a *punishment?* Is God, in causing such a divine experience in humanity, inflicting a punishment? There can be but one answer.

Reflecting on that answer, and seeing it to be impossible to regard suffering, of which such is the nature, as penal, I find myself forced to distinguish between an atoning sacrifice for sin and the enduring as a substitute the punishment due to sin - being shut up to the conclusion, that while Christ suffered for our sins as an atoning sacrifice, what he suffered was not - because from its nature it could not be - a punishment. I say, I find myself shut up to this conclusion, and that I am obliged to recognise a distinction between an atonement for sin and substituted punishment - a distinction, the necessity of which might have been expected to force itself upon the attention of those who, in endeavouring to conceive of Christ's sufferings, have found themselves constrained to seek for these in His holiness and love - Divine Holiness and Divine Love feeling in Him in humanity towards man and man's sin and man's misery through sin, what in God they eternally feel.

Reader, permit me to ask you to pause here and consider what the question is to which I have led your mind. It is not a question as to the fact of an atonement for sin. It is not a question as to the amount of the sufferings of Christ in making atonement. It is not a question as to the elements of these sufferings. It is not so even between me and those who believe in the imputation of our sin to Christ in the strictest sense. Even they introduce no element into His consciousness which amounted to His being in His own apprehension the personal object of divine wrath. The question to which I have led you is this: The sufferings of Christ in making His soul an offering for sin being what they were, was it the pain as pain, and as a penal infliction, or was it the pain as a condition and form of holiness and love under the pressure of our sin and its consequent misery, that is presented to our faith as the essence of the sacrifice and its atoning virtue?

The distinction on which this question turns appears to me all-important in our inquiry into the nature of the atonement, and we shall be greatly helped by keeping it steadily in view; for my conviction is, that the larger and the more comprehensive of all its bearings our thoughts of the atonement become, the more clear will it appear to us, that it was the spiritual essence and nature of the sufferings of Christ, and not that these sufferings were penal, which constituted their value as entering into the atonement made by the Son of God when He put away sin by the sacrifice of Himself - making His soul a sacrifice for sin - through the eternal Spirit offering Himself without spot to God.

It has been in the free consideration of the actual elements of the sufferings of Christ as these have been represented by men who had themselves quite another conception of the subject, that the important distinction between an atonement for sin, and substituted punishment, has now been arrived at; and so, it is in the way of studying the atonement by its own light, and of meditation on what it is revealed to have been, that I propose to proceed in seeking positive conclusions as to its nature, its expiatory virtue, and its adequacy to all the ends contemplated. And surely this is the right course in order that untested preconceptions may not mislead us; for even as to the abstract question - "What is an atonement for sin?" it is surely wise to seek its answer in the study of the atonement for sin actually made, and revealed to our faith as accepted by God.

But before proceeding thus to consider the atonement made by Christ for the sins of men by the light that shines in itself, there is a ray of light on the nature of atonement for sin afforded to us by an incident in the history of the children of Israel, which claims our attention because of the marked way in which it is recorded, viz. the staying of the plague by Phinehas.

As compared with any other light that the Old Testament Scriptures shed on the subject of atonement, this incident has the special importance of not being a mere instituted type, but a reality in itself. Phinehas had no command to authorise what he did, or promise to proceed upon. That which he did was a spontaneous expression of feeling. But that feeling was so in accordance with the mind of God, that God acknowledged it by receiving what he did as an atonement. "And the Lord spake unto Moses, saying, Phinehas, the son of Eleazar, the son of Aaron the priest, hath turned my wrath away from the children of Israel, while he was zealous for my sake (margin, with my zeal) among them, that I consumed not the children of Israel in my jealousy. Wherefore say, Behold, I give unto him my covenant of peace: and he shall have it, and his seed after him, even the covenant of an everlasting priesthood; because he was zealous for his God, and made an atonement for the children of Israel." (Numbers xxv. 10-13)

Here we see a man turning away the wrath of God, and staying the plague which was the manifestation of that wrath, by an act of which the essence was, condemnation of sin and zeal for the glory of God. This act, done in the sight of all Israel, ("zealous for my sake among them") was immediately accepted by the God of Israel - may we not say, in mercy taken

hold of by the God of Israel? - as a justification of Himself in turning away
His wrath from the children of Israel - an atonement for the children of Israel.

There can be no uncertainty as to the atoning element here. It was not
the mere death of the subjects of the act of Phinehas. Had they died by the
plague, their death would have been no atonement - the death of the twenty-
four thousand who so died was none. But the moral element in the
transaction - the mind of Phinehas - his zeal for God - his sympathy in God's
judgment on sin, this was the atonement, this its essence. Surely we have here
a ray of light shed on the distinction between making an atonement for sin
and bearing the punishment of sin; - nor can we rightly weigh the words in
which God has put His seal upon the atonement made by Phinehas, "Behold,
I give unto him *my covenant of peace:* and he shall have it, and his seed after
him, even the covenant of an *everlasting priesthood,*" without feeling, that the
contemplation of this incident is intended to be a help toward our understanding of the foundation laid in atonement for *the* covenant of peace, the
covenant of *the* everlasting priesthood - a help which prepares us to find in
the moral and spiritual elements in the sufferings of Christ, the atoning
power that was in them; and to see how, though there is nothing of an
atoning nature in death, the wages of sin - not in the death of all who have
died since death entered the world, nor in all death that may yet be endured;
yet was the death of Christ, who tasted death for every man, because of the
condemnation of sin in His spirit, an atonement for the sin of the whole
world.

When I speak of the light of the atonement itself I mean, the atonement
as accomplished; I do not mean the atonement as foretold merely and
typically prefigured. For, although the typical sacrifices of the Mosaic
institutions intimated the necessity for an atonement and in some sense its
form, they did not, for they could not, reveal its nature. After we have traced
and recognised the points in which the types prefigured the antitype, we have
still to inquire and to learn by the study of the antitype itself, what the reality
is of which such and such things were the shadow. In the type all was
arbitrary and of mere institution. The perfection required in the victim - a
perfection according to its own physical nature - had no relation whatever
to sin, but as the type of that moral and spiritual perfection in the antitype,
of which sin is the negation and the opposite. In no real sense did the
confession of the sins of the people over the victim, thus selected as
physically perfect, connect these sins with it, or lay them upon it; for in no
real sense could it bear them. Therefore, while that confession indicated and
foretold the laying of men's sins on Christ, it shed no light upon that which
these words express - no light either on the capacity for bearing our sins
which was in Christ because of His moral and His spiritual perfection, or on
that reality of coming under their weight which was to be in His consciousness in making His soul an offering for sin. The shedding of the blood of the

victim declared that without shedding of blood was no remission of sins; but
the blood of bulls and of goats could not take away sins, and therefore, how
through the shedding of blood remission of sins would be, remained to be
learned from the knowledge of that blood which really has this virtue.

It may seem superfluous to insist upon this inadequacy in the type to
reveal that which, from the nature of things, can only be learned from the
antitype. But how often have the points of agreement between the type and
antitype been dwelt upon, as if to see that agreement was to understand the
atonement, although the fullest recognition of that agreement leaves the
questions still to be answered - Why must He who is to be the atoning
sacrifice for sin, be Himself the Holy One of God? How does His being so
qualify Him for bearing our sins? In what sense could they be, and have they
been laid upon Him? Being laid upon Him, how is the shedding of His blood
an atonement for them? How is His moral and spiritual perfection so
connected with, and present in His bearing of men's sins, and in His tasting
death for every man, as that "we have redemption through His blood, even
the forgiveness of sins," *because* He, "through the eternal Spirit, offered
Himself without spot to God?"

These questions are not answered by tracing the points of agreement
between the type and the antitype, and therefore the seeming progress made
in the understanding of the atonement by such tracing is altogether illusory;
- and if we are contented to remain in the darkness in which it leaves us, we
are refusing to pass on from the type to the antitype, from the shadow to the
reality. In the Epistle to the Hebrews, it is not upon the coincidence between
the type and the antitype, but upon that in which they differ, that the Apostle
insists; - and the antitype is recognised by him as indeed the antitype
contemplated, because it is seen to have in it that reality of atoning efficacy
which was not in the type. This comparing and contrasting of course implies,
that he who engages in it is in a light in which he can say what is atoning
efficacy. In such light he claims to be, equally in judging that the blood of
Christ can take away sin, as in judging that the blood of bulls and of goats
could not. Not that the Apostle knew beforehand what would be an
adequate atonement, and so was qualified to judge of the claims of the
sacrifice of Christ to that character; - but that, apprehending the atonement
made by Christ as it was revealed to him, he, in the light of the atonement
itself, had clear discernment of its adequacy.

That light of the atonement itself, in which the Apostle wrote, pervades
the whole argument of the Epistle to the Hebrews. But the first principle and
essence of his reasoning is contained in these verses of the tenth chapter, 4
to 10:

For it is not possible that the blood of bulls and of goats should take
away sin. Wherefore when He cometh into the world, He saith,
Sacrifice and offering thou wouldest not, but a body hast thou

prepared me. In burnt offerings and sacrifices for sin thou hast had no pleasure. Then said I, Lo, I come (in the volume of the book it is written of me), to do thy will, O God. Above when He said, Sacrifice and offering and burnt offerings and offering for sin thou wouldest not, neither hadst pleasure therein, which are offered by the law; then said He, Lo, I come to do thy will, O God. He taketh away the first that He may establish the second. By which will we are sanctified, through the offering of the body of Jesus Christ once for all.

The will of God which the Son of God came to do and did, this was the essence and substance of the atonement, being that in the offering of the body of Christ once for all which both made it acceptable to Him who in burnt offerings and sacrifices for sin had no pleasure, and made it fit to "sanctify" those whose sin the blood of bulls and of goats could not take away.

Let us then receive these words, "Lo, I come to do thy will, O God," as the great key-word on the subject of the atonement. The passage in full, as it is in the 40th Psalm, is,

I delight to do thy will, O my God: yea, thy law is within my heart. I have preached righteousness in the great congregation. Lo, I have not refrained my lips, O Lord, thou knowest. I have not hid thy righteousness within my heart; I have declared thy faithfulness and thy salvation: I have not concealed thy lovingkindness and thy truth from the great congregation, 7-11;

and I quote the context of the psalm because it brings out so clearly, that the *will* of God contemplated is that WILL which immediately connects itself in our thoughts with what *God* is, that will, the nature and character of which we express when we say, "God is good," - or, explaining what we mean by good, say, "God is holy, God is true, God is just, God is love." This expression of the purpose of the Son of God in coming into this world, is therefore coincident with His own statement of His work when in the world, viz. "I have declared thy name, and will declare it." (John xvii. 26) Some have understood the will of God here to mean the plan of redemption, and so the purpose expressed would be the purpose to execute that plan. So understood, of course, the words would throw no light on the nature of the atonement, being only the declaration of the intention of making it. But the mind of the Apostle is manifestly occupied with *that in the work of Christ* which caused the shedding of His blood to have a virtue which was not in that of bulls and goats, which he represents as being the will of God done, the mind of God manifested, the name of the Father declared by the Son.

We have therefore to trace out the fulfilment of this purpose, Lo, I come to do thy will. In what relation to God and to man did it place the Lord as partaking in humanity? - especially, in what relation to men's sins and the evils consequent upon sin to which they were subject? How did it imply His having all men's sins laid upon Him - His bearing them as an atoning sacrifice - His being an accepted sacrifice - His obtaining everlasting redemption?

It will simplify our task in considering Christ's doing of the will of God, if we remember the relation of the second commandment to the first, as being "like it;" that is to say, that the spirit of sonship in which consists the perfect fulfilment of the first commandment, is one with the spirit of brotherhood which is the fulfilment of the second. Loving the Father with all His heart and mind and soul and strength, the Saviour loved His brethren Himself. He, the perfect elder brother, unlike the elder brother in the parable, sympathised in all the yearnings of the Father's heart over His prodigal brethren; and the love which in the Father desired to be able to say of each of them, My son was dead, and is alive again; he was lost, and is found; in Him equally desired to be able to say, My brother was dead, and is alive again; he was lost, and is found.

President Edwards, in tracing out the fitness and suitableness of the mediation of our Lord, dwells upon His interest in the glory of God with whom He was to intercede, and because of which He could propose nothing derogatory to it; and His love to those for whom He was to intercede, because of which He felt so identified with them that what touched them touched Him. There is something which surely commends itself to us in this recognition of love as that which identifies the Saviour with those to whom he is a Saviour, and this, as Edwards traces it out, both in His own consciousness and in the Father's thoughts of Him as the mediator. May we not go further and say, that as love was thus a fitness for the office, so it necessitated the undertaking of the office, moving to the exercise of this high function, as well as qualifying for it? And seeing love *to all men* as that law of love under which Christ was, must we not both wonder and regret, that his deeply interesting thoughts in this region did not lead Edwards to see, that by the very law of the spirit of the life that was in Christ Jesus He must needs come under the burden of the sins of all men - become the Saviour of all men, and, loving them as He loved Himself, seek for them that they should partake in His own life in the Father's favour - that eternal life which He had with the Father before the world was?

When God sent His own Son in the likeness of sinful flesh to accomplish our redemption, the Apostle says He sent Him as "a sacrifice for sin." (Romans viii. 3, margin) To send Him in the likeness of sinful flesh was to make Him a sacrifice for sin, for it was to lay the burden of our sins upon Him. Thus related to us, while by love identified with us, the Son of God necessarily came under all our burdens, and especially our great burden - sin. And this not merely as President Edwards represents our sins as being laid upon Christ, in that a vivid sense of their evil oppressed His Holy Spirit, nor even in that through love to us (as he speaks with reference to the elect) the realisation of the misery to which we were exposed would give Him pain;

but that living the life of love in humanity He must needs care for all humanity, for all partaking in humanity even as for Himself: so being affected by the evil of the life of self, and enmity in humanity according to His own consciousness of the life of love - and at once condemning that life of self, desiring its destruction, and feeling Himself by love devoted to the work of delivering man from it, at whatever cost to Himself.

Thus moved by love, and in the strength of love, must we conceive of the Saviour as taking upon Him all our burden, undertaking our cause to do and suffer all that was implied in obtaining for us redemption. The love that came into humanity had manifested its own nature even in coming into humanity - its self-sacrificing nature; though this we can less understand or measure. Being in humanity, it acts according to its own nature, and must needs bear our burden and work and suffer for our salvation, and this in ways which we who are human may understand, and shall understand in the measure in which the life of love becomes our life.

The active outgoing of the self-sacrificing love in which the Son of God wrought out our redemption presents these two aspects, first, His dealing with men on the part of God; and, secondly, His dealing with God on behalf of men. These together constitute the atonement equally in its retrospective and prospective bearing. Therefore it will be necessary to contemplate them not only severally, but also, first in reference to our condition as sinners under the condemnation of a broken law, and then in reference to the purpose of God to bestow on us the adoption of sons.

The unity of the life that was in Christ as love to God and love to men - the unity of the ends contemplated in His sacrifice of Himself, viz. the glory of God and the salvation of men - the unity also of the intermediate results, in that the same work which was an adequate ground on which to rest our being taken from under the law, making that consistent with the honour of the law and the character of the law-giver, was also the adequate preparation for our receiving the adoption of sons; this pervading unity, which is "the simplicity that is in Christ," will not be veiled by this orderly consideration of the different aspects of the works of Christ, while it will prepare us for the closer consideration of the details of the sacred history, at once shedding light on these details and being confirmed by them.

CHAPTER VI

RETROSPECTIVE ASPECT OF THE ATONEMENT

The atonement considered in its retrospective aspects is-

1. Christ's dealing with men on the part of God.

It was in our Lord the natural outcoming of the life of love - of love to the Father and of love to us - to shew us the Father, to vindicate the Father's name, to witness for the excellence of that will of God against which we were rebelling, to witness for the trustworthiness of that Father's heart in which we were refusing to put confidence, to witness for the unchanging character of that love in which there was hope for us, though we had destroyed ourselves.

This witness-bearing for God, ("I have given him for a witness to the people,") was accomplished in the personal perfection that was in Christ, His manifested perfection in humanity, that is to say, the perfection of His own following of the Father as a dear child, and the perfection of His brotherly love in His walk with men. His love and His trust towards His Father, His love and His longsuffering towards His brethren - the latter being presented to our faith in its oneness with the former - were together what He contemplated when He said, "He that hath seen me hath seen the Father."

This witness-bearing for the Father was a part of the self-sacrifice of Christ. The severity of the pressure of our sins upon the Spirit of Christ was necessarily greatly increased through that living contact with the enmity of the carnal mind to God into which Christ was brought, in being to men a living epistle of the grace of God. His honouring of the Father caused men to dishonour Him - His manifestation of brotherly love was repaid with hatred - His perfect walk in the sight of men failed to commend either His Father or Himself - His professed trust in the Father was cast up to Him, not being believed, and the bitter complaint was wrung from Him - "reproach hath broken my heart."

Not that His task in doing the Father's will, "not hiding His righteousness within His heart," but "declaring His faithfulness and His salvation," was altogether cheerless: on the contrary, the Man of sorrows could speak to the chosen companions of His path, those who knew Him most nearly, of a peace which they had witnessed in Him - nay, of a joy, a peace and a joy as to which He could expect that they would receive as the intimation of a precious legacy the being told that these He would leave with them - could even expect that the prospect of having these abiding with them would reconcile them to that tribulation which was to come to them through their relation to Him. That which He had presented to their faith would not have been a true and successful witnessing for the Father, had this not been so; - it would have been less than that of the Psalmist, "O taste and see that God is good." Whatever sorrow may have been seen as borne by the Son of God in confessing His Father's name in our sinful world - and this could not have been but in sorrow - yet must a joy deeper than the sorrow have been present, as belonging to that oneness with the Father which that living confession implied; and to have hidden that joy would have been to have marred that confession - leaving imperfect that condemnation of sin which is by the manifestation of the life that is in God's favour, and the shining forth of which in Christ is the light of life to man. Therefore the peace, the joy of which our Lord speaks as what the disciples had witnessed in Him, and what would be recalled to them when He used the expressions, "My peace," "My joy," were a most important element in His declaration of the Father's name.

But not less important as an element of that declaration, not less essential to its perfection, were the sorrows of the Man of sorrows, of which also they were the chosen witnesses. It has been said, "If God should appear as a man on this sinful earth, how could it be but as a man of sorrows?" The natural outward expression of Christ's inward sorrow from the constant pressure of our sin and misery on His spirit - a pressure under which, as God in our nature, with the mind of God in suffering flesh He could not but be - would of itself have been enough to justify the appeal to those who saw Him nearly, "Look, and see if there be any sorrow like unto my sorrow?" But to the vindication of the name of God, and to the condemnation of the sin of man, that actual meeting of the eternal love with the enmity of the carnal mind, which took place when Christ came to men in the Father's name - in the fellowship of the Father's love, was necessary; and therefore, however much it added to Christ's suffering as bearing our sins, it was permitted; and the Father ordered the path in which He led the Son so as to give full and perfect development and manifestation to the self-sacrificing life of love that was in Christ, in fulness and perfection to His declaration of the Father's name.

We have been prepared for recognising our Lord's honouring of the Father in the sight of men, as an element in the atonement in its retrospective aspect, by the power to arrest the course of judgment, and stay the plague which expressed the divine wrath, found in that outcoming of zeal for God, and sympathy in His condemnation of sin, by which Phinehas, the son of Eleazar, made atonement for the children of Israel. If the principle of the divine procedure in that case be recognised, we shall have no difficulty in seeing the place which the perfect zeal for the Father's honour, the living manifestation of perfect sympathy in the Father's condemnation of sin, the perfect vindication of the unselfish and righteous character of that

condemnation as the mind of Him who is love, which were presented to men
in the life of Christ, being perfected in His death - we shall, I say, have no
difficulty in seeing the place which this dealing of Christ with men on the
part of God has in the work of redemption.

If we at all realise the cost to Christ, we can have no difficulty in
contemplating as included in the expression, "a sacrifice for sin," what Christ
endured in this witnessing for God. But I am anxious that *the way* in which
the sufferings of Christ now before us entered into the atonement, and not
the fact only that they did enter into it, may be distinctly understood - that
it was as being necessary to the perfection of His witness-bearing for the
Father.

For, while these sufferings have also received a place in the atonement,
in the systems which have been considered above as forms of Calvinism, it
has been on the entirely different ground that they were a part of what our
Lord endured in bearing the punishment of our sins; and I have already urged
the impossibility of regarding as *penal* the sorrows of holy love endured in
realising our sin and misery - the impossibility of believing that He who said,
"Rivers of water run down mine eyes, because men keep not thy law," could
have felt the pain of the holy sorrow which caused His tears to flow, to have
been *penal* suffering, seeing that that pain was endured in sympathy with
God, and in the strength of the faith of the divine acceptance of that
sympathy.

But apart from the objection to our regarding the sufferings of Christ
now contemplated as *penal* presented by the very nature of these sufferings,
is there any reason to feel, that they would be a more fitting element in the
atonement had they been penal, than as being, what we know they were, the
perfecting of the Son's witnessing for the Father?

The distinction between *penal* sufferings endured in meeting a demand
of divine justice, and sufferings which are themselves the expression of the
divine mind regarding our sins, and a manifestation by the Son of what our
sins are to the Father's heart, is indeed very broad; and I know that the habit
of thought which prevails on the subject of the atonement is such as will
cause minds, under the power of that habit, to think it more natural to
connect remission of sins with sufferings having the *former*, than with
sufferings having the *latter* character. But, independent of the necessity
which the *nature* of the sufferings which we are considering impose upon us
to refuse to them the *former* character - while we know that they certainly
had the *latter* - is not the habit of mind which creates any difficulty here,
delusive?

We are accustomed to hear it said, that the law which men had violated
must be honoured, and the sincerity and consistency of the lawgiver must
be vindicated. But what a vindicating of the divine name, and of the character
of the lawgiver, are the sufferings now contemplated, considered as them-

selves the manifestation in humanity of what our sins are to God, compared to that to which they are reduced if conceived of as a punishment inflicted by God! No doubt, even in this view, there would remain to us a ray of light in the love that is contented to endure the infliction; but, however precious the thought of love willing so to suffer, the full revelation of God is *not* that divine love has been contented thus to suffer, but that the suffering is the suffering of divine love suffering from our sins according to its own nature; a suffering, therefore, in relation to which the sufferer could say, "He that hath seen me hath seen the Father."

2. But Christ's honouring the Father in the sight of men, which was His dealing with men on the part of God, is only one aspect of His mediatorial work. **We have to consider also His dealing with God on behalf of men.** And this, indeed, is the region in which *penal* suffering should meet us, if penal suffering had entered into the atonement. We cannot conceive of the Son of God as enduring a penal infliction in the very act of honouring His Father. But when we contemplate Him as approaching God on behalf of man - when we contemplate Him as meeting the divine mind in its aspect towards sin and sinners, and as dealing with the righteous wrath of God against sin, interposing Himself between sinners and the consequences of that righteous wrath - we feel, that here we have come to that which men have contemplated when they have conceived of Christ as satisfying divine justice in respect of its claim for vengeance upon our sins.

Here, therefore, we feel was the place for outcoming of wrath upon the Mediator, and penal infliction, if such there had been - and, as such there has not been, that here is the place in which we should find that dealing of the Mediator with the divine wrath against sin which has had the result which men have referred to His assumed bearing of the punishment of sin; and which, being understood, will be felt to meet all that was right, and according to truth, in the feelings which men have expressed by the words, "appeasing divine wrath" - "expiating the guilt of sin."

I say, "all that was according to truth in these expressions", for there was truth in them, though mingled with error - how much error, the separating of the truth will best shew. But the wrath of God against sin is a reality, however men have erred in their thoughts as to how that wrath was to be appeased. Nor is the idea that satisfaction was due to divine justice a delusion, however far men have wandered from the true conception of what would meet its righteous demand. And if so, then Christ, in dealing with God on behalf of men, must be conceived of as dealing with the righteous wrath of God against sin, and *as according to it that which was due:* and this would necessarily precede His intercession for us.

It is manifest, if we consider it, that Christ's own long-suffering love was the revelation to those who should see the Father in the Son, of that forgiving

love in God to which Christ's intercession for men would be addressed; and
so also, I believe, does Christ's own condemnation of our sins, and His holy
sorrow because of them, indicate that dealing with the aspect of the divine
mind towards sin which prepared the way for intercession.

That oneness of mind with the Father, which towards man took the
form of condemnation of sin, would in the Son's dealing with the Father in
relation to our sins, take the form of a perfect confession of our sins. This
confession, as to its own nature, must have been *a perfect Amen in humanity
to the judgment of God on the sin of man*. Such an Amen was due in the truth
of things. He who was the Truth could not be in humanity and not utter it
- and it was necessarily a first step in dealing with the Father on our behalf.
He who would intercede for us must begin with confessing our sins.

This all will at once perceive. But let us weigh this confession of our sins
by the Son of God in humanity. And I do not mean in reference to the
suffering it implies viewed as suffering. Christ's love to the Father, to whom
He thus confessed the sin of His brethren - His love to His brethren whose
sin He confessed - along with that conscious oneness of will with the Father
in humanity, in the light of which the exceeding evil of man's alienation from
God was realised; these must have rendered His confession of our sins before
the Father a peculiar development of the holy sorrow in which He bore the
burden of our sins; and which, like His sufferings in confessing His Father
before men, had a severity and intensity of its own. But, apart from the
question of the suffering present in that confession of our sins, and the depth
of meaning which it gives to the expression, "a sacrifice for sin," let us
consider this Amen from the depths of the humanity of Christ to the divine
condemnation of sin. What place has it in Christ's dealing with that wrath?

I answer: He who so responds to the divine wrath against sin, saying,
"Thou art righteous, O Lord, who judgest so," is necessarily receiving the full
apprehension and realisation of that wrath, as well as of that sin against which
it comes forth into His soul and spirit, into the bosom of the divine
humanity, and, so receiving it, He responds to it with a perfect response - a
response from the depths of that divine humanity - and *in that perfect response
He absorbs it*. For that response has all the elements of a perfect repentance
in humanity for all the sin of man - a perfect sorrow - a perfect contrition -
all the elements of such a repentance, and that in absolute perfection, all -
excepting the personal consciousness of sin - and by that perfect response in
Amen to the mind of God in relation to sin is the wrath of God rightly met,
and that is accorded to divine justice which is its due, and could alone satisfy
it.

In contending "that sin must be punished with an infinite punishment,"
President Edwards says,* that "God could not be just to Himself without this

***

* *On Satisfaction for Sin*, Chap II.1-3

vindication unless there could be such a thing as a repentance, humiliation and sorrow for this (viz. sin), proportionable to the greatness of the majesty despised," - for that there must needs be, "either an equivalent punishment or an equivalent sorrow and repentance" - "so," he proceeds, "sin must be punished with an infinite punishment," thus assessing that the alternative of "an equivalent sorrow and repentance" was out of the question.

But, upon the assumption of that identification of Himself with those whom He came to save, on the part of the Saviour, which is the foundation of Edwards' whole system, it may at the least be said, that the Mediator had the two alternatives open to His choice - either to endure for sinners an equivalent punishment, or to experience in reference to their sin, and present to God on their behalf, an adequate sorrow and repentance. Either of these courses should be regarded by Edwards as equally securing the vindication of the majesty and justice of God in pardoning sin. But the latter equivalent, which also is surely the higher and more excellent, being a moral and spiritual satisfaction, was, as we have now seen, of necessity present in Christ's dealing with the Father on our behalf. Therefore, to contend for the former also would be to contend for two equivalents.

This of course Edwards had no intention of doing. For, though the thought of that moral and spiritual atonement which would be presented to God in the adequate confession of sin, passed through his mind, he did not recognise the presence of this "equivalent repentance" in the work of Christ. He had set out with the assumption of Christ came to bear the punishment of our sins, and to work out a righteousness to be imputed to us; and, as we have seen that the latter part of this assumption hindered his so seeing the Father in the Son as to recognise that law of love to all men which was fulfilled in Christ, as in truth the law of God's own being, so here we see that, in consequence of the former part of that assumption, it has come to pass, that notwithstanding all his deep and earnest study of the work of redemption, and notwithstanding his feeling constrained to recognise moral and spiritual elements as alone present in the sufferings of Christ, the thought of an atonement for sin by an equivalent repentance has suggested itself to him only in connection with the manifest impossibility of such a repentance being presented by the sinner himself to God in expiation of his guilt. And in the connection in which the idea of repentance as an expiation for sin presented itself to the mind of Edwards, his conclusion was just. A condemnation and confession of sin in humanity which should be a real Amen to the divine condemnation of sin, and commensurate with its evil and God's wrath against it, only became possible through the incarnation of the Son of God.

But the incarnation of the Son of God not only *made possible* such a moral and spiritual expiation for sin as that of which the thought thus visited the mind of Edwards, but indeed caused that it *must be*. Without the assumption of an imputation of our guilt, and in perfect harmony with the unbroken consciousness of personal separation from our sins, the Son of God, bearing us and our sins on His heart before the Father, must needs respond to the Father's judgment on our sins, with that confession of their evil and of the righteousness of the wrath of God against them, and holy sorrow because of them, which were due, due in the truth of things, due on our behalf though we could not render it, due from Him as in our nature and our true brother; - what he must needs feel in Himself because of the holiness and love which were in Him - what He must needs utter to the Father in expiation of our sins when He would make intercession for us.

I have said that in approaching the dealing of Christ with God on behalf of men, we approach the region in which we should have met *penal* infliction as endured by Christ for our sins, had such infliction entered into the atonement; and, as it has not, where we should see *that*, whatever else it was, which has been Christ's dealing with God's righteous wrath against our sins. What I believe that dealing to have been, I have, I trust, expressed with sufficient clearness - while I have laboured more to illustrate the *nature* of this expiation by confession of our sins, than the *intensity of suffering* to the soul of Christ thus made an offering for sin, which it involved.

Yet is it needful that we should, in realising the elements of these sufferings, endeavour to realise also their intensity - that it was according to the perfection of the divine mind in the sufferer, and the capacity of suffering which is in suffering flesh. And this meditation, as I trust the reader will feel, is a very different thing from weighing the sufferings of Christ in scales against the sufferings of the damned. *That* belongs to the following out of the conception of the Son of God suffering the punishment of our sins. But what I contemplate is the following out of the conception of the Son of God suffering in suffering flesh that which is the perfect response of the divine holiness and divine love in humanity to the aspect of the divine mind in the Father towards the sins of men. No thought unworthy of the faith that the sufferer is God in our nature, comes through exalting our conceptions of the measure of the suffering endured on account of sins, when such exalting is thus but the raising of our apprehension of what our sins is to the heart of God.

And I may here refer to what has been urged by some as a reason for holding that the sufferings of Christ were penal, viz. that otherwise there is no explanation of the sufferings of one who was without sin, as endured under the righteous government of God. Do we never see suffering that we must explain on some other principle than this? Surely the tears of holy sorrow shed over the sins of others - the tears, for example, of a godly parent over a prodigal child, are not penal, nor, if shed before God in prayer, and acknowledged in the merciful answer of prayer in God's dealing with that prodigal, are they therefore to be conceived of as having been penal. But the fact is, that the truth that God grieves over our sins, is not so soon received into the heart as that God punishes sin - and yet, the faith that He so grieves is infinitely more important, as having power to work holiness in us, than the faith that He so punishes, however important. But there is much less spiritual apprehension necessary to the faith that God punishes sin, than to the faith that our sins do truly grieve God. Therefore, men more easily believe that Christ's sufferings shew how God can punish sin, than that these sufferings are the divine feelings in relation to sin, made visible to us by being present in suffering flesh.

Yet, however the former may terrify, the latter alone can purify, because the latter alone perfectly reveals, and in revealing vindicates the name and character of God, condemning us in our own eyes, and laying us prostrate in the dust because we have sinned against such a God. The entrance of sin has been the entrance of sorrow - not to the sinful only, and as the punishment of sin, but also to the holy and the loving, and as what holiness and love must feel in the presence of sin. That such suffering as the suffering of Christ should have existed in the universe of God in connection with innocence and holiness, moral and spiritual perfection, must indeed, be felt to suggest a solemn question, and one which must receive an answer, if we are to be in a condition to glorify God in contemplating that suffering. The answer that it was penal, is precluded by the nature of the suffering itself. Yet, that it was for sin is also implied in that very nature, and for the sin of others than the sufferer, for He was without sin; therefore was it vicarious, expiatory, an atonement - an atonement for sin as distinguished from the punishment of sin.

And with this distinction, how much light enters the mind! We are now able to realise that the suffering we contemplate is divine, while it is human; and that God is revealed *in it* and not *merely in connection with it*; God's righteousness and condemnation of sin, being in the suffering, and not merely what demands it - God's love also being in the suffering, and not merely what submits to it. Christ's suffering being thus to us a form which the divine life in Christ took in connection with the circumstances in which He was placed, and not a penal infliction, coming on Him as from without, such words as, "He made His soul an offering for sin" - "He put away sin by the sacrifice of Himself," - "By Himself He purged our sins," grow full of light; and the connection between *what He is* who makes atonement, and the atonement which He makes, reveals itself in a far other way than as men have spoken of the divinity of the Saviour, regarding it either as a strength to endure infinite penal suffering, or a dignity to give adequacy of value to any measure of penal suffering however small.

Not in these ways, but in a far other way, is the person of Christ brought before us now as fixing attention upon the divine mind in humanity as that which alone could suffer, and which did suffer sufferings of a nature and virtue to purge our sins. By the *word of His power all else* was accomplished, by *himself He purged our sins - by the virtue that is in what He is;* and thus is the atonement not only what was rendered possible by the incarnation, but itself a development of the incarnation.

Luther says, that all sin of man, and the eternal righteousness of God, being met in Christ in mutual opposition, the one of these must prevail; and it must be the righteousness, for it is divine and eternal. His conception seems to have been:- sin being there present calling for judgment, and righteousness calling for life, the righteousness, being divine, must triumph. When, in explaining this presence of sin, he speaks of the consciousness that was in Christ in relation to man's sin, as if it were, with reference to all the sin of man, identical in nature with what in measure the perfectly awakened sinner feels as to his own sin, Luther certainly *seems* to lose the sense of the personal separation from sin of that Holy One of God, in whose inner being all the sin of humanity was thus realised. And yet I venture to think, that he only seems to do so, and that his meaning has not been beyond that sense of man's sin, and what is due to it, and of the righteousness of God's judgment upon it, of which I have spoken above.

At all events, the view now taken of the way in which the Saviour met and dealt with the Father's wrath against sin, may be expressed in language akin to that of Luther, and we may say that the divine eternal righteousness in Christ used confession of the sinfulness of sin, as the weapon of righteousness in its conflict with sin calling for judgment; and so, that righteousness prevailed. The divine righteousness in Christ appearing on the part of man, and in humanity, met the divine righteousness of God condemning man's sin, by the true and righteous confession of its sinfulness uttered in humanity, and righteousness as in God was satisfied, and demanded no more than righteousness as in Christ thus presented.

It might be too bold to assert that this was Luther's meaning. But at all events - and this alone is important - I believe this to be a conception according to the truth of things; and that the feelings of the divine mind as to sin, being present in humanity and uttering themselves to God as a living voice from humanity, were the true atonement for the sin of humanity - the "equivalent sorrow and repentance" of which the idea was in the mind of Edwards, though the fact of its realisation in Christ he did not see.

But, though Edwards saw not that the equivalent sorrow and repentance, of which the thought passed before his mind, was actually present in these sufferings of Christ which he was considering, yet am I thankful that the conception of such an equivalent as the alternative to infinite punishment has been recognised by him. For he is the great teacher of a demand for infinite punishment as implied in the essential and absolute justice of God; and, as I have said above, in his dealing with absolute justice and righteousness on the subject of the atonement I have much more sympathy than with the teaching that makes rectoral justice or public justice the foundation of its reasoning. For of this I feel quite certain, that no really awakened sinner into whose spirit the terrors of the Lord have entered, ever thinks of rectoral justice, but of absolute justice, and of absolute justice only. "Against thee, thee only have I sinned," is language, in using which the soul is alone with God, and thinks not of any other bearing of its sin, but its bearing on the individual in relation to God.

That due repentance for sin, could such repentance indeed be, would expiate guilt, there is a strong testimony in the human heart, and so the first attempt at peace with God, is an attempt at repentance - which attempt, indeed, becomes less and less hopeful, the longer, and the more earnestly and honestly it is preserved in - but this not because it comes to be felt that a true repentance would be rejected even if attained, but because its attainment is despaired of - all attempts at it being found, when taken to the divine light, and honestly judged in the sight of God, to be mere selfish attempts at something that promises safety - not evil, indeed, in so far as they are instinctive efforts at self-preservation, but having nothing in them of the nature of a true repentance, or a godly sorrow for sin or pure condemnation of it because of its own evil; nothing, in short, that is a judging sin and a confessing it in true sympathy with the divine judgment upon it. So that the words of Whitefield come to be deeply sympathised in, "our repentance needeth to be repented of, and our very tears to be washed in the blood of Christ."

That we may fully realise what manner of an equivalent to the dishonour done to the law and name of God by sin, an adequate repentance and sorrow for sin must be, and now far more truly than any penal infliction such repentance and confession must satisfy divine justice, let us suppose that all the sin of humanity has been committed by one human spirit, on whom is accumulated this immeasurable amount of guilt, and let us suppose this spirit, loaded with all this guilt, to pass out of sin into holiness, and to become filled with the light of God becoming perfectly righteous with God's own righteousness - such a change, were such a change possible, would imply in the spirit so changed, a perfect condemnation of the past of its own existence, and an absolute and perfect repentance, a confession of its sin commensurate with its evil. If the sense of personal identity remained, it must be so.

Now, let us contemplate this repentance, with reference to the guilt of such a spirit, and the question of pardon for its past sin, and admission now to the light of God's favour. Shall this repentance be accepted as an atonement, and the past sin being thus confessed, shall the divine favour flow out on that present perfect righteousness which thus condemns the past? or, shall that repentance be declared inadequate? shall the present perfect righteousness be rejected on account of the past sin, so absolutely and perfectly repented of? and shall divine justice still demand adequate punishment for the past sin, and refuse to the present righteousness adequate acknowledgment - the favour which, in respect of its own nature, belongs to it? It appears to me impossible to give any but one answer to these questions. We feel that such a repentance as we are supposing would, in such a case, be the true and proper satisfaction to offended justice, and that there would be more atoning worth in one tear of the true and perfect sorrow which the memory of the past would awaken in this now holy spirit, than in endless ages of penal woe. Now, with the difference of personal identity, the case I have supposed is the actual case of Christ, the holy one of God, bearing the sins of all men on His spirit - in Luther's words, "the one sinner" - and meeting the cry of these sins for judgment, and the wrath due to them, absorbing and exhausting that divine wrath in that adequate confession and perfect response on the part of man, which was possible only to the infinite and eternal righteousness in humanity.

I have said that my hypothetical, and indeed impossible case, and that case which the history of our redemption actually presents, differ only in respect of the *personal identity* of the guilty and the righteous. And, to one looking at the subject with a hasty superficial glance, this difference may seem to involve all the difficulties connected with imputation of guilt and substituted punishment. Yet it can only so appear to a hasty and superficial glance. For, independent of the higher character of the moral atonement supposed, as compared with the enduring as a substitute a penal infliction, this adequate sorrow for the sin of man, and adequate confession of its evil implies no fiction - no imputation to the suffer of the guilt of the sin for which He suffers; but only that He has taken the nature, and become the brother of those whose sin He confesses before the Father, and that He feels concerning their sins what, as the holy one of God, and as perfectly loving God and man, He must feel.

In contemplating our Lord as yielding up His soul to be filled with the sense of the Father's righteous condemnation of our sin, and as responding with a perfect Amen to that condemnation, we are tracing what was a necessary step in His path as dealing with the Father on our behalf. His intercession presupposes this expiatory confession, and cannot be conceived of apart from it. Not only so - but it is also certain that we cannot rightly conceive of this confession, or be in the light in which it was made, without seeing that the intercession that accompanied it was necessary to its completeness, as a full response to the mind of the Father towards us and our sins.

I have endeavoured to present Christ's expiatory confession of our sins to the mind of the reader as much as possible by itself, and as a distinct object of thought, because it most directly corresponds, in the place it occupies, to the penal suffering which has been assumed; and I have desired to place these two ways of meeting the divine wrath against sin, as ascribed to the Mediator, in contrast. But the intercession by which that confession was followed up, must be taken into account as a part of the full response of the mind of the

Son to the mind of the Father - a part of that utterance in humanity which propitiated the divine mercy by the righteous way in which it laid hold of the hope for man which was in God. "He bare the sins of many, and made intercession for the transgressors."

In the light of that true knowledge of the heart of the Father in which the Son responded to the Father's condemnation of our sins, the nature of that condemnation was so understood that His love was at liberty, and was encouraged to accompany confession by intercession:- not an intercession which contemplated effecting a change in the heart of the Father, but a confession which combined with acknowledgment of the righteousness of the divine wrath against sin, hope for man from that love in God which is deeper than that wrath - in truth originating it - determining also its nature, and justifying the confidence that, its righteousness being responded to, and the mind which it expresses shared in, that wrath must be appeased.

Therefore, when we would conceive to ourselves, that Amen to the mind of the Father in its aspect toward us and our sins, which, pervading the humanity of the Son of God, made His soul a fit offering for sin, and when we would understand how this sacrifice was to God a sweet-smelling savour, we must consider not only the response which was in that Amen to the divine condemnation of sin, but also the *response which was in it to the divine love in its yearnings over us sinners.*

In itself, the intercession of Christ was the perfected expression of that forgiveness which He cherished toward those who were returning hatred for His love. But it was also the form his love must take if He would obtain redemption for us. Made under the pressure of the perfect sense of the evil of our state, this intercession was full of the Saviour's peculiar sorrow and suffering - a part of the sacrifice of Christ: its power as an *element of atonement* we must see, if we consider that it was the voice of the divine love coming from humanity, offering for man a pure intercession according to the will of God, offering that prayer for man which was the utterance alike of love to God and love to man - that prayer which accorded with our need and the Father's glory as seen and felt in the light of the Eternal love by the Son of God and our Brother.

We do not understand the divine wrath against sin, unless such confession of its evil as we are now contemplating is felt to be the true and right meeting of that wrath on the part of humanity. We do not understand the forgiveness that is in God, unless such intercession as we are now contemplating is felt to be that which will lay hold of that forgiveness, and draw it forth. It was not in us so to confess our own sins; neither was there in us such knowledge of the heart of the Father. But, if another could in this act for us - if there might be a mediator, an intercessor - one at once sufficiently one with us, and yet sufficiently separated from our sin to feel in sinless humanity what our sinful humanity, could it in sinlessness look back on its sins, would feel of

Godly condemnation of them and sorrow for them, so confessing them before God - one coming sufficiently near to our need of mercy to be able to plead for mercy for us according to that need, and at the same time, so abiding in the *bosom of the Father*, and in the light of His love and secret of His heart, as, in interceding for us to take full and perfect advantage of all that is *there* that is in our side, and wills our salvation; - if the Son of God has, in the power of love, come into the capacity of such mediation in taking our nature and becoming our brother, and in that same power of love has been contented to suffer all that such mediation, accomplished in suffering flesh, implied - is not the suitableness and the acceptableness of the sacrifice of Christ, when his soul was made an offering for sin, what we can understand?

In truth, we cannot realise the life of Christ as He moved on this earth in the sight of men, and contemplate His witness-bearing against sin, and His forgiveness towards sinners, and hear the Father say of Him, "This is my beloved Son in whom I am well pleased," and yet doubt that that mind towards sin and sinners which he thus manifested, and the Father thus acknowledged, would be altogether acceptable, and a sacrifice to God of a sweet-smelling savour, in its atoning confession of sin and intercession for sinners.

I know that the adequacy of the atonement to be a foundation for the remission of sins cannot be fully apprehended, or the righteousness of God in accepting it as a sacrifice for sin be fully justified, apart from its prospective reference to the divine purpose of making us through Christ partakers in eternal life. Yet I will, even at this point, express the hope, that the purpose of God to extend mercy to sinners being realised, and the considerations connected with the name of God and the honour of His law, which had to be taken into account, being present to the mind, it will be felt, that the atonement, as now set forth, was the suitable preparation for that contemplated manifestation of mercy; and I venture to express this hope here, and thus early, because, I am not unwilling that the atonement as now represented, and while considered only in its retrospective reference, should be compared with the conception of the atonement as Christ's bearing, as our substitute, the punishment of our sins - the rather, that that is a retrospective conception exclusively. But, I repeat it, I feel that it is placing the atonement, as now set forth, under a disadvantage as to its power to commend itself to the conscience, to look at its retrospective adequacy thus apart from its prospective reference; to the consideration of which I now proceed.

CHAPTER VII

PROSPECTIVE ASPECT OF THE ATONEMENT

I have said above, that the atonement is to be regarded as that by which God has bridged over the gulf which separated between what sin had made us, and what it was the desire of the divine love that we should become. Therefore its character must have been determined as much by the latter consideration as by the former; and, on this ground, I have complained of the extent to which the former consideration, rather than the latter, has been taken into account in men's recognition of a need-be for an atonement.

Yet an atonement such as they contemplate, and consisting in substituted punishment, might allowably be so regarded, being like the paying of a pecuniary debt, at least as to the definite relation of the payment to the debt, the latter determining the former without direct reference to the ulterior results involved in the debt's being paid. But such an atonement as that which the Son of God has actually made, cannot be contemplated but as in its very nature pointing forward to the divine end in view.

Accordingly, I have not been able now to enter freely upon the subject of that intercession for transgressors, which the prophet mentions as an element in the atonement, because that intercession cannot be conceived of as limited to the remission of past sins, but must necessarily have had reference to what Christ, in His love to us, loving as He did Himself, desired for us. So also the confession of our sin, in response to the divine condemnation of it, must, when offered to God on our behalf, have contemplated prospectively our own participation in that confession as an element in our actual redemption from sin. And even the witnessing of Christ for the Father in the sight of men, as connected with the righteousness of God in the extension of the divine mercy to us rebels, must have had its place in the atonement, not *merely* as a light *condemning* our darkness, but as the *intended light of life for us.*

All views of the work of Christ of course imply that its ultimate reference was prospective. Whether conceived of as securing, in virtue of a covenanted arrangement, the salvation of an election from among men, or as furnishing, in reference to all men, a ground on which God may extend mercy to them, the work of Christ has equally been regarded as what would not have been but with a prospective reference. But on neither of these views is the justification of God's acceptance of the propitiation itself, bound up with the question of the results contemplated. On the one view, the penal infliction is complete in itself as a substituted punishment; the righteousness wrought out is complete in itself as conferring a title to eternal blessedness, irrespective of results to be accomplished in those in the covenant of grace.

On the other view, a meritorious ground on which to rest justification by faith is furnished, which is complete in itself, irrespective of any effect which is anticipated from the faith of it. But, what I have now been representing as the true view of the atonement, is characterised by this, that it takes the results contemplated into account in considering God's accept-ance of the atonement. Not that the moral and spiritual excellence of the work of Christ, could have been less than infinitely acceptable to God, viewed simply in itself; but that its *acceptableness in connection with the remission of sins*, is only to be truly and fully seen in its relation to the result which it has contemplated, viz. our participation in eternal life; - or, in other words, that the justification of God in "redeeming," as He has done, "us who were under the law," is only clearly apprehended in the light of the divine purpose, "that we should receive the adoption of sons."

This *direct* reference to the end contemplated, which distinguishes the view of the atonement now taken, as compared with those other systems in which that reference is more remote, I lay much weight upon. It explains, as they cannot otherwise be explained, those expressions in Scripture in which the practical end of the atonement is connected so immediately with the making of the atonement - as when it is said, that "Christ gave Himself for us, that He might redeem us from all iniquity," - that "we are redeemed from the vain conversation received by tradition from our Fathers, by the precious blood of Christ," - that "Christ suffered for us, the just for the unjust, that He might bring us to God."

Men have been reconciled by the seeming necessity of the case to the idea that such language is employed because these are the *ultimate* and *remote* consequences of that shedding of Christ's blood, which, it is held, immedi-ately contemplated delivering us from the punishment of sin by His enduring it for us. But I regard as a great scriptural argument in favour of the view now taken of the atonement, that it represents the connection between these results and Christ's suffering for our sins as not remote, but immediate. While, as to the internal commendation of the doctrine itself, my conviction is, that the pardon of sin is seen in its true harmony with the glory of God, only when the work of Christ, through which we have "the remission of sins that are past," is contemplated in its *direct* relation to "the gift of eternal life."

The elements of atonement, which have now been considered in relation to the remission of sins, contemplated in their relation to the gift of eternal life, teach us how to conceive of that gift. The atonement having been accomplished by the natural working of the life of love in Christ, and having been the result of His doing the Father's will, and declaring the Father's name in humanity, we are prepared, as to the prospective aspect of the atonement, to find that the perfect righteousness of the Son of God in humanity is *itself* the gift of God to us in Christ - to be ours as Christ is ours - to be partaken in as He is partaken in - to be our life as He is our life: instead of its being, as has been held, ours by imputation - precious to us and our salvation, not in respect of what is inherent in it, but in respect of that to which it confers a legal title; or, according to the modification of this conception, (the transference of righteousness by imputation being rejected), our salvation in respect of effects of righteousness transferred for Christ's sake to those who believe in Him.

Abstractly considered, and viewed simply in itself, the divine righteousness that is in Christ must be recognised as a higher gift than any benefit it can be supposed to purchase. In the immediate contemplation of the life of Christ, seen as that on which the Father is fixing our attention when He says of Christ, "This is my beloved Son, in whom I am well pleased," it cannot be questioned, that the choice being offered, on the one hand, to partake in this divine righteousness, or, on the other, either to have it imputed to us, and on account of such imputation, to have a title to any supposed rewards of righteousness, or to have these rewards without such imputation trans- ferred to us, there could be no hesitation what choice to make. Apart altogether from the difficulties involved in the conception of the imputation of righteousness, or the transference of its effects, it would manifestly be a dishonour done to the divine righteousness, to prefer to it any good of any kind external to it, not inherent in it but separable from it, which might be conceived of as its reward.

I may be reminded, that the reward of righteousness, thus placed in contrast with the divine righteousness itself, and assumed to be a lower thing, includes spiritual benefits, includes sanctification; and that this in effect is a participation in the mind and life of Christ, and might be spoken of as substantially righteousness imparted - the purchase of righteousness im- puted, or, according to the modification of the doctrine, apart of God's gracious dealing with us on the ground of Christ's righteousness: and although this is a complication altogether foreign to the simplicity that is in Christ, I thankfully recognise the degree to which the elements of righteous- ness - all that God delights in - holiness, truth, love, may be the objects of spiritual desire, and be welcomed as a part of the unsearchable riches of Christ, even in connection with this system, and when not seen simply as the elements of the eternal life given to us in Christ our life, and in respect of which He is "made of God unto us wisdom, and righteousness, and sanctification, and redemption."

But a righteousness imparted as that to which a right has been conferred by a righteousness imputed; - divine favour and acceptance first resting upon us, irrespective of our true spiritual state, and then a spiritual state in harmony with that favour, bestowed as an expression of that favour; - a right and title to heaven made sure irrespective of a meetness for heaven, and then the meetness - the holiness necessary to the enjoyment of heaven - bestowed upon us as a part of what we have thus become entitled to:- this is a complication which the testimony of God, that God has given to us eternal life, and that this life is in His Son, never could suggest.

Its natural effect is to turn the mind away, in the first instance at all events, from the direct contemplation of eternal life as the salvation given in Christ. The elements of that life may come to be taken into account afterwards; but the evil effect of the first separation between the favour of God and the actual condition of the human spirit in its aspect towards God, never can be altogether remedied - while this root error will always tend to develop itself in reducing the meaning of the words, "eternal life," to the conception of an unproved future endless blessedness that awaits us as those who trust in Christ's merits, not a spiritual state into which we enter in receiving the knowledge of God in Christ. Thus confusion and perplexity are introduced into the whole subject of righteousness and eternal life, when, this life being admitted to be given, righteousness is not recognised as simply an element in that gift, or rather an aspect of it.

In tracing, in their prospective relation to the gift of eternal life, the elements of atonement now considered in relation to the remission of sins, we shall find the simplicity that is in Christ delivering us from all this perplexity and confusing complication; while the immediate and direct occupation of our spirits with eternal life itself as salvation, will favour our intelligent apprehension of that gift, and strengthen us in the faith that God has given it, and also in the faith of the remission of our sins as seen in connection with it - the glory of God and the gift of eternal life in His Son, shedding back its light on the Father's acceptance of the Son when He made His soul an offering for sin.

I would recall here the illustration which I have offered above, of the conception which I have sought to convey of the atoning virtue of Christ's expiatory confession of man's sin, viz. the supposition that all the sin of man had been committed by one human spirit, and that that spirit, preserving its personal identity, and retaining the memory of what it had been, should become perfectly righteous. Had such a case been possible, how would the righteous God deal with such a spirit? In the language of Luther, sin and righteousness being thus met in one person, which would prevail? Would the absolute repentance and sorrow for the past sin, which is necessarily implied in the present righteousness, be an atonement for that past sin, and leave the righteous God free to receive that present righteousness with the favour due to it, or would justice still call for vengeance?

This would be a perplexing dilemma, on the assumption of the correctness of the theory of divine justice that represents that attribute of God as a necessity of the divine nature which necessitates the giving to every spirit that which is righteously due to it - which, in this case, would imply the necessity both to punish the past sin and reward the present righteousness, and this for ever - an impossible combination. The great advocate of that theory has, however, as we have seen, recognised a principle which would extricate him from this dilemma, when he recognises as alternatives an infinite punishment, or an adequate repentance; and he therefore would have consented to the answer assumed above to be clearly the right answer in the case supposed.

I go back on this illustration, because, while stating it formerly, I felt embarrassed, so far as the supposition was one of present righteousness as well as of past sin. In order to the completeness of the parallel between the hypothetical case and the constitution of things in Christ which the Gospel reveals, Christ's confession of our sin must be seen in connection with our relation to the righteousness of Christ, and the sin confessed, and the righteousness in which it is confessed, be seen as if they were in the same person - being both in humanity; though the sin really exists only in humanity as in us, and used in rebellion by us rebels, and the righteousness only in humanity as in Christ, "who through the Eternal Spirit offered Himself without spot to God." But the glory of God in this constitution of things, is only seen when the gift of eternal life to man, in the Son of God, is understood - and this gift we had not then before our minds.

I admitted, in representing Christ's confession of our sin as accounted of to us, that I might, on a superficial view, seem to be stating what was open to the same objections that I have recognised as valid against the doctrine of penal infliction endured by Christ as bearing our sin by imputation; and I offered, in reply, the broad distinction between a state of mind in Christ which implied no legal fiction, no relation to our sins but what was necessarily the result of His being in our nature in the life of love - a mind which, call it an *atoning* confession of our sin or not, was most certainly *a confession of our sins* which *must have been present* in His intercession for us - the broad distinction between this and the infliction on Christ, by the Father, of penal suffering, because, by imputation, He was accounted guilty of our sins. This distinction, if clearly before the mind, is too palpable not to satisfy. But still, that identifying of Christ with us, and that giving to us, so to speak, the benefit of what He was in humanity, which is implied in representing His confession of our sins as an element in the atonement, is not, as I have now said, fully justified to the mind, apart from that further identifying of Christ with us through which His righteousness is ours.

Yet, thus to speak of Christ's righteousness, will as readily recall the doctrine of imputation of righteousness, as the place given to Christ's confession of our sins might recall that of imputation of sin. How wide apart the two conceptions are, and what the true vindication of the divine counsel in this dealing of the Father with Christ, as with the one man who bears the weight of all men's sins upon His spirit, atoning for them by confessing them before the Father in a divine righteousness in humanity, which the Father receives on behalf of all men as the righteousness of humanity; - this we shall understand in the light of the relation of the atonement to the gift of eternal life.

When we consider humanity in the light shed upon it by the life of Christ in humanity, we see together revealed to us the great evil of its condition as possessed by us sinners, and its great capacity of good as that capacity is brought out by the Son of God. now, this is not the same thing with seeing the same person first sinful and then righteous; nor is the problem which it presents the same exactly, as in that hypothetical case:- but, still, what we are thus contemplating involves a closely analogous question for the determination of the righteous Lord who loveth righteousness. As the dishonour done to God in humanity cries out against it, so does the honour done to God plead in its favour - not in the way, certainly, of an off-set in respect of which the honour may cover over, gild over, the dishonour, and so humanity be regarded with acceptance as one whole; not thus - although the honour be divine as well as human, while the dishonour is simply human - but as the revelation of an inestimable preciousness that was hidden in humanity, hidden from the inheritors of humanity themselves, but not hid from God, and now brought forth into manifestation by the Son of God. For the revealer of the Father is also the revealer of man, who was made in God's image.

This high capacity of good pertaining to humanity, is not indeed to be contemplated as belonging to us apart from our relation to the Son of God. For although in one sense it is quite correct to speak of the righteousness of Christ as the revelation of the capacity of righteousness that was in humanity, a capacity that remained to man although hidden under sin; - in truth, humanity had this capacity only relatively, that is, as dwelt in by the Son of God; and therefore, there was in the righteousness of Christ in humanity no promise for humanity apart from the Son of God's having power over all flesh to impart eternal life. We cannot, therefore, see hope for man in the righteousness of Christ, apart from the contemplation of this power as possessed by Christ. Therefore, there must be a relation between the Son of God and the sons of men, not according to the flesh only, but also according to the spirit - the second Adam must be a quickening spirit, and the head of every man be Christ.

But if we see this double relation as subsisting between Christ and men, if we see Him as the Lord of their spirits, as well as a partaker in their flesh, that air of legal fiction, which, in contemplating the atonement, attaches to our identification with Christ and Christ's identification with us, so long as this is contemplated as matter of external arrangement, will pass away, and the depth and reality of the bonds which connect the Saviour and the saved will bear the weight of this identification, and fully justify to the enlightened conscience that constitution of things in which Christ's confession of our sins expiates them, and Christ's righteousness in humanity clothes us with its own interest in the sight of God: for thus, that divine righteousness of the Son of God is seen as necessarily shedding to the mind of the Father its own glory and its own preciousness over all humanity - but in a way as remote from the imputation of righteousness as Christ's bearing our sins, as this has now been illustrated, and confessing them, is from imputation to Him of our sins.

And this, indeed, is infinitely far; and yet some vague feeling corresponding to this truth of things - some vague feeling of the standing which the human spirit needs to find in another than itself - not having it in itself - and which God has given to men in Christ, has been present, working in men's minds, and commending to them the system of imputation with all its moral repulsiveness and intellectual contradiction; - insomuch that one truly knowing his own dependence on Christ, feels more sympathy and unity with those who in the spirit cherish that dependence - though conceiving of it intellectually in the erroneous form which it has in the system of imputation - than with those whose sense of the moral and intellectual objectionableness of that system, is connected with the taking of a standing of independent self-righteousness before God. For, as to all whose trust is truly in Christ, and in the Father's delight in Him, spiritually apprehended, I am assured that, however I may seem to them - as to many such I shall seem - touching the apple of their eye, I am not touching that which is their life.

I proceed to consider, in relation to the gift of eternal life, the two aspects in which we are contemplating the life of love in the Son of God, in His making His soul an offering for sin.

1. The atonement by which Phinehas stayed the plague, prepared us for recognising the vindication of the divine righteousness in **the Son's honouring the Father in the sight of man** as a necessary step in the manifestation of mercy, and we see a true element of propitiation for the sin of man in Christ's glorifying God in humanity. Yet, in studying the manner of Christ's witnessing for the Father, we have the conviction continually impressed upon us, that this revealing of the Father by the presentation to us of the life of sonship has as its object our participation in that life of sonship, and so our participation in that knowledge and enjoyment of the Father, and that inheriting of the Father as the Father, which fellowship in the life of sonship can alone bring.

Let us mark how immediate was the relation of this hope for man to what Christ was suffering in making His soul an offering for sin. He knew that that life of love which was then in Him a light condemning the darkness from which He was suffering was yet to overcome that darkness and take its place. His own consciousness in humanity witnessed within Him that humanity was capable of being filled with the life of love. The more perfectly

He realised that these were His brethren whose hatred was coming forth against Him, the more did He realise also that hatred was not of the essence of their being - that there was hope in giving Himself for them to redeem them from iniquity - that there was hope in suffering for them the just for the unjust - hope that He would bring them to God.

How manifestly has the joy of this hope underlain all His sorrow! It was, indeed, the joy that was set before Him, for which He endured the cross, despising the shame. He bore the contradiction of sinners against Himself, not only in the meekness and patience of love, and the unselfishness of love, which was more deeply grieved that they should offend, than that itself was offended against; but also, in the prophetic faith of love that looked forward to yet becoming itself the life of those who now rejected it. There is hope for the future, as well as deep sadness because of the present, in the words, "O righteous Father, the world hath not known thee, but I have known thee." If the world could continue to be the world after coming to know the Father, there would have been no hope for the world. But, in the consciousness of being in a light in which the world was not was there hope to His heart for the world - therefore did He pray on the cross, and when the enmity had manifested itself to the utmost, "Father forgive them; for they know not what they do."

I know we more frequently refer to these words, as the precious record of the perfection of that forgiveness of His enemies, which was in Him who by His life and death, as by His precepts, has taught us to forgive our enemies, to love them, to pray for them - and in this view the record is precious. But, there is important light in the footing on which He puts His prayer for forgiveness to them, viz. "for they know not what they do." Had the full power of light been expended on them, and without result, there would have been no room to pray for them, because there would have been no possibility of answering the prayer. But, let us thankfully hear Him who knew what is in man, thus praying; and let us mark how to the close He was sustained in making his soul an offering for sin, by the consciousness in His own humanity of a knowledge of the Father which, being partaken in, had power to redeem humanity. "I have declared thy name, and will declare it, that the love wherewith thou has loved me, may be in them, and I in them."

I do not forget the words, "now they have no cloak for their sin," - "now they have seen and hated both me and my Father." But, however great the measure of light thus recognised as received and abused, and bringing condemnation, the possibility of a light beyond it is clearly implied in the words which I have been quoting. These evil men were of the world, of which He says to the Father, that it hath not known Him. They were included in the prayer, "Father, forgive them; for they know not what they do." And so the apostle John teaches, "He that saith he is in the light, and hateth his brother, is in darkness even until now. He that hateth his brother, is in darkness, and *walketh in darkness*, and *knoweth not whither he goeth, because that darkness hath blinded his eyes*." This our Lord knew, and He knew also, that He had come a light into the world, that he that should believe in Him should not abide in darkness was therefore cheered by the consciousness of not only being light in Himself, but "the light of the world," that is, a light for men, a light which His own human consciousness ever testified to be a light for men.

Therefore was the consciousness of having glorified the Father on the earth the foundation of the prayer that the Father would glorify Him in the exercise of the power over all flesh to give eternal life to as many as the Father should give to Him - to all who, having heard and been taught of the Father, should come to the Son; and we know that while walking in His sorrowful path, with the hope of being the channel of eternal life to those for whose sins He was making atonement, the comfort was granted to him of being able to say of some, that the light that was in Him had in some measure been received by them; that in a true sense, however small the measure, they "were not of the world, even as He was not of the world;" that His revealing of the Father by being in their sight the Son honouring the Father, had not been in vain; that at least it had quickened so much life in them as when* Philip could say, "Shew us the Father, and it sufficeth us;" that in truth, though they so little understood what His living ministry of love had accomplished in their spirits as not to understand Him when He bare testimony to it, still a great result had been accomplished, for that He could say, "Whither I go ye know, and the way ye know," though they themselves were so little aware of this as to rejoin, "Lord, we know not whither thou goest; and how can we know the way?"

Thus, a measure of present comfort of the nature of the joy set before Him was granted to our Lord even in the time of His making His soul an offering for sin. Thus are we to conceive of Him as contented to be through suffering made perfect as the Captain of our salvation - welcoming all by which He was receiving fitness to be to us the channel of eternal life. "For their sakes I sanctify myself that they also might be sanctified through the truth."

For, He welcomed that ordering of His path by the Father, which had reference to the development of the life of love that was in Him, according to all the need of man; not withholding His face from shame and spitting, when opening His ear as the learner, that in Him we might have all the treasures of wisdom and knowledge; though a Son, yet learning obedience by the things which He suffered, that being made perfect, He might become the author of eternal salvation unto all that obey Him; submitting to be tempted in all points as we are tempted, that, sinlessly passing through such

---

* Third edition has "...as in Philip could say..."

trial, He might be able, as our high priest, to succour us when we are tempted. In all ways of manifestation of the life of sonship, and at all cost to Himself, He declared the Father's name in life and in death, that the love wherewith the Father had loved Him might be in us and He in us.

It is certain that the atonement has its right interest to us, and quickens in us the hope which it has been intended to quicken, only when that interest and that hope are one as to nature and foundation with what were present in the mind of Christ in making the atonement. We must be in the light of His honouring of His Father's name in all that He presented in humanity to the faith and spiritual vision of men. And this honouring was not only universal as to the outward form of his life, but went to the depth of the inner man of the heart, to the full extent of making His life in humanity a "serving of the living God." "I do nothing of myself: as I hear, I judge," - "My works are not mine, but His that sent me," - "The Father who dwelleth in me, He doeth the works," - "My Father worketh hitherto, and I work," - "The Son doeth nothing of Himself; but whatsoever the Father doeth, the same doeth the Son likewise," - "Why callest thou me good? there is none good but one, that is God." So deep was the honouring of the Father in humanity by the Son, when "through the Eternal Spirit He offered Himself without spot to God."

Nor is it by what He presented in Himself as under His Father's guidance alone, that the Son of God reveals to us the Father. He vindicates the name of the Father, and condemns our sin as rebellious children, by all that we see the Father to be to Him through His following God as a dear child walking in love. I have, in this view, noticed above the place which our Lord's "peace" and "joy," of which He speaks to the disciples as known to them, had in His witnessing for the Father: for, indeed, the Son would have been an imperfect witness for the Father if He was not, by those who saw Him truly, seen to have peace and joy in the Father - a peace and a joy to which often an unclouded expression would be permitted - but which would abide in His spirit, however His sorrows from all else might abound; and in respect of which all such sorrows, though they might be what would justify the appeal, "Look, and see if there be any sorrow like unto my sorrow," would be but the trial of faith, and the more abundant manifestation of what the Father was to the Son. Now, as to all by which the Son thus honoured the Father, we are to see that it all entered into His hope for us in His making His soul an offering for sin, because it was in humanity that He was having all this experience.

I have said above that we are to understand that He who is the revealer of God to man is also the revealer of man to himself. Apart from Christ we know not our God, and apart from Christ we know not ourselves: as, indeed, it is also true, that we are as slow to apprehend and to welcome the one revelation as the other - as slow to see man in Christ, as to see God in Christ.

We have seen how much loss even earnest and deep thinking and holy men have suffered through not looking upon the life of love in Christ as the revelation of the Father; - how it has thus come to pass that, looking upon Christ's love to men merely as the fulfilment for man of the law under which man was, they have dwelt on that fulfilment, and enlarged on the circumstances which prove how perfect it was, and yet have not read the heart of God - the love of God to all men, in that record of the life of Christ which they were studying.

And so also, these same men, through the assumption that in the life of Christ they were contemplating the working out of a legal righteousness for man, to be his by imputation, as they were turned away from seeing God in Christ, so have also been turned away from seeing man in Christ, seeing themselves in Christ, seeing the capacities of their own being in Christ. Not for His own sake but for our sakes did the Son of God reveal the hidden capacity of good that is in man by putting forth in humanity the power of the law of the Spirit of His own life - the life of sonship. "For what the law could not do, in that it was weak through the flesh, God sending His own Son in the likeness of sinful flesh, and as a sacrifice for sin, condemned sin in the flesh, that the righteousness of the law might be fulfilled in us who walk not after the flesh, but after the spirit." We, then, for whose sake this has been, must learn to see in this revelation of what humanity is when pervaded with the life of sonship that redemption of which we were capable, and which we have in Christ, and set ourselves to the study of the twofold discovery of God and of man in Christ, with the conviction that in it are hid for us all the treasures of wisdom and knowledge.

I have said above that the Son alone could reveal the Father - for, indeed, manifested sonship can alone reveal fatherliness, being that in which the desire of that fatherliness is fulfilled - which therefore reveals that desire by fulfilling it. Thus are we to understand the voice of the Father saying of the Son, "This is my beloved Son, in whom I am well pleased" - which voice, when heard in our hearts, is that drawing of the Father through which we come to the Son. And in this light are we to receive the words, "hear ye Him," which declare the purpose of that drawing. For we are called to hear the Son that we may know the Father through knowing the Son in whom He is well pleased, and so may know what is the Father's desire as to ourselves, and what He has given to us in the Son, that that desire of His heart for us may be fulfilled in us.

Let the reader examine his own heart as to the measure in which this is the ground of the interest with which he regards the divine righteousness in humanity, and the Father's testimony to the Son. For, assuredly, it ought to be so; and we ought to be jealous of every thought and view that divides attention with the gift of eternal life - jealous of our going *out* of the circle of the life that is in Christ in search of the unsearchable riches which we have *in* Christ; above all, jealous of occupying our imagination with an unknown future blessedness to be bestowed on us for Christ's sake, instead of keeping to what is included in Christ, in the mind revealed in Christ, and so is addressed to the will in man as what we are to partake in in yielding our will to be guided by the law of the Spirit of the life that is in Christ - the life of sonship: which is in itself riches, unsearchable infinite riches, because it, and it alone, enjoys the Father as the Father, making us heirs of God - heirs of God, and joint heirs with Jesus Christ.

One has spoken of difficulty in joining, in anticipation, "himself and glory in one thought." The greater difficulty is to join ourselves and eternal life in one thought now, although God has already in Christ so connected us in the very truth of things. But, as I have said, we are alike slow of heart to receive Christ's revelation of ourselves, and to receive His revelation of God - to believe that God has given to us eternal life in His Son, and to believe that God is love.

I know, indeed, that the difficulty felt in believing that our humanity and its capacity of good in respect of the eternal life which we have in Christ, is what the life of Christ reveals it to be, is what we are tempted to excuse on the ground of the felt sinfulness of our own nature. Yet, is not the deepest knowledge of that sinfulness expressed in the verses just before those in which the Apostle recognises the power of the law of the Spirit of the life that is in Christ to make us free from the law of sin and death? Has, in this matter, experimental knowledge ever gone further than what the words express - "I find a law in my members warring against the law of my mind, and bringing me into captivity to the law of sin that is in my members. O wretched man that I am, who shall deliver me from the body of this death?" This was the question, and this the state of mind in relation to which the knowledge of the power of the life of sonship in humanity moved the Apostle to thank God through Jesus Christ. We know not the truth of humanity - we know only its perversion while we are living the life of self and enmity and are as gods to ourselves. What it is to be a man, what we possess in humanity, we never know until we see humanity in Him who through the eternal Spirit offered Himself without spot to God.

Let us understand it. The difficulty of believing the revelation of man that is in Christ, and the difficulty of believing the revelation of God that is in Christ, is one difficulty. To believe that God *is love*, as this is revealed by His manifestation of *love to us*, is to believe that love, as ascribed to God in relation to man, means that desire for man which is fulfilled in the humanity of Christ, and can in that alone be satisfied. Therefore, those general conceptions of the divine mercy and benevolence which are formed when God is contemplated only as so feeling for our misery and desiring our happiness as that He gave Christ to die for us that we might be saved from misery and partake in everlasting bliss, although they are true conceptions so far as they go, *come altogether short of the love of God to us in Christ Jesus*. For the element of fatherliness is wanting - what it craves for - what alone can satisfy it. But on fatherliness, as ascribed to God, is the attention kept continually fixed in the Gospel. That God has a Father's heart, may not, indeed, be admitted as a proof that the capacity of sonship has remained to us. But at least the manifestation of that fatherliness by the Son as the *light of life to us* does prove it.

Let us not think of Christ, therefore, simply as revealing how kind and compassionate God is, and how forgiving to our sins, as those who have broken His righteous law. Let us think of Christ as the Son who reveals the Father, that we may know the Father's heart against which we have sinned, that we may see how sin, in making us godless, has made us as orphans, and understand that the grace of God, which is at once the remission of past sin, and the gift of eternal life, restores to our orphan spirits their Father and to the Father of spirits His lost children.

I have dwelt above on the difference between a filial standing and a legal standing. I have spoken also of what Christ's being our example in the life of faith implies as to the footing on which we are to draw near to God, and the nature of the confidence which Christ desires to quicken in us. Yet I feel it necessary thus to insist upon the faith of the sonship in humanity, which is revealed in Christ, as the necessary supplement and complement of the faith of the fatherliness, revealed to be in God: and I must often recur to this because, in truth, my hope of helping any out of the perplexities and confusions which I feel to prevail on the subjects of justification and sanctification, is simply the hope of helping them to see the contradiction between coming to God in the spirit of sonship, with the confidence which the faith of the Father's heart sustains, and coming to God with a legal confidence as righteous in His sight, because clothed with a legal righteousness, or at least accepted on the ground of such a righteousness.

In speaking of that which he had come to experience through knowledge of the eternal life which was with the Father and was manifested in the Son - that experience into the fellowship of which he desired to bring others, the Apostle says, "And truly our fellowship is with the Father and with His Son Jesus Christ." "Father" and "Son" here do more than indicate persons: they indicate that in these persons with which the fellowship is experienced. Eternal life is to the Apostle a light in which the mind of fatherliness in the Father, and the mind of sonship in the Son, are apprehended and rejoiced in.

This teaching as to the nature of salvation is the same which we receive from the Lord Himself when He says, "This is eternal life, to know thee the only true God, and Jesus Christ whom thou has sent;" as also when he says, "If a man love me, he will keep my words: and my Father will love him, and WE will come unto him, and make our abode with him."

Let the reader think of this, and take his own experience to this light. To me it appears that the temptation to stop short of the light that shines to us in the communion of the Son with the Father in humanity is strong, and greatly prevails. But this light is the very light of life to us; for this communion is the gift of the Father to us in the Son. In the experience of this communion in our nature and as our brother, did our Lord look forward to our partaking in it as what would be our salvation. The seventeenth chapter of the Gospel of St John most fully declares this. Indeed the evidence abounds that it was this which was ever in the contemplation of Christ in glorifying the Father on the earth; while of anything like the consciousness of being working out a righteousness to be imputed to me to give them a legal ground of confidence towards God there is no trace.

I have already referred to President Edwards' legal representation of the righteousness of Christ, assumed to be imputed in faith, as perfected in His obedience unto death, and that of which God manifested His acceptance when He raised Christ from the dead. But the testimony to the Saviour was deeper and higher. Christ was *declared to be* the Son of God by the resurrection from the dead. The righteousness then acknowledged was none other than what the Father had previously borne testimony to when He said, "This is my beloved Son, in whom I am well pleased;" - on the sonship, the life of sonship that was in Christ, was attention thus fixed, and not on the legal perfection of the righteousness which it fulfilled. How then can we think of the Father's testimony to the Son as other than a commending of sonship to us, or think of the Father's delight in the Son otherwise than as what justifies His imparting the life of sonship to us?

Let us in this light regard Christ's being delivered for our offences, and raised again for our justification. The offences for which He made expiation were ours - that expiation being the due atonement for the sin of man - accepted on behalf of all men. His righteousness, declared in His resurrection from the dead, is ours - the proper righteousness for man, and in Him given to all men: and that righteousness is NOT the *past fact of legal obligation discharged*, but the *mind of sonship towards the Father*; for in the beloved Son is the Father seen to be well pleased, and in our being through Him to the Father dear children will it come to pass that the Father will be well pleased in us.

2. All that we thus learn as to the prospective reference of the atonement in considering Christ's own manifested life in humanity as His witnessing for the Father to men, is confirmed, and further light shed upon it, when we consider with the same prospective reference the atonement as **the Son's dealing with the Father on our behalf.**

We cannot conceive of our Lord's dealing with the Father on our behalf without passing on to its prospective reference. We could not formerly speak freely of that intercession for sinners which the Prophet has conjoined with

His bearing of their sins, because that intercession could not be conceived of as stopping short of the prayer for our participation in eternal life, to which the expiatory confession of our sins, and prayer for the pardon of our sins necessarily led forward, and in connection with which alone they could have existed. We now approach the subject of this dealing of Christ with the Father in the light of Christ's own perfection in humanity, and connect His laying hold of the hope for man which was in God with the Father's testimony that He was well pleased in the Son. What we have thought of Christ as necessarily desiring for us, was the fellowship of what He Himself was in humanity. This, therefore, was that which He would ask for us; and we can now understand that He would do so with a confidence connected with His own consciousness that *in humanity* He abode in His Father's love and in the light of His countenance. Thus would His own righteousness be presented along with the confession of our sins when He asked for us remission of sins and eternal life.

And this is the right conception of Christ pleading His own merits on our behalf. Our capacity of that which He asked for us was so implied in these merits, and the Father's delight in these merits so implied His delight in their reproduction in us, that the prayer which proceeds on these grounds is manifestly according to the will of the Father - to offer it as a part of the doing of the Father's will - to offer it in the faith and hope of an answer is a part of the trust in the Father by which He declared the Father's name, and is to be contemplated as completing that response to the mind of the Father towards us in our sin and misery, which was present but in part in the retrospective confession of our sin.

And these - the confession and the intercession - so harmonise, are so truly each the complement of the other, that we feel in passing from the one to the other our faith in the Father's acceptance of each confirmed by seeing it in connection with the other; that is to say, we more easily believe in the Father's acceptance of Christ's expiatory confession of our sins when we see that confession as contemplating our yet living to God - our partaking in eternal life; and we more easily believe in the gift of eternal life to those who have sinned, when we see it in connection with that due and perfect expiation for their past sin.

It is in the dealing of the Son with the Father on our behalf, thus in all its aspects before us, that the full light of the atonement shines to us. In the life of Christ, as the revelation of the Father by the Son, we see the love of God to man - the will of God for man - the eternal life which the Father has given to us in the Son - that salvation which the gospel reveals as the Apostle knew it when he invited men to the fellowship of it as fellowship with the Father and with His Son Jesus Christ. Proceeding from this contemplation of the light of eternal life as shining in Christ's own life on earth, to consider the Son in His dealing with the Father on our behalf, and contemplating Him now as bearing us and our sins and miseries on His heart before the Father, and uttering all that in love to the Father and to us He feels regarding us - all His divine sorrow - all His desire - all His hope - all that He admits and confesses as against us - all that, notwithstanding, He asks for us, with that in His own human consciousness, in His following the Father as a dear child walking in love, which justifies His hope in making intercession - enabling Him to intercede in conscious righteousness as well as conscious compassion and love - we have the elements of the atonement before us as presented by the Son and accepted by the Father, and see the grounds of the divine procedure in granting to us remission of our sins and the gift of eternal life. We are contemplating what the Son, who dwells in the bosom of the Father, and whom the Father heareth always, offers to the Father as what He knows to be according to the Father's will, which, receiving the Father's acknowl-edgment as accepted by Him, is sealed to us as the true and perfect response of the Son to the Father's heart and mind in relation to man, the perfect doing of His will - the perfect declaring of His name.

In the light of what God thus accepted when Christ through the eternal Spirit offered Himself without spot to God, we see the ultimate ground - the ultimate foundation in God - for that peace with God which we have in Christ. I say the *ultimate* ground *in God* for that peace with God which we have in our Lord Jesus Christ; for, while the *immediate* ground is the atonement thus present to our faith, that is to say, the purpose as *fulfilled* which our Lord expressed, when coming to put away sin by the sacrifice of Himself, He said, "Lo, I come to do thy will, O God;" yet clearly it is, that *eternal will itself* which He thus came to do, and which by doing it the Son has revealed, even that *name of God* which the Son has *declared*, which is itself the *ultimate peace and rest of our spirits*.

In this full light of the atonement our first conviction is, that in this divine transaction in humanity, through which we have the remission of our sins and the gift of eternal life, there has been nothing arbitrary. We see a righteous and necessary relation between the remission of our sins and Christ's expiatory confession as the due and adequate confession of them - a perfect expiation in that it was divine - perfect in relation to us in that it was human. We see a righteous and necessary relation between the gift of eternal life and Christ's righteousness; God's delight in that righteousness in humanity justifying to us the Son's offering it, and the Father's accepting it on behalf of man to be the righteousness of man.

We see further that what is thus offered on our behalf is so offered by the Son and so accepted by the Father, entirely with the prospective purpose that it is to be reproduced in us. The expiatory confession of our sins which we have been contemplating is to be shared in by ourselves: to accept it on our behalf was to accept it as that mind in relation to sin in the fellowship of which we are to come to God. The righteous trust in the Father, that following Him as a dear child walking in love which we have been contemplating as Christ's righteousness, is to be shared in by us: to accept it on our behalf as the righteousness of man, was to accept it as what pleases God in man - what alone can please God in man - therefore as that in the fellowship of which we are to draw near and live that life which is in God's favour.

In the light of the atonement this is seen clearly; and the light, as our eyes become able to bear it, reconciles us to itself. We soon are thankful that what God has accepted for us in Christ, is also what God has given to us in Christ. As to our past sins, we not only see that the atonement presented to our faith is far more honouring to the righteous law of God against which we had sinned than any penal infliction for our sins, whether endured by another for us, or endured by ourselves in abiding misery, could have been; but are further able to accept, as a most welcome part of the gift of God in Christ, the power to confess our sins with an Amen to Christ's confession of them, true and deep in the measure in which we partake in His Spirit. We are contented and thankful to begin our new life with partaking in the mind of Christ concerning our old life, and feel the confession of our sins to be the side on which the life of holiness is nearest to us, the form in which it naturally becomes ours, and in which it must first be tasted by us: for holiness, truth, righteousness, love must first dawn in us as confessions of sin.

So we welcome the fellowship of the mind in which Christ, by the grace of God, tasted death for every man as the first breathing of that life which comes to us through His death. As to our interest in the righteousness of Christ, we see that God's acceptance of that righteousness on behalf of man, with the purpose of imparting it to man, is more glorifying to the divine delight in righteousness than any other conception that has been entertained; while we also feel the confidence toward the Father which we cherish in receiving Christ as our life to be the only confidence towards God which can meet alike the desires of His heart for us, and the need of our own spirits as God's offspring.

And thus we are in a light in which all drawing of us by the Father to the Son - that is to say, all testifying to our spirits by the Father of our spirits that He has given to us eternal life in His Son - comes to us as the personal application to ourselves of that eternal will of God which we have seen revealed in Christ's dealing with the Father on our behalf. This drawing is felt to accord with, and to be interpreted by, the offering of the Son, and the acceptance of that offering by the Father; and as our faith realises the work of atonement - Christ's confession of our sins, Christ's presentation of His own righteousness in humanity in relation to us, and the Father's acceptance of both on our behalf - we are more and more able to understand and to believe the testimony of God in the Spirit, that God has given to us eternal life, and that this life is in His Son.

In proportion as the light of the divine counsel thus strengthens to us, and in proportion to the growing awakenedness of our spirits to the proper

consciousness of God's offspring and realisation of what the divine fatherliness must be - what it must desire - what alone can be satisfying to it - we
come to see the work of redemption in the light of our ultimate and root
relation to God as the Father of spirits, with whom abides the fountain of
life. We see that, however we had departed from God, our true well-being
continued to be, and must ever continue to be, so bound up in what God is
to us in Himself, and what the aspect of our mind is towards Him, as that
nothing external to this - nothing in God's outward dealing with us - nothing
that He can give or we can receive - nothing that is not included in the state
of our own spirits towards God, and the response in our own hearts to that
which is in His heart towards us - can be our salvation.

I have noticed above how much we may deceive ourselves if we expect
that light from the typical sacrifices under the law which can only be shed
upon us by the antitype itself. But there is an error from which these services
might have saved men, which yet has been fallen into. What these services
present to us as the picture of God's spiritual kingdom is, a temple and a
worship - the participation in that worship being the good set forth,
disqualification for that worship the evil - and sacrifices, and participation in
these sacrifices, the means of deliverance from that evil and participation in
that good. Not to deliver from punishment, but to cleanse and purify for
worship, was the blood of the victim shed. Not the receiving of any manner
of reward for righteousness, but the being holy and accepted worshippers,
was the benefit received through being sprinkled with the victim's blood. In
the light of this centre idea of worship, therefore, are we to see the sprinkling
of all things with blood, and the remission of sins to which this related.

Accordingly, when we pass from the type to the antitype, we find
worship the great good set forth to us - that worship in spirit and in truth
which the heart of the Father craves for - that worship which is sonship - the
response of the heart of the Son to the heart of the Father. We find the
disqualification for worship to be not a mere fact of guilt, but the carnal mind
which is enmity against God - the law in man's members warring against the
law of his mind, and bringing him into captivity to the law of sin that is in
his members. We find that when the Son of God came to be the needed
victim, and to put away sin by the sacrifice of Himself, He indicated the
nature and virtue of His contemplated sacrifice by the words, "Lo, I come
to do thy will, O God;" so that by this will it is that we are sanctified through
the offering of the body of Christ - the blood shed for the remission of sins being
the blood of Christ, who, through the eternal Spirit, offered himself without
spot to God, which *purges the conscience from dead works to serve the living God.*

Thus we are taught the strictly moral and spiritual relation of the
sacrifice to the worship, we see the fitness of the blood shed to fit the spirits
which shall be washed in it to partake in that worship, we see the mind of
Christ, which is in that blood, to be that mind in the *light* of which and in

the *fellowship* of which the worshipper will cry, Abba, Father. Finally, we see why the High Priest and the head of this worship is the Son of God; and why His relation to the worshippers is not "the law of a carnal commandment," - not a mere institution or arrangement, but a spiritual relation, viz. "the power of an endless life," - so that He is their High Priest in that He is their life.

All this, while it accords with the place of sacrifices under the law, is to us, when we see it in the light of our relation to God as the Father of our spirits, of the nature of necessary truth; that is to say, we see that that access to God which shall indeed be to us a way into the holiest, must accord with the spiritual constitution of our being, with the nature of holiness, and with the nature of the separation from God which sin causes; therefore, that no permission or authority to come to God can be of any avail to us, apart from the mind in which alone he who has sinned can in truth draw near to God; and this mind we see is just that into which the sinner enters in the Amen of faith to the voice that is in the blood of Christ, viz. Christ's confession of our sins. In the faith of God's acceptance of that confession on our behalf, we receive strength to say Amen to it - to join in it - and, joining in it, we find it a living way to God; and at the same time we feel certain that there is no other way - that we get near to God just in the measure in which in the Spirit of Christ we thus lovingly adopt His confession of our sins - in this measure and no further.

Permission to draw near to God, seen thus in the light of the mind in which to draw near - that is to say, the remission of our sins seen in connection with Christ's confession of our sins - *this* is the way of life open before us; - a way which is to our faith a part of the gift of eternal life. For though the right feelings for us to cherish, though the suitable feelings in which to approach to God, and in truth, the only feelings in which the consciousness of having sinned can coexist with the experience of communion with God, still these feelings altogether belong to the Son of God - to the Spirit of sonship - and are possible to us only in the fellowship of the Son's confidence in the Father's fatherly forgiveness, being quickened in us by the faith of that fatherly forgiveness, as uttered in God's acceptance of Christ's confession and intercession on our behalf.

I have above insisted upon the importance of the difference between a legal standing and a filial standing, and on the necessity, in considering the nature of the atonement, of keeping continually in view that in redeeming us who were under the law and divine purpose was that we should receive the adoption of sons. This necessity is becoming, I trust, more and more clear as we proceed. The virtue required in the blood of Christ is seen to be necessarily spiritual - a power to influence the spirits washed in it by faith, when our need is seen as the need of those whose life lies in God's favour, whose well-being must consist in communion with God, whose salvation is joining in that worship of God which is in spirit and in truth. And the spiritual virtue needed is determined to be the law of the Spirit of the life that is in Christ, the life of sonship, when it is understood that the worship in spirit and in truth is that which the Father seeketh as the Father - the worship which is sonship, that of which the son is High Priest and head.

But it further appears to me, that this conception of the worship for which the blood of Christ is to qualify, sheds back a light on the atonement, in which we are justified in saying that Christ's confession to our sin was not only the expiation due to the righteous law of God, but also the expiation due to the fatherly heart of God.

To speak of an atonement as due to the fatherly heart of God is foreign to our habits of mind on the subject of atonement. Yet I believe that in proportion as we see the expiation that is in Christ's confession of man's sin to be that which has truly met the demand of the divine righteousness, we must see that the *filial* spirit that was in that confession, and which necessarily took into account what our being rebellious children was to the Father's heart, constituted the *perfection* of the *expiation*. This is no uncalled for refinement of thought. The pardon which we need is the pardon of the Father of our spirits - the way into the holiest which we need is the way into our Father's heart; and therefore, the blood of Christ which hath consecrated such a way for us, must have power to cleanse our spirits from that spiritual pollution which defiles rebellious children, that is to say, must contain the new mind in which it pertains to rebellious children to return to the Father.

And this consideration manifestly confirms the view now taken of the atonement. In proportion as it is seen that that which expiates sin must be something that meets a demand of the divine righteousness, the superiority of a moral and spiritual atonement, consisting in the right response from humanity to the divine mind in relation to sin, becomes clear. But that superiority is surely rendered still more unequivocal when, from the conception of God as the righteous ruler, we ascend to that of God as the Father of spirits. It is then that we fully realise that there is no real fitness to atone for sin in penal sufferings, whether endured by ourselves or by another for us. Most clearly to the Father's feelings such sufferings would be no atonement; and yet are not these the feelings which call for an atonement - is it not to them that expiation is most righteously due?

And I would ask some attention to this question, because I know that weakness has been supposed to be introduced into our conceptions of the divine requirements, by giving prominence to the idea that God is our Father. Those who have this impression, and who fear the weakening of our sense of the divine authority, through giving the root place in our system to our relation to God as the Father of our spirits, would say, "It is the righteous ruler and judge who calls for an atonement, not the Father; the Father would receive us without an atonement." Certainly, such an atonement as they have before their minds in saying this, would be no response to any demand that we can ascribe to the Father's heart - as neither, indeed, I believe would it be to any demand which, in the light of the divine righteousness, we can ascribe to the Judge of all the earth.

But this associating of moral weakness, and, as it were, *easiness*, with the idea of the fatherliness that is in God, is altogether an error; neither should any place be given to it. "If ye call on the *Father*, who, without respect of persons, judgeth according to every man's work, pass the time of your sojourning here in fear." The Father's heart did demand an atoning sacrifice. Is not this clear, if the worship in relation to which the victim's blood was shed is, indeed, sonship? The Father's heart did demand the shedding of blood in order to the remission of sins, because it demanded blood in which justice would be rendered to the fatherliness which had been sinned against, and which, therefore, would have virtue in it to purge our spirits from their unfilial state, and to purify us in respect of the pollution that attaches to us as rebellious children.

We might, indeed, say that the Father's heart asked for an atonement for our sin, simply on the ground that it desired us back to itself, and therefore, desired a living way of return for us, and one related in its nature to the nature of our departure, in order that our return might be a real return; and that such a way could only be that which was opened by the Son of God, when He confessed the sins of God's rebellious children as to the Son, who abides ever in the bosom of the Father, alone could: for He, indeed, alone could know the exceeding sinfulness of our sins, and feel regarding them in that mind, the fellowship of which would be to us our purgation from them. But this moral and spiritual impossibility of our returning to the Father of our spirits, except on such a path as this which Christ has opened for us through the rent veil of His flesh, and in the power of that endless life in which He is related to us as our High Priest over the house of God - this impossibility in respect of the very constitution of our spiritual being, can only be the counterpart of a necessity in the divine nature, in respect of which, the right feelings of the Father of spirits must be conceived of as demanding that expiation which we are now contemplating, rendering it impossible that He should receive us with welcome and acknowledgment, if coming by any other path than the fellowship of that expiation. God's righteous glory in us, no less than our special and peculiar blessedness in God as redeemed sinners, implies that in our consciousness in drawing near to God, our future shall not be cut off from our past. Therefore, that is not to be in time or in eternity; nor is our life of sonship in its highest development to be without the element of the remembrance, that we did not from the first cry Abba, Father; "Unto Him that loved us, and washed us from our sins in his own blood, and hath made us kings and priests unto God and His Father; to Him be glory and dominion, for ever and ever, Amen." We may say, that without the shedding of the blood of Christ, the Father of spirits could not receive back to the bosom of His love His rebellious children, as well as that without the shedding of the blood of Christ, it was morally and spiritually impossible for them to return. For these, indeed, are but two aspects of one spiritual truth.

What I thus labour to impress on the mind of my reader is, that the necessity for the atonement which we are contemplating, was moral and spiritual, arising out of our relation to God as the Father of spirits; and not merely legal, arising out of our being under the law. In truth, its existence as a legal necessity arose out of its existence as a moral and spiritual necessity; therefore, the legal difficulty is to be contemplated as what could be, and has been, removed only in connection with, and because of, the removal of the spiritual difficulty. In other words, we have remission of our sins in the blood of Christ, only because that blood has consecrated for us a way into the holiest, and in this relation, and in this alone, can remission of sins be understood.

Therefore, it is altogether an error to associate weakness and easiness with the fatherliness of God, and severity and stern demand with His character as a moral governor. What severity, what fixedness of righteous demand has to be calculated upon, is to be seen as first in the Father, and then in the moral governor, because in the Father. And, although there had been in the universe but one moral being related to God as each of us is, and though God should be contemplated in His dealing with that individual being as acting exclusively as the Father of that spirit, seeking to realise the yearning of His fatherly heart in relation to that spirit - the necessity for the atonement would, as respected that individual, have been still what it has been; nor could the fulfilment of the Father's desire for that one man have been possible, otherwise than through the opening of that fountain for sin and for uncleanness which is presented to our faith in the shedding of Christ's blood. And I never expect to see the real righteous severity of God truly and healthfully realised, and the unchangeable and essential conditions of salvation apprehended, and hope cherished only in being conformed to them, until the blood of Christ is thus seen in its direct relation to our participation in eternal life.

So far is it from being the case, that giving the root place to our relation to God as the fountain of life and the Father of spirits, and subordinating the relation in which we stand to Him as a Lawgiver and as a Sovereign - so far is this from introducing weakness into our conceptions of the moral and spiritual laws of the kingdom of God, that it is the seeing the Father in the Son, and the desire of the Father for us realised in the Son, which ultimately and absolutely shuts us up to the faith, that there is for us but one path of life, because but one path to the Father. "I am the way, the truth, and the life; no man cometh unto the Father, but by me." These words of the Son, who dwelleth in the bosom of the Father, heard as shedding light on the kingdom of God, reveal a fixed and immutable constitution of things. No words can be more exclusive, more unbending, more remote from all opening of a door to the hope of being easily dealt with - the hope of experiencing a soft, accommodating indulgence, that in weak tenderness would bend the divine requirement to what we are.

"No man cometh unto the Father but by me," - these words raise us up to a region in which there is, there can be nothing arbitrary. A sovereign Lord and moral governor, appointing laws and enforcing them by the administration of a system of rewards and punishments, may be contemplated as severe and uncompromising in the exercise of his righteous rule - but he may also be thought of as merciful and considerate of individual cases; and the outward and arbitrary nature of the rewards and punishments which he is believed to dispense makes his awarding the former on easier terms, and withholding or mitigating the latter according to circumstances - and, it may be, under the influence of mercy - what can be supposed, and what, in thinking of God as such a governor and Lord, and of ourselves as the subjects of His rule, we can turn to the thought of with a vague hope. And such a governor and Lord God is in the ordinary thoughts of men, and such a vague hope towards God is the ordinary hope of men. And on such a conception of their relation to God have men ignorantly engrafted the gospel - conceiving of it as giving a special and definite form to the indefinite combination of judgment and mercy, which has sustained that vague hope of salvation which they had cherished.

But the gospel, truly apprehended, raises us into another and a higher region - a region, indeed, in which divine mercy or clemency, as previously conceived of, is felt to have been but as the dimmest twilight of kindness and goodwill towards men, in comparison of the noonday light of the love of the Father of spirits to His offspring - but a region also in which no arbitrary dealing with us can find a place. In the light that shines in that region it is clear to us that the relation between the blessedness that is seen there, and the rightness that is recognised there, is fixed and immutable. So that the liberty which, in the lower region, we ascribed to mercy, is here found not to belong to love; nor the discretion which we ventured to attribute to the righteous governor, found to pertain to the loving Father; but, on the contrary, the law of the Father - the principle on which happiness is dispensed by Him to His offspring as His offspring - is found to be fixed and altogether unbending, incapable of accommodation in a way of pity, or indulgence, or consideration of circumstances. "No man cometh unto the Father but by the Son." All modification of this law is impossible; for sonship and fatherliness are mutually related in an eternal relation. The Father as the Father, can only receive His offspring to Himself as coming to Him in the spirit of sonship; - neither otherwise than as coming in the spirit of sonship can they in spirit and in truth draw near to Him.

I have spoken of a way into the holiest as what must have its nature determined by the nature of holiness; so a way to the Father must have its nature determined by the nature of fatherliness. These are two aspects of one spiritual reality; a reality, reader, which we must steadfastly contemplate, to the certainty and fixedness of which we must be reconciled - a reality in the light of which we must see the free pardon of sin and redeeming love, and all the divine mercy to us sinners which the gospel reveals. In that lower moral region to which I have referred, in which men are not dealing with the Father of spirits but with the moral governor of the universe (but whose moral government, while thus not illumined by the light of His fatherliness, is never understood) we may be occupied with the punishment of sin and the rewards of righteousness, in a way that permits us to connect the atonement directly with the idea of punishment and reward, and invests it simply with the interest of that desire to escape punishment and to be assured of happiness, which may, even in the lowest spiritual state, be strong and lively in us. But if we will come to the atonement, not venturing in our darkness to predetermine anything as to its nature, but expecting light to shine upon our spirits from it, even the light of eternal life; if we will suffer it to inform us by its own light why we needed it, and what its true value to us is, the *punishment* of sin will fall into its proper place as testifying to the existence of an evil greater than itself, even *sin*; from which greater evil it is the *direct* object of the atonement to deliver us - deliverance from punishment being but a secondary result. And the reward of righteousness will be raised in our conceptions from the character of something that can be ours by the adjudication of the judge on arbitrary grounds which mercy may recommend, to its true dignity as that blessedness which is essentially inherent in righteousness, and in that glorifying and enjoying of God of which righteousness alone is the capacity, and which no name, nor title, nor arbitrary arrangement can confer.

The atonement, thus seen by its own light, is not what in our darkness we desired; but it soon reconciles us to itself, for it sets us right as to the true secret of well being. A spiritual constitution of things that would have been more accommodating to what we were through sin, we soon see as precluded alike by the nature of God, and the nature of man in its relation to the nature of God - a relation, to violate which would not be the salvation, but the destruction of man. We, indeed, see ourselves encompassed by necessities, instead of flexible, compromising, weak tenderness; but they are necessities to which we are altogether reconciled, for we are reconciled to God. One has said, "It is a profitable sweet necessity to be forced on the naked arm of Jehovah." That "no man cometh to the Father but by the Son" is the great and all-including necessity that is revealed to us by the atonement. But, as combined with the gift of the Son to us as the living way to the Father, we rejoice to find ourselves shut up to "so great salvation."

CHAPTER VIII

FURTHER ILLUSTRATION OF THE FIXED AND NECESSARY CHARACTER OF SALVATION AS DETERMINING THE NATURE OF THE ATONEMENT AND THE FORM OF THE GRACE OF GOD TO MAN.

I have said that the character of the Mosaic institutions, as commented upon in the Epistle to the Hebrews, ought to have saved us from the direct connecting of the atonement with the subject of rewards and punishments, and more especially from that direct connecting of forgiveness through the blood of Christ with exemption from punishment which has so prevailed, seeing that the blood of the victim was intended to purify and cleanse for participation in worship.

In this light as to the relation of the sacrifice to worship, and seeing the worship typified to be that worship which is sonship, we see how perfectly that which our Lord taught in saying, "No man cometh unto the Father but by me" - meaning to fix the attention of His disciples on what He Himself was in their sight, as the revealer of the Father by the manifested life of sonship - accords with the elements of confidence in drawing near to God, which the Apostle enumerates in exhorting men to "draw near in the full assurance of faith, having their hearts sprinkled from an evil conscience, and their bodies washed with pure water." That our Lord and the Apostle must have contemplated the same thing as the due and accepted worship we cannot doubt. But it is only when we understand that the shedding of the blood of Christ had direct reference to our relation to God as the Father of our spirits, and to the opening of a way in which we as rebellious children can return to the bosom of the Father's love, according to the truth of what the Father is, and what sonship is, that we see that "having boldness to enter into the holiest by the blood of Jesus, by a new and living way which He hath consecrated for us through the veil, that is to say His flesh, and having an High Priest over the house of God," is the same thing with the Son of God being to us a living way to the Father.

The doctrinal form of thought which the language of the Apostle presents, would probably have been more difficult of apprehension to the disciples, who had yet to learn that "it behoved Christ first to suffer and afterwards to enter into His glory," than even their Lord's language as to their own favoured position as the chosen companions of the path of Him who could say, "He that hath seen me hath seen the Father." Yet, afterwards, they could look back and see the identify of what they subsequently learned with what had been presented to their faith in their personal acquaintance with Christ.

These disciples, indeed, knew not then the form which the work of redemption must take in being perfected, but they had received under the Lord's personal acquaintance with Christ. These disciples, indeed, knew not then the form which the work of redemption must take in being perfected, but they had received under the Lord's personal ministry that spiritual teaching, for the want of which, no familiarity with the full record of the finished work of Christ can compensate, and in the absence of which, our study of that record never is safe; for already they were fit subjects for that high testimony from their Lord, "They are not of the world, even as I am not of the world;" they had received the Son as coming to them in the Father's name, and that was quickened in them which was according to the truth of our relation to God as the Father of our spirits. Their attraction to their Master was that they felt that He "had the words of eternal life;" - their cry was, "Shew us the Father, and it sufficeth us;" and so, when the true worship, of which their temple service had been a type, was subsequently clearly revealed to them as that worship which is sonship, and when they learned distinctly to contemplate the heart of the Father as the Holy of Holies, they were prepared to know the Son of God as both the sacrifice and the High Priest.

This unity of their recollections of the Lord as they knew Him so nearly, with the light that afterwards shone to them in His blood shed for the remission of sins, and in His relation to them as the High Priest over the house of God, is illustrated to us by that opening of the first Epistle of John which has already engaged our attention. The fellowship with the Father and with His Son Jesus Christ, which the Apostle had entered into in receiving the knowledge of eternal life, we have already noticed. This divine fellowship he proceeds at the 5th verse to speak of as calling Him to declare to men as the divine message - the Gospel - "that God is light, and in Him is no darkness at all."

This statement in the connection in which it is made has clearly the same fixedness of character, as respects the terms of grace and the way of salvation, which we have seen in the Saviour's own words, "No man cometh unto the Father but by me." For he adds, "If we say that we have fellowship with Him, and walk in darkness, we lie, and do not the truth: but if we walk in the light, as He is in the light, we have fellowship one with another." This is, indeed, but the same spiritual law or necessity elsewhere declared in the words, "there is no communion between light and darkness." But the experimental character of the Apostle's language is used by one claiming to have the fellowship with God of which he speaks - fellowship with the Father and with His Son Jesus Christ - claiming through knowledge of Christ both to know that God is light, and to be walking in that light, and making His own experience in this spiritual region known to us with the purpose and hope of our coming into the fellowship of it, and so being saved; - this brings the truth that "there is no communion between light and darkness" - very near to us - very home to us: the felt unity of what the disciples came to know, when they came to understand that "it behoved Christ to suffer and afterwards to enter into His glory," with what had been presented to their faith in the life of Christ, and what their Lord had commended to them as the light of life when He said, "I am the way, the truth, and the life: no man cometh unto the Father, but by me," coming fully out in the words which follow, "If we walk in the light, as He is in the light, we have fellowship one with another, *and the blood of Jesus Christ His Son cleanseth us from all sin.*"

Not surely - what I fear these words too often suggest - a cleansing having reference to our exposure to the punishment of sin, but a cleansing having reference to the pollution of sin itself. Not, therefore, a cleansing spoken of in a legal sense, and as something *over* and *above* the spiritual cleansing implied in walking in the light of God and having fellowship with God, but a cleansing *having effect in that fellowship*, and which is referred to as *explaining* that fellowship, explaining how it comes to pass in a way that gives the glory of that fellowship to the blood of Christ in which such cleansing power is found. For we cannot doubt that the power to cleanse which here the words, "the blood of Jesus Christ His Son cleanseth from all sin," declare, is the same that is contemplated where it is said, "If the blood of bulls and of goats, and the ashes of an heifer sprinkling the unclean, sanctifieth to the purifying of the flesh: how much more shall the blood of Christ, who through the eternal Spirit offered Himself without spot to God, purge your conscience from dead works to serve the living God?" To say that the blood of Christ "cleanseth us from all sin," and to say that it "purges the conscience from all sin," and to say that it "purges the conscience from dead works, to serve the living God," are but different ways of declaring the spiritual power of the atonement when apprehended by faith - asserting its fitness for being partaken in by us as the mind of Christ in relation to our sin. And so the words are added in relation to our own participation in Christ's expiatory confession of our sin, "If we say that we have no sin, we deceive ourselves, and the truth is not in us. If we confess our sins, He is faithful and just to forgive us our sins, and to cleans us from all unrighteousness."

So he proceeds to speak of Christ as our advocate with the Father, and the propitiation for our sins: "My little children, these things write I unto you, that ye sin not," for he has been shutting them up to a salvation which is walking in the light of God, and is fellowship with God. And, that they may feel the reasonableness of proposing to them "that they sin not," he reminds them that "if any man sin, we have an Advocate with the Father, Jesus Christ the righteous;" and that "He is the propitiation for our sins." Of course, if any man sin and then find comfort in remembering that he has an advocate with the Father, this implies that with the thought of that advocate will rise the thought of the pardon of sin; but it is clear that the pardon of sin is here rather implied than expressed, for the value and use of the advocate *directly contemplated* is His value to those who are called "not to sin;" therefore is the *"righteousness"* of the advocate that on which attention is fixed: for He is made of God unto us righteousness, and righteousness is in Him for us as the sap is in the vine for the branch. On the ground of the sap that is in the vine, therefore, are the branches here exhorted to bear fruit; which also determines the light in which the Saviour is contemplated when it is added, "He is the propitiation for our sins;" and that this is spoken in direct reference to Christ's righteousness, and the fitness of that righteousness to meet the need of the sinner as being deliverance from sin. In other words, Christ is the propitiation for our sins as He is the way into the holiest - the living way to the Father.

And He *is* the propitiation: for propitiation is not a thing which He has accomplished and on which we are thrown back as on a past fact. He *is* the propitiation. Propitiation for us sinners - reconciliation to God - oneness with God abides in Christ. When we sin, and so separate ourselves from God, if we would return and not continue in sin we must remember this. For it is in this view that the Apostle, writing to us "that we sin not," reminds us of the propitiation - not a work of Christ, but the living Christ Himself: and so he proceeds - "Hereby we do know that we know Him if we keep His commandments;" the *direct* effect of knowing Christ the *propitiation* for sin being *keeping Christ's commandments.* And because of the power to keep Christ's commandments, which is ours in Christ as the propitiation for our sins, the Apostle, in words similar to those which he had just used with reference to the claim to fellowship with God who is light, adds, "He that saith I know Him," that is Christ the propitiation for our sins, "and keepeth not his commandments is a liar, and the truth is not in him. But whoso keepeth His word, in him verily is the love of God perfected," - the end of this gift of love accomplished. "Hereby know we that we are in Him. He that saith he *abideth in Him ought himself also so to walk even as He walked.*"

We need not then be uncertain what the reference is in which the "righteousness" of the Advocate with the Father is here contemplated, or doubt that, by *abiding in Christ* is here meant, that abiding in which the branch receives the sap of the vine, that it may bear fruit. And yet I know that this *directness* of relation between knowing Christ as the propitiation for our sins, and walking as He walked, some may deny, and that, retaining that meaning for the word "propitiation" which the conception of an atonement as substituted penal suffering has given to it, it may be said that it is as a motive to gratitude, because of the deliverance from punishment through the sufferings of Christ, that a moral power is here ascribed to Christ's being the propitiation for our sins. The impression of directness in this matter, that is, of direct dealing with sin itself as the evil, and of recognition of Christ as the deliverer from sin, which not only the verses I have quoted, but the whole Epistle gives, is, however, so strong that I cannot but hope that, in spite of associations of old standing, I may not in vain have directed the reader's attention to it.

And, with a similar hope, though with the same knowledge that deep-rooted associations stand in the way, I would now take the reader to a parallel passage in the Epistle to the Hebrews. I refer to the 2nd chapter, verses 17, 18, "Wherefore in all things it behoved Him to be made like unto His brethren, that He might be a merciful and faithful High Priest in things pertaining to God, to make reconciliation for the sins of the people. For in that He Himself hath suffered being tempted, He is able to succour them that are tempted."

To succour us when we are tempted is manifestly to do for us that very service which I have just represented the Apostle John as leading those to whom he writes "that they sin not," to expect from that righteous Advocate with the Father, who is the propitiation for our sins. For this service of love, Christ is *here* represented as fitted, in that He Himself hath suffered, being tempted - as *there* by being righteous. Both thoughts are combined when it is said, that "He was tempted in all points like as we are, yet without sin." Now, going back from the 18th verse to the 17th (the 18th, "For," &c. being given as the justification of the comfort offered in the 17th), it is clear, that "making reconciliation for the sins of the people," is the same thing with "succouring us when we are tempted," - in other words, is a dealing with our spirits as worshipping God - calling Him Father, in a way of merciful and faithful aid, such as the High Priest, who is related to us according to the power of an endless life - the Son of God, in whom we have eternal life - has been qualified for ministering to us through having "been made in all things like unto His brethren."

I know that this view of making reconciliation for our sins as being the ministering to us a present help, according to our spiritual need - enabling us to be at peace with God spiritually, and therefore, truly - enabling us to worship God, who is a spirit, in spirit and in truth - is not that usually taken. And that thus to interpret Christ's making reconciliation by the reference made to His experience of our conditions as what has qualified Him for this office of an High Priest, is as great a departure from prevailing associations with the sacred language, as there is in the view just taken of what is taught when Christ is said to be the propitiation for our sins. Yet there is no case in which there is to my mind a more painful illustration of the power of system, than in the way in which the 18th verse has seemed to have been lost sight of in fixing the meaning of the 17th, and in which, indeed, I may say the tone of the 17th itself as a whole has been misunderstood.

If the interpretation of the expressions, "propitiation" and "reconciliation," now adopted in harmony with the view taken of the nature of the atonement, commends itself to the reader, he will be prepared to receive a corresponding interpretation of the expression "peace", as applied to Christ, when He is said, to be "our peace," - making it equivalent to His claim to being the only "way to the Father." (Eph. ii. 14)

In the teaching by which the Saviour comforted the disciples in the near prospect of His being taken from them, we find Him, in words referred to already, encouraging them by the prospect of passing through the trials that awaited them in the fellowship of the inward consolation by which they had seen their Lord Himself sustained in all they had seen Him pass through. "Peace," says He, "I leave with you, my peace I give unto you." That He could speak to them of His own peace, has been already noticed, as a part of the perfection of His witnessing for the Father. That He could promise to them the fellowship of that peace which He thus claims as His own, has been also already noticed as one of the forms in which He made them to know that the life of sonship which they witnessed in Him, was in Him the Father's gift to them. If they were to be sons of God in Spirit and in truth, the peace of the Son in following the Father as a dear child, would be their portion also.

Further, as they were to live the life of sonship, not as independent beings, following the example of the Son of God, but as abiding in the Son of God, as branches in the true vine, this peace which He bequeathed to them they were not to have apart from Himself. In abiding in Him were they to have it as a part of the fulness that was in Him for them - a part of the all things pertaining to life and to godliness. "In me ye shall have peace."

Thus are we to understand the word "peace" in the promises of the Lord to the disciples before His departure; thus are we to understand the word "peace" in the promises of the Lord to the disciples before His departure; thus are we to understand it when, on those occasions on which He appeared to them between His resurrection and ascension, still further to comfort their hearts and to strengthen them for what was before them, He stood in the midst of them and said, "Peace be unto you; as the Father hath sent me, even so send I you." Doubtless, thus also are we to understand the "peace" intended in the apostolic prayer and benediction, "Grace be unto you, and peace from God the Father, and from the Lord Jesus Christ." Nor has the word any other meaning than this in the song of the heavenly host at the nativity, "Glory to God in the highest; on earth peace, and good-will toward men." Now the reader is prepared to understand that in accordance with the nature of the atonement as now represented, it is the same peace, the peace of sonship, the peace that is "from God the Father and the Lord Jesus Christ;" being peace "in fellowship with the Father and with His Son Jesus Christ," - it is this same peace that I understand to be the peace spoken of when it is said that Christ "*is* our peace."

The parallelism of the 2nd chapter of the Epistle to the Ephesians, with the portion of the 10th chapter of the Epistle to the Hebrews, considered above, is obvious. The language of the temple service is not so closely adhered to, nor is salvation so exclusively contemplated as the condition of true and accepted worship: for with the idea of "a holy temple," is united that of "citizenship," and a "household," verses 19, 20, 21, 22; but the summing up of the evil of the state in which the gospel had found the Ephesians, in the words "without God in the world," verse 12 - the setting forth, as the grace revealed to them, their being "made *nigh* by the blood of Christ" - the purpose ascribed to Christ, to reconcile us to God, by slaying the enmity; - all express the same conception of the evil of man's state as a sinner as consisting in his spiritual distance from God, and of the salvation revealed in the gospel as consisting in spiritual nearness to God. In this connection the peace with Christ is said *to be*, and which is said to be preached to men, can only be understood to be a spiritual peace with God - a spiritual destruction of the previous enmity - a spiritual reality present in the humanity of Christ, and proclaimed to men as the gift of God to them in Christ - one with the way into the holiest, which He has opened up for us - the way to the Father, which He is to us. And this spiritual conception of the peace spoken of, suggested by the tone of the whole passage as what alone accords with the spiritual realities of distance from God and nearness to God, is sealed to us as the true conception by the explanatory words of the 18th verse. "For through Him we both have access by one spirit unto the Father." "For," that is to say, because of this condition of things, viz. our having, both Jew and Gentile, through Christ, access by one spirit unto the Father - therefore, is peace preached to us, for in this is peace for us.

Looking more closely into the passage, there is a complication foreign to our present purpose introduced by the mention of Jew and Gentile. This has arisen from its being an Epistle to Gentiles. But we see that the Apostle is taking us deeper than the distinction between Jew and Gentile. He is taking us down to our common humanity, and presenting to our faith the Son of God by one work doing away with the separation between Jew and Gentile, and reconciling both Jew and Gentile - all humanity - unto God in one body by the cross, having slain the enmity thereby.

Paul says to the Galatians, "We who are Jews by nature, and not sinners of the Gentiles, knowing that a man is not justifies by the works of the law but by the faith of Jesus Christ, even we have believed in Jesus Christ, that we might be justified by the faith of Christ, and not by the works of the law; for by the works of the law shall no flesh be justified." So here he takes the Ephesians to the contemplation of that dealing of the Son with the Father on behalf of all humanity, in which Jew and Gentile were alike interested, and in which they must alike see their interest if they would see the veil rent that separated them from each other, and separated them from God; for indeed, the veil is one and the same that separates man from God, and that separates man from man.

I will not anticipate that tracing of the atonement in connection with the actual history of our Lord's work to its close on the cross which I contemplate, and by which I hope the view I am presenting of the nature of the atonement will be felt to be illustrated and confirmed. In no view of the atonement can the crucifixion be separated from the previous life of which it was the close. Yet, it is only the view now taken that identifies the peace to which our Lord was conscious throughout His own life on earth, and which He promised to His disciples, with the peace which He fully accomplished and vindicated for humanity in that death on the cross, which was the perfecting of the Lord's work of redemption, the perfected fulfilling of the purpose, "Lo, I come to do thy will, O God," the perfecting of His declaration of the Father's name.

But the gospel does not proclaim two manners of peace with God: one legal, the result of Christ's bearing the penalty of our sins; the other spiritual, to be known in our participation in Christ's spirit. That oneness of mind with the Father in the aspect of the divine mind towards man, which was fully developed and perfected in humanity in the Son of God when His confession of the Father before men, and His dealing with the Father on behalf of men, were perfected on the cross - this was that divine and spiritual peace for man in His relation to God, which is to be contemplated, first, as in its own nature and essence spiritual; and then, because spiritual, also legal - a perfect answer to all the demands of the law of God - a perfect justification of God in regard to the grace in which we stand.

And thus was the atonement adequate to whatever victory of Christ on our behalf is implied in His "leading captivity captive," when "through death destroying him that had the power of death, that is, the devil; and delivering them who through fear of death were all their lifetime subject to bondage," Hebrews ii. 14, 15. The power of evil adverse to us to which this language refers we imperfectly understand. Definite conceptions of the manner of our bondage we have not beyond this, that "the strength of sin was the law." But, if the honour regarded as done to the law by the death of Christ conceived of as implying the enduring of penal infliction for our sins, have seemed a sufficient explanation of the power thus ascribed to Christ's cross, how infinitely more adequate to the results accomplished, because infinitely more honouring to the law of God, and a real living deal with that in the heart of the Father of spirits to which the law refers, is the moral and spiritual atonement of which the cross was the perfecting! Christ said to Pilate, "Thou couldest have no power at all against me, except it were given thee from above;" and this we know of all subordinate power, wherever present, for "power belongeth to God alone." Therefore has the power ascribed to the accuser of the brethren - our adversary the devil - been always, and rightly regarded, as what could only rest upon the fixedness of that moral constitution of things of which the law is the formal expression, and our rebellion against which had given him advantage over us. But the root of that constitution of things is the Fatherliness of the Father of our spirits: nothing, therefore, could truly honour that constitution which did not do due honour to that Fatherliness in which it has its root; while that Fatherliness in which it has its root; while that Fatherliness being duly honoured, the law must of necessity have been therein honoured, and with the highest honour.

While, therefore, that formal literal meeting of the demands of the law which men have seen in Christ has been to them the spoiling of the power of the devil, because it was a meeting of the law seen simply as the law: in the light in which we are now contemplating the work of redemption, it is the Son's dealing in humanity directly with the Fatherliness that is in God - and so dealing with the violation of the law in relation to the ultimate desire of the heart of the Father, who gave the law - by which we see ourselves, who were under the law, redeemed, that we might receive the adoption of sons; this true doing of the Father's will by the Son, and not a mere literal fulfilling of the law, being the spiritual might by which our captivity is seen to be led captive.

This deliverance wrought out for all humanity - the peace accomplished on the cross - is, in respect of its being *first* spiritual, and *then*, as a *consequence*, legal, in striking accordance with the order that is observed in our individual participation in it. "Verily, verily, I say unto you, He that heareth my word, and believeth on Him that sent me, hath everlasting life, and shall not come into condemnation; but is passed from death unto life." (John v. 24)

But to this order men do not easily conform. There is a state of mind in which it will be asked,

> If the relation of the atonement to our participation in the life of Christ be thus direct and immediate - if it be such as necessitates our giving a moral, a spiritual meaning, as distinguished from a mere legal meaning, to the expressions, "peace with God," "reconciliation with God," "propitiation for sin" - if the immediate and only natural reflection in seeing the pardon of our sins as the gospel reveals it, be, that we are free to draw near to God, to join in the services of the true sanctuary, and in the spirit of sonship to have communion with our heavenly Father - if Christ's suffering for us, the just for the unjust, thus simply suggest the purpose of bringing us to God - then is the gospel to us sinners the good news which it claims to be? The wrath of God has been revealed against all unrighteousness of men; we are sinners under condemnation - our first need is pardon, as a discharge from the sentence upon us. Granting that our true well-being is to be ultimately found in peace and reconciliation in the spiritual sense of the words, have we not at first need of peace and reconciliation in a

legal sense? Our fears of wrath may not be holy feelings, or what pertain to the divine life in man; but are they not natural, allowable, nay, right feelings in us sinners? And if they are, are they not to be taken account of and must not this be done in the first place?

I have said above that what of severity is in the moral governor of the universe has its root in the heart of the Father of spirits. We cannot therefore believe in an atonement that satisfies the heart of the Father - we cannot believe in blood shed for the remission of our sins, which has power to purge our spirits for that worship which is sonship - and yet be uncertain whether, partaking in the fruit of such an atonement, and joining in this worship, we are still exposed to the righteous wrath of God. If an atonement be adequate morally and spiritually, it will of necessity be legally adequate. If it be sufficient in relation to our receiving the adoption of sons, it must be sufficient for our redemption as under the law.

To think otherwise would be to subordinate the gospel to the law, and the love of the Father of spirits to His offspring to that moral government which has its origin in that love. We are not under the law, but under grace. Let us receive this gracious constitution of things in the light of the love that has ordained it. Let us understand that He was made sin for us who knew no sin, that we might be made the righteousness of God in Him. Let us conform to this purpose of God - let us receive the righteousness of God in Christ, and *be* the righteousness of God in Him - let us be reconciled to God and we shall find all questions as to our exposure to the wrath of God to have been fully taken into account in that divine counsel which we have welcomed, for we shall understand the experience of the Apostle - "Herein is our love made perfect, that we may have boldness in the day of judgment; because as He is, so are we in this world."

Surely Philip was right when he said, "Shew us the Father, and it *sufficeth us*." Surely we do not know to what we are listening when we are listening to the testimony of God concerning His Son, viz. that "God has given to us eternal life, and that this life is in His Son," if we can answer, "But if we receive this life to be our life, will that be enough for us; shall we not need something besides to save us from the wrath to come?" Oh, my brother, "there is no fear in love; but perfect love casteth out fear." If you are "reconciled to God by the death of His Son," how shall you not be "saved from wrath through Him?" It is, indeed, unbelievable - no man can believe - that receiving Christ as our life, we can feel that His blood does indeed cleanse from all sin, in relation to that worship of God which is in spirit and in truth; but that we cannot feel secure as engaged in this worship, unless that blood of Christ, under the power of which our spirits have come by faith, speak to our consciences of penal sufferings, endured for us, and so assure us that the law has no claim against us.

But the difficulty felt is not that of persons seeing the subject from this point of view. One once said to me, when urging on him the evidence of the universality of the atonement, in opposition to his own faith of an atonement for an election only - "Were I to believe that Christ died for all, it would destroy the peace which I have in the faith of the atonement, for this is my peace - He suffered, therefore, I shall not suffer." This was the same idea which we have seen urged on Arminians by Dr Owen, in that dilemma which appears unanswerable, on the assumption that the atonement was the enduring of penal suffering by Christ as our substitute. Yet, however inconsistently, and though not in the strong form - "He suffered, therefore I shall not suffer," - many feel as if they were less obnoxious to suffering, because of the penal suffering which they assume to have been endured by Christ even when their faith in the universality of the atonement necessarily qualifies their comfort from this source. I do not now recur to the inconsistency which Dr Owen has so well exposed, but will deal directly with the state of mind which desires, if it does not quite venture to cherish, the peace of saying, "He suffered, therefore I shall not suffer."

This state of mind only exists through not seeing our relation to God as a moral governor, in its true subordination to our relation to Him as the Father of our spirits. I have asked, "Can the moral governor remain unsatisfied if the Father of spirits is satisfied?" The converse of this question is, "Can the moral governor be satisfied while the Father of spirits is not?" To suppose that peace can ever be justifiable on the ground, "He suffered, therefore I shall not suffer," is to answer this question in the affirmative - it is to suppose that when Christ suffered, the just for the unjust, the *direct* end was that the unjust should not suffer.

Now, we cannot doubt the pain which the exposure of the unjust to suffering was to God, or the desire of His heart to save them from suffering; but we must not forget that the original reason for connecting sin and misery still continued, that that connection was not arbitrary, that the wrath of God revealed against all unrighteousness of men was not a feeling that has passed, or could pass away: no revelation of the unchanging God could. Therefore, when the just suffered for the unjust, it was with the direct purpose of bringing the unjust to God, - that is, bringing the unjust to the obedience of the just, *leaving the connection between suffering and injustice, or sin, undissolved, the righteousness of that connection being unchanged.*

Here we are met by another necessity, corresponding to that already dwelt on as declared in the words, "No man cometh unto the Father, but by me." But how could it be otherwise? If departure from the Father be the ultimate root evil, which it was righteousness - the righteousness of love - to visit with wrath, how should deliverance from wrath be experienced otherwise than in returning to the Father, or mercy to those who had departed take any other form than opening for them the way of return?

I have said that the atonement reconciles us to the spiritual necessities, the laws of the kingdom of God which it reveals. We should in our darkness be willing to lose the Father in the moral governor if we could think of the moral governor in a way that would permit to us the feeling of security under His government; and all the demand that we should make on the fatherliness of the Father of our spirits would be for such mercy as would qualify His moral government and modify it in accommodation to what we feel ourselves to be. But in the light of the atonement which reveals the Father to us in the Son we bless God that not our wishes in our darkness, but God's own fatherliness and our capacity of sonship have determined the nature of the grace extended to us. Nor would we now desire to see one terror that is connected with sin separated from it, or one token of the divine displeasure against it withdrawn. For Christ's sufferings have revealed to us the nature, and the depth, and the righteousness of God's wrath against sin - what our sins are to His heart, and what that mind in relation to sin is to which it is His sole desire in the matter to bring us, and which mind is His gift to us in Christ, in whom it is revealed. Therefore, the pardon of sin in any other sense than the revealing, and the opening to us of the path of life, is now to us as undesirable as, in relation to the moral government of the Father of spirits, it is inconceivable.

To some whose serious thoughts are occupied with the punishment of sin as an object of terror, rather than with the sin itself on which it is God's mark, this tone may seem high, and, it may be, even presumptuous, and in relation to themselves, unfeeling; more like the self-congratulation of the pharisee, than the humility of the publican, and sounding like self-righteousness, however it may be but that "giving of thanks at the remembrance of God's holiness" of which the Psalmist speaks. Others again, entirely occupied with their own newly-discovered and dimly apprehended exposure to divine wrath, will not venture to judge those on whom they look as more in the light of God than themselves, or to doubt that their professed sympathy in the mind of God towards sin, may be genuine, and consistent with humility, but they are still disposed to say, "Shew us something more suited to our present position, some ground of safety to rest upon - to trust to at once; and then teach us to worship, and direct us to the provision for doing so in spirit and in truth; for doubtless such worship belongs to Christianity."

As to the first of these states of mind, the misconstruction of confounding the righteousness of faith with self-righteousness is not strange to those who are the subjects of it; nor, as to the second, is the temptation to seek a ground of peace in relation to God's law - thinking only of the lawgiver, and not thinking of the Father of spirits, what any one can have difficulty in understanding, who knows how much religious earnestness exists which has no deeper root than the sense of our dependence on God as our sovereign

Lord, the judge of all the earth. But whether judging the spirits of those who preach the true gospel of peace to them, or withholding from judging, the feeling of awakened sinners "that the ground taken is too high for them," is altogether a misconception on their part. We beseech men by the meekness and gentleness of Christ; we are ambassadors for Him who would not break the bruised reed nor quench the smoking flax: but our word, the word which He has put into our mouth is, "Be ye reconciled to God."

Is this a hard saying, too high a demand to make on the awakened, self-condemned spirit? It is not made except in connection with that which God has done to make such a demand reasonable - yea hopeful, as addressed to the chief of sinners, viz. the peace for man in his relation to God which is in the blood of Christ: but in connection with this prepared and revealed peace it is made, and we may not change or modify this demand, or in any way accommodate ourselves to a state of mind in which alienation from God is not felt to be the great, the all-embracing evil of our state as sinners, and reconciliation to God the very first dawn of light, and breathing of the breath of a new life.

So that however awful our sense of all secondary evils that come in the train of men's alienation, or high our conception of the secondary good that will follow on their being reconciled to God, we must forbid all *direct* dealing with wrath and judgment as if these might be *first* disposed of, and *then* attention be turned to other considerations. We have here to do with PERSONS - the Father of spirits and His offspring. *These are to each other more than all things and all circumstances.* We know that the desire of the Father's heart is toward His offspring - that it goes forth to them directly - that it is not a simple mercy pitying their misery - that it seeks to possess them as dear children. We know that to be restored to Him, and to possess Him as their Father, is to these alienated children themselves not merely a great thing, but every thing. He, the Father, has done all towards their reconciliation in perfect fatherliness, and all the provisions of His love have been dictated, and have had their character determined by His fatherliness. They therefore must hear nothing, be occupied with nothing, but what pertains to their character as His offspring. They must see His grace as that outcoming of fatherliness, which it is - they must see its provisions for them as what belong to the adoption of sons which He contemplates for them.

And so they must hear the call addressed to them in the words, "Be ye reconciled to God," as not only a reasonable call in respect of the grace manifested, but as, indeed, the gracious invitation to the benefit of that grace - as equivalent to, "Be saved, receive salvation." As to wrath - terror - these they have not *directly* to do with; they are to think of them as connected with the region of distance from God, of alienation from God, back from which they are called: they will cease as to them in their being reconciled to God. They belong to that which is without: but the invitation to be reconciled to

God is the invitation to return and enter into their Father's house, into their Father's heart. This is what is put before them, freely, unconditionally. Does the word "unconditionally" cause difficulty? Is it said - "Is not to be *reconciled* to comply with a condition? Yes, such a condition as drinking of the water of life is in relation to living. Not in any other sense a condition - not assuredly as giving the right to drink, for that is the grace revealed, the grace wherein we stand. But as to wrath and safety from wrath, if questions arise it is a proof that what is presented is not understood. "He that believeth *shall not* come into condemnation, but *hath passed* from death unto life."

The peace-speaking power of the blood of Christ is to be conceived of as a direct power on the spirit in its personal relation to the Father of spirits, revealing at once the heart of the Father, and the way into the heart of the Father, even the Son. The blood that reveals this imparts peace, makes perfect as pertains to the conscience - yea, purges it from dead works to serve the living God. Indeed, that the relation of that blood to God's law, and the honour it rendered to that law, have had, as we have seen, a direct reference to our receiving the adoption of sons implies that it has not come directly between man and judgment, or taken him, by the fact of its being shed, from beneath the righteous rule of God; and, therefore, that it ministers no peace, being rejected - but, on the contrary, only a fearful looking for of judgment, so assuredly giving no place for the direct confidence, "He suffered, therefore I shall not suffer."

But, apart from the fact that the shedding of the blood of Christ had its direct reference to the perfecting of the conscience, and the reconciling us to God truly and spiritually as the Father of our spirits, is not the idea of a direct immunity from judgment, the idea of a ground of peace in the thought of judgment which may be contemplated by us as ours, so to speak, antecedent to our being reconciled - a legal reconciliation to be rested on antecedent to a spiritual reconciliation - inconsistent with giving our alienation from God its true place as the great evil and what must be directly dealt with? - And is there not, however terrible the thought, yet is there not in the very sense of gratitude for the mercy which is believed to be in such a direct deliverance from wrath to come, a source of delusion as to our true interest, our true well being? Does it not tend to confirm in us the tendency to lose the Father of our spirits in the moral governor, and so to misunderstand, as in that case we must do, the ends of His moral government? Does it not tend to smother in us the cry of the orphan spirit for its long lost Father? Does it not take from God the attribute that life lies in His favour - making Him important to us because of what He has to bestow, and not because of what He feels towards us viewed in itself, and as the feeling of the Father to His offspring?

Nor is there any room for feeling as if some lower ground should be taken at first, and in tenderness to newly awakened sinners. We cannot too soon present the Father to them. We cannot too soon lay their weakness on the everlasting arms of the Eternal Love. To furnish them, in accommodation to their darkness, with any ground of confidence towards God other than what the Son has revealed as the heart of the Father, would be to seal them in that darkness, and to counteract the end of that revelation.

No doubt the words, "No man cometh unto the Father but by me," which reveal that fixed constitution of things to which our vague hope of salvation must conform, or cease, were spoken to the chosen companions of our Lord's path, and towards the close of His personal ministry, but they express the manner of Gospel which had breathed from His life all along. And so those gracious words to all the weary and heavy laden - "Come unto me, and I will give you rest," are both spoken in immediate reference to what He had just declared, "No man knoweth the Father save the Son, and he to whomsoever the Son shall reveal Him," - clearly teaching that the promised rest would be found in knowledge of the Father; and, more, are followed by the clear intimation that in their participation of Himself as their life, participating in what He was, was the Son to be to men the channel of this rest-giving knowledge of the Father - "Take my yoke upon you, and learn of me; for I am meek and lowly in heart: and ye shall find rest unto your souls."

The nature of that hope which was in God for man, and which the atonement has brought within the reach of our spirits, has indeed been necessarily determined by our ultimate and primary relation to God as the Father of our spirits. And we must take all our preconceptions to this light, and more especially those thoughts of God as the moral governor of the universe, in which the divine fatherliness has been left out of account, and to which is to be referred men's listening to the gospel simply as those who were under the law, and not as God's offspring.

When the apostle argues, Gal. iii. 17, that "the covenant which was confirmed before of God in Christ, the law, which was four hundred and thirty years after, cannot disannul," he deals with the legalism with which he was contending on a principle which may guide us here. If we recognise in the words "by the deeds of the law shall no flesh living be justified," a reference to that universal law under which all men are, and in relation to which God has concluded both Jew and Gentile alike as all under sin; if we take this universal ground in teaching justification by faith, then must we in vindicating the superiority of the gospel ascend to our original relation to the Father of our spirits, whose law it is that we have broken, and see that gospel in the Father's heart - that promise for man - that hope abiding for man in God - which the law could not disannul.

Is it not thus that we are to understand the Apostle Peter when in the full light of redeeming love he says, "Wherefore let them that suffer according to the will of God commit the keeping of their souls to Him in well doing, as unto a faithful Creator?" We are justified in the ground we take in teaching justification by faith, only because in faith the hope which remained in God for man is apprehended, and, being apprehended, becomes in man a living hope towards God.

I formerly complained of a subordinating of the gospel to the law. I am now contending for the due subordinating of the law to the gospel. When the apostle says, "If there had been a law given which could have given life, verily righteousness should have been by the law," it seems to me that he is speaking in the light of the subordination of the law to the gospel, for he is recognising the *giving of life* as what *must be the end of God*; and therefore, that our being taken from under the law, and placed under grace, has been in order that we should be alive to God. Therefore righteousness would not have been by faith any more than by the deeds of the law, had it not been because of the life which in faith is quickened in us. "He that believeth hath passed from death unto life." It is in this view of faith that God the father of spirits is just in justifying the ungodly who believe. These words I have considered before; but, at the point at which we now stand, it seems to me that we are contemplating, as the justifying element in faith, not only *not* an imputation, but that which is the most *absolute opposite* of an imputation, viz. *life from the dead*.

Although the expression "justification by faith" be associated in our mind with all preaching of the atonement, the teaching of Luther is that alone of all the forms of thought on this subject considered above with which that expression really harmonises, for him alone have we found teaching that it is faith itself which God recognises as righteousness: and how excellent a manner of righteousness faith is in Luther's apprehension, and how righteous it is in God to count it righteousness, has been sufficiently illustrated, even by the quotations to which I have limited myself. In what he so writes, the words of the Apostle, "was strong in faith giving glory to God," are the text - the axiom I should rather say - from which Luther reasons. That condition of the human spirit in which most glory is given to God he regards as self-evidently the highest righteousness, and that condition is faith.

But the glory given to God in faith must be in proportion to the depth and fulness of the apprehension of what God is which faith embraces, and to which it responds. In proportion, therefore, as God is revealed by the atonement, and as, in consequence, he that believes is in the light of what God is, and by his faith trusts and glorifies God as He is, in that proportion is the righteousness faith enhanced and exalted. "No man hath seen God at any time. The only-begotten Son, who dwelleth in the bosom of the Father, He hath declared him." He that hath seen the Son hath seen the Father, and he who, seeing the Father in the revelation of Him by the Son, hath faith in Him as the Father, attains the highest form of faith - a faith which is the fellowship of the Son's apprehension of the Father - indeed, is sonship - and utters itself in the cry, Abba, Father. This is its nature; this, whatever its measure.

But, when the subject of justification by faith takes this form in our thoughts, we have no longer any difficulty in recognising faith as "the highest righteousness;" for how can we otherwise conceive of that which is the fellowship of Christ's own righteousness, the righteousness given to us in the gift of Christ, who is "made of God unto us wisdom, and righteousness, and sanctification, and redemption?"

I have intentionally kept before the reader's mind longer than was necessary for the simple expression of it, the distinction between contemplating the blood of Christ as shed with *direct* reference to the purging of our consciences from dead works to serve the living God, and contemplating it as shed with *direct* reference to our deliverance from the punishment of sin. In addition to the character of the whole Epistle to the Hebrews, as setting forth the well-being of man as standing in his being an accepted worshipper, and, therefore, the atonement for sin needed as the shedding of blood that would make perfect as pertains to the conscience, I may recall to the reader the relation to righteous judgment in which the typical and the antitypical shedding of blood are both represented in the words, "He that despised Moses' law died without mercy under two or three witnesses: of how much sorer punishment, suppose ye, shall he be thought worthy, who hath trodden underfoot the Son of God, and hath counted the blood of the covenant, wherewith he was sanctified, an unholy thing, and hath done despite unto the Spirit of grace?"

But in dwelling as I have done upon the distinction between a man's not coming into condemnation, because the blood of Christ is known by him as a living way into the holiest, and, through the faith of it, he has passed from death unto life; and a man's not coming into condemnation because the blood of Christ was shed for him, and the punishment of his sins borne by Christ - my great anxiety has been to get to the right point of view in considering man's well-being - that point from which God is seen as the fountain of life, in whose favour is life; and, therefore, the question of salvation is seen to be simply the question of participation in that favour as it is the outgoing of a living love, the love of the Father's heart, and not as the mere favourable sentence of a judge and ruler, setting the mind at ease in reference to the demands of the law of His moral government.

With this same purpose have I above entered as I have done into the questions connected with justification; and if I have appeared to forget, as I have not for a moment done, the distinction made between justification and sanctification, it is that I have hoped that the real spiritual truth that is in justification being once seen, the subject would take its right form in the mind of itself. That "righteousness" as a part of what Christ is said to be "made of God unto us," has come to be dealt with on a principle entirely distinct from that on which men have dealt with "wisdom," and "sanctification," and "redemption," has been owing to the exigencies of a legal system;

but such an error has been possible only because it has not been seen that these are all alike elements of the eternal life which we have in Christ. For Christ is all these to us just in that He is our life, nor otherwise than as living by Him are we "righteous" any more than we can otherwise be "wise," "holy," "redeemed," that is, free men - free with the liberty wherewith the Son of God maketh free.

Nothing, indeed, has done more to confirm the mind in that tendency to seek in the atonement what will come *directly* between us and the punishment of sin, instead of seeking in it the secret and the power of returning to God - recognising sin and all misery as what are together left behind in returning to God - than the distinction made between justification and sanctification, when justification is connected with a demand in the mind of our judge which may be met in an arbitrary way as by imputation or imagined transferred fruits of righteousness, while sanctification is recognised as having its necessity in the truth of things, in that without holiness no man shall see God; as if righteousness in man had no such relation to righteousness in God, as holiness in man has to holiness in God.

As to the supposed necessity for God's imputing righteousness that He may see us as perfectly righteous, why must our participation in Christ's righteousness be the meeting of a demand for perfection, any more than our participation in His holiness, or His wisdom or the freedom that is in Him? All is perfect in Him, and He and His perfection belong to us; but all in the same sense. But, when the righteousness contemplated is understood to be the righteousness of faith, faith in the Father's heart as revealed by the Son - of the faith, therefore, by which the life of sonship is quickened and sustained - this demand for a legal perfection is seen to be altogether foreign to that with which we are occupied. The feeblest cry of the spirit of sonship is sure of a response in the Father's heart, being welcome from its own very nature, as well as for that of which it is the promise, as it is also the fruit; for it both comes from and grows into the perfect sonship which is in Christ. Confidence is of the essence of this cry - hope in the fatherliness towards which is its outgoing.

Reader, say, does it not jar with this cry, does it not mar its simplicity, its truth, to be required to pause and say, "I would cry to my Father, I see His heart towards me - the Son reveals it; but I must remember that to be justified in drawing near with confidence I must think of myself as clothed by imputation with a perfect righteousness, because the Father of my spirit must see me as so clothed in order that He may be justified in receiving me to His fatherly heart?" Would not this thought mar the simplicity of the child's cry - would it not indeed altogether change the essence of the confidence cherished? But the thought of the righteousness which God has accepted in accepting Christ, the righteousness to which the words, "This is my beloved Son, in whom I am well pleased, hear ye Him," turn the mind, altogether encourages the child's cry in us - indeed, is its source; for to cherish, to utter that cry, is the spiritual obedience of the word, "hear ye Him." But I almost repeat what I said before. Only I hope that in that light of the elements of the atonement in which justification is now before us, the oneness of the confidence which the faith of Christ's work quickens in us with the confidence in which He went before us in that path of life which He has opened up for us, and which He Himself is to us, will be more clearly recognised.

I have now asked, why should the divine demand for righteousness in men, which God has Himself met and provided for by the gift of Christ, giving us in Him all things pertaining to life and to godliness, making us complete in Him - why should this demand of the divine mind for righteousness be seen as met on another principle than that on which the demand for holiness is met? All these demands are truly, fully met. Christ came not to destroy the law but to fulfil. But if in connection with all that varied perfection in humanity which is in the Son of God, all humanity may be dealt with, and is dealt with, by God, the preciousness of that perfection shedding its own glory over all humanity, and being ever to the heart of a Father a promise for all humanity, and if the heart of the Father waits in hope for our "growing up into Him in all things, which is the head even Christ," (Ephesians iv. 15), why should a fiction be introduced to give a character of perfection to our individual righteousness before God which has no place in relation to our part in the other elements of the perfection that is in Christ?

I have already expressed my conviction that that in us which in full light welcomes this ordination of a kingdom in the hands of a mediator, is what has, in part at least, made the reception of this doctrine of the imputation of Christ's perfection to those who believe, possible.

But in the light of the atonement the heart feels no need of any fiction for its peace. The confidence in the Father, which the revelation of the Father by the Son quickens, has its witness in itself - its sanction in its own nature. Its spiritual relation to that in God towards which it goes forth justifies it to the conscience.

For, in truth, it is but the due response to the Father testifying to us that He has given to us eternal life in the Son - that testimony of God in the spirit, which being heard by us in the spirit effectually calls us to the confidence of sonship. Therefore does one Apostle say, "if our hearts condemn us not, then have we confidence towards God," and another Apostle, "the Spirit beareth witness with our spirit that we are the sons of God." And such expressions accord with what I have urged above, viz. that our knowledge that we are justified should be of the same spiritual nature with the true knowledge that we are sinners, and not be sought in that way of inference from the fact that we believe combined with the doctrine that those that believe are justified, to which men have had recourse and on which, indeed, they have necessarily been thrown when artificial conceptions of justification by faith have been adopted.

That nothing artificial, but something the deep reality of which is proved in the consciousness of the individual justified, is contemplated in the beginning of the 8th chapter of the Epistle to the Romans, it is impossible to doubt. The misery recorded in the close of the 7th chapter is not more real, more a matter of consciousness, than the salvation for which thanks are rendered; nor is the law of sin in the members causing that misery more a thing known by the individual than "the law of the Spirit of life in Christ, which makes free from the law of sin and death." Therefore, the freedom from condemnation, in other words, the justification through being in Christ Jesus, spoken of, is clearly one with that cleansing by the blood of Christ, that purging of the conscience, on which I have dwelt so much; nor can it be at all separated from that "fulfilment of the righteousness of the law" in those "who walk not after the flesh, but after the Spirit," which the Apostle goes on to mention as the direct end which God has contemplated in sending His Son in the likeness of sinful flesh, and as a sacrifice for sin, and so condemning sin in the flesh. The *subjective* character of this passage - that is to say, the relation between freedom from condemnation and the condition of a man's own spirit which it recognises - and the place which it ascribes to the law of the Spirit of the life that is in Christ in connection with this freedom, that is in connection with justification, is too broadly marked to permit its being quoted in favour of the doctrine of justification by an imputation of righteousness.

But the conditions of true peace of conscience must always be the same; and therefore, although the first verse of the fifth chapter is so quoted, we must believe that that in Christ in respect of which thanks are rendered that "there is no condemnation to them who are in Christ Jesus," is present to the mind of the Apostle when he speaks of "peace with God through our Lord Jesus Christ" in connection with "being justified by faith."

This language, indeed, occurs in immediate connection with that reference to the glory given to God in the faith of Abraham which sheds such clear light on the righteousness of God in recognising *faith* as *righteousness:* while, in saying that faith shall be imputed to us for righteousness, "if we believe on Him that raised up our Lord Jesus from the dead, who was delivered for our offences, and raised again for our justification," the Apostle has brought before us *that* in God which the faith by which we are to glorify God must apprehend and trust. For faith, in trusting God, does so in response to that mind of God in relation to man which is revealed to us in our being embraced in Christ's expiatory confession of our sins, when, by the grace of God, He tasted death for every man, and in that perfect righteousness of sonship in humanity which Christ presented to the Father on behalf of all humanity as the true righteousness of man, and, which, in raising Him from the dead, the Father has sealed to us as our true righteousness. This gracious mind of God in relation to us it is that our faith accepts and responds to; for our faith is, in truth, the Amen of our individual spirits to that deep, multiform, all-embracing, harmonious Amen of humanity, in the person of the Son of God, to the mind and heart of the Father in relation to man - the divine wrath and the divine mercy, which is the atonement.

This Amen of the individual, in which faith utters itself towards God, gives glory to God according to the glory which he has in Christ; therefore does faith justify: and this justification is not only pronounced in the mind of God, who accepts the confidence towards Himself, which the faith of His grace in Christ has quickened in us, imputing it to us as righteousness, but is also testified to by the Spirit of truth in the conscience of him in whom this Amen is a living voice - a spiritual mind - the fellowship of that mind in the Son of God by the faith of which it is quickened. The Amen of the individual human spirit to the Amen of the Son to the mind of the Father in relation to man, is saving faith - true righteousness; being the living action, and true and right movement of the spirit of the individual man in the light of eternal life. And the certainty that God has accepted that perfect and divine Amen as uttered by Christ in humanity is necessarily accompanied by the peaceful assurance that in uttering, in whatever feebleness, a true Amen to that high Amen, the individual who is yielding himself to the spirit of Christ to have it uttered in him is accepted of God.

This Amen in man is the due response to that word, "Be ye reconciled to God;" for the gracious and gospel character of which word, as the tenderest pleading that can be addressed to the most sin-burdened spirit, I have contended above. This Amen is sonship; for the gospel-call, "Be ye reconciled to God," when heard in the light of the knowledge that "God made Him to be sin for us who knew no sin, that we might be made the righteousness of God in Him," is understood to be the call to each one of us on the part of the Father of our spirits, "My son, give me thine heart," addressed to us on the ground of that work by which the Son has declared the Father's Name that the love wherewith the Father hath loved Him may be in us, and He in us. In the light itself of that Amen to the mind of the Father in relation to man which shines to us in the atonement, we see the *righteousness of God in accepting the atonement*, and in that same light the Amen of the individual human spirit to that divine Amen of the individual human spirit to that divine Amen of the Son of God, is seen to be what the divine righteousness will necessarily acknowledge as the *end of the atonement accomplished*.

I have illustrated above the distinction between the righteousness of faith and self-righteousness, and the way in which faith excludes boasting, while introducing us into the light of God's favour, and have anticipated what would have been urged with advantage here as the justification of God in accounting faith righteousness. I only add now, that, as in illustrating the elements of the atonement, I have desired that the reader should see by its own light the suitableness and adequacy of the moral and spiritual expiation for sin which Christ has made, and should see all such expressions as "A way into the holiest," - "Propitiation," - "Reconciliation," - "Peace with God," - in that light of our spiritual relation to the Father of our spirits which demands for them a spiritual, as distinguished from a mere legal meaning; so, now I have sought for "Justification by faith" a spiritual and self-evidencing character, and that the attitude towards God of a human spirit in the light of that will of God which the Son of God came to do and has done cherishing a confidence towards God in harmony with that light shall be felt to be the right attitude towards God of spirit of man - that in which are combined God's glory in man and man's salvation in God.

I have sought for justification by faith this self-evidencing character, not fearing by this to open the door for a self-righteous and presumptuous confidence - believing that the true confidence alone can preclude the false in all its measures and forms. The Amen of faith - the being reconciled to God - peace with God through our Lord Jesus Christ - these, in meekness and lowliness, are known in the light of the atonement. For that light of eternal life harmonises us with itself and so with God; and in it it is impossible to trust in self - impossible not to trust in God - impossible to doubt that this trust in God is true righteousness - impossible to doubt that God is just in being the justifier of him that believeth in Jesus.

CHAPTER IX

THE INTERCESSION WHICH WAS AN ELEMENT IN THE ATONEMENT CONSIDERED AS PRAYER

In recognising at the outset a need-be for the atonement I sought to separate between what is sound and true in the feelings of awakened sinners and what is to be referred to their remaining spiritual darkness. At the same time I have desired that we should be in the position of learning from the atonement itself why it was needed, as well as how it has accomplished that for which it was needed.

The error which in its grossest form has amounted to representing the Son as by the atonement exercising an influence over the Father to make Him gracious towards us, (but which, even when such a thought as this would be disclaimed, has still led to seeking in the atonement a ground of confidence towards God distinct from what it has revealed as the mind of God towards man), has become very manifest in the light of the nature of the atonement as a fulfilling of the purpose of the Son "Lo, I come to do thy will, O God," - His "declaring of the Father's Name." In the light of that will as fulfilled - that Name as declared, our faith has been raised to the Eternal Will itself thus revealed, to the Unchanging name thus declared: as the Apostle speaks of those that believe in Christ as those "who by Him do believe in God, who raised Him from the dead, and gave Him glory; that our faith and hope might be in God." (1 Peter i. 21)

Yet it seems to me that in this high spiritual region some of the difficulties which we experience in all our deeper meditations on the ways of God are more realised when we are fully delivered from the error to which I have now referred than they were before. I say this, contemplating especially the aspect of the atonement as a dealing of the Son with the Father on our behalf - a mediation, an intercession. I have spoken of the nature and ground of this intercession, of its combination with the confession of our sins and of its relation to our Lord's own consciousness in humanity - His experience of sonship in humanity - His experience of abiding in humanity in the Father's favour. But a more close consideration of what is implied in intercession as intercession seems called for - a more close consideration, that is, of the hope for man in which the Son of God made His soul an offering for sin, as that hope was a hope in God, sustained by faith and prayer.

We are so much in the way of looking on the work of Christ as the acting out of a pre-arranged plan, that its character as a natural progress and development, in which one thing arises out of another, and is really caused by that other, is with difficulty realised. Yet we must get deliverance from this temptation - the painful temptation to think of Christ's work as almost a scenic representation - otherwise we never can have the consciousness of getting the true knowledge of eternal realities from the atonement. All light of life for us disappears from the life of Christ unless that life be to us a life indeed, and not the mere acting of an assigned part.

Unless we realise that in very truth Christ loved us as He did Himself, we cannot understand how near an approach to a personal feeling there has been in His feeling of our sins, and of our misery as sinners. Unless we realise that His love to Himself and to us was the love of one who loved the Father with all His heart, and mind, and soul, and strength, we cannot understand the nature of the burden which our sins were to Him, what it was to His heart that we were to the Father rebellious children, or how certainly nothing could satisfy His heart as a redemption for us, but that we should come to follow God as dear children in the fellowship of His own sonship. Unless we contemplate His sense of our sin and His desire to accomplish for us this great salvation as lovingly working in Him and practically influencing Him, we cannot understand how truly He made His soul an offering for sin, when, receiving into Himself the full sense of the divine condemnation of sin, He dealt on behalf of man with the ultimate and absolute root of judgment in God, presenting the expiation of the due confession of sin, and in so doing at once opening for the divine forgiveness a channel in which it could freely flow to us - and for us a way in which we could approach God.

And, finally, unless we apprehend the encouraging considerations by which the love of Christ was sustained in making this expiatory offering - unless we have present to our minds His faith in the deep yearnings of the Father's heart over men His offspring, joined with His own conscious experience in humanity which testified that these yearnings could be satisfied - unless we conceive to ourselves how naturally and necessarily these thoughts took the form of prayer, laying hold of that hope for man which was in God - unless, as it were, we hear the intercession thus made for man, and see the grounds on which it proceeds, we cannot understand what is made known to us of the Name of God by the success of this pleading on our behalf - we cannot see how this appeal to the heart of the Father becomes, in being responded to, the full revelation of the Father to us; and that in proportion as we apprehended the nature and grounds of that intercession, and realise that it has been perfectly responded to, we know the grace wherein we stand, what that faith in God is to which we are called, what the grounds are on which we are to put out trust in Him. Faith must make us present to the work of our redemption in its progress as well as in its result, so that the love which is working for us - the difficulties which that love encounters - the way in which it deals with them - the salvation which it accomplishes - all may shed their light on our spirits and be to us the light of life.

But the faith that makes this history a reality to our spirits, while difficult as to every part of this realisation, is most difficult when we are occupied with that intercession of Christ which is the perfecting element in the atonement - making it literally an offering. It is not so difficult to realize how to the perfect holiness and love which were in Christ our sins should be so heavy a burden - nor is it difficult to realise His intercourse with the Father while He bore our sins on His spirit as that response to the Father's mind concerning them which has now been represented as an expiatory confession of our guilt. We also easily see how the Saviour's own conscious experience in humanity, doing His Father's commandments, and abiding in His love, would both determine the character of the redemption which He would seek for us and be an element in His hope towards God for us - a hope which He would cherish in conscious oneness with His Father.

But when we consider Christ's hope for man as taking the form of intercession, and see that His knowledge of the Father's will is so far from suggesting an inactive waiting in the expectation that all will necessarily be as the Father wills, that on the contrary, that knowledge only moves to earnest pleading and entreaty - the hope cherished seeking to realise itself by laying hold in a way of prayerful trust on that in the heart of the Father by which it is encouraged - then the difficulty that always haunts us as to the ordinance of prayer - the difficulty, I mean, of the idea of God's interposing prayer between His own loving desire for us and the fulfilment of that desire instead of fulfilling that desire without waiting to be entreated - this difficulty is felt to be present with our minds in this highest region in which the Son is represented as by prayer, and intense and earnest and agonising prayer, obtaining for us from the Father what the Father has infinitely desired to give - what He has given in giving Him to us as our Redeemer to whose intercession it is yielded. Here we have the divine love in Christ pleading with the divine love in the Father, and thus obtaining for us that eternal life, which yet in giving the Son to be our Saviour the Father is truly said to have given. The difficulty is that which haunts us in our own prayers; but it is the same, and no other: and if we are enabled to deal rightly with it as it meets us here it will be an increase of practical freedom to us in our individual walk with God.

What I have now been attempting has been to see and trace the atonement by its own light, viz. the light of the life which was taking form in it according to the words, "In Him was life, and the life was the light of men." Proceeding in this way the intercession of Christ has presented itself as a form which His love must naturally take. That it would take the form of *desiring* for us what His intercession asked for us was quite clear. But we could not conceive of that desire as cherished in conscious weakness and dependence on the Father and yet in conscious oneness with the Father, without conceiving of it *as uttering itself to the Father in prayer*. With all the weight of all our need upon His spirit - bearing our burden - that He should cast this burden upon the Father appeared the perfection of sonship towards the Father and brotherhood towards us. And as this intercession seemed a natural form for the love of Christ to take, so did it seem what must be to the Father a sacrifice of a sweet-smelling savour; and we felt that no aspect of the perfect sonship in humanity which the life of Christ presented to the Father could be more welcome to the heart of the Father than that of love to men, His brethren, as thus perfected in intercession; especially as being intercession for brethren who also were enemies, making the intercession to be the perfection of forgiving love.

This indeed was to God, who is love, a sacrifice of a sweet-smelling savour from humanity which must have been infinitely grateful in itself; while as part of the perfection that was in Christ this intercession was a most excellent part of that promise for humanity in respect of which Christ's perfection is to be contemplated as pleading for humanity. Any father who has ever been privileged to have one child pleading for forgiveness to another child for an offence which has been unkindness to the interceding child himself has here some help to his faith in his own experience.

But though all this is felt by us to be natural and what arises out of the life of love which was in Christ, yet, approaching it not by this path but by the path of meditation on Christ as the gift of the Father - meditation on all that interest in us which Christ's love is feeling, and under the power of which it is interceding, as already in the Father and already desiring to impart all that Christ is asking for us - nay, as having really bestowed it in the gift of Christ - the difficulty of which I have spoken suggests itself. We ask, how Christ should have felt it necessary?

A Christian philosopher of our own time has said that whereas once he had thought of prayer as the expression of a want of faith in God's goodness he afterwards came to understand that prayer was the highest expression of faith in God's goodness. Assuredly He who came to make known the goodness of God and that towards us men it is the highest form of goodness, even fatherliness, which on a superficial view might seem most to supersede all prayer - leaving room only for thanksgiving and praise - has been as distinguished by the depth and intensity of His praying to the Father as of His faith in the Father's fatherliness: nor is there any part of His testimony for the Father as He was the witness for God more marked than His testimony that God is the hearer and answerer of prayer. In Him we see that knowledge of the Father's will and confidence in His love supersede not prayer, but, on the contrary, only move to prayer, giving strength for it - making it the prayer of faith and hope and love - love perfected in thus flowing back to its own fountain.

The fact of Christ's "intercession for the transgressors" accords with and confirms what we feel in meditating on the life of love that was in Him, viz.

that such intercession was the fitting form for His bearing of our burdens to take, what in the light of the knowledge of the hope that was for us in God it must take; while to give place to the thought of anything dramatic - the acting out of a pre-arranged part - in regard to that recorded intercession, (and the intercession indicated is infinitely beyond what is recorded), would be to lose all sense of life and reality in Christ.

But let us try to approach this great and fundamental fact in the history of our redemption really from God's side. Let us try to realise what we are contemplating when we are rising to the contemplation of that hope for man which was in God antecedent to the atonement, and which the atonement has brought within the reach of our spirits. Let us see the love that man needs as in God before it has come forth in the atonement. Let us see the Fatherly heart as yet unrevealed - waiting to be revealed. Let us contemplate the Son as coming forth to reveal it. Let us distinguish between the purpose to reveal the Father's heart and a purpose to realise any predetermined train of events. Let us see, as that which is to be brought to pass, not certain facts, events, or circumstances thought of merely as such, but a knowledge of the heart of the Father brought within reach of us His offspring - destroyed by the lack of this knowledge but to whom this knowledge will be salvation. Let us consider in this view the Son of God in humanity bearing upon His spirit our burden, and dealing with the Father concerning it; let us see all our need made visible to us in Christ's feeling of it, and let us listen to the cry of this need as ascending to the Father from Christ addressing itself to what the Father feels in relation to that need, and let us ask ourselves how but as the answer to that cry could that in the Father which answers that cry have been made known, or our need and that in the Father which meets our need have been revealed to us together?

It is the cry of the child that reveals the mother's heart. It is the cry of sonship in humanity bearing the burden of humanity, confessing its sin, asking for it the good of which the capacity still remained to it, which being responded to by the Father has revealed the Father's heart. Without taking the form of that cry the mind that was in Christ would have failed by all its other outgoings to declare the Father's name.

There is nothing scenic or dramatic in this. Were such its nature it would be valueless. It would be nothing, and could reveal nothing. But no feeling in the Son, no desire, no prayer, is other than what is natural and inevitable to holy love so placed. The response of the Father is in like manner a real response, and therefore the nature and character of the heart that responds is seen in the nature and character of that to which it responds. As that confession of man's sin is justly due, so the demand for it in God is real as well as His acceptance of it is gracious. As that intercession is a natural form of love in Him that intercedes, the response to that intercession is a natural form for the love addressed to take - its living and real outcoming.

To say that what ascends to God from humanity has come from God, that God has Himself in the person of the Son furnished humanity with the pleading that would prevail with Him, that the life of sonship is already in humanity antecedent to the atonement which it makes - this in no way affects the truth of the atonement as indeed the due and true expiation for sin, nor the truth of the grounds of the Intercessor's pleading as really the grounds on which the grace of God is extended to men.

We may indeed go further back: we may contemplate the mere capacity of redemption that was in humanity as a cry - a mute cry, but which still entered into the ear and heart of God; we may contemplate the gift of Christ as the divine answer to this cry; but it is not the less true that when Christ under our burden and working out our redemption confesses before the Father the sin of man and presents to the Father His own righteousness as the divine righteousness for man, and the Father in response grants to men remission of sins and eternal life - that confession which humanity could not have originated but which the Son of God has made in it and for it, and that righteousness which humanity could not itself present, but which the Son of God has presented in it and for it, are the grounds on which God really puts His own acting in the whole history of redemption.

It is the tendency to deal with God as a fate and with the accomplishment of the high designs of His grace for man simply as the coming to pass of predetermined events which is the real source of our difficulty in regard to prayer as a law and power in the kingdom of God; whether we think of it contemplating its place in the history of our redemption as the intercession of Christ, or as an element in our own life of sonship through Christ. In consequence of that tendency, "asking things according to the will of God" comes to sound like asking God to do what He intended to do - a manner of prayer for which we have no light - as it is a manner of prayer, indeed, which would be felt to be superseded by that very light as to the future which would make it possible.

But God is not revealed to our faith as a fate, neither is His will set before us as a decree of destiny. God is revealed to us as the living God, and His will as the desire and choice of a living heart, which presents to us not the image or picture of a predetermined course of events to the predestined flow of which our prayer is to be an Amen, but a moral and spiritual choice in relation to us His offspring to which our prayer is to respond in what will be in us the cry of a moral and spiritual choice. That knowledge of the Father which the prayer of Christ implied - the knowledge of the Son who dwelleth in the bosom of the Father - was not the knowledge of a certain future, predestined and sure to be accomplished, but was the knowledge of the unchanging will of the Father concerning man - a will which in all rebellion is resisted, in all obedience of love is fulfilled. If we are able to see and realise this distinction we shall see the dealing of the Son with the Father on our behalf as that response to the mind of the Father in relation to us which in our participation in the spirit of the Son is to be continued and perpetuated in our own prayers.

And, it seems to me, that these things mutually illustrate each other to us; I mean our own prayers in the spirit of sonship and the great original intercession of the Son on behalf of all humanity which was to spread itself through humanity and which we partake in as a part of the eternal life which we have in the Son of God. For that cry for things according to the Father's will - that cry for holiness, and truth, and love, which is the cry of Christ's spirit in us, and which is not repressed or discouraged by the knowledge that it is according to the will of God, as if therefore it was superfluous, nay, is only quickened and sustained by that knowledge, may throw light to us upon the infinite intensity of that cry as in Christ on behalf of all humanity - enabling us to understand that in Him it was infinitely intense just because of His perfect oneness of mind with the Father in regard to what He asked, and perfect knowledge of that will of the Father according to which the cry was. While, on the other hand, nothing is such a help against all temptation to deal with the living God as with a fate, and with His will as a decree which we are passively to allow to take its course, instead of putting forth that prayerful trust which is the necessary link between His will for us and its fulfilment in us, as the believing meditation of the place which prayer had in the work of Christ in accomplishing our redemption.

And it is not merely in order that we may not come short in our realisation of the large place which prayer must have in our personal religion, if when we attempt to follow God as dear children we would really walk in the footsteps of the Son of God, that it is so important that we should realise the part which the intercession of Christ has in the atonement. Our doing so is, I would venture to say, even more needed in reference to the *nature* of our prayers, and that we may be found really praying *according to the will of God* - according to the light of the gospel - according to the knowledge that the true worshippers worship in spirit and in truth, for that the Father seeketh such to worship Him. Small as the amount of prayer is, its usual character is a still sadder subject of thought than its small amount. I mean its being so much a dealing with God simply as a Sovereign Lord, a Governor, and Judge, and so little a dealing with Him as the Father of our spirits.

There is much feeling that "power belongeth to God alone" combined with the encouraging persuasion that "to Him also belongeth mercy" moving to prayer and sustaining prayer, which yet is not enlightened and exalted by the knowledge of God as a Father, and the apprehension of our true well-being as all embraced in the sonship which we have in Christ. Reader, let me ask you, do you pray as a child of God whose first and nearest relationship is to God your Father, whose most deeply felt interests are bound up in that relation in what lies within the circle of that relation contemplated in itself? Do you pray as one to whom the mind of God towards you and your own mind towards Him are the most important elements of existence, and whose other interests in existence are as outer circles around this central interest - so that you see yourself, and your family, and your friends, and your country, and your race, with the eyes, because with the heart, of one who "loves the Lord his God with all his heart, and mind, and soul, and strength?"

Is this at least your ideal for yourself, what you are seeking to realise - to realise for its own sake, not for any consequences of it in time or eternity? For whatever the blessed consequences of its realisation will be, they shall be far, and for ever, inferior and secondary to itself.

CHAPTER X

THE ATONEMENT, AS ILLUSTRATED BY THE DETAILS OF THE SACRED NARRATIVE

Regarding the atonement as the development of the life that was in Christ I have now considered its nature in the light of that life - and the unity of a life has, I trust, been felt to belong to the exposition offered. But the life of Christ had an external history and took an outward form from the successive circumstances in which our Lord was placed, from the manger to the cross, according to the divine ordering of His path. And while the history can only be understood in the light of that inward life of which it has been the outward form, the contemplation of the outward form must help our understanding of the inward life; and if the view taken of the nature of the atonement be the true view must both confirm it and illustrate it.

We are thus prepared to find the outward course of life appointed for the Son of God as that in which He was to fulfil the purpose of doing the Father's will determined by the divine wisdom with special reference to that purpose. Another condition, also, we expect to find fulfilled in the circumstances in which the Son is seen witnessing for the Father, viz. that they shall accord with the testimony of the Father to the Son. The witnessing of the Son for the Father would have manifestly been incomplete as to us without the Father's seal to it. But this sealing was an essential part of the divine counsel - not only that outward testimony, however solemn and authoritative, which was in the words of the angel to Mary, the voice from heaven at the Lord's baptism by John, and again on the mount, but that also to which these special testimonies of the Father to the Son in humanity direct our minds, viz. that testimony of the Father to the Son in the Spirit which *always is*, and out of which all responsibility for faith in the Son of God arises, being that on which such faith must ultimately rest.

With this testimony of the Father to the Son, as well as with the witnessing of the Son for the Father, the divine ordering of our Lord's path would necessarily accord; so that, although the aspect of that path, judged according to the flesh, might seem in contradiction to the words, "This is my beloved Son, in whom I am well pleased," seen in the light of God it would be known to harmonise with that acknowledgment. What would accord with the Father's testimony to the Son must manifestly be one with what would accord with the Son's honouring of the Father in our sight; so that we have not really here two conditions to be fulfilled, but one only; nor does the need-be that there should be fitting scope for the manifestation of brother-hood in relation to men, add any new element, seeing the unity of sonship towards God and brotherhood towards men. But it is important that we approach the consideration of the course of our Lord's life, realising that we are to contemplate it in relation equally to the Father's acknowledgment of the Son, and to the Son's witnessing for the Father - "No man knoweth who the Son is, but the Father; and who the Father is, but the Son, and he to whom the Son will reveal Him."

This, therefore, is the aspect in which we are to contemplate the actual history of the work of redemption. We are to contemplate it as the Son's witnessing for the Father by the manifestation of sonship towards God and brotherhood towards men, in circumstances which divine wisdom ordained with reference to the perfection of that manifestation, and which we are to see in the light of the Father's testimony to the Son.

As our Lord "increased in wisdom and stature," so the elements of the atonement gradually developed themselves with the gradual development of His humanity, and corresponding development of the eternal life in His humanity. The sonship in Him was always perfect sonship. At no one moment could He have said more truly than at another, "The Son doeth nothing of Himself; but whatsoever things the Father doeth, the same doeth the Son likewise." But submitting at once, both to the Father's inward guidance, "opening His ear as the learner, morning by morning," and to His outward guidance, "not hiding His face from shame and spitting," Christ's inward life of love to His Father and love to His brethren was constantly acted upon by the circumstances appointed for Him, receiving its perfect development through them: so that, tracing our Lord's life as thus a visible contact with men while an invisible abiding in the bosom of the Father, and endeavouring to realise the bearing and operation of outward things upon His inward life, we may expect the light of the atonement to shine forth to us with increased clearness, as the light of that life which is the light of men.

We are not told much of the course of our Lord's life before He entered on His public ministry; we may say we have its general character in the words, He "increased in wisdom and stature, *and in favour with God and man*. His doing the Father's will, His following God as a dear child, had then that attraction in the eyes of men which goodness often has while it commends itself to men's consciences without making any positive demand upon themselves. And this record concerning our Lord - that at this time, and while His life was to men's eyes the simple filling of His place in relation to Joseph and Mary, and His kindred and neighbours, according to the perfect form of childhood and youth in a young Hebrew, He had the acknowledgment of human favour - should put as on our guard against hastily concluding that the favour of men may not even now, in certain circumstances, follow the favour of God.

When, however, our Lord entered on His public ministry, and the words which He spake and the miracles which He wrought constrained men to attend to and consider the demand which He made for His Father, and the condemnation on men which the righteous demand implied - we see the darkness soon disturbed by the light, and beginning to manifest its enmity to the light. Yet neither was this universal - and not only did some attach themselves to Him as immediate disciples and followers, but many more rejoiced in His teaching; and the response which His testimony had in their hearts commanded an outward acknowledgment of Him, which indeed was so general and so strong, that those in whom enmity was most moved were restrained as to the manifestation of their ill will by "the fear of the people."

How superficial the hearing was with which the great multitudes that followed Him listened to His words, we know, both from His own care to warn them of the cost of discipleship (Luke xiv. 25-33) which He saw they were not counting, and from the subsequent history of that favour, when the cry "Hosanna to the Son of David" so soon gave place to the cry, "Crucify Him, crucify Him." But doubtless between those who, as Peter says of himself and the rest, "forsook all and followed Him," and those who early set themselves against Him, knowing that His word condemned them, and that the acceptance of His teaching with the people would be the subverting of their own consequence and influence, there were many shades of feeling - the internal witness in men's hearts to the outward word of Him who spake as never man spake, being dealt with in many different measures of reverence and rebellion.

On the whole, however for a time, the power of evil came forth but in measure; and though He could early say, "I honour my Father, and ye do dishonour me," and though so much of even what was of another character was to Him who knew what was in man but a shew of good which did not deceive Him, yet it was but gradually and towards the close that He had to taste in all its bitterness that enmity to God to which He was exposing Himself in coming to men in His Father's name. The public ministry of the Lord, with its mixed character of favour and dishonour, of loud acclamations of those who at the least believed Him to be a teacher sent from God, and secret machinations of enemies whose malice could not calculate enough on sympathy to make its expression safe, was ordered of God to continue for a time; and "no man could lay hands on Him for His hour was not yet come."

It was however but a brief time, much briefer than the previous period of private life in which the favour of men was conjoined with the favour of God; and it was followed by another distinctly marked period, of which the character is the patient endurance of all the full and perfected development of the enmity which the faithfulness of the previous testimony for the Father's name had awakened. This last is much the briefest division of our Lord's life on earth; and its darkest portion is to be measured by days, or rather by hours: as if He who spared not His own Son, but gave Him to the death for us, yet spared Him as much as possible, making the bitterest portion the briefest.

We cannot doubt the importance of that portion of the fulfilment of the purpose, "Lo I come to do thy will," which constitutes the private life of our Lord, antecedent to His entering upon His public ministry. The scantiness of the record is no reason for doing so. We know how that scantiness has been attempted to be compensated for by fictitious narratives, intended to meet the natural desire to know more of what was so large a proportion of our Lord's whole life on earth.

But this has been a part of the error of not seeing that *that life itself as it abides in Him who lived it* and *not the mere written record* of that life is our unsearchable riches which we have in Christ. When the promise is fulfilled to us, that the Comforter would take of that which is Christ's, and shew it unto us, this acting of the Comforter is not limited to what is recorded. He takes from the treasures of wisdom and knowledge, stored up for all humanity in the humanity of the Son of God - revealing the life of Him who "was in all points tempted like as we are, yet without sin," in its relation to our individual need, with that minuteness of application of which that life, thus revealed to us in the Spirit, is capable, but of which no written record could be capable.

How many a little child, remembering that Jesus was once a little child, and grew in wisdom, and in stature, and in favour with God and man, and looking to Him for help according to the need felt in seeking to follow God as a dear child, and be in obedience to those related to him as Joseph and Mary were to the child Jesus, has found his trust met, and felt no want of "a gospel of the infancy of Jesus." Let the divine favour, testified as resting upon that first portion of our Lord's life, sanctify to our hopes private life - the large proportion of the life of all, the whole of the life of most; and let us see that on which that favour rested, as a part of the eternal life given to us in the Son of God, which is to be God's glory in us in private life, a store from which to receive all that pertains to life and godliness as we are individual Christians - as truly as His life as a preacher of the kingdom of God, is that to a special participation in which those who are called in this to walk in His steps, are to look - as truly as His witnessing before Pontius Pilate a good confession, is for strength according to their need, to those who are called to suffer as martyrs for His name.

As to our Lord's personal ministry, its distinguishing character is to be seen in this, that that ministry was the *outcoming of the life of sonship.* By this character of a life was His ministry distinguished from that of all who were only "teachers sent from God." In this respect was it that He "spake as never man spake." What He spake, as what He did, was a part of what He was. His words were spirit and life, and not a mere testimony concerning life. As now in the inner man of our being, when the Son of God is known as present in us claiming lordship over our spirits, there is a testimony of the Father to the Son in the Spirit, which in calling Jesus Lord we are welcoming, so we cannot doubt that then in Judea the man Jesus, in His living witnessing as the Son for the Father, had a testimony of the Father born to him, which men heard according as they welcomed the teaching of God. This testimony was a testimony to what He was, to the life that was shining forth in His deeds and words. And the unconscious sense of this has manifestly gone beyond the intelligent recognition of it; so that we find men unable to resist the authority and power with which He spake, even though not beholding, as the disciple did, "His glory as the glory of the Only-begotten of the Father."

Unless we realise this, and that *that* was presented to men's faith, if they could receive it, which pertained to one who could say, in reference to His own conscious life, "I am the light of the world," we cannot enter into that immediate presenting to men of *what He Himself was as the Gospel*, which we have seen in the words, "Come unto me, all ye that labour and are heavy laden, and I will give you rest. . . . Learn of me; for I am meek and lowly in heart: and ye shall find rest unto your souls." And in that testimony as to who are "blessed," with which the discourse which we call the Sermon on the Mount opens, we are to recognise the same thing. All these declarations as to the blessedness of the several conditions of spirit which our Lord there specifies are rays of the light of the life that was in Him; and will be such to us, being heard as utterances of that life - utterances of Christ's own consciousness in humanity, a part of His confessing the Father before men, being testimonies in humanity to the blessedness of sonship in doing the Father's will.

Accordingly the whole discourse keeps the Father before us. The foundation of every counsel is our filial relation to God. All is in harmony with the prayer which He teaches, putting the words, "Our Father," in our lips, and adding, as the first petitions which we are to present, the expression of an interest in the Father's "name" and "kingdom" and "will," - an interest which, if these petitions are to proceed from unfeigned lips, must imply our participation in that life of sonship which is presented to us in Him who teaches us so to pray.

Nor are we to leave out of account, in contemplating our Lord's ministry as giving glory to the Father in being manifested sonship, that not only was this in our nature and in our circumstances, but that the consciousness of its being so, and the full knowledge of the amount of the demand made on us when called to learn of Him, is distinctly expressed - the knowledge that to call on us to follow Him, is to call upon us to take up the cross. When we in very truth betake ourselves to Him, as to that high priest who is "touched with the feeling of our infirmities, and was in all points tempted like as we are, yet without sin" and who in that He Himself hath suffered, being tempted, is able to succour us when we are tempted, we then learn to value the tone of full conscious entering into the amount of the demand which He makes upon men in calling upon them to hate their life in this world which pervades our Lord's teaching equally with the consciousness of being Himself living that life in the Father's favour which He is commending.

But that life of which our Lord's ministry was thus the living outcoming, in the consciousness of which He testified who are blessed, in the consciousness of which He declared to the weary and heavy laden what is the true rest - speaking to us also in all this as our very brother - that life needed, in order to its perfect development, as the light of life to us, to have the depth of its root in God - its power to overcome the world - the nature of its strength and victory - the weight of the cross which it bore in suffering flesh - revealed, as even the living teaching of the Lord's ministry did not reveal it. Therefore was that hour and power of darkness permitted which the closing period of our Lord's course presents, in which sonship towards the Father and brotherhood towards man have had their nature manifested and their power displayed to the utmost.

As the time drew near the Lord prepared the disciples for this hour and power of darkness.

> And Jesus, going up to Jerusalem, took the twelve disciples apart in the way, and said unto them, Behold, we go up to Jerusalem; and the Son of man shall be betrayed unto the chief priests and unto the scribes, and they shall condemn Him to death, and shall deliver Him to the gentiles to mock, and to scourge, and to crucify Him; and the third day He shall rise again (Matt. xx. 17, 18, 19).

His own feelings in looking forward to what, as to its outward form, He thus foretold, were such as to impress their minds with the most solemn anticipations, and His words then, so far as they are recorded, remain to us a portion of Scripture on which we mediate as bringing us near to a region of feeling into which we scarcely dare to venture: and yet these expressions of mental agony are recorded for our instruction as belonging to that life of Christ which is the light of life to us.

"I have a baptism to be baptised with; and how am I straitened till it be accomplished," Luke xii. 50. "Now is my soul troubled; save me from this hour: but for this cause came I unto this hour. Father, glorify thy name," John xii. 27. And even after the conclusion which the words "For this cause came I to this hour" seem to express, when the awful hour was close at hand it again became the subject of earnest pleading with the Father - pleading, the earnestness of which, while it reveals to us the measure of the apprehended bitterness of the cup, and terror of the hour to which it refers, makes a demand upon our faith as to the reality of life which was in our Lord's prayers, and how truly, in dealing with the Father, He dealt with a *living will and heart*, and *not with a fate*, which blessed are those who are able truly and fully to respond to.

And they came to a place which was named Gethsemane: and He saith to His disciples, Sit ye here, while I shall pray. And He taketh with Him Peter and James and John, and began to be sore amazed, and to be very heavy; and saith unto them, My soul is exceeding sorrowful unto death: tarry ye here, and watch. And He went forward a little, and fell on the ground, and prayed that, if it were possible, the *hour* might pass from Him. And He said, Abba, Father, all things are possible unto thee; take away *this cup* from me, nevertheless not what I will, but what thou wilt. (Mark xiv. 33-36)

And being in an agony He prayed more earnestly: and His sweat was as it were great drops of blood falling down to the ground. (Luke xxii. 44)

In this awfully intense prayer we have to mark its alternative nature, and that the latter part was as truly prayer as the former: the former uttering the true and natural desire to which He was conscious as contemplating that which was before Him in the weakness and capacity of suffering proper to suffering flesh; the latter uttering the desire of the spirit of sonship, being that which was deepest, and to which the other, while consciously realised, was perfectly subordinated.

After being offered the third time, our Lord's prayer was answered and the mind of the Father, which was the response to His cry, was revealed to Him in the Spirit. He was not to be spared the dreaded hour. The cup was not to pass from Him; and therefore, in that truth of sonship in which He had said, "Nevertheless not as I will, but as thou wilt," the Father's will was welcomed, the bitter cup was received from the Father's hand *as the Father's hand*, and in the *strength of sonship* the Lord drank it:

And He cometh the third time, and saith unto them, "Sleep on now, and take your rest: it is enough, the *hour is come; behold, the Son of man is betrayed into the hands of sinners.*" And *immediately, while He yet spake,* cometh Judas one of the twelve, and with him a great multitude with swords and staves, from the chief priests and the scribes and the elders. (Mark xiv. 41, 43)

Then Simon Peter having a sword drew it, and smote the high priest's servant, and cut off his right ear. Then said Jesus unto Peter, "Put up thy sword into the sheath: *the cup which my Father hath given me to drink, shall I not drink it?*" (John xviii. 10,11)

To those who had come with Judas He said, "When I was daily with you in the temple, ye stretched forth no hands against me: but *this is your hour, and the power of darkness.*" (Luke xxii. 53)

The precise point of time at which the anticipated hour and power of darkness had its commencement is thus clearly indicated - the moment in which the cup, in reference to which He had prayed, was put into our Lord's hand - the moment at which the baptism began as to which He was straitened until it should be accomplished. And I ask attention to this, because the record clearly separates between the actual experience which these expressions, "hour," - "cup" - "baptism," refer to, and the agony in the garden in which that experience was only anticipated, being still the subject of the prayer, if it were possible, that it should not be, as well as of the prayer that if the Father so willed, it should be.

The history of the hour and power of darkness, now come, follows, and is given with a fulness of detail commensurate with its importance; while it is widely separated from all recorded suffering of man from man by the preternatural circumstances that accompanied it; circumstances which, in their awfulness, accorded with that relation which the sufferings of the sufferer bore to the sin of man; yet which, in their connection with what was visible of Christ's bearing under His sufferings, had that character impressed upon them which drew from the Roman centurion the acknowledgment, "Truly this was the Son of God."

CHAPTER XI

HOW WE ARE TO CONCEIVE OF THE SUFFERINGS OF CHRIST, DURING THAT CLOSING PERIOD OF WHICH SUFFERING WAS THE DISTINCTIVE CHARACTER

The sufferings of Christ during the hour and power of darkness have been dealt with in two quite opposite ways.

1. They have been regarded in their simply physical aspect; and aid to the imagination and the heart in realising their terrible amount has been eagerly sought in pictured representations or picturing words; and thus a lively feeling of the pain endured by our blessed Lord under the hands of wicked men has been cherished as a help in measuring the evil of our sins and our obligations to the Saviour.

I am not afraid to regard all that was attained of knowledge of the sufferings of Christ in this way as only a knowing Christ after the flesh, and therefore what had no virtue to accomplish any *spiritual development* in men - no virtue to impart a true knowledge of sin, or to raise the spirits of men into the light of what our sins are in the sight of God - what they are to the heart of God. Feelings of a strong and solemn, as well as tender character, have, doubtless, been thus cherished; and doubtless, the element of gratitude has been present: yet there was not, for there could not be, in images of physical suffering anything of the nature of spiritual light - however such light may have been present along with them, being received otherwise.

2. But there has been manifested also, and this especially recently, a tendency to deal with the detailed sufferings of Christ, as these were endured at the hands of wicked men, in the quite opposite way of making as little account of them as possible; I do not mean denying their reality - denying that our Lord's flesh was suffering flesh - but rashly admitting the justness of a comparison of them with other cases of suffering inflicted by man on man.

Of such other cases it is not difficult to find many recorded that would bear the comparison; cases in which the cruellest tortures have been submitted to with such fortitude and patience of endurance, as if this way of viewing the subject had been admissible, would excuse the sneer of the infidel. Indeed, dealing with the sufferings of the Saviour on this principle, those who have done so have escaped from justifying that infidel sneer only by referring the language of our Lord, in relation to the cup given Him to drink, to an apprehension of what the cup contained, altogether unrelated to His being delivered into the hands of sinful men. Nay, because of its seeming to shut us up to the view which they have taken of what that cup contained, viz. that it was filled with the wrath of God, the concession has been willingly made of the alleged disproportion between our Lord's agony in the Garden of Gethsemane in looking forward to the coming hour and power of darkness, and those sufferings which the history of that hour records.

And here let me say that I entirely feel that our Lord's physical sufferings, viewed simply as physical sufferings and without relation to the mind that was in the sufferer, could not adequately explain the awful intensity of the feelings which accompanied His prayer in the garden of Gethsemane.

But, on the other hand, apart altogether from the insuperable objection that presents itself on other grounds to the conception that the cup which was the subject of Christ's prayer contained the Father's wrath, it seems impossible, without putting aside the record, not to connect that cup with these minutely detailed sufferings, foretold, as they had been, to the disciples on the way up to Jerusalem, and having their commencement *immediately after* the answer of His prayer in the garden was revealed to the Lord; being also, as we have seen, met and submitted to by Him with words which identified them with the cup as to which He had prayed.

While John records the words already quoted addressed to Peter, "The cup which my Father gives me to drink shall I not drink it?" Matthew gives these - "Thinkest thou that I cannot now pray to my Father and He shall presently give me more than twelve legions of angels?" words which, as well as all else, suggest, not a wrath coming forth from the Father, but a power of evil which the Father permitted to have its course. We cannot indeed doubt what the impression on the disciples as to that to which their Lord was subjected must have been; and accordingly, after our Lord's resurrection, in that interview of touching tenderness with the two disciples on the way to Emmaus, when He joined Himself to them and said, "What manner of communications are these which they have one to another, as ye walk, and are sad" - their sad thoughts were "concerning Jesus of Nazareth, which was a prophet mighty in deed and word before God and all the people: and how the chief priests and our rulers delivered Him to death, and have crucified Him." On these events were their minds going back, and on these events did He give them light. "O fools, and slow of heart to believe all the prophets have spoken: ought not Christ to have suffered these things, and to enter into His glory? And beginning at Moses and all the prophets, He expounded to them in all the Scriptures the things concerning Himself." (Luke xxiv. 17, 19, 20, 25, 26, 27)

But both the errors now noticed - the minute dwelling on the physical suffering as such on the one hand, and on the other hand, the turning away from it altogether, for the explanation of the intensity of our Lord's agony in the garden, and seeking that explanation in the assumption that the wrath of the Father was the bitterness of the cup given to the Son - both these very opposite errors have alike originated in the root error of regarding our Lord's sufferings as penal, and so being occupied with their aspect *as suffering merely*, when they were truly a moral and spiritual sacrifice, to which the sufferings were related only as involved in the fulness and perfection of the sacrifice.

In St Matthew xvi. 21, we have the record of an intimation to the disciples of the sufferings to which the Lord looked forward, earlier than that quoted above. And both the outburst of natural feeling in Peter at the thought of his Master's suffering such things, and our Lord's rebuke that in so feeling he savoured not the things that be of God but the things that be of men, connected with the teaching that is immediately added - "Then said Jesus unto them, If any man will come after me, let him deny himself, and take up his cross, and follow me: for whosoever will save his life shall lose it, and whosoever will lose his life for my sake shall find it" - illustrate to us the relation of the sufferings foretold to the *life* which the Son of God was presenting to the faith of the disciples, and to the *fellowship of which* He sought to raise their desires and their hopes.

The later occasion of His speaking of His anticipated sufferings to His disciples already quoted is also marked by an incident which is in its teaching to us entirely to the same effect, I mean the request of the two sons of Zebedee. They, with Peter, were the three privileged to be present with our Lord during His agony of prayer in the garden; as they had also been to be with Him on the Mount of Transfiguration, when "as He prayed, the fashion of His countenance was altered, and His raiment was white and glistening. And behold there talked with Him two men, which were Moses and Elias, who appeared in glory, and spake of His decease which He should accomplish at Jerusalem."

Whether the scene on the Mount, along with the words with which their Lord's intimation of His approaching suffering had concluded - "And the third day He shall rise again" - though not fully understood, had carried their thoughts at once beyond the sufferings to the glory that should follow, and so moved the desire which the request to "sit the one on His right hand, the other on His left in His kingdom," expressed, we know not; but nothing can be more conclusive as to the relation - the *abiding relation* of the sufferings which the Lord foretold to the development of the life that was in Him, than His reply to this request.

First, in accordance with the awful impression of what He looked forward to which it was His intention to convey, He says - "Ye know not what ye ask. Are ye able to drink of the cup that I shall drink of, and to be baptised with the baptism that I am baptised with?" But when they reply, "We are able," He adds "Ye shall drink indeed of my cup, and be baptised with the baptism that I am baptised with:" plainly preparing them for that fellowship in His anticipated sufferings which His words on the former occasion, as to the necessity of "bearing His cross," had equally implied.

For, indeed, although this period of which the *distinctive* character is *suffering in connection with a permitted hour and power of darkness* is so clearly marked off to us; yet had the disciples been, as we have seen, before this time taught to see their Lord as bearing the cross, and to understand that they were called to take up the cross and follow Him. And now, when they were taught to associate a deeper meaning than it had yet to them, with their Lord's cross, it was still as that cross which they would have themselves to bear in following their Lord that they were to contemplate it.

The *continuity of life of sonship*, therefore, is unbroken in the transition to this third and last period, the character of the Father's dealing with the Son as what related to the development of that life is unchanged, and the interest of the progress of that development to us as the development of the life given to us in the Son of God, and which we are ourselves to partake in, is unaltered. We are to meditate on the details of our Lord's sufferings with that personal reference to ourselves, and, therefore, with that expectation of light as to their nature, which is justified by the words, *"Ye shall drink indeed of my cup, and be baptised with the baptism that I am baptised with."*

If we ponder these words well, they will indeed give a peculiar character to our consideration of the cup given the Son of God to drink; and realising in their light something of the depth of our calling as a call to fellowship in Christ's sufferings - as in the light of the transfiguration we may realise something of the high hope set before us - we shall, in our ignorance of the forms of trial which our Father's love may yet take in accomplishing in us the good pleasure of His goodness, feel it needful to fall back, as we may peacefully do, on the faith that "the height and the depth and the breadth and the length of the love of God in Christ passeth knowledge;" for that its end is, that we may be "filled with the fulness of God."

The faithfulness of our Lord's personal ministry and the unclouded light of His life had been already the realisation in humanity of a loving trust in the Father and a forgiveness towards men, which were a victory of sonship and brotherhood in the sight of God of great price. But the extent to which sonship could trust the Father, the extent to which the true brother could exercise forgiving love, and to be further manifested - or, rather, this life of love had to be further developed; and if we enter into the reason for Christ's suffering *at all* through being exposed to the enmity of the carnal mind to God, instead of being protected from its malice by "twelve legions of angels," we can see how it should please the Father to bruise Him, and put the Son of His love to grief, such as the restraint put upon the power of the wicked up to a certain point had not permitted. We can see how it was fit that He should be exposed to suffer at the hands of wicked men what would be a measure at once of man's rejection of God, "This is the Son, let us kill Him, and the inheritance shall be ours," and of the forgiving love of Him who could die for His enemies: and we can see how as *a revealing of the Father* this must take place in the *power of the life of sonship,* that is to say, in the strength of the Son's conscious oneness of mind with the Father, in the strength of the life which is in the Father's favour.

Therefore, in following the path of the Son as the Father orders it, and keeping our ear open to the voice which says, "This is my beloved Son," we can, without feeling it a contradiction to that voice, contemplate the coming to the Son of "the hour and power of darkness." But we should feel very differently if called to believe in any outcoming of the Father's mind towards the Son, or any aspect of His countenance towards Him that did not accord with the words, "This is my beloved Son." For this we should feel quite unprepared.

When Satan was permitted to try Job, it was with this reservation, "but save his life." In our Lord's case, it is the higher life, *the life in the Father's favour,* that we are prepared to see untouched. That He should die, by the grace of God tasting death for every man, so dying as through death to destroy him who had the power of death, that is the devil, we can understand, seeing in this the triumph of the eternal life. Whatever can have been contained in the permission of an hour and power of darkness we can believe to have entered into the divine counsel, because anything that these words can express could only prove the might of the eternal life; - for nothing simply permitted - nothing external to God Himself - nothing that was not in *the divine aspect towards Christ* could reach that life to touch it as a life in God's favour, or suspend its flow from God. But the wrath of God as coming forth towards Christ would be indeed *the touching of that very life in the Father's favour, whose excellence and might was to be proved at so great a cost.* Accordingly we have seen that it was as a *cup from the Father's hand* that Christ received the cup given Him to drink, and that the *unbroken sense* of the *Father's favour* was expressed in the rebuke to the unbelieving, though affectionate zeal of Peter, "Thinkest thou that I cannot now pray to my Father, and He shall presently give me twelve legions of angels?"

And, most conclusive of all, we have the revelation of the nature of the strength in which the anticipated trial was met, and in which doubtless it was victoriously borne, in the express words of our Lord in reference to one most bitter element of its bitterness - "Behold, the hour cometh, yea, is now come, that ye shall be scattered every man to his own, and shall leave me alone: and yet *I am not alone, because the Father is with me.*"

We can understand, then, the permission of an hour and power of darkness as what could only prove the might of the eternal life presented to our faith in the Son of God. We do not so easily understand the *measure* of the proof which such an hour was fitted to be. And it is here that the error and shortcoming have been which have permitted the comparison of our Lord's sufferings during the hour and power of darkness with the ordinary case of man's suffering at the hands of man.

The actual treatment to which our Lord was subjected is but one of two elements in His suffering; and it has surely been a grave error to leave the other element, which is, indeed, the important element, out of account. We may find cases where the physical infliction and the indignities offered have been as great or greater, but how shall we calculate the infinite difference that the mind in which Christ suffered has made?

That mind, indeed, made Him equal to what He had to bear, for its might was the might of the eternal life which is in God's favour; but this great might was not the might of mere power, nor was it that the life of sonship imparted an insensibility to His humanity, or that because of the light of God which belonged to it it made all that He had to encounter to be to Him as nothing. On the contrary, the very opposite of all this was the truth. It was not a might of power at all, but the might of *realised perfect weakness*, whose *only strength* was the *strength of faith*. It was not a bearing of the things that came upon Him in insensibility. The most tender sensitiveness proper to humanity, as possessed and lived in in the truth of humanity, was there open to all that came to wound it.

It was not that in the light of God, and in the knowledge that He came from God and went to God, there was a raising of the Lord above His circumstances, making them to Him as nothing. In the light of God, which is the light of love, all these circumstances as they were indeed the form taken by an hour and power of darkness had their true import and magnitude and awful substance of sin and enmity as these are estimated by the divine love. In truth, we are to judge that according as was the love which, in the strength of love to God and man, was able to drink that cup, so was the bitterness of that cup. And that according to the measure of the true sense and conscious-ness of humanity in Christ, was the sensibility to that bitterness, the capacity of suffering through it. And that according to the absolute felt weakness of the flesh to which no strength at all remained was the need of sustaining faith, as the need of one believing in "the dust of death."

If we are not turned away from meditating on this subject in the light of the life itself which we are seeing tried and triumphing, and do not unwisely occupy ourselves with the record of physical sufferings, as if we were called on to look at what could be known according to the flesh - until the unsatisfactory result cast us upon the opposite error of supposing that our Lord's agony in the garden could not really have its explanation in His anticipation of what the hour and power of darkness would be to Him - we shall find even our ordinary experience of human suffering as connected with man's inhumanity to man, giving a right direction to our thoughts.

We are familiar with the fact, that unkindness affects quite differently a meek, gentle, loving spirit, and a proud, independent, self-relying spirit. The comparative ease with which some men encounter all manner of ungracious and unbrotherly treatment at the hands of others in the conflict of life is because they meet pride and unbrotherliness in the strength of pride and unbrotherliness. This too often passes for manliness; - and it would be unjust to say that it may not often be combined with, and upheld by, the instinctive feeling of manhood, and of what is due to oneself. But assuredly the state of mind, as a whole, tends to make the apparent victory not so much a victory as an insensibility. The evil treatment experienced does not really, in these cases, cause the pain it would cause to that brotherliness in which it should be met, and which, being recognised, has always a witness in men's consciences as the right and highest way of meeting injuries; though the pride that hinders a man from feeling it himself makes him slow to give another credit for it.

But it is surely not difficult to see that, if our feeling of what is due to ourselves be free from pride, and only commensurate with our feeling of the love due from us to others - if our sense of manhood be in harmony with the true and pure feeling of the oneness of all flesh, and if the claim of others on love from us be felt to be *altogether untouched by failure in love on their part* - being discharged by us in the reality of a love that, notwithstanding such failure, loves them still - loves them as we love ourselves, making their sin our burden, as well as also their unkindness to be felt as the disappointing response of hatred to love; then must unkindness be to us, so minded, a suffering and trial just commensurate with the measure of the unkindness to which we are subjected, on the one hand, and the measure of this life of love in us, on the other.

But it is not alone the *amount* of suffering implied in the treatment to which our Lord was subjected that we must fail to estimate aright, unless we see that suffering in the light of the life that was in Him. It is still more as to the *nature* of that suffering that we shall err. This we feel the moment we turn from contemplating it as physical infliction on the part of men and physical endurance on the part of Christ, to contemplate it in its spiritual aspect as *the form of the response of enmity to love.*

There is surely very special instruction for us here in the fact that shame - indignity - is so marked a character of the injuries inflicted on Christ. I need not illustrate this point. The Apostle speaks of "the shame of the cross," as if the great victory through the faith of the joy set before our Lord was victory over that shame: and, both in the historical narrative, and in the related Psalms, indignity and contumely, that is to say, all that would most touch that life which man has in the favour of man, and which strikes more deeply than physical infliction, because it goes deeper than the body -

wounding the spirit - is the most distinguishing feature of the evil use made by sinful men of the power that they received over the Son of God when He was betrayed into the hands of sinners.

All along, the relation of the *cross* to *shame* was ever present to our Lord's mind. It is against the consequences of being *"ashamed of* Him and of His words" as the opposite of "confessing Him before men," that His warnings are given. He knew in His own honouring of the Father as bringing upon Him, as its consequence, dishonour to Himself from men, the shame of which He spake, according to the words, "The reproaches of them that reproached thee, fell upon me."

How related the shame against which He warned men was to their laying down their life in this world, so that being content to bear it was identical with being contented to lay down that life, our Lord plainly declares, when preparing men for the sacrifice that would be implied in becoming His disciples. So the desire of the honour which is the correlative of that shame is represented by Him as hindering the faith to which he called men - "How can ye believe, which receive honour one of another, and seek not the honour that cometh from God only?" (John v. 44).

What are we taught by all this in relation to the cup of suffering which our Lord received from His Father's hand? For the shame that was an ingredient in that cup would not have the place it has if it were not peculiarly the occasion of suffering to the suffering Saviour.

Here we feel that, notwithstanding all our great our sinful bondage to what others think of us, a bondage of which the measure is never known until we attempt to assert our freedom, as the strength of an iron fetter is not known until the attempt is made to break it, still we little realise what the shame to which our Lord was subjected was to His Spirit. And this is the case partly because *our own bondage* in this matter, however real, and however excused by us to ourselves because of its universality all around us, never has the *sanction of conscience*, never is what we can confess before God, or confess to ourselves without a certain sense of degradation. How different the feeling with which a man says, "I must do as others do," from that with which he says, "This is the will of God. I must do it." The former obedience is, I say, felt to be a degradation even while it is rendered, while the latter, being rendered, is felt to exalt and ennoble. But because of the sinful and polluted form of that reference to the thoughts of others regarding us, to which we are conscious in ourselves, we have the more difficulty in entering into "the *shame* of the cross" as an element in Christ's sufferings. And yet the importance assigned to it is, as I have said, undeniable.

I have already had occasion to quote that which is said in reference to our Lord's early life at Nazareth, and He grew in favour with God and man. In the book of Proverbs iii. 4, the virtues commended are commended with this promise annexed, "So shalt thou find favour and good understanding in the sight of God and man." The first and great commandment is, "Thou shalt love the Lord thy God with all thine heart, and mind, and soul, and strength," and the second is like unto it, "Thou shalt love thy neighbour as thyself." As our life in God's favour is related to the first commandment, and our capacity of that life is the preparation of our being for our having that command addressed to us - so is there a life like unto that life related to the second commandment, having also preparation made for it in the constitution of humanity, viz. a life in man's favour - a life like, I say, to the life which is in God's favour in that it is a life *in favour*, i.e. a life not in possession, but in the feelings of a heart towards us.

As, then, it is proper to the life of sonship - the perfect love to God as the Father of our spirits - to desire His favour, and know what favour as the light of life, so it is proper to the life of brotherhood, which is the perfect love to our neighbour, to desire our brother's favour, to desire that living oneness with him which is only possible in unity of *spirit*, such as "favour," if a spiritual reality, implies. Therefore our Lord, the true brother of every man, desired this response of heart from every man; and the refusal of it, the giving of contempt instead of favour, and scorn instead of that accord of true brotherhood which would have esteemed Him, as was due to Him, as "the chief among ten thousand, and altogether lovely," was as a death to that life which desired the favour thus denied.

No doubt, as it was, that favour was withheld on grounds that quite strengthened the Son of God to submit to the loss of it. He "came in His Father's name, and they received Him not." No doubt it was thus peculiarly an ingredient in His bitter cup which He was enabled to drink in the strength of sonship; but it was not the less on that account bitter to the heart of perfect brotherhood. He was able to bear the loss of the life that is in man's favour, in the strength of the higher life which is in the Father's favour. But in itself that loss was bitter in proportion to the pure capacity of life in brotherhood which was in Him.

God is not the author of confusion, but of order. In giving us two commandments, He has not placed us under two masters. The first commandment is absolute, and its requirements reach to the whole extent and circle of our being, *leaving nothing to the man that it does not claim for God*; the second our Lord says is like unto it and, coming after so extensive a first commandment, would be what we could not meet with obedience, had not "likeness" amounted to such a relation to the first, as that obedience to the second commandment must flow out of obedience to the first. Therefore, as the strength to obey the second commandment must be in that love to God which is the obeying of the first commandment, when the obedience of that second commandment is not followed by its due response from those in relation to whom it is fulfilled, the consciousness that pertains to obeying the first commandment must still sustain the spirit. But that second commandment has not been really obeyed, the love it calls for has not been truly cherished, unless the refusal of that due response, and the return of enmity for love in that most trying form of scorn and contempt, be painful. And painful it must be in the measure of the love that is thus put to grief.

As to our fleshly experience in this matter - our experience of life in the favour of others - it is but too clear, that, though the desire of that favour has a true root in humanity, yet not love, but selfishness, renders that desire the occasion of the bondage to which we are conscious. But in Christ's case the love to men to which men made so evil a response - that very love itself was what demanded that coming to them in His Father's name because of which they refused Him. His so coming to them was true love to them, as well as faithfulness to His Father - the true brotherhood, which, while seeking men's favour, seeks their good still more than their favour. Therefore, if we would understand the forgiveness which by giving occasion for its exercise, our Lord's sufferings during the hour and power of darkness developed in Him, we must see that His love was forgiving injuries which were, in the strictest sense, injuries *against itself* - injuries sustained by the *love as love*, and not merely touching Him against whom they were directed in some more outward and lower part of His being, some inferior capacity of suffering.

But there was a reason, though not this, why our Lord, having taken suffering flesh, and being subjected to suffer in it under an hour and power of darkness, should prove its full capacity of suffering. For He was to manifest to the utmost the power and courage of love refusing the favour of man when that follows not the favour of God; as well as the forgiveness of love, when those who can kill the body, but after that have no more that they can do, put forth that power in enmity.

Among the comparisons which have been so unwisely permitted of our Lord's sufferings under this hour and power of darkness with what others have suffered, the sufferings of His own martyrs have been mentioned. As to the sufferings of martyrs *suffering in His spirit* and *sustained by His strength*, they are obviously a part of the fulfilment of the word, "Ye shall drink indeed of my cup, and be baptised with the baptism that I am baptised with:" but, unless we are prepared to claim for them the life of love, in the fulness in which it was present in Him from whom it has flowed in them, we cannot conclude as to the comparative amount of their sufferings from the external circumstances of suffering in which we see them.

But, apart from this, though His church be called to fill up what is behind of Christ's sufferings, and though the counsel of God, in that Christ is the vine, we the branches, He the head, we the members, implies that, in a sense, and an important sense, there is that behind which remains to be filled up; yet in suffering, as in all else, there was a fulness and perfection in Christ Himself, of which we severally receive but a part. Accordingly, measures of comfort under sufferings, even to the extent of partially neutralising these sufferings, have been often granted to martyrs, though not to their Lord.

Nay, even in more ordinary cases of physical suffering as a cup which our Father may give us to drink, while it is good for us though children to learn obedience by the things which we suffer, yet it is sometimes our Father's will, in seasons of suffering, to reveal in the spirit so much of His glory in Christ as neutralises the physical suffering. Thus David Brainerd, to whom a very unusual measure of physical pain was appointed, sometimes when that pain was most acute, had granted to him, along with it, a joy in the Holy Ghost, which so counterbalanced that pain, that on the whole he judged that condition far happier than an ordinary measure of religious joy, with ordinary health. But as to our Lord's experience during that hour and power of darkness, it would seem inconsistent with the purpose of subjecting Him to the experience of the weakness of suffering flesh at all, to conceive of this experience as other than, so to speak, perfect. In this view, the reason that has been assigned for His refusing the drink offered to deaden pain commends itself to us.

I believe these thoughts as to the elements of our Lord's sufferings as suffered at the hands of men, and as to the weakness of suffering flesh in which He bore them, are true; and will help us to realise the trial to which forgiving love in which He endured the trial, the manner of the victory of love. This it concerns us to know, because it is with this same love as in Him towards ourselves, and as, alas! tried by our sins, that we have to do. This it concerns us to know, also, because it is this same love as in us through participation in Him as our life that we are called to manifest towards others, and for the developing of which in us, it may be the Father's will that we shall have a personal experience of drinking of our Lord's cup and being baptised with His baptism even in outward form of trial, which, if it comes to us, we, without this light, are ill prepared to welcome.

In thinking of what has been, and may yet be, of literal conformity to the sufferings of Christ, and in considering the probable history of any attempt to persecute for Christ's name, or to constrain men to deny Christ - an hour and power of darkness coming to the church towards the close as to her Lord - it is a solemn thing to think that of the many who would be found prepared to die rather than deny Christ, few might be found so partaking in the life of Christ as that dying would be to them the true fellowship of His cross - the fellowship of His love to those who crucified Him - of that love as in itself the deepest capacity of suffering - of that love as in its deepest experience of suffering, proving its fountain to be in God by being forgiving love. And yet such a victory of love would be but what Christ is daily calling us to prove in measure in calling us to take up our cross daily and follow Him.

CHAPTER XII

THE SUFFERINGS OF CHRIST, IN WHICH THE ATONEMENT WAS PERFECTED, CONSIDERED IN THEIR RELATION, 1ST, TO HIS WITNESSING FOR GOD TO MEN, AND 2DLY, TO HIS DEALING WITH GOD ON BEHALF OF MEN

1. These sufferings were the perfecting of **the Son's witnessing for the Father**, being the perfected manifestation of the life of love as sonship towards God and brotherhood towards man.

The trial of our Lord's love to men, and its triumph in the prayer on the cross, "Father, forgive them; for they know not what they do," and the trial of His love to the Father, and trust in the Father, of which the final and perfected expression was these words in death, "Father, into thy hands I commend thy spirit," - were accomplished together by one and the same elements.

The power of the life of sonship and of conscious oneness with the Father in His mind towards His brethren to enable Christ to abide in love and overcome evil with good, is in truth that which we have now been contemplating. The sense of His Father's fatherliness was the strength in which He manifested this perfection of brotherhood. For that perfection of brotherhood was just His following of the Father as a dear child, and all He suffered in this path came to Him as doing His Father's commandments, and abiding in His love; and thus was the Father in all this glorified in the Son. The very words, "*Father*, forgive them," testify how *within* the light of the Father's love and favour the Intercessor abode while suffering; finding in that favour strength to suffer, and not only to suffer, but to intercede. And as the experience of the utter weakness of suffering flesh was necessary to the completeness of the trial of His love to men, so was it also essential to the development of perfect trust in the Father - for there remained to the sufferer no strength but the strength of faith.

The outward history of the hour and power of darkness we have detailed to us by the Evangelists. We have not, however, much from them to help us to see that "hour" *as from Christ's side*. But there is a portion of Scripture, one of the Psalms, which is usually received as having this special interest to us, and which therefore is taken in supplement of the gospel narrative; and our Lord's own partial quotation of this psalm on the cross, as well as its own contents, seem to justify our so receiving it. I refer to the 22nd psalm, which I believe to be confirmatory of the view now taken of the cup given our Lord to drink as being a permitted trial of the faith of the Son in the Father. The first words of this psalm, as quoted by our Lord, have been regarded as the Son's utterance of the sense of the Father's wrath endured under the imputation of our sins. Such an interpretation seems to me a violent straining of the words taken alone; but when we take them as a part of the psalm, it becomes altogether untenable, being directly opposed to the tone and character of the psalm, as a whole. The concluding verses of this psalm, by the largeness of the reference of men connect it with the character of the cross as a trial of the love of brotherhood in Christ. But the first and larger portion of it places the suffering Saviour before us as an individual sufferer, drinking the bitter cup given Him to drink, and uttering the trial of faith which He is experiencing in drinking it.

The psalm opens with a cleaving appropriation on the part of the Sufferer of God as His God: "My God, my God." He asks God, *His* God, why He leaves Him in the hands of the wicked, and interposes not on His behalf, delaying to answer His prayer: "Why hast thou forsaken me? why art thou so far from helping me, and from the voice of my roaring? O my God, I cry in the day-time, but thou hearest not; and in the night-season, and am not silent."

He refuses any explanation of this silence that would be dishonouring to God: "But thou art holy, O thou that inhabitest the praises of Israel." He refers to God's former justifying of faith in the case of others of old: "Our fathers trusted in thee; they trusted, and thou didst deliver them. They cried unto thee, and were delivered. They trusted in thee, and were not confounded." But the acknowledgment of God is delayed in His case as it had not been in theirs, and the delay is exposing the sufferer to contempt and scorn and the bitter reproach that His professed trust in God has been a delusion or a false pretension: "But I am a worm, and no man; a reproach of men, and despised of the people. All they that see me laugh me to scorn. They shoot out the lip, they shake the head, saying, He trusted on the Lord that He would deliver Him: let Him deliver Him, seeing He delighted in Him." Therefore does the Tried One go back on that which God has been to Him - therefore does He fall back on the faithfulness of God, as the "faithful Creator:" "But thou art He that took me out of the womb: thou didst make me hope when I was upon my mother's breasts. I was cast upon thee from the womb. Thou art my God from my mother's belly."

Thus His faith is strengthened, and the prayer, the delay in answering which has been the subject of the opening question, is renewed; for His hope in God, His God, is not let go: "Be not thou far from me; for trouble is near; for there is none to help." The trouble is very great. The outer circle of His being is possessed by His enemies. He turns from it to that inner region where God's nearness is to be known, for elsewhere there is no help: "Many bulls have compassed me; strong bulls of Bashan have beset me round. They gaped on me with their mouths, as a ravening and roaring lion." And this is while the depths of the utter and absolute weakness of humanity are proved by the Sufferer as by one cast entirely upon God and who puts not forth one effort on His own behalf, nor gives place to one movement of self-relying energy or self-dependent strength of the flesh: "I am poured out like water, and all my bones are out of joint: my heart is like wax; it is melted in the midst of my bowels. My strength is dried up like a potsherd; and my tongue cleaveth to my jaws; and thou hast brought me into the dust of death."

Thus low in suffering at the hands of the wicked is He brought: "For dogs have compassed me: the assembly of the wicked have enclosed me: they pierced my hands and my feet. I may tell all my bones: they look and stare upon me. They part my garments among them, and cast lots upon my vesture." All this is permitted to the wicked; for "they would have had no power at all, unless it had been given them from above." All this is received as therefore to Him from God: "*Thou* hast brought me into the dust of death." But God is *Himself* to Him "*His God*" still; so He is only the more cast upon God, made the more to cleave to Him: "But be not thou far from me, O Lord: O my strength, haste thou to help me. Deliver my soul from the sword; my darling from the power of the dog. Save me from the lion's mouth."

And now we meet the returning answer of prayer - the justification of the Sufferer's unbroken trust - the clearing up of God's faithfulness and truth in the whole transaction: "Thou hast heard me from the horns of the unicorns. I will declare thy name unto my brethren; in the midst of the congregation will I praise thee." His experience of God was not found to be in contradiction to God's justification of the trust of the fathers, to which He had referred. That of God to which they were witnesses, has been, through the divine dealing with Him, only more deeply revealed:- as we see in the Epistle to the Hebrews, the testimony of the cloud of witnesses, connected with that of our Lord Himself, as "the author and finisher of faith," *i.e.* He whose faith perfects the revelation of that in God which we have to trust. Therefore he proceeds, "Ye that fear the Lord, praise Him; all ye the seed of Jacob, glorify Him: and fear Him, all ye the seed of Israel. For He hath not despised nor abhorred the affliction of the afflicted; *neither hath He hid His face from Him*; but when He cried unto Him, He heard."

Then follows the expression of the purpose to declare to men what in this great trial of faith He has been experiencing of God's faithfulness, and a prophesying of the result that would follow, viz. universal trust in God, who had not hid His face from the afflicted, but had heard His prayer:

My praise shall be of thee in the great congregation: I will pay my vows before them that fear Him. The meek shall eat and shall be satisfied: they shall praise the Lord, that seek Him: your heart shall live for ever. All ends of the world shall remember and turn unto the Lord; and all the kindreds of the nations shall worship before thee, &c.

The character of this psalm as a whole is, therefore, quite unequivocal, viz. a dealing of the Father with Christ in which the cup of man's enmity is drank by Him to its last drop, in the experience of absolute weakness - the true weakness of humanity realised, whereby scope is given for the trust of sonship towards the Father; and we may add, considering the reference to men and their salvation with which the psalm closes, the love of brotherhood to men.

But trust in God, personal trust, is that of which the trial is most conspicuous as pervading the psalm - trust in utter weakness - trust in the midst of enemies - trust which the extremity of that weakness and the perfected enmity of these enemies tries to the utmost - trust which the Father permits to be thus tried; but trust the root of which in the Father's favour has not been cut off, nor even touched by any act of the Father or expression of His face as if He were turned into an enemy - as if He looked on the suppliant in wrath - as if He regarded him as a sinner, imputed sin to him. Not this, not the most distant approach to this. Nay, on the contrary, language is put into the mouth of the Tried One that would seem to preclude the possibility of such a misconception as completely as if chosen for that purpose; and the very ground on which the exhortation is given "Ye that fear the Lord, praise Him; all ye the seed of Jacob, glorify Him; and praise Him, all ye the seed of Israel," is, "For He hath not despised nor abhorred the affliction of the afflicted; *neither hath He hid His face from him*; but when he cried unto Him, He heard," leaving no place even for that negative wrath, if the expression be not a contradiction, which, in clinging to the idea that the cup given to Christ was the cup of the Father's wrath, while yet shrinking from what such words should mean, has, as we have seen above, been set forth as a hiding of the Father's face.

A measure of freedom of pleading with the Father while drinking of the bitter cup is indeed here recorded which is of the same character and has the same special impress of a life upon it which the words, "if it be possible let this cup pass from me" as used in the anticipation of drinking it, have. But that we meet here an interruption of the continuity of that life which was in the consciousness of the Father's favour, an exception to the experience of abiding in the Father's love because keeping His commandments - that a moment had arrived in which the confidence was disappointed which He had expressed when He said, "Ye shall flee every man to his own, and shall leave me alone: and *yet I am not alone, because the Father is with me*," - that having said, "I lay down my life that I may take it up again, *therefore my Father loveth me*," the love of which He thus spoke was not His strength in dying, but that He tasted death under the Father's wrath; of this, or anything in the most distant way suggestive of this, there is no trace.

And this remains true whatever width of meaning we may give to the expression "hour and power of darkness." Many have dwelt upon the part that he who is said to have the power of death, viz. the devil, may have had in our Lord's sufferings on the cross and in all this season. Considering the manner of trial which he was permitted to be to our Lord at His entering on His ministry, there is nothing that we need be repelled by in the thought that, in the invisible, a part of the trial appointed for our Lord may have been a permission to him to express his malice. But on this supposed element in the cup given Christ to drink I must be silent as to positive statement, not seeing that anything is revealed.

Only this much may be confidently asserted, that anything permitted now could only be what that permitted formerly was, that is, a *trial* of the *faith of sonship*; for indeed as to the former trial, while the devil is represented as met by the Saviour with quotations from Scripture for which the tempter's appeal to Scripture was one reason, we shall lose much if we do not mark that the bringing forth of the meaning of the words quoted by the enemy by placing them in their true harmony with other passages, is a use of Scripture for which no verbal knowledge of Scripture can qualify, but of which those alone are capable who are the children of wisdom.

That the fiery darts of the wicked of which so many have had experience may be a participation in one element of our Lord's cup, it is not difficult to understand. But if so, these fiery darts have been met by Him with the shield of faith in the Father's fatherliness, and can have had nothing at all to do with the real aspect of the Father's face towards Him; nor could any supposed amount of such an element as this in His cup be in the smallest degree an approach to what has been conceived of as the wrath of God. This is certain, as neither could any suffering from this supposed source, whatever its amount, be consistent with the idea of penal suffering, any more than any other element of suffering which was painful because of the holiness of the sufferer - however it might accord with the purpose of making our Lord perfect through suffering as the Captain of our salvation and He who led captivity captive.

If the 22nd psalm helps us to conceive more truly of what our Lord felt while suffering at the hands of the wicked, it must, in the measure in which it does so, add to the value to us of the words of forgiving intercession which He uttered on the cross - as all unadvised depreciating of what men's treatment of Him was to Christ must lessen their value. In proportion, also, as this psalm presents to us the trial to which the faith of sonship in Christ was subjected, it helps us to realise the victory of that faith which is revealed in the peace of the words in death, "Father, into thy hands I commend my spirit."

But the triumphant close of the psalm, and its large prophetic intima-tions shed important light back on the purely individual tone of the earlier part of it. We are not told in the psalm itself what the answer to "the cry of the afflicted" has been: only the language of supplication so accords with what is said in the Epistle to the Hebrews, (v. 7), of our Lord's having "in the days of His flesh offered up prayers and supplications with strong crying and tears unto Him that was able to save Him from death, and being heard in that He feared," - that we cannot hesitate in assuming the relation of these passages, or in connecting the last with what is said in the 21st psalm, ver. 4, "He asked life of thee, and thou gavest it Him even length of days for ever and ever;" an answer according with the peace of the words "Father, into thy hands I commend thy spirit."

The comfort of this answer is indeed, so far as the language goes, as purely individual as the tone of the agony and the pleading. Yet the prospect for men which is seen to open to the suppliant reveals an interest of all men in the answer of His prayer, as well as the consciousness of a relation to all men in the previous suffering in which the cry was uttered, the divine response to which is thus salvation to men. So that, notwithstanding the individuality of the tone of the earlier part of the psalm, we are justified in ascribing to the sufferer an inward sense of His relation to all men corresponding with the expression used by Him in anticipating His sufferings: "and I, if I be lifted up, will draw all men unto me," - a reference such as the words imply, "who for the joy set before Him endured the cross." Notwithstanding, therefore, the individual tone of this psalm which, at first sight, does not seem to accord with its unquestionable reference to the crucifixion of Christ, we see in its close that it indeed belongs to Him who bore our sins in His own body on the tree, and who, having made peace by the blood of His cross, came and preached peace to them who were afar off, and to them that were near.

But it is not only as indicating to us that the interests of all humanity were involved in that suffering and that cry of the afflicted and in the divine response to that cry, that the latter part of this psalm is so important. It is still more important, as shedding light upon the atonement by the representation made of the way in which the happy result as to men which is prophesied is to be accomplished. It is the Father's acknowledgment of the faith of the Son, which, being made known to men, is to cause "all the ends of the world to remember and turn unto the Lord, and all the kindreds of the nations to worship before him." However much the Afflicted One whose cry had been heard was, as the Holy One of God, separated from all men: however it might be assumed that He had grounds to plead in prayer peculiar to Himself; however free also He was from all that cause of fear and hesitation in lifting up the heart to God in prayer, which ordinary men are conscious to as sinners: still His prayer must have been offered on a ground that all may occupy, and from which sin need exclude none.

This is clear; otherwise, that His prayer was heard, would not have been that Gospel to a sinful world, which it is here set forth as being. We must believe that any sinner of the human race to whom the nature of that cry and the grounds of it, and that which it sought from God, would be revealed in the Spirit, would see the divine answer that would quicken faith and hope towards God in that sinner. He who in coming to this world had said, "Lo I come to do thy will, O God," - who could, as to the fulfilment of this purpose, say to the Father, "I have glorified thee on the earth, I have declared thy name, and will declare it," is seen here at the close of His course, as one holding fast the beginning of His confidence, and in this last trying time, and while subjected to the hour and power of darkness, sustained by the simple faith of that original fatherliness of the Father's heart, which He had *come forth to reveal* and TO REVEAL BY TRUSTING IT.

Thus, the Holy One of God, God's holy child Jesus, having glorified his Father on the earth in all living righteous fulfilment of His will, now perfects His glorifying of the Father's Name, by being seen trusting in that Name alone when brought into the extremest need of a sure hold of God - trusting simply in that Name, and not raising a claim of merit on having so perfectly honoured that Name. The Sinless One is seen trusting simply in that Name which he had come to reveal to sinners, that they also might trust in it and be saved; and thus the Father's response to that trust is preached as the gospel to the chief of sinners.

When one who has seen the glory of God in the face of Jesus Christ, and who through Christ has faith and hope towards God, invites a brother sinner to share in his joy in the Lord, to share in his confidence through Christ, it is not an uncommon reply to be told, "But you are much better than I am. If I were only as religious as you are, and obeyed God as you seem to do, I should cherish hope." And when such a person replies, "But you do not understand the secret of my peace. I am not trusting to my own merits. I am trusting simply and entirely to the free grace of God: the mercy of God revealed in Christ and which has just the same relation to you that it has to me is the source of all my peace. I indeed do seek to please God. Indeed I seek my life in His favour. But I do so altogether in the strength of that mind and heart of God towards me which the gospel reveals, and my doing so is only my welcoming of the salvation which is given me in the Son of God;" - he has often the pain of finding all he thus urges going for nothing, because it is set down as only Christian humility on his part - only the effect of the high standard which he is setting before himself; and so, while it is thought to be very becoming in him to be thus humble, yet it still is felt that he must be trusting to that in which he is seen to differ from others; and so his peace is no gospel to those who feel themselves so unlike him.

To meet this is painful and embarrassing when one would say with the Psalmist, "O taste and see that *God is good*: blessed is the man that trusteth in Him." But it may surely serve to clear up this matter, and to remove all darkness from the subject of peace with God, to consider that our Lord Himself at the last as at the first, trusted simply and purely in the fatherliness of the Father. "But thou art He that took me out of my mother's womb. Thou didst make me hope when I was upon my mother's breasts."

That which is not understood while men's conceptions of salvation are self-righteous, whether they are still flattering themselves with the hope that they are in some measure succeeding in recommending themselves to God's favour, or are less or more disturbed by the sense of failure in this attempt, is the simple nature of trust in God as the response of sonship to the heart of the Father apprehended by faith. The oneness of sonship as perfect in Christ, and as in measure in us through participation in Christ, I have sought to keep before my reader's mind all along. To understand this oneness is what is needed to enable us to understand how the Father's response to the cry of the Son, as "the afflicted," the trial of whose faith is so far set before us in this psalm, is expected to have power, being made known, to cause "all the ends of the world to remember and turn unto the Lord, and all the kindreds of the nations to worship before Him."

2. The sufferings of Christ, which thus perfected His witnessing for God to men, had an equally close relation to **His dealing with the Father on our behalf** - giving its ultimate depth to His confession of our sins, and the excellence of a perfect development of love and faith to His intercession for sinners, according to the will of God.

The expectation as to the great results that were to follow, because "God had not despised nor abhorred the affliction of the afflicted, neither had hid His face from Him, but when He cried unto Him He heard," with the expression of which the 22nd psalm concludes, is in effect the preaching to us of the gospel that God has given to us eternal life in His Son; - for it is the declaration that the knowledge of the Son's trust in the Father will introduce us to the fellowship of that trust. But we are to learn from what we know otherwise of that cross of the Redeemer, which, in one aspect of it, this psalm so sets before us, how this should be so.

It was in making His soul an offering for sin that this terrible trial of the faith proper to sonship came to Christ. He was wounded for our transgressions, and bruised for our iniquities - that which He suffered was the chastisement that was to issue in peace to us, and His stripes were for the healing of our souls; for He suffered the just for the unjust that He might bring us to God - bearing out sins in His own body on the tree, that we, being dead to sins, should live unto righteousness. In accomplishing these results, we have now seen that, in order to the perfection of the work of Christ as witnessing for God to men, it has appeared to the divine wisdom necessary to subject His love and trust towards the Father, and His long-suffering forgiveness in bearing the contradiction of sinners against himself, to the trial of the hour and power of darkness. Nor was the bitter cup thus appointed by the Father for the Son less important to the full development of the other element in the atonement, viz. the dealing of the Son with the Father on our behalf, as confessing our sins and making intercession for us, according to the will of God.

The intercession of forgiving love in the words, "Father, forgive them; for they know not what they do," has already engaged our attention, as it was the expression of Christ's own righteousness of His enemies - and so also a part of His testimony for the Father as He says, "Love your enemies, bless them that curse you, do good to them that hate you, and pray for them that despitefully use you and persecute you; that *ye may be the children of your Father which is in heaven.*" But contemplating our Lord as bearing us on His Spirit before the Father, and dealing on our behalf with the righteousness and mercy of God, confessing our sin with that confession which was the due response to the divine wrath against sin, and interceding for us according to the hope that was for us in God; this prayer on the cross - "Father, forgive them; for they know not what they do," belongs to the perfecting of this intercession of redeeming love in making our peace with God - that peace which, because perfected on the cross, is set forth to us as made there.

It is obvious that all by which the pressure of our sins on the Spirit of Christ was increased and He was brought into closer contact with them and deeper experience of the hatred of the darkness to the light must have given a continually deepening character to Christ's dealing with the Father on our behalf; - giving an increasing depth to His response to the divine condemnation of our sin, causing that response to be rendered in deeper agony of spirit, and, at the same time, rendering His preserving intercession a casting Himself more and more on the further, and deeper depths of fatherliness in the Father.

Adhering to the conception of a progressive development of the eternal life in our Lord's human consciousness, and looking at all that was appointed for Him by the Father as adapted by the divine wisdom for the end of forwarding this development, we indeed see abundant reason for that perfected personal experience of the enmity of the carnal mind to God to which our Lord was subjected. Without this the Son could never have proved in human consciousness, as we have just been contemplating Him as doing the forgiveness that is in love; - or the strength to overcome evil with good, which brotherly love can exercise, sustained by the faith of sonship trusting in the love of the Father; or the sufficiency that is in the Father's favour for the life of sonship, however absolutely cast upon God. And so neither without this could an adequate confession of man's sin have been offered to God in humanity in expiation of man's sin, nor intercession have been made according to the extent of man's need for forgiveness.

Therefore, though not as filling a cup of penal suffering, yet as essential to the living reality of a moral and spiritual atonement for sin, are all those painful experiences which President Edwards has so fully entered into in his illustrations of Christ's suffering for our sins when He bore them in His own body on the tree, to be weighed equally by us also.

I have already noticed the limits which Edwards has recognised as to be observed in conceiving to ourselves the elements of the inward mental sufferings to which our Lord was subjected while the malice of the wicked was poured upon Him from without - being thankful that he has recognised such limits; nor, as I have said above, is it to his representation of the amount of Christ's sufferings, or of their nature, that I object, but to the conception that these sufferings were *penal*. Assuming *that* idea to be precluded, as urged above, by the very nature of the sufferings endured, I am only the more anxious that we should not come short in our apprehension of the terrible reality that was in these sufferings, or of the *real* and *necessary proportion* that was between our *sins* and the *wounding to which Christ submitted*, in making His soul an offering for sin.

The *peace-making* between God and man, which was perfected by our Lord on the cross, required to its reality the presence to the spirit of Christ of the *elements of the alienation* as well as the possession by Him of that eternal righteousness in which was the virtue to make peace. All the considerations that had a claim in the truth of things to be taken into account must have been taken into account: and though God's wrath against sin was not felt by the Son of God as coming forth against Himself personally, as if the Father saw Him as a sinner; yet must that wrath in the truth of what it is have been present to and realised by His spirit; - and though He suffered not from it as "having its revenges inflicted on Him," yet must the realisation of it and confession of its righteousness, in perfect sympathy with that righteousness, have been a suffering proportioned to His spiritual perfection; and while He interceded in the faith of the infinite love of the Father and knowing that the will of God was our salvation, yet must the love that was taking this form have suffered in itself, while interceding, all the pain proper to the heart of perfect sonship, in its sympathy with the feelings of perfect fatherhood against which His brethren had sinned.

Surely the soul that was made to be filled with the consciousness which these thoughts imply was made a sacrifice for sin. Surely, while freed from all that it is so impossible to harmonise with the faith of a true consciousness in this great transaction - either in contemplating the mind of the Father towards the Son, or the mind of the Son towards the Father - which is implied in the imputation of our sins to Christ and the assumption that His sufferings were penal, there is seen still in this great peace-making an awful coming together in the inner man of the Son of God of moral and spiritual elements; the harmonising of which in the result of peace between man and God - a peace in God realised in humanity for man to know and partake in, a peace to be preached to the chief of sinners - has been a work of love, in which the Son of God is seen bearing the chastisement of our peace; suffering for us, the just for the unjust, to bring us to God.

Let it not seem to any as if while rejecting the conception of *penal* suffering as the atonement I were still anxious to keep the idea of *suffering* before the mind, and to raise as high as possible the conception of that suffering, as feeling a demand for suffering in the history of the pardon of our sins to be what is to be ascribed to God, a demand for suffering as suffering. That would indeed be to cherish indirectly the wrong conception of atonement, deliverance from which I feel so important. I am only anxious that the elements of the dealing of the Son with the Father in His intercession for us should be realised by us, so that the mind of God in relation to us and our sins should be truly apprehended; and the hatefulness of our sins, as well as our personal preciousness to the Father of our spirits, be revealed to us through the apprehension of the elements of the peace which Christ accomplished on the cross.

Nothing can be more vague or practically unsuited to the real need of our spirits, polluted with the pollution of sin, than the kind of meaning associated with our being "washed in the blood of Christ," while the thought of the shedding of His blood is the thought of the punishment of our sins, as endured by Christ for us. The nearest approach to a meaning which the common prayer, "to be washed in the blood of Christ," has, as used in this connection, is, I think, the expression of the feeling in the suppliant that he deserves wrath, and a recognition of the sufferings of Christ for his sin as the only ground on which he can expect pardon; and a certain element of self-despair, and of hope in free grace, may be present, and, I doubt not, often is present in this form of thought. But if the blood of Christ be to our thoughts the spiritual reality which was in Christ's making His soul an offering for sin, then, to be washed in the blood of Christ must be to have the moral and spiritual elements of that offering revealed in our spirits, so bringing us into spiritual harmony with them, making us to partake in them; which to call a spiritual cleansing is no figure of speech but the simplest and most natural expression for a spiritual reality.

But in this view every element in the great peace-making, which the Gospel proclaims as having been altogether and perfectly successful and as resulting in a true spiritual peace for man - a peace for man to be enjoyed in fellowship with the Father and the Son in the Spirit - is of the utmost importance; and to leave any one element out unembraced by our faith is to be practically without the knowledge and so without the use of a part of the unsearchable riches which we have in Christ.

In the full and clear apprehension of the moral and spiritual atonement made by the Son of God, in the faith of the peace made by Him on the cross, then perfected, but in relation to which He was all along "the blessed peace maker," it is most surely felt that the true and perfect atonement, expiation, and satisfaction for man's sin is known; that we are in the light of it; and that that light is the light of life.

As respects what the atonement is in itself, and Christ's consciousness in making it, we see that, if Christ had been literally, as Luther has attempted to believe, made the reality of sin for us - if He had been in personal consciousness the one sinner, guilty of all the sins of all men, and under this load of guilt had sought, in the strength of conscious perfect righteousness, the Father's face; such confession of the evil of sin, such entrance into the Father's mind regarding it, such responsive unity with the Father in the condemnation of it, as we have been ascribing to Him as presented by Him to the Father with reference to our sins, would have been the atonement He would have made; and such trust in the fatherliness of the Father as we have assumed to have encouraged and sustained His intercession for us would have been the strength of hope in which He would have made that atonement.

Therefore, being the holy one of God, and separate from sin, in personal consciousness as well as in reality, yet bearing our sins on His heart before the Father, dealing with the Father's righteousness and mercy on our behalf, asking for us that which was according to the Father's will, we feel that the confession and the intercession made by Him - divine, while human - must have been made with the consciousness of its suitableness, and the assurance of its acceptance. "I said, I will confess my transgressions unto the Lord; and thou forgavest the iniquity of my sin." (Psalm xxxii. 5)

As to ourselves and the light in which we see all that concerns our relation to God in contemplating the Son's dealing with the Father on our behalf, if we understand the elements of that which we contemplate we must feel that it is what, could we have offered it to God, was due from ourselves; and that, could we have offered it, it would have been an atonement such as no endurance of punishment could ever have been; this we must feel, though at the same time we feel that to have made it was as impossible for us as to have made ourselves divine; while yet we also see that we must partake in it, and must have its elements reproduced in us, for that these elements constitute the mind in which we who have sinned against God and been rebellious children must return to the Father of our spirits if we are to return at all; that Christ is indeed the way and the truth and the life; that no man can come to the Father but by Him.

In the way opened for us into the holiest by the blood of Christ we see what in its own light is discerned by us to be at once *a way* into the holiest and *the only way*. In exercising faith in that blood we are consciously under a cleansing and purifying power, the only power that could cleanse and purify us, but as to which we feel that it has *in itself no limit*, and that its result in us will only be limited as the measure of our being yielded up to it is limited. In our begun life of sonship through the faith of the Son of God, in our feeble lisping of the Father's name, we have consciously the earnest of the eternal inheritance. The perfecting of our conscience as worshippers by the sprinkling of the blood of Christ we discern to be the commencement of that experience which will hereafter utter itself in the song, "Unto Him that loved us, and washed us from our sins in His own blood, and hath made us kings and priests unto God and His Father; to Him be glory and dominion for ever and ever. Amen."

Finally, when from thus contemplating the atonement as accomplished by Christ, and seeing ourselves in its light - realising how hopeless our state had been apart from it, while conscious to the living faith and hope towards God which the faith of it is quickening in us - we lift up our thoughts to the Father, and consider what the great work of redeeming love has been to Him, and hear in relation to it the testimony of the Father to the Son, "This is my beloved Son in whom I am well pleased, hear ye Him," we are, indeed, filled with the glory of God in the face of Jesus Christ. Seeing the Father in the Son, the divine elements of the work of the Son in the Father - that what we are contemplating in Christ is, indeed, but the perfect doing of the Father's will, the perfect declaring of His name, and raised up by the faith of the will of God as done, of the name of God as declared, to the apprehension of the Eternal Will, the Unchanging Name, we understand the complacency of the Father in the Son, and how it pleased the Father to bruise the Son and put Him to brief, how the Father saw it good to put into the hands of the Son of His love the cup concerning which He had prayed that if it were possible it should pass from Him; we understand the value to God who is love of the manifestation of love in all its long-suffering, forgiving, self-sacrificing depth and might; while yet we understand that this manifestation of love neither was nor could have been but in relation to the results which were contemplated - that it was as being "bringing many sons to glory," that "it became Him for whom are all things, and by whom are all things, to make the Captain of their salvation perfect through sufferings:"

And the identity of the life of sonship as seen accomplishing the atonement and as partaken in by men through participation in the atonement, and the excellent glory of the hope of sonship in its inheriting of the Father - as it is said, "heirs of God, heirs of God and joint heirs with Christ," - are to use the *full* justification of the Father in all that travail of the soul of Christ of which our salvation is the fruit.

CHAPTER XIII

THE DEATH OF CHRIST CONTEMPLATED AS HIS "TASTING DEATH," AND "FOR EVERY MAN"; AND THE LIGHT IT SHEDS ON HIS LIFE, AND ON THAT FELLOWSHIP IN HIS LIFE, THROUGH BEING CONFORMED TO HIS DEATH, TO WHICH WE ARE CALLED

I have nothing to add in direct elucidation of the view now taken of the nature of the atonement; but both the necessity for the perfecting of the atonement in the death of our Lord on the cross, which the fact of His death in connection with His prayer in the garden implies, and the constant reference to the cross as suggestive of the whole work of redemption, are reasons for presenting here to the reader's attention some thoughts in relation to the death of our Lord, viewed in itself and in the light of His consciousness in passing through death, which may be profitable, and especially, practically.

The words of our Lord in death, "Father, into thy hands I commend my spirit," are given to help us to understand the life of sonship which we are seeing passing out of our sight, and to reveal to us in this its final triumph the secret of its victory all along. For, in this trust in death we are not contemplating a new manner of faith. The perfection of its development and measure of its manifestation only are new. The faith which this last utterance of the voice of sonship presents to our faith is not anything else than that trust in the Father manifested in death which had pervaded the Lord's whole life; for, Christ's following of God as a dear child, walking in love, always implied that direct and immediate living by the Father which these words used in death expressed. He ever through the Eternal Spirit offered Himself without spot to God. To hold and use this life in the flesh in sonship, and to yield it up in sonship, these were diverse actings of one faith. Therefore, the words, "Father, into thy hands I commend my spirit," should shed light back to us on the whole of our Lord's path on earth. There was a saying "Not my will, but thine be done," a dying to live, in all our Lord's life, as well as at the close.

I have already spoken of the shame of the cross in its relation to that second commandment of which Christ's perfect brotherhood towards man was the fulfilment, as His sonship towards the Father was the fulfilment of the first. If we know anything of life as a meeting in the strength of sonship the call which the first commandment makes on us, and know that rejection of all independent life in self and our neighbour which this implies, our own experience will help us in endeavouring to realise the oneness of the faith in which Christ lived, seeking not His own glory but His glory who had sent Him, with the faith in which in death He said, "Father, into thy hands I commend my spirit." The Apostle speaks of "dying daily;" and, if we are attempting to "follow God as dear children, walking in love," we know that *this* implies such a dying daily as is possible only in a faith which is a constant commending of our spirit into the Father's hands. For lonely as death is, not less lonely is true life at its root and core - I mean lonely as respects the creature, a being left alone with God.

But, while the faith tried and proved in our Lord's tasting death was the same that had been tried and proved in His whole life, yet was the trial peculiar and extreme and in its nature fitted to be the final trial, as well as to shed light back on all former trials. I have already noticed the sinless - I should rather say righteous - desire of the life that is in man's favour which our Lord's fulfilment of the second commandment implied, and which explains to us the intenseness of feeling under the injustice done to Him in men's estimate of Him expressed in the words "Reproach hath broken my heart." In bearing the contradiction of sinners our Lord was continually drinking of cups which naturally and sinlessly, nay, because of love and therefore righteously, He must have desired not to drink; which yet as presented to Him by His Father He desired to drink, and which, in the strength of the eternal life which is in the Father's favour, He did drink.

Now death itself, as the close of life so lived and passed through in the strength which the words reveal, "Father, into thy hands I commend my spirit," was in harmony with such a life and its fitting close; for it was the perfect manifestation and consummation of the faith in the Father which was the secret of that life.

(1) I say, it was the "perfect manifestation" of that faith, because it revealed the strength in which our Lord had been able to do without the honour which cometh from man - the life that is in man's favour - and how it was that He had not feared those whose power can go no further than to kill the body. The life which was common to them and to Him, the life through which they could reach Him and cause Him pain, *that* life had conferred upon them no power over His spirit; for that life He had held, as He now parted with it, in the strength and freedom of sonship.

(2) I have also said, "consummation," because it was the perfected development of that faith. I cannot help having the words in reference to Abraham's offering up of Isaac here recalled to me, "Now I know that thou lovest me." "By works was faith perfected." The faith that could offer up Isaac was there before it was proved; yet something further had come to pass in the spirit of Abraham, and in the sight of God, when it was proved. So of all our Lord's sufferings, in that though a Son He learned obedience by the things which He suffered. The sonship was there perfect all along; yet

something came to pass, something was developed in the humanity of the Lord in each successive outcoming of the obedience of sonship under suffering; something which the Father had desired to see in humanity and now saw, and which the incarnation, simply as such, had not accomplished, but which was being accomplished as the life of the Son in humanity progressed under the Father's educating of Him as the Captain of our salvation. And if this be a true apprehension as to the previous sufferings of the Lord and their progressive intensity, so also must it be of His tasting death. In substance, in spirit, He had all along said, "Father, into thy hands I commend my spirit." In actual death He now said so.

The simplest positive idea which I am able to form of the glory given to the Father, in saying, in death, "Father, into thy hands I commend my spirit," I receive in realising the nakedness of simple being, stripped of all possession but what is possessed in the heart of the Father, which is suggested to us as that in the consciousness of which this trust is exercised. It is the most perfect and absolute form of that experience, "I am not alone, for the Father is with me." It takes away creation and leaves but God. It is not difficult to see the glory given to God in this faith. Never does the Son who dwells in the bosom of the Father, utter more to our hearts what it is to possess the Father as our Father, and to be sons of God, than when He says in death "Father, into thy hands I commend my spirit."

And we must note that this is not said in simple naked existence, as it might be the utterance of sonship in a spirit just awakened to the consciousness of existence, knowing yet no possession but God who has given it being. It is an utterance *in death*. He who thus puts trust in the Father is *tasting death* while doing so.

It is very difficult for us, though most desirable, to apprehend what this should add to our conception of that declaring of the Father's name which is in Christ's death. When I think of our Lord as tasting death it seems to me as if He alone ever truly tasted death. And this, indeed, may be received as a part of the larger truth that He alone ever lived in humanity in the conscious truth of humanity. But when I think of death as tasted by our Lord, how little help to conceiving of His experience in dying do any of our own thoughts or anticipated experiences seem fitted to yield!

What men shrink from when they shrink from death, is, either the disruption of the ties that connect them with a present world, or the terrors with which an accusing conscience fills the world to come. The last had no existence for Him who was without sin: neither had the world, as the present evil world, any place in His heart. And even as to that purer interest in the present scene, which the relationships of life, cherished aright and according to God's intention in them, awaken, and the trial that death may be from this cause, there was in our Lord's case nothing parallel to it; unless that care of His mother, which He devolved upon the beloved disciple.

But death, *as death*, is distinct from such accompanying considerations as these, and our Lord tasted it in the truth of that which it is. For, as He had truly lived in humanity, and possessed and used the gift of life according to the truth of humanity, so did He also truly die; death was to His humanity the withdrawal of the gift of that life which it closes. As men in life know not life as God's gift, neither realise what it is to live; so neither do they in death know God's withdrawal of that gift, nor consciously realise what it is to die. "For as a man liveth, so he dieth."

But it was altogether otherwise with our Lord. It was a part of His sinless consciousness in humanity to possess life in the pure sense of it as God's gift; and, therefore, it was a part of His sinless consciousness in humanity to cleave to it - to desire to retain it. This desire was in Him a true and sinless utterance of humanity. And as we have seen in what truth of humanity, and how intensely, Christ was affected by the malice of the wicked, though as respected the perfection of His faith He could say, "I have overcome the world;" so are we to understand that the eternal life in which He passed through death did not make death as nothing to Him, but that the true conception is, that it enabled Him perfectly to taste of death - to taste of it as was only possible in the strength of eternal life.

Further, as our Lord alone truly tasted death, so to Him alone had death its perfect meaning as the wages of sin, for in Him alone was their full entrance into the mind of God towards sin, and perfect unity with that mind. We have seen before, that the perfect confession of our sins was only possible to perfect holiness; and so we may see also, that the tasting of death in full realisation of what it is that God who gave life should recall it, holding it forfeited, was only possible to perfect holiness.

How much this thought should suggest to us as to the bitterness which belonged to the cup which Christ drank in tasting death for every man, we may not measure. Yet we can see the fitness of the presence of this element in Christ's cup of suffering, and that His perfect realisation of the relation of death to sin naturally connected itself with the confession of the righteousness of the divine condemnation on sin, and the fulness and perfection of that confession - the fulness of meaning of the response, "Thou art righteous, O Lord, who judgest so. For, thus, in Christ's honouring of the righteous law of God, the *sentence of the law* was included, as well as *the mind of God* which that sentence expressed.

In this light are we to see the death of Christ, as connected with His redeeming those that were under the law, that they might receive the adoption of sons. Had sin existed in men as mere spirits, death could not have been the wages of sin, and any response to the divine mind concerning sin which would have been an atonement for their sin could only have had spiritual elements; but man being by the constitution of humanity capable of death, and death having come as the wages of sin, it was not simply sin that had to be dealt with, but an existing law with its penalty of death, and that death as already incurred. So it was not only the divine mind that had to be responded too, but also, that expression of the divine mind which was contained in God's making death and wages of sin.

This honouring of the law, while it was being made to give place to that higher dispensation to which it was subordinate from the first in the divine purpose, being also subordinate in its own nature has, indeed, been followed out to its fullest measure, in that our Lord not only tasted death, but, that that death was the death of the cross - as the Apostle says, "Christ hath redeemed us from the curse of the law, being made a curse for us: for it is written, Cursed is every one that hangeth on a tree." (Galatians iii. 13)

He who endured the cross, despising the shame, did so as He tasted death, of which the cross was for this reason the selected form, in that oneness of mind with God which rendered His doing so truly a fitting element in the atonement; and thus in respect even of all that was most physical and external, the real value and virtue was most physical and external, the real value and virtue was strictly moral and spiritual: for the tasting of death for us was not as a substitute - otherwise He alone would have died; nor as a punishment - for, tasted in the strength of righteousness and of the Father's favour, death had to Him no sting; but as a moral and spiritual sacrifice for sin. And thus, as I have said above, while death taking place simply as such, and the wages of sin, had been no atonement, neither could come to be through the subjection to it of the countless millions of our sinful race, death *filled with that moral and spiritual meaning in relation to God and His righteous law* which it had as tasted by Christ, and *passed through in the spirit of sonship*, was the *perfecting of the atonement*. That personally our Lord was conscious to perfect freedom in relation to death, "Therefore doth my Father love me, because I lay down my life, that I might take it again. No man taketh it from me, but I lay it down of myself. I have power to lay it down, and I have power to take it again. This commandment have I received of my Father," John x. 17, 18; *this* accords with the difference between death coming as the wages of sin, and passing upon all men, for that all have sinned, and death as tasted by the Son of God; tasted in the strength of eternal life, not as a punishment, but, on behalf of men in righteous Amen to the judgment on sin, of which as the wages of sin death is the expression.

In this view we see the suitableness of the awfully solemn circumstances with which it seemed right to the Father to accompany the death of Christ. That darkness, which the evangelists record to have been over the earth from the sixth hour to the ninth hour, has been regarded as what in the natural world harmonised with and was intended to symbolize, what was taking place in the spiritual world, when the vials of the Father's wrath were pouring out on the Son. Minds in which this association has long found a place will not easily receive any other explanation of that darkness, as any other explanation must be felt to come so infinitely short of that most awful and terrible conception. Yet in itself, and apart from this association as already in possession of the mind, this darkness no more than accords with the presence and place of our sins as borne on the spirit of the Redeemer, in that awful though blessed peace-making the elements of which we have been considering, and which had its consummation on the cross; while the language of the Roman centurion under the power of the whole scene, when the baptism in the prospect of which the Lord was so straitened received its accomplishment, "Surely this was the Son of God," recalls to us the testimony of the voice from heaven at His baptism by John in Jordan, "This is my beloved Son," - recalls this testimony to us as one with that which reached the spirit of the centurion, making itself heard in spite of the permitted hour and power of darkness, and prevailing over the seeming meaning of that hour.

We can, indeed, have no difficulty, apart from a fixed habit of thought, in seeing the harmony of the darkness recorded, with the relation of Christ's death to our sins as that relation has now been represented; while the response from the spirit of the centurion to that which was the true expression of the awful scene as a whole accords with the unbroken and continuous acknowledgment of the Son by the Father implied in the conception of the atonement, as altogether and throughout, "Grace reigning through righteousness unto eternal life."

Realising the relation of the death of Christ to our sins, we thus feel all that was dark and terrible in the circumstances of His death justified to our minds; while the peace in which He is seen tasting death illustrates to us the life of sonship in which He does so. But, realising further, that He who is putting this peaceful trust in the Father in death is "by the grace of God tasting death for every man," we are learning much more than how the spirit of sonship can trust the Father even in death, though this by itself is a most important lesson, fitted to help us to realise the truth of our relation to God as "He on whose being our being reposes." This we are learning, but we are further learning how adequate and accepted the atonement for our sins which, in tasting death for us, the Son of God is perfecting, is in His own consciousness before the Father. That relation to us in which the Son of God is seen tasting death - which relation, indeed, alone explains His being tasting death at all - gives this largeness of reference to the words, "Father, into thy hands I commend my spirit," as we have seen in considering the 22nd Psalm.

And so we are to connect the words just quoted as to our Lord's personal freedom in relation to death, "Therefore doth my Father love me, because I lay down my life that I might take it again," with the words, "Except a corn of wheat fall into the ground and die, it abideth alone; but if it die, it bringeth forth much fruit." And "I, if I be lifted up, will draw all men unto me." (John xii. 24, 32)

Therefore, in endeavouring to conceive of our Lord's consciousness in cherishing this hope in death in humanity, and in relation to all humanity, that is, as a hope which His death was opening up to all men, we must have before our minds the atoning elements present in that consciousness as entering into that hope; for upon this depends the measure in which the death of Christ shall be filled for us with the light of life. Faith, it is said, will be imputed to us for righteousness, "if we believe on Him that raised up Jesus our Lord from the dead; who was delivered for our offences, and was raised again for our justification." Therefore, the faith in God by which we become righteous, must embrace our seeing our sins in the light shed upon them by the death of Christ, and our seeing our justification in the light shed upon it by His resurrection from the dead.

And the first part of this statement is presupposed in the second. We cannot understand the ground of confidence for us in God which Christ's resurrection from the dead reveals, unless we understand the mind of God in relation to our sins which His death reveals, and in response to which He tasted death for us. That ground of confidence is the heart of the Father, because with that heart the words deal, "Father, into thy hands I commend my spirit;" but the *death itself*, no less than the hope in death, is an element in the Son's revelation of the Father; and unless that revelation is seen in that death, as well as in that hope in death, the true confidence of sonship to which that hope in death calls, is not understood.

The condemnation of our sin in that expiatory confession of our sin which was perfected in the death of Christ is not less a part of the revelation of the Father by the Son, than the trust in the depths of fatherliness in which life was asked and received for us. Indeed, these are ultimately but two aspects of one mind of God who must condemn our life as rebellious children according as He chooses for us and desires for us the life of true sonship.

Our being planted in the likeness or fellowship of Christ's death is, therefore, a prerequisite to our fellowship in His resurrection from the dead. For, not only was His death no substitute for our death - superseding the necessity for our dying - but, more than this, His death, as differing from death coming as the wages of sin - His death as a propitiation for sin, tasted in the spirit of sonship, and in unity with the Father in His condemnation of sin, that is to say, death, *as tasted by Christ* - must be not only apprehended by our faith, but also spiritually shared in by us. And such participation in the death of Christ is, because of the unity that is in His life and death, necessarily implied in receiving Christ as our life; for the mind in which He died is the mind in which He lived, and that condemnation of sin in the flesh, which was perfected and fully told out in His death, pervaded His life.

Therefore is our "bearing about in the body the dying of the Lord Jesus," implied in "the life of Jesus being manifested in our mortal bodies." Therefore must we knowing Christ, and experiencing the power of His resurrection from the dead as what enables us to have faith and hope in God, have *fellowship in Christ's sufferings*, and *be conformed to His death*.

The close and direct consideration of the death of Christ, and of His consciousness in tasting death for every man, saying, "Father, into thy hands I commend my spirit," now attempted, may as I have said, help us practically; illustrating the directly and absolutely practical aspect in which the cross of Christ is contemplated in the Scriptures. I have already noticed how we are taught by the hope for men expressed in the 22nd psalm, in connection with God's hearing the cry of the afflicted and not hiding His face from him, that that fatherliness in God, in which the Sinless One is trusting, is a fatherliness in which the sinful may trust. It is in the light of the confession of our sins as one aspect of the life of sonship in Christ - that side, as I have said above, on which the life of Christ is nearest us - that this is clear to us.

That confession being understood, we feel that in receiving it, as a part of the mind of Christ, to be in us and be our own mind, we can freely breathe the life of sonship as confidence towards the Father - we can share in the mind which the words express, "Father, into thy hands I commend my spirit;" we can share in that mind, both as it was through life the inmost element in the victory of the Son of God over the world, and as it was His victorious peace in death. Acting on this apprehension, taking to ourselves this confession, and saying Amen to it, entering by this path into the liberty of sonship, and in that liberty meeting life and meeting death, we come to know in ourselves what the Apostle meant when He said, "God forbid that I should glory, save in the cross of our Lord Jesus Christ, by whom the world is crucified unto me, and I unto the world." (Galatians vi. 14)

The fleshly life which the death of Christ condemns, the spiritual life which Christ's hope in death commends to our spirits, these are present to us in the enlightened contemplation of Christ as dying that we might live; and, therefore, our uniting in the condemnation that His death expresses in relation to the life which it condemns, welcoming that life to be our life which His hope in death reveals and commends - this, and our receiving Christ as our Saviour, are one and the same movement of our being - a practical movement in the deepest sense - a choice of the will, not as to *acts*, but as to *life* - a choosing the life given to us in Christ that we may live; being that same practical judgment which the Apostle Paul expresses when he says, "For the love of Christ constraineth us; because we thus judge, that if one died for all, then were all dead" - or, rather, then have all died - "and that He died for all, that they which live should not henceforth live unto themselves, but unto Him which died for them, and rose again." (2 Cor. v. 14, 15)

And the Apostle Peter also, when he says, "Forasmuch then as Christ hath suffered for us in the flesh, arm yourselves likewise with the same mind. For He that hath suffered in the flesh hath ceased from sin; that He no longer should live the rest of His time in the flesh to the lusts of men, but to the will of God." (1 Peter iv. 1, 2)

How such practical, living dealing with the cross of Christ as these quotations express, will confirm us in the faith to which it belongs; how the "bearing about in the body the dying of the Lord Jesus," and "the manifestation of the life of Jesus in our mortal bodies," will progress together and deepen in intensity; how the counsel of God in connecting us with Christ as He has done, and identifying us with Him in His death, and in His resurrection from the dead, will be more and more clearly seen to be to the glory of God according as we are conforming to this gracious constitution of the kingdom of God, dead in the death of Christ, and living that life which we have hid with Christ in God - this, in the light of the atonement as now represented, we easily understand.

But one caution my reader will here bear from me, supposing the teaching of these pages to be commending itself to his understanding, and so to be giving me some claim on his weighing what I urge - viz. that it is the *conscience* much more than the *understanding* that is concerned in a right reception of teaching, which, if true at all, is pre-eminently, and in the deepest sense, *practical teaching.* I shall not feel it nothing that the argument should commend itself; but this consent of the understanding is a small matter unless the conscience feel, that *that* is presented to it which has power to purge it from dead works, to serve the living God; - unless the spirit which has dwelt in the darkness and death of sin, see the path of life open before it, shining in the light of the divine favour; unless the orphan spirit find itself brought into the presence of its long lost Father, who is waiting to receive it graciously, whose heart yearns to hear it cry, Abba, Father. To this result it is as necessary that the death of Christ, as filled with the divine judgment on sin, shall commend itself to the conscience, as that the life of Christ and His resurrection from the dead, revealing the hope which, when we had destroyed ourselves, remained for us in God, shall so commend itself.

And let no man deceive himself, as if it were his experience that conscience responded to the latter revelation, and welcomed the light of life, while it responded not to the former, nor said "Amen" to that amen to the divine judgment in relation to sin which was in the death of Christ, and gave it its atoning virtue. That would be to say that light may be light, and yet not make the darkness manifest. I have dwelt above on the fixedness of that law of the kingdom of God which the words express - "No man cometh to the Father but by the Son." But no man cometh by the Son who cometh not in the fellowship of His death - "Thou hast washed us in thy blood, and made us kings and priests unto God."

The deep and awful impression of what sin must be in the eyes of God, which men have received while contemplating the suffering of Christ for our sins as His having the vials of divine wrath poured out on Him, has been recognised above as in itself a great gain, notwithstanding the darkness in which the mind of God towards sin and sinners was left by that view, and even the positive misconception which it contained. So real a gain has that deep and awful impression on the subject of sin been, that it would be an indication of having gone out of the right path to find that we were parting with it. But, assuredly, not less profound or awful, while accompanied by a light of the glory of God not seen in that other system, is the sense of the evil and guilt of sin which is received when the sufferings of Christ become to our minds *not* the *measure* of what God *can inflict*, but the *revelation* of what *God feels*; that which the Son of God in our nature has felt in oneness with the Father, that into the fellowship of which He calls us in calling us to be sons of God.

I freely confess that to my own mind it is a relief, not only intellectually, but also morally and spiritually, to see that there is no foundation for the conception that when Christ suffered for us, the just for the unjust, He suffered either "as by imputation unjust," or "as if He were unjust." I admit that *intellectually* it is a relief not to be called to conceive to myself a double consciousness both in the Father and in the Son, such as seems implied in the Father's seeing the Son at one and the same time, though it were but for a moment, as the well-beloved Son to whom infinite favour should go forth, and also as worthy in respect of the imputation of our sins to Him of being the object of infinite wrath, He being the object of such wrath accordingly; and in the Son's knowing Himself the well-beloved of the Father, and yet having the consciousness of being personally through imputation of our sin the object of the Father's wrath. I feel it intellectually a relief nether to be called to conceive this, nor to assume it as an unconceived mystery.

Still more do I feel it *morally* and *spiritually* a relief not to be required to recognise legal fictions as having a place in this high region; in which the awful realities of sin and holiness, spiritual death and spiritual life, are the subjects of a transaction between the Father and the Son in the Eternal Spirit. And though it may seem to some that this admission may excuse in the reader the fear that I have been less free of bias in considering this subject than was desirable, and that I have been less able to weigh justify the claims of the system which I have rejected, in proportion as I feel it a relief to be justified in concluding that it is not true, I must still in fairness make the admission.

But while so many, as we have seen above, of those who believe in an atonement have latterly made the same avowal on the subject of imputation, and transferred guilt, and merit, that I now make - to whom therefore this avowal on my part will be no source of distrust as to the conclusions at which I have arrived - it is to my own mind and additional source of freedom of feeling, besides the positive weight of the intellectual and moral difficulties involved in the system which I am rejecting, that the conception of the nature of the atonement which I have seemed to myself to receive in seeking to see it by its own light is altogether independent of the question of imputation, neither needs the denial of imputation for its commendation.

Whatever be supposed to have been the nature of the link between Christ and our sins, it was needful that He should on our behalf deal with the righteous wrath of God against sin *in that way which accorded with the eternal and unchanging truth of things*. And that which has now been represented as the way in which He has actually done so, commends itself, as I have said above, as what would *still* have been the right and God-glorifying way had the *identification of Christ* with us and our sins, been of a nature to justify even the boldest and most unbelievable language ever ventured on this subject.

The point of divergence of the two conceptions of the atonement is that at which, as we have seen, President Edwards stood when these two ways of satisfying divine justice in relation to sin were together before his mind, viz. an infinite punishment and an adequate repentance. Had these alternatives been dwelt on, even in connection with that manner of taking of the place of those whom He came to save on the part of Christ which Edwards conceived of, the latter alternative would have commended itself as most to the glory of God; although its claim to be, as I hold, the only satisfaction to divine justice that could be called an atonement or propitiation were not at once perceived: for it would be felt to be the higher and more real satisfaction to the divine righteousness, while the former could be contemplated only as an infinitely unwelcome necessity.

But these alternatives could not be fully realised, and their different natures considered, without the mind's being led to that perception of the deep and fundamental distinction between the conception of Christ's enduring as a substitute the penalty of sin, and Christ's making in humanity the due moral and spiritual atonement for sin; and this perception, once reached, would have commanded for the truth the assent both of the understanding and of the conscience, and would have claimed for it all the varied expressions of Scripture on the subject as what, although they had clothed another conception in men's systems, belonged *of right to it*, and expressed *it* - and it *alone - naturally and truly*.

It would be a suitable and satisfactory sequel to what I have now presented to the reader's attention, to examine all those portions of Scripture which are most identified in men's minds with the conception of the atonement as penal suffering endured by Christ as our substitute, and to shew how much more naturally they express a moral and spiritual atone-ment, and how they are by the conception of such an atonement filled with light; but I must satisfy myself for the present with what I have incidentally done in this way already. Nor, assuming the view expounded to be truth, can the reader who has fully received it have difficulty in doing this for himself.

Of the passages to which I refer, those as to which I would most urge the reader to engage in this task are those in which the death of Christ is made the measure of the evil of sin; earnestly desiring as I do that His death may be that measure to our spirits, and feeling that it never can be so as God has intended, unless we are understanding our calling to die to sin in the *fellowship of His death*, unless to us, as to the Apostle, to "win Christ, and be found in Him, not having our own righteousness, which is of the law, but that which is through the faith of Christ, the righteousness which is of God by faith," be identified with "knowing Christ, and the power of His resurrection, and the fellowship of His sufferings, being made conformable to His death."

CHAPTER XIV

COMPARATIVE COMMENDATION OF THE VIEW NOW TAKEN OF THE NATURE OF THE ATONEMENT AS TO (1) LIGHT, (2) UNITY AND SIMPLICITY, (3) A NATURAL RELATION TO CHRISTIANITY, AND (4) HARMONY WITH THE DIVINE RIGHTEOUSNESS

My conception of the nature of the atonement, and of its relation to the remission of sins and the gift of eternal life, being now before my readers, I might stop here, and leave it to receive that measure of consideration which, in the naked statement of it, it may be felt to claim for itself. If it come with that self-evidencing light to others with which it has come to me, it will not only commend itself as the truth, but also by its light, reveal the root of error in any erroneous view which it may find in possession of the mind. Yet I cannot conclude without pointedly directing attention to some of the aspects in which it contrasts with the system with which it will be most compared.

1. Understanding the words "Lo, I come to do thy will, O God," to be the key to the atonement, and to contemplate that Eternal Will of God, in respect of which it is true that "God is love;" and that therefore the doing of this will by Christ is to be seen in this, that love was the law of the spirit of the life that was in Him which took form in its outcomings according to its own nature, and as the path in which the Father led Him gave it development and manifestation - the conception of the atonement received in tracing the work of redemption, has been *full of light*.

For, however imperfectly I have executed the high task which I have attempted, I hope it has been felt that the path in which I have led the reader has been one in which the mind has advanced in conscious light. I do not, of course, mean the light of the conviction that what I have set forth as the atonement has been the atonement; this has been my own consciousness and may, I trust, have been that of many of my readers: but I mean a conviction distinct from this, and which, I hope, has been felt even when that further conviction may not have been imparted, viz. the conviction that all the elements of the work of Christ stated, were really present in that work; are seen clearly to have arisen out of the life that was in Him; and are all what, in the light of that life, we can as to their nature understand, though their measure be beyond the grasp of our capacity. For this has been so, whether these elements in the work of Christ do, or do not, constitute its atoning virtue.

Now this is an important point of contrast between what has now been taught and the conception of the atonement as Christ's being, in respect of the imputation of our sins, the object of the Father's wrath; and so bearing, as our substitute, the punishment of our sins. Whatever light may be recognised in that system as shining from the work of Christ *as a whole*, the great *central fact* in it is so represented, as to remain necessarily shrouded in darkness. But what our Lord would feel in bearing our sins as His doing so has now been represented, we can in measure enter into; and that, too, a measure which must enlarge, as the life of Christ progresses in us: while, as to its fulness, as it is our blessedness, in contemplating the work of our redemption, to be occupied with the height, and depth, and breadth, and length of a love which passes knowledge; so it is also to an experience of suffering and self-sacrifice on our behalf, which passes knowledge, that our faith is directed; the measure as well as the nature of Christ's sufferings being that of the divine love which experienced them.

But the difference is immense, even the difference between light and darkness, between *knowing in measure* what *passeth knowledge*, and *not knowing at all*: and this, and nothing less, is the difference between knowing, as to their nature, the elements of Christ's sufferings, being ourselves called to the fellowship of them, and knowing nothing of their nature at all. And, assuredly, whatever elements of Christ's suffering are still held to be what we are to understand and to share in, that *special* suffering which was proper to the assumed consciousness of having our sin imputed to Him and its punishment inflicted on Him, that which is represented as the personal sense of the Father's wrath coming out on Him personally - the wrath of God coming forth on the Son of His love: *this* is, and must be to us, simply darkness - a horror of darkness, without one ray of light.

The conception that Christ suffered as our *substitute* - so by His suffering *superseding the necessity for our suffering*, itself implies that the sufferings of His which such expressions contemplate, must remain in their nature unknown to us; an experience in our Lord's humanity which, though it has been an experience in humanity, we have not been intended to share in: a conception that seems to me improbable in the bare statement of it. For an experience of the Son of God in humanity not within reach of man's vision as partaking in the divine nature is to me what there is a strong presumption against.

How much that deeply-meditating believer in Christ, President Edwards, has ventured to expect in the way of understanding the elements of Christ's sufferings, we have seen above; while we have also seen how unsuited to his conception of their being penal sufferings the sufferings which he has specified are, though altogether in accordance with the conception of the atonement now advocated. But *all beyond* what he has thus specified, which the words "the Father's wrath" may be expected to suggest, however awful it must be supposed to be, must be felt to remain - necessarily to remain - unconceived of. Men's minds are indeed accustomed to this darkness as resting upon the central point in the great work of redemption. Yet surely it is a presumption in favour of the view of the atonement now taken, that it makes that central point no longer darkness, but light - the light of the life of Christ concentrated in His death; or rather present in His death, in a fulness which sheds back light on all His life.

2. The life of Christ being the light of life to us, and the atonement being the form of that life, it must needs be light, and not darkness. That which sheds light on all else must needs be light in itself, and be visible in its own light; as we not only see all things by the light of the sun, but also the sun itself. Further, that in the nature of the atonement which imparts to it this character of light, also imparts that of simplicity and unity.

Although I have found it necessary to consider the work of Christ in the two aspects of a dealing with man on the part of God, and with God on behalf of man; and in the two references of a retrospective relation to the remission of sins, and a prospective relation to the gift of eternal life; I trust the unity and simplicity and natural character of a life has been felt to belong to all that has been thus traced. It is all *grace reigning through righteousness unto eternal life*. All is in harmony with the purpose "Lo, I come to do thy will, O God;" and is its natural development terminating in its perfect accomplishment. An unbroken testimony on the part of the Father to the beloved Son in whom He is well pleased; an unbroken consciousness in the Son as hearing the Father's voice, abiding in the Father's love, strong in the strength of the life that is in the Father's favour, able to drink the cup of suffering given Him to drink because receiving it from his Father's hand, the last utterance of His inner life in man's hearing being the words in death, "Father, into thy hands I commend my spirit;" from first to last the Son doing nothing of Himself, all His speaking the result of an inward hearing of the Father, all His works the doing of the Father that dwelleth in Him, all His strength the strength of faith, all His peace, all His joy - peace and joy in conscious oneness with the Father, all His consolation in the prospect of desertion drawn from the assurance, that, though all forsake Him, He is not alone, because the Father is with Him; the bearing of the heavy burden of our sins accomplished in the might of a hope sustained by the consciousness that what of pain they were to his heart, they were also to the Father's heart: that what of interest we were to His heart we were also to the Father's heart: therefore His separating between us and our sins, His intercession, "Father, forgive them; for they know not what they do," - a separating, an intercession, in the assurance of the response of the Father's righteous mercy:- in all this I say is unity, and harmony, and divine simplicity. We can trace all this back to the purpose, "Lo, I come to do thy will."

Had it been given to us to hear the expression of that purpose, and were it permitted us to follow its fulfilment with a perfect spiritual vision, all would be seen to be in accordance with it, and to be made clear to us, step by step, by *its light*. The path thus trod we should expect to find all lying within the light of the Father's favour; and it has been so. Suffering and sorrow we should not anticipate, apart from what we might understand of the nature of sin, with which the Son of God was come to deal in the might of the eternal righteousness; but for suffering and sorrow and self-sacrifice in accomplishing the end of righteous love, we should understand that love was prepared. And if any difficulty should be felt as to suffering coming to the Holy One and the True, it must pass away - I can only express my own experience by saying it has passed away - in contemplating these sufferings as they arise, and in considering and apprehending their nature; the unity with the Father out of which they spring, the unity with the Father in which they are borne; and the justification of the Father in relation to them, in their divine fitness to accomplish the ends of the Father's love in sending the Son to do His will in humanity, and reveal His name to men - even as they were thus justified to the sufferer Himself, "Now is my soul troubled; and what shall I say? Father, save me from this hour; but for this cause came I unto this hour. Father, glorify thy name."

What is thus seen endured in conscious oneness with the Father as a necessary element in the Son's glorifying of the Father, and in the strength and with the comfort of the Father's acknowledgment, we can believe in as a cup which the Father gave the Son to drink, and which the Son welcomed from the Father's hand. But if we are asked to see the path which the Son is treading in doing the Father's will, declaring His name, as, at a certain point, passing out of the Father's favour into His wrath, and that a demand is made on us for the faith of a consciousness both in the Father and in the Son, in their relation to each other, which would make this statement a reality: or if the conception be not that of transition, but that we are asked to combine with the faith of a favour always resting upon the Son, the faith of a wrath from the Father as also proceeding forth upon Him; however other grounds for this faith may be urged, or whatever weight may be asserted for them - which question I am not at this moment considering - it is clear that the unity and harmony and natural character of what we have been contemplating as the fulfilment of the purpose, "Lo, I come to do thy will," is marred, and the commendation on this ground at least, of that which is presented to our faith, ceases.

3. This unity and simplicity and natural character of the atonement, contemplated as the form which the life of love in Christ took - the natural development of the incarnation - is still further commended to us by its imparting a corresponding unity and simplicity to the relation of the atonement to Christianity. If the atonement be the form which the eternal

life took in Christ, that eternal life which the Father has given to us in the Son, then, as the atonement is the development of the incarnation, so is Christianity the development of the atonement; and this is only what the words, "I am the vine, ye are the branches," express.

The fitness of all the elements that have been now recognised as present in the personal consciousness of Christ in humanity in making His soul an offering for sin, to enter into the experience of Christians, and be the elements of their lives, must have been commending itself to the reader as we have proceeded. These elements of our Lord's consciousness as the rays of the light of the life that was in Him, have that relation to us and our state, that, shining in us in faith, they necessarily reproduce themselves in us, that is, according to the measure of our faith; man and God, sin and holiness, becoming to us in the light of Christ what that light reveals them to be, and the confession of sin and the choice of holiness, self despair and trust in God, springing up in us: a confession of sin in unison with Christ's confession of our sins, a trust in God quickened by the faith of His trust in the Father on our behalf and laying hold on that in the Father's heart on which His intercession laid hold. The atonement thus through faith reproduces its own elements in us, we being raised to the fellowship of that to which Christ descended in working out our salvation. "We are crucified with Christ" in actual consciousness, as we were in the death of Christ for us in the counsel and grace of the Father: "Nevertheless we live; yet not we but Christ liveth in us."

Let our minds rest on this unity between the atonement and Christianity. How natural a sequel to the atonement is Christianity thus seen to be! Christ's work shared in through being trusted to, or rather trusted to with a trust which is of necessity a sharing in it. No need here to watch ourselves that we may not only trust to Christ, but also receive Him as our life; for in the light in which we are, these are but two forms of expression for one movement of our inner man. For, as I would ever keep before the reader's mind, trust in the work of Christ is, in its *ultimate* reference, trust in that fatherly heart in God which that work reveals, and such trust is the pulse and breath of our new life - the life of sonship.

But this natural relation of Christianity to the atonement, and which I believe to be a part of the simplicity which is in Christ, disappears when we would pass to Christianity from that other conception of the work of redemption according to which the atonement and the life given to us in Christ, are totally distinct and diverse in their nature; so that we are taught to keep them distinct in our thoughts, trusting to the one while we welcome the other.

To any seeking a clear, intelligent consciousness in religion, the complexity of this teaching appears to me to involve practically difficulties which have been unaccountably little felt. As to the sufferings of Christ, whatever sufferings of His may still be considered as what we are to share in (and the words "if we suffer with Him we shall also reign with Him," must be held to imply that such sufferings there are), it is clear, that sufferings assumed to have been the punishment of our sins, endured by Christ as our *substitute*, we cannot be *intended to share in*, not even though, as to their outward form and circumstances, they should be repeated in our history; for still they would not be sufferings endured as the wrath of God and the punishment of sin, inflicted on us as having the guilt of sin imputed to us. Indeed, were we to see one professing trust in Christ, suffering with this consciousness, we should feel that he was therein denying Christ, and making His death for sin of none effect. Therefore any consciousness that is ascribed to Christ, on the assumption of His being consciously bearing our sins as what the Father imputed to Him, and what drew forth the Father's wrath upon Him personally, must be excluded from what the example which Christ is to us comprises.

But even as to the righteousness of Christ as that is conceived of, how was He in fulfilling all righteousness, as His doing so is represented in this system, an example to us? He is supposed as one *under the law* to be consciously engaged in meeting its demands, working out a legal righteousness to be imputed to us. But this is not a consciousness which we are supposed to be called to share, being *not under the law* but under grace. So while His righteousness is represented as a perfect legal righteousness, it is as such put in opposition to the righteousness contemplated for us, which is the righteousness of faith.

Now I am not at present considering the objections otherwise to this manner of conception; I here consider it only in relation to the recognition of Christ as *our example*, and I request those who, while adopting these distinctions, propose to themselves to follow Christ as an example, to consider how, adhering, to these distinctions, they can attempt to follow Christ as an example in relation to His inner life - the springs of His action - the conscious rightness of His righteousness - His conscious confidence towards God - His walk with God. I do not see how they can do so with conscious inward consistency. No doubt Christ did fulfil the law - did fulfil all righteousness; not, however, in a *legal spirit*, but as *the Son* of God *following God as a dear child*. Therefore, in the true conception of this matter there is no practical difficulty, Christ's righteousness as the form of the law of the spirit of the life that was in Him, being, in the strictest and most absolute sense, an example for us who have the life of sonship in Him and in whom the righteousness of the law is to be fulfilled in our walking in His spirit.

The complication introduced in consequence of this departure from the simplicity of the truth, is obviously still further increased when we add to the assumed presence in Christ of the sense of an imputation of sin, the presence in us of the sense of the imputation of righteousness; a consciousness which could have had nothing corresponding with it in the consciousness of Christ.

But, in whatever way these practical difficulties in walking in the footsteps of the Son of God, in the highest sense which these words can bear, may be dealt with, the fitness of the atonement, as now contemplated, to be reproduced in us, and on the other view of its nature, its unfitness to be so reproduced, are alike clear; and, apart from other and more fundamental aspects of the subject, I certainly feel that greater simplicity, a more natural character in the transition from the work of Christ to our calling as Christians, is a consideration to which weight is due.

4. I say "apart from other and more fundamental aspects of the subject." For, while it certainly accords to my mind with the assumption that the true conception has been reached, that the atonement is thus seen filled with the light of the life of Christ - characterised by the simplicity and unity proper to a life - and standing to Christianity in the natural relation of the life that is in the vine to the life that is in the branches; yet these appearances are comparatively superficial, and must be delusive, however beautiful, unless the atonement which they commend is in harmony with the divine righteousness, and such as meets the demands of the eternal laws of the kingdom of God. Therefore an appeal to these must still remain.

I have already expressed my accordance with President Edwards in his founding on the absolute righteousness of God, and my greater sympathy with him than with those who ascend no higher than what they express by the words "rectoral justice." Doubtless what meets the requirements of absolute righteousness must secure the interests of rectoral justice; while it is not easy to see - I cannot see - how the interests of rectoral justice can be felt secure if the requirements of absolute righteousness are compromised, or even are not seen to be taken into account. But in whichever relation the atonement is contemplated, the superiority of the moral and spiritual atonement, which I have now attempted to illustrate, seems to me clear. That such an atonement lay within the limits of the principles of eternal rectitude on which Edwards builds, we have seen in the alternatives which he states. And, being contemplated as within these limits, I have no doubt that, if realised, its higher character must be recognised. I would indeed rather speak of its *exclusive* claim to meet adequately the demand of the eternal righteousness; but its *higher* character as a meeting of that demand is beyond question; and, if so, then also its superiority as that moral demonstration and vindication of God's rectoral government which the teachers of the modified Calvinism regard as what was called for.

This much I feel justified in saying, even looking at the question with exclusive reference to the honouring of the divine law. But when we consider, that the highest honouring of the law cannot be recognised as an atonement for sin *apart from the prospective result contemplated* - as, indeed, but with a view to such a result an atonement could never have been - the natural relation of the atonement to Christianity now illustrated, and which in its first aspects so commends itself to us, is seen, when more deeply considered, to be of fundamental importance.

Some, I know, are so far from feeling that a natural relation between the atonement and Christianity is necessary, or to be looked for, that they draw back from the attempt to trace such a relation as what they would call reducing the work of atonement to the mere setting an example before us - and, considering the associations which exist with making the example of Christ the sum and substance of Christianity, great jealousy on this subject may well be excused.

Yet that jealousy may go too far. If to represent the atonement as what we are intended to participate in, having its elements reproduced in us, be to lower the conception of an atonement, must it not be held also that it is a lowering of our conception of the divine nature to say that the gospel contemplates our participation in it - that it is a lowering of our conception of the divine nature to say that the gospel contemplates our participation in it - that it is a lowering of our conception of what is said when it is said "God is love," to speak of men as "dwelling in love," and so "dwelling in God?" I know that such thoughts of the relation of the human to the divine may be so entertained as to lower our conceptions of God, rather than to raise our conceptions of that to which God calls man; but that the latter, and not the former, ought to be their operation, is unquestionable.

So of the atonement as now represented, if it has been a form which the eternal life took in Christ, a form determined by the nature of that life and the circumstances in which it was developed, it follows, that in the measure in which we partake in that eternal life, we shall partake in the atonement, and have it reproduced in us: though not with the same personal consciousness as in the Saviour, who, as I have said, came down in saving us to that to which in being saved we are raised. But so to conceive is surely not to have our conceptions of the atonement lowered, but only our conceptions of Christianity exalted. And let not the expression "example" turn us away. For as to the dignity that may belong to an example let us remember the exhortations "Be ye therefore followers of God as dear children," "Be ye therefore perfect even as your Father which is in heaven is perfect."

But, indeed, apart from this, the truth is that the use of the expression "example" is misleading. The relation of our participation in the atonement to the atonement is radically a different thing from what the words "following an example" suggest. Each slender branch, each leafy twig of the tree, with its fruit-blossom or ripened fruit, may recall the plant in its first form as a single stem, yet with all its proper nature and beauty already visible in it, with that richness of leaf, and blossom, and fruit which belongs to the first development of the life of plants; but these reproductions of the original plant in its branches are not individual, independent, self-reliant plants. It drew, as it draws, its life from the ground; they draw their life from it: Christ is the vine; we are the branches. As it is no depreciating of the life seen in the plant while yet a single stem, to say that that same life is the contemplated life of its future branches; so neither is it a depreciation of the atonement to say that that eternal life, which glorified God and wrought redemption for man, in the personal work of Christ on earth, is the same that is to be seen bearing fruit to the glory of God in us in our participation in redemption.

Such conceptions neither depreciate the atonement nor affect the absoluteness of our dependence on Christ; on the contrary, the relation of the branch to the vine alone represents that dependence adequately. And this will, I trust, meet a difficulty which really arises from feeling the expression "example" suggestive of individuality, and individual independence, as if we were to be individually each another Christ, and our participation in the atonement itself an atonement, our participation in the propitiation itself a propitiation.

But, it is not only that this recognition of a natural relation between the atonement and Christianity is in itself no objection to the view which implies it, and can only under misapprehension of what is taught, be regarded as reducing the work of Christ to a mere example. The truth is, that the discernment of this natural relation *becomes essential to our faith in the adequacy of the atonement* in proportion as we see the subject of atonement in the light of God.

No doubt the perfect response from humanity to the divine mind in relation to our sins, which has been in Christ's confession of our sins before the Father, has been the due and proper expiation for that sin - an expiation infinitely more glorifying to the law of God, than any penal suffering could be; but that confession, as it would not have been at all, but in connection with that intercession for the transgressors which laid hold of the divine mercy on our behalf, so neither would it have been the suitable and adequate atonement for *our* sin apart from its fitness to be reproduced *in us*, and the contemplated result of its being so reproduced.

No doubt the perfect righteousness of Christ seen as the perfection of sonship in humanity, and acknowledged in the words, "This is my beloved Son in whom I am well pleased," is a higher righteousness than obedience in any legal aspect of it; and, if fruits of righteousness could be dispensed to us, either in connection with imputation, or without imputation, on the ground of the righteousness of another, otherwise than in the reproduction of that righteousness in ourselves, here was the highest righteousness, the divine righteousness in humanity: but that righteousness could never have been accounted of in our favour, or be recognised as "ours," apart from our capacity of partaking in it; that is to say, apart from its being a righteousness in humanity, and, therefore, for all partaking in humanity.

In order that the importance of this natural relation between the atonement and Christianity may be clearly seen, the relation in which the joy of God in Christians stands to his perfect delight in Christ must be understood.

I have already had occasion to express my objection to what is held on this subject in connection with imputation of righteousness, or the transference of the fruits of righteousness, assumed to be implied in justification by faith. There has been in this matter a subverting of the natural relation of things which has caused much darkness. The end has been represented as valued for the sake of the means; not the means for the sake of the end.

The very excellence inherent in the means has partly led to this. When we look at the work of Christ, viewed simply in itself, it is seen filled with a divine glory, and a moral and spiritual excellence is felt to belong to it so great that God alone can perfectly appreciate it. To say that it is the Eternal Will of God fulfilled, is to say that it is in itself infinitely acceptable to God. When, then, the remission of our sins, and the gift of Eternal life, are preached to us in connection with that excellent glory to God in humanity, we feel that any acknowledgment of it that can be, is to be looked for; and, also, that nothing granted on the ground of it can be otherwise than safely granted, for that mercy flowing through such a channel must be holy: so that we easily receive the statement, that pardon of past sin, and prospective blessings, are all given to us for Christ's sake, and because of the perfect atonement which Christ has made for our sin, and God's perfect delight in him; and this if we are in the light of God in the matter, we cannot do too readily or too confidently. And yet our lack of spiritual discernment, and of participation in the mind of God, combined, also, I would say, with our unenlightened sense of the evil and danger of our condition as sinners, may lead to our resting in notions of the meaning of the expression, "for Christ's sake," which are superficial and even erroneous. And this is sure to be the case if we enter not into these two great truths, viz.

(1) Though, in a true sense and one which it is most important that we should apprehend, remission of sins, and the gift of eternal life, are presented to our faith as resting on the atonement, and as the redemption which Christ has accomplished for us; yet is the ultimate ground of these, and of the atonement itself in its relation to these, to be seen in God, who is to be conceived of, not as moved to give us remission of sins and eternal life by the atonement, but as self-moved to give us remission of sins and eternal life, and as giving them through the atonement as what secures that what is given shall be received, *on the ground of that in God which moves Him to this grace*, and *in harmony with His mind in bestowing it*. So that to stop at the atonement, and rest in the fact of the atonement, instead of ascending through it to that in God from which it has proceeded, and which demanded it for its due expression, is to misapprehend the atonement as to its nature, and place, and

end. It has been truly said, that men have perverted creation, and instead of using it as a glass through which to see God, have turned it into a veil to hide God. I believe the greater work of redemption has been the subject of a similar perversion. It is the commendation of the light in which Christ's doing of the Father's will, Christ's declaring of the Father's name, has now been contemplated, that, as I have said, it ever raises the mind to the Eternal Will, the Unchanging Name.

(2) As it is thus necessary, in order that we may not misunderstand the expression "for Christ's sake," that we ascend from the work of Christ, and through it, to that in God because of which that work has itself been, and to which, therefore, we must refer all that springs out of it; so is it necessary that, on the other hand, we descend from the work of Christ to its results, and, viewing these as its fruits, see that work as means to an end, and, therefore, as having its ultimate value in the sight of God in the excellence of that end, and its adequacy to accomplish it.

This going forward to the result is inevitable if we go back to where redemption has its origin in the divine mind. We cannot stop between. For the work of Christ, while of infinite excellence in itself, has its special value as the work of redemption in the excellence of its result. If Christ were a mere man, His excellence in Himself, could such excellence have been in a mere man, would have been enough to satisfy the mind as to God's glory in Him: but, seeing the *perfection of sonship* - like the perfection of fatherliness - as divine, and eternal, and, as respects the Son of God, only *manifested* in humanity and *not then come into existence*, this divine excellence in humanity in the person of Christ is seen as in humanity with a view to results in all humanity. Therefore these results are not to be regarded as excellent in the sight of God, and justified because of that divine excellence in humanity; but rather the existence of that divine excellence in humanity is to be seen by us in the light of these results, and God's ultimate glory in it is to be seen in them. This is saying no more than what our Lord plainly teaches when He says, "I am the vine, ye are the branches. Herein is *My Father* glorified that *ye* bear much fruit."

Now the origin of the atonement in God, and its result in man, have been kept constantly before the mind in the view now given of the nature of the atonement; and any misconception of the expression "for Christ's sake" has been precluded: as it is also obvious, that all practical using of the atonement as now represented - all turning the knowledge of it to account in our personal intercourse with God - must be in the way of an ascending through it to that in God from which it springs, and a yielding ourselves to God to have that which it has contemplated accomplished in us.

This movement in our inner being - this moulding of us to itself - the atonement, apprehended by a true and living faith, necessarily accomplishes; and its tendency to secure this result, is one element in our faith, when we first believe; as also the experience of this power in it is the great subsequent strengthening of our faith.

Ascending upwards to the mind of God, into the light of which the atonement introduces us, and descending again to the ultimate fulfilment of that mind in men washed from their sins in the blood of Christ, and made kings and priests unto God, and reigning with Christ, we not only feel a harmony and simplicity and beauty in the natural relation of the atonement to Christianity, but we are also conscious to finding in that natural relation a chief and most sure ground for our faith in the atonement, and in remission of sins, and eternal life, as presented to us in connection with it. Every time we are enabled, in spirit and in truth, through participation in the spirit of Christ, to confess sin before God, and meet His mind towards sin with such a response as, in the faith of pardon and liberty of sonship, we are enabled to give, we have a clearer glimpse of the excellence of Christ's expiatory confession of our sins, and of the righteousness of God in accepting it on our behalf, to the end that we might thus share in it. Every time we lisp, in whatever feebleness, the cry, Abba, Father, having that cry quickened in us by the revelation of the Father by the Son, we see with the peculiar insight which the experience of the fulfilment of the divine counsel in ourselves can alone give, the excellence of that kingdom ordained in the hands of a Mediator, according to which eternal life in the Son is the Father's free gift.

But this direct occupation of our own conscience with the elements of the blood of Christ, and with the nature of the hope in God in which He tasted death for every man, is a source of deep certainty as to the glory of God in our redemption through Christ, which exclusively belongs to the view of the atonement, according to which our trust in it is necessarily fellowship in it - that fellowship a light in which the sure grounds of our trust are ever more and more clearly seen. For this character can only belong to an atonement whose nature admits of its reproduction in us, so that its elements become matter of consciousness to ourselves.

CHAPTER XV

THAT GOD IS THE FATHER OF OUR SPIRITS, THE ULTIMATE TRUTH ON WHICH FAITH MUST HERE ULTIMATELY REST

That natural relation of the atonement to Christianity on which so much weight has now been laid is the full meeting of a demand which must be more or less felt in any deep realisation of the divine righteousness; the demand which is so far met when those who represent our acceptance with God as turning upon our trust in the merits of Christ's work are still careful to illustrate the moral tendency of such trust, founding systems of "Christian Ethics" on the atonement; the demand which is recognised when those who regard the actual imputation of Christ's righteousness as what justifies us in the sight of God are careful to deny the character of justifying faith to any faith that does not sanctify: for Luther alone have we found setting for the excellent righteousness which is in the faith which justifies viewed in itself.

In truth, all care to exclude antinomianism, in whatever way that care is expressed, is an indication of the depth and authority of the feeling which forbids our ascribing to the righteous God any constitution of spiritual and moral government, which does not contemplate results in harmony with the divine righteousness, and which has not its justification in these results. So that, though, in form of thought, a near approach is made to saying, that the great husbandman values the fruitful branch, not because of His delight in the fruit it bears, but because of His delight in the imputed excellence of the vine; still the real feeling of the heart is in harmony with the words of our Lord, "Herein is my Father glorified, that ye bear much fruit." But, as these words "Herein is *my Father* glorified, that ye bear much fruit," indicate, we find that it is only in the light of the relation in which the scheme of redemption stands to the *fatherliness* of God that the necessity for a natural relation of the atonement to Christianity can be adequately conceived of.

The great and root-distinction of the view of the atonement presented in these pages is the relation in which our redemption is regarded as standing to the fatherliness of God. In that fatherliness has the atonement been now represented as originating. By that fatherliness has its end been represented to have been determined. To that fatherliness has the demand for the elements of expiation found in it been traced. But the distinction is broad and unmistakeable between simple mercy proposing to save from evils and bestow blessings, and finding it necessary to deal with justice as presenting obstacles to the realisation of its gracious designs - which conception is that on which the other view of the atonement proceeds; and this of the love of the Father of our spirits going forth after us, His alienated children, lost to Him, dead to Him through sin, and desiring to be able to say of each one of us, "My son was dead and is alive again, He was lost and is found."

Not, indeed, that supposing the only elements of the divine character concerned in determining the nature of the atonement to have been mercy and righteousness, the conception to which I object, would meet the requirements of these attributes more adequately than that which I offer instead. On the contrary, the moral and spiritual expiation for sin which Christ has made, has dealt with the justice of God, whether contemplated as absolute or as rectoral, in a way infinitely more glorifying to the law of God, and more fitted to open a free channel for mercy to flow in, than an atonement consisting in the endurance of penal sufferings by the Son of God as our substitute would have done. But while this lower ground is tenable, we should not be justified in coming down from the point of view to which the gospel raises us, to what, while true, is not the *ultimate* truth revealed. So to do, would be to forget that the gospel, and not the law, affords us full light here; the law being subordinate to the gospel, as our relation to God as our righteous Lord is subordinate to our relation to Him as the Father of our spirits - the original and root-relation, in the light of which alone all God's dealings with us can be understood.

How far, indeed, this subordinating of our relation to God as we are the subjects of His righteous rule, to our relation to Him as we are His offspring, is from depreciating that which is subordinated, has, I trust, been made abundantly manifest, seeing that it is the law of the spirit of the life that is in Christ Jesus, that is to say, sonship, in which alone the power is found to accomplish the fulfilment of the righteousness of the law in us, and that our being reconciled to God, whose law we have violated - the writing of His law on our hearts, so that it becomes to us a law of liberty - is the result of revealing to us our Father in our Lawgiver, and shewing us the law of the Lawgiver in its fountain in the Father's heart.

But while to reveal the Father in the Lawgiver is that which reconciles us to the Lawgiver, the only adequate statement of the high result accomplished, is, that it is reconciliation to the Father - the quickening in us of the life of sonship. However high a conception it is that the "disobedient should be turned to the wisdom of the just," that alone is commensurate with the excellence of the salvation granted to us which is conveyed by the words "Following God as dear children walking in love."

As to the place now recognised as belonging to the fatherliness of God in the history of our redemption, viz. that it is the *ultimate* ground for faith, I would add to what I have urged above these two considerations:

(1) It is a special glory to God that the fatherliness which originates our salvation and determines its nature - that it shall be the life of sonship - is *itself* that in which the *saving power* resides. For, as we have seen, the Son of God

saves us by a work whose essence and sum is the declaring of the Father's Name. A result so high, accomplished by the power over our spirits found to be in the Name of God - that is to say in *what God is*, is manifestly the highest glory to God. No result referable to simple Almightiness could be the same glory. That God should by a miracle change a rebellious child into a loving child would be no such glory to God as that the knowledge of the fatherliness rebelled against should, by virtue of the excellence inherent in that fatherliness, accomplish this result. "We love Him because He first loved us."

The power to quicken love in us is here ascribed to the love with which God regards us, considered simply as love. For it clearly is not the meaning, that, because God loved us, He wrought a miracle of Almighty power to make us love Him. And do we not feel a special glory to accrue to the divine love from this, as the history of our love to God? a special glory which vanishes, whatever other manner of glory may be supposed to remain, the moment the fact of our loving God is resolved into a miracle of Almighty power.

(2) But not only is this history of our being reconciled to God what is full of glory to God. If we consider well we must see that our being reconciled to God *must* have this history. We have seen that the words "Lo, I come to do thy will, O God," indicate the difference between that blood of Christ which cleanseth from all sin and the blood of bulls and of goats which could not take away sin. And so the Apostle, when illustrating this, goes on to say, "*By the which will we are sanctified*, through the offering of the body of Jesus Christ once." Our sanctification therefore is accomplished by the *will of God* as *acting on our will* by the *moral* and *spiritual power* of what that divine will *is in itself*. For the will of God, in order to be welcomed with that welcome which is holiness, i.e. *the free consecration of our will*, must be welcomed *just because of* WHAT IT IS.

This is a point which it is most important that we should see clearly. *Nothing extraneous to the nature of the divine will itself to which we are to be reconciled, can have a part in reconciling us to that will.* Fear of punishment, hope of reward, have here no place. However they may have been included in the history of our awakening to the importance of the relation in which our will stands to the divine will, they must go for nothing - they have ever been found to go for nothing - when the soul is alone with God, feeling itself under His searching eye, all its self-consciousness quickened by the realisation of the divine knowledge of its thoughts "when yet afar off." Simple earnestness, intense desire to be safe and assured of happiness, is then valued only at its true value; neither is it self-deceivingly supposed to generate anything better than itself.

In the light of God, all that springs from the desire of safety and happiness is seen to continue but the desire of safety and happiness still; and this, though not wrong - nay, though in a lower sense right, as the working of an instinct in our being which God acknowledges, and which God addresses - yet assuredly is *not holiness*, nor any approach to a delight in God's holy will. Nor, if we should, on any ground, have come to conclude that we are assured of the safety and happiness which we have desired, and, in consequence, should feel grateful to God for this great boon, is such gratitude, though a higher feeling than mere fear, or hope, to be recognised as holiness, or as what implies our being reconciled to God *spiritually and truly*.

At how great a distance from all oneness of will with the Holy God a human spirit may still be, even when esteeming itself saved and thanking God for salvation, is most instructively illustrated by President Edwards, in his analysis of delusive appearances of conversion which had come under his own observation, occurring under the awakening power of much urging of the importance of salvation. But, indeed, clearly understood, the statement is felt to be self-evident, that the will of God must reconcile us to itself *by the power of what it is, or not at all*. Therefore that the Son reconciles us to the Father by revealing the Father is not only a way of salvation full of Glory to God, but is, in truth the only possible way. So that our salvation would have been impossible had there not been in the heart of the Father what, being revealed to us, and brought to bear on our spirits, would reconcile us to Him, making His condemnation of our sin to become our own condemnation of it, His choice for us our own free choice for ourselves, his love the light of life to us, His fatherliness the quickening of sonship in us. There being that in God which was adequate to this result, our salvation was not only possible, but the way and manner, as well as the nature of our salvation, were thereby fixed and determined.

The Apostle John says, "And we have seen and do testify that the Father sent the Son to be the Saviour of the world." (1 John iv. 14) I have had occasion above to notice the way in which the Divinity of the Saviour has been contemplated in relation to the atonement in the two forms of Calvinism; in the one as implying a capacity of infinite suffering, adequate because infinite; in the other, as giving infinite value to any suffering in respect of the dignity of the sufferer; instead of recognising the divinity of the sufferer as what has determined the nature of His sufferings, and has given them their moral and spiritual fitness to expiate sin and purge it away. There has not been the same result of positive error, but there has beyond doubt been great loss of light of truth, through an *unwise resting of attention* on the *simple fact* of the divinity of Christ, which has veiled the teaching of the words "the Father sent the Son to be the Saviour of the world," chosen by the Apostle to express that light of eternal life in which He consciously was. Labour has been bestowed on proving the divinity of the persons thus spoken of in connection with our salvation - that the Father is God, that the

Son is God; and the excellent dignity and importance of salvation have doubtless been in this way magnified. But the special teaching intended by the Apostle is clearly that which is received in contemplating the Father as the Father, and the Son as the Son. Thus considered the statement that the Father sent the Son to be the Savour of the world, sheds light on the whole scheme of redemption, its origin, its end, and that by which that end is accomplished.

Exclusive occupation with the personal dignity claimed for the Saviour by the name "the Son of God," has, indeed, had the general result of causing men to lose the teaching contained in that name, so that it has suggested the *greatness* only of the love of God to man revealed in Christ, and *not* its *manner* and *nature*; and yet neither is its greatness known while its nature is not understood. "In this was manifested the love of God toward us, because that God sent His only begotten son into the world, that we might live through Him:" let the name "Son" here suggest to us what it has been intended to suggest, and the nature of the life which it has been intended that we should "live through Him" will be taught by it. "Herein is love, not that we loved God, but that He loved us, and sent His Son to be the propitiation for our sins:" let the name "Son" here teach us what it should teach, and it will shed light upon that propitiation for sin which Christ is, and illustrate to us the relation of the life of sonship to the atonement - the relation of the revelation of the Father by the Son to our being reconciled to God.

Fatherliness in God originating our salvation: the Son of God accomplishing that salvation by the revelation of the Father; the life of sonship quickened in us, the salvation contemplated; *these* are conceptions continually suggested by the language of scripture if we yield our minds to its natural force; and they are conceptions which naturally shed light on each other, and which, in their combined light, and contemplated together, so illustrate the nature of the atonement, as to impart a conviction like that produced by the internal light of axiomatic truth. Our Lord complains that He had come in His Father's name, and they had not received Him: yet as coming in the Father's name must He be ultimately received; any other reception is not the reception of the Son of God by which we become sons of God. "He came unto His own, and His own received Him not. But as many as received Him, to them gave He power to be the sons of God, even to them that believe on His name." This those understand whose deepest conviction of having found salvation in Christ is as the experience of *orphans who have found their long lost Father*. For, corresponding to the yearning of the Father's heart over us while yet in our sins, is the working of the misery of our orphan state as the *ultimate contradiction to the original law of our being*: some measure of conscious realisation of which misery is the truest preparation for receiving the gospel, being the first yielding to the teaching of the Father drawing us to the Son who alone reveals the Father - that inarticulate groaning of our spirits to which Philip gave expression in saying, "Shew us the Father, and it sufficeth us."

It is justly held that the faith that there is a God, has a root in us deeper than all inferential argument, a root in relation to which all inferential argument is but so to speak, complemental; owing its authority rather to that root than that root at all to it, though being what that root demands and prepares us to expect. And surely those who deal with men who are attempting to be atheists act most wisely when they throw them back on this root of faith in God in their own inner being, instead of permitting a course of argument which allows their thoughts to run away to find without them what unless found within them will never be found at all.

That this God, in whose existence we necessarily believe, is the Father of our spirits, is to be regarded as a *further truth*, the faith of which has a *corresponding depth of root in us:* and this I understand the Apostle to recognise in the use he makes, in preaching to the Athenians, of the expression as used by one of their own poets, "For we are also His offspring." That one of their own poets had said so would have been no reason for assuming that they ought to have believed that it was so, and to have determined their manner of worshipping God accordingly, unless these words of the poet had been the utterance of a truth that was deep in all their hearts.

In assuming, as I have been doing, a relation of men to God as the Father of spirits, antecedent to, and to be regarded as underlying their relation to Him as their moral governor, I have, in like manner, been calculating on a response from the depths of humanity. And it is in the hope of awakening that response into a distinct consciousness that I have proceeded in treating our relationship to God as the Father of our spirits, as the ultimate truth, in the light of which we are to see the scheme of our redemption, the Father's sending the Son to be the Saviour of the world. If we are in very truth God's offspring, if it is as the Father of our spirits that He regards us while yet in our sins, it accords with this that the Father should send the Son to save us, that the Son should propose to save us by the revelation of the Father, and that our salvation shall be participation in the life of sonship.

There is a corresponding witness of truth in the results which the faith of the atonement accomplishes. These in being the truth of sonship towards God and the truth of brotherhood toward men deepen the conviction that it is the very truth of God that our faith is receiving.

1. Sonship quickened in us by the revelation of the fatherliness that is in God is sonship in the true and natural sense of the expression. If our redemption has its origin in the feelings with which God regards us as the Father of our spirits, if the Son of God accomplishes our salvation by revealing the Father to us, then is our salvation necessarily the truth of sonship. In living harmony with the light of life, drawn by the Father to the Son, knowing the Son as He

is present in our inmost being - our true life, and ever seeking to be our actual life - yielding our hearts to Him to reign in them, "receiving with meekness the engrafted word, which is able to save our souls," we call God "Father;" and the utterance is from us a true and natural and simple approach to the Father of our spirits, such as He desires, a speaking to Him according to the truth of what He is to us, the cherishing of an immediate direct confidence in His fatherly heart. For indeed our right confidence in the Father is direct, and is confidence in His fatherly heart towards us, as also is our confidence in the Son direct, viz. a direct confidence in Him as our proper life; which several manners of confidence in the Father is to confide in Him as our Father, so to exercise confidence in the Son is to welcome the life of sonship which we have in Him. And this is the manner of our being alive to God through Jesus Christ, and it is self-evidenced to my mind as the truth of sonship, as what and what alone we can believe to meet and satisfy that fatherliness in God which presupposes, and by the revelation of which to our spirits by the Son it is quickened.

I cannot recognise this truth of sonship, in what, in connection with the other conception of the atonement, is held as "adoption;" of which I desire to speak plainly, yet warily, knowing how much more difficult it is to do justice in the choice of one's words to the faith of others, than to one's own faith; and having, also, the awe on my spirit of the true savour of the life of sonship, which it has been my privilege to meet in connection with the form of thought on this subject which yet I feel constrained to reject.

The adoption of us as sons, as superadded to justification by faith, no element of sonship being present in the faith that justifies us, nor exercise of fatherliness contemplated as an element in the divine acceptance of us, the adoption itself a boon bestowed upon us in connection with the imputation of Christ's merits to us, - *this* is a manner of sonship as to which it is obvious that the confidence with which we may so think of ourselves as sons of God, and draw near to Him expecting to be acknowledged as such, is *no direct trust in a Father's heart at all, no trust in any feeling in God of which we are personally the objects as His* OFFSPRING, but is in reality a trust in the *judicial grounds on which the title and place of sons is granted to us.*

I know that it is held that, when in connection with the faith that justifies God bestows on us the adoption of sons, He gives us also the spirit of sonship, that we may have the spiritual reality as well as the name and standing. But the spirit of sonship is the *spirit of truth*, the Son himself is *the truth* - "I am the way, the *truth*, and the life." That the Son should say, "I am the *way*" - no man cometh unto the Father but by me," teaches us that *sonship alone* deals with fatherliness *as fatherliness*; that we must *come to God as sons, or not come at all.*

On this co-relativeness of sonship and fatherliness I have dwelt above. So also that He should say, "I am the *life*," fixes our faith on Him as *our proper life*, according to "the testimony of God, that God has given to us eternal life, and that this life is in His Son," - but that He should say, and say *in humanity*, "I am the *truth*," teaches us, that not only is it the case that to come near to the Father we must come near in the Son, and that the life of sonship is the life to which we are called, but, besides, that to come to God in the Son, and so to come to Him as sons, *is*, and *alone* is, *in harmony with THE TRUTH of our relation to God*.

I have in some measure anticipated this contrast between sonship towards God as quickened in us by the revelation to us of the Father by the Son, and sonship conceived of as added to our legal standing of justified persons through the imputation to us of Christ's merits, when noticing above the practical difficulty of harmonising in conscious experience two manners of confidence so opposite in their nature as a legal confidence on the ground of the imputation to us of a perfect righteousness, and a filial confidence such as the faith of a Father's heart is fitted to quicken. In truth the assumed filial confidence being cherished in this dependence on the legal confidence, and the fatherliness conceived of being, not a *desire of the heart of God going forth towards us as His offspring* to which *sonship* is the *true and right response*, but the divine acknowledgment of a standing granted to us according to the arrangement assumed, though our conception of the mercy and grace of which we assume ourselves to be the objects may still be high, the *true and simple feeling of dealing with a Father's heart is altogether precluded*.

But thus to think of the intercourse with God which eternal life implies as resting for its peace and security on another ground than its own essential nature; - to think of sonship as cherished freely otherwise than as the natural response to the Father's heart, to think of the Father as rejoicing in this sonship as present in us otherwise than as the Father; - to feel that the prodigal son feels secure in the welcome of his forgiving father on any other ground than the fatherly forgiveness itself which has embraced him, falling on his neck and kissing him; - to feel that the Father is justified in his own eyes, or would justify himself in the eyes of the rest of His family, in the gracious welcome which he accords to the returning prodigal, on any other ground than that which he expresses when he says, "My son was dead, and is alive again;" - to suppose that the filial standing must rest on a legal standing, and that all this intercourse between the Father of spirits and His redeemed offspring must be justified by the imputation to them of Christ's righteousness, and that this reality of communion with the Father and the Son must be reconciled, in this way of at least seeming fiction, with the moral government of God, instead of recognising that *communion itself* as what is the *highest fulfilment of moral government*, and the *ultimate* and *perfect justification* of all *the means* which God has employed in bringing it to pass: *these* are thoughts which can have no place in the light in which the Apostle says - "It *became Him* for whom are all things, and by whom are all things, *in bringing many sons unto glory* to make the Captain of their salvation perfect through sufferings."

The natural character now claimed for the consciousness of sonship as belonging to our communion with God in Christ - that is to say, that it shall be felt the due response to the Father's heart, and not the mere using of a privilege and right graciously conferred upon us, corresponds with, or, I should rather say, is one with the self-evidencing character claimed above for justifying faith.

The liberty to call God Father, which we feel in the light of the revelation of the Father to us by the Son, we in that light *cannot but feel*: for in that light we not only apprehend the divine fatherliness, through the perfect response of sonship yielded to it by the Son of God in humanity, and, at the same time, the sonship itself, which is that response, but we have this apprehension necessarily with a *personal reference to ourselves*.

How important this statement is - assuming its truth - those will feel who are acquainted with the questionings on the subject of adoption by which the most earnest and deeply exercised spirits have been most tried, while their right to call God Father has been conceived of by them as turning upon the previous question of their justification through imputation of Christ's righteousness, and that again upon the soundness of the faith from which justification has been expected. What is here taught is that to call God Father, and draw near to Him in the confidence of sonship, is simply to conform to, and walk in, the light of life which shines to us in Christ.

Assuredly that word from heaven - "This is my beloved Son, in whom I am well pleased: hear ye Him" - each man that hears is called to hear as a word addressed to himself - a revelation of a will in God in relation to him. This is not to be questioned. Why is this divine sonship manifested in humanity? Why, brother man, is *our* attention called to it? Why are *we* told of the Father's being pleased in the Son and in this connection bade to "hear the Son?" Surely the fatherliness thus presented to our faith is fatherliness in which we are interested, for surely it is interested in us - has desires with reference to us; and surely the sonship on which our attention is thus fixed concerns us, yea, can be nothing else than the very condition of humanity which these desires of the Father contemplate and seek for us. Therefore when we are turned to *the kingdom of God within us* - when that spiritual constitution of things, which the words that have raised our eyes to the Father and our hopes to sonship have pre-supposed, is revealed to our spiritual apprehension; - when we know "that the Father sent the Son to be the Saviour of the world," as these words state a condition of things with the advantages of which we are encompassed, and the truth and reality of which is to be known by us in our own inner being; - when that testimony of the Father to the Son, and of the Son to the Father, which *pervades the Scriptures* is known by us as *also in ourselves*, then what is contemplated by the call addressed to us - "Hear ye Him," is understood by us; - we understand how, in the love of the Father of our spirits, the Son, in whom the Father is well pleased, has in Him the life of sonship for us, and how, through Him, and in Him, we also may be sons in whom the Father shall be well pleased.

Thus are the outward preaching of the kingdom of God, and the revelation of that kingdom within us, known in their unity, in the experience of salvation; and the light shining in the Scriptures and the light shining in man are known as one light - at once universal and individual, as is the nature of light. When I hear, in the most general reference to men, the words "God has given to us eternal life, and this life is in His Son," - "This is my beloved Son, in whom I am well pleased: hear ye Him," - I hear what connects me in my own thoughts, as by *a revelation of truth*, with the fatherliness that is in God the Father, and the sonship that is in the Son of God: and so, still, as the light dawns on me and brightens, and I become a child of light and of the day, when I know, in my own inner being, the Father drawing me to the Son, and the Son moving and quickening in me the cry, Abba, Father, and have the illustration of a personal experience shed upon the words of Christ - "No man knoweth the Son but the Father; neither knoweth any man the Father save the Son, and He to whomsoever the Son will reveal Him;" still the fatherliness that is thus calling me to sonship, the sonship that is enabling to respond to that fatherliness, I know as one *receiving knowledge of the truth of things*; my experience is that of conforming to what is a *revelation* to me at once *of God* and *of man* - that is to say, as I am a man, of *myself*. *In obeying* I am *obedient to the truth*. I do not, I should say, I dare not, doubt the voice of that fatherliness by which I am drawn to the Son, or doubt that the Son is revealed to me by the teaching of the Father for this very end, that I may know the desire and choice of the Father of my spirit *for me*. I do not, I dare not, doubt the light of that sonship, or that the Son is truly teaching me, as well as lovingly teaching me, how it is *right for me to feel* towards the Father of my spirit - the response to His heart which *accords with the truth of what that heart is in relation to me*. I do not ask, "Have I exercised a faith in Christ which has justified me, and am I certain that that faith is so sound as to warrant me to believe that now I am a child of God, and entitled to call Him Father?" I am exercising a faith to which it is a contradiction to doubt the fatherliness of my Father, or the welcome that awaits me in coming to Him as a child. I am exercising a faith in which it is impossible for me to be disobedient to the Son, quickening the cry, Abba, Father, in my spirit.

I have been at pains, in relation to justification by faith, to shew how faith excludes boasting; not by any artificial arrangement, nor at all by denying to the faith itself the attribute of righteousness, but, on the contrary, because it is itself the true righteousness, and that boasting is impossible in that light of the truth into which faith introduces; for in faith we are beholding the glory of God in the face of Jesus Christ, and no flesh shall glory in His sight. I would add here, that the life of sonship, as now represented as quickened in us, excludes boasting.

That faith is trust in God, as He is revealed in Christ, excludes, as we have seen, boasting, and makes the righteousness of faith to be the opposite of self-righteousness; - that this faith apprehends the fatherliness of God, and that its responsive trust is sonship, this yet more and more excludes boasting. The trust of a child in a Father's heart is just the perfect opposite of a self-righteous trust; for it is a *going back* to the *fountain of our being* - a dealing with that interest in us which was before we did good or evil; and, as cherished by us sinners towards God, against whom we have sinned, such trust deals with fatherliness as what has survived our sins; so that our trust, so far from being self-righteous, implies, commences with the confession of sin. Doubtless this trust is in itself holy - the mind of the Son; but it is not on that account less lowly - less remote from boasting. Are we not, in cherishing it, "learning of Him who is meek and lowly in heart?"

There is, indeed, a further exclusion of boasting, in the consciousness that it is in the Son that we are approaching the Father - that He, who made atonement for our sins and brought into humanity the everlasting righteousness of sonship, is not the mere pattern of our life, but is Himself that life in us in which we are able to confess our sins, and to call God Father; that He is the vine, that we are the branches. But I feel it important that we should realise that in its own nature, and apart from its derived character as existing in us, the confidence of sonship is essentially and necessarily the opposite of self-righteousness.

I the more insist upon this, while also desirous to fix attention on that deepest sense of dependence on Christ, which, in knowing Him as our life, our spirits prove, because I believe, that the whole attraction to conscience which has been found in the conception of an imputation of Christ's merits to us, has been its seeming fitness to secure the result of a peace with God free from self-righteousness, and which shall be really a *trust in God* and *not in ourselves*; the doing away with what Luther calls "the monstrous idea of human merit, which must by all means be beat down;" and in reference to which he values the law as "a hammer with which to break it in pieces." This right result, essential to the glory of God in us, and to our being in harmony with the truth of things in the attitude of our spirits towards God, the truth of the life of sonship in us secures, and alone can secure.

Nay more, the life of sonship is not only the purest and simplest trust in the heart of the Father, but its nature is, because of the experience which it implies, to be a *continually growing trust in God*. I must see a Father's heart in God towards me before I can call Him Father; but, in calling Him Father, the consciousness which comes with so doing is itself a fresh proof to me that He is my Father, and that in so believing I am not welcoming a cunningly devised fable; and thus progress in the life of sonship is not the coming to have a new ground of confidence towards God, but an experience which enables us to "hold fast the beginning of our confidence" more and more firmly. Experience, in calling God Father in spirit and in truth, becomes a source of increased freedom in doing so; not because it has created any further or fresh title to do so, for it has not, but because the rightness that is in this mind towards God, its harmony with the truth of our relation to Him, and the glory which it gives to Him, become clearer to us in that increased light as to what it is to follow God as dear children which is implied in the experience of doing so.

And, as this holds true as to our trust in the Father, so also, as to our trust in Christ as our life, all experience of life in abiding in Him as a branch in the vine, only develops into deeper consciousness the sense of dependence upon Him, shutting us up to so abiding for all expectation of well being; for the more I know what it is to be able to say, "I live, yet not I, but Christ in me," the more simple, and absolute, and continuous will be my living by Him. The mystery of God both of the Father and of Christ, being thus experimentally known as our fellowship with the Father and with His Son Jesus Christ, abounds, the fulfilment of God's purpose in us enlightens us more and more in that purpose, and thereby deepens our faith in it as His purpose.

I do not feel that the *ground for faith*, which is thus found in the *experience of faith*, has been sufficiently valued, especially when the object has been to save us from looking for a ground of peace in ourselves. We cannot be too jealous of looking to self, if we rightly discriminate. But beyond all question, *eternal life experienced* must have *its own proper consciousness*; and the apprehension of it as given in Christ, and the consciousness of receiving it and being alive in it as a conscious life, must be trusted to exclude self-righteousness as light excludes darkness, and not otherwise.

It seems to me that Luther, notwithstanding his high estimate of the righteousness that is in faith, and notwithstanding the power to prevail with God which he recognises as being in the feeblest utterance of the cry "Father," has not given its true place to the subjective experience of the life of sonship. I have felt justified in saying above, that the great Reformer was the preacher of justification by faith, according to a truer and stricter meaning of the expression than it has had, or could have had, in the teaching of those who have not understood as he did, either that condition of things which the gospel reveals to our faith, and which by its very nature excludes boasting, or that excellent glory which God has in the faith which apprehends and trusts God, according to the revelation of Himself which He has granted to us in Christ, and in the exercise of which our souls "make their boast in God." The difference is indeed broad and unmistakeable between the faith that would correspond with the revelation of work of Christ performed on behalf of an elected number, by which he purchased and secured for them certain benefits to be in due time imparted to them -

according to the teaching of Dr Owen and President Edwards; or the faith that would correspond with the modified Calvinism, which preaches a work of Christ for all men, by which a foundation has been laid on which God may righteously proceed in dispensing benefits to those who will receive them on that footing; and that faith to which Luther called men, when he proclaimed a work of Christ by which He had redeemed us, even all men, "from the law and death and all evils," and procured for us the adoption of sons, so that we are not under the law, but under grace, and are called to believe, directly and personally, and with appropriation to ourselves, because it is so in truth, that Christ is the Father's gift to us, that He is made of God unto us wisdom, and righteousness, and sanctification, and redemption. For, however far Luther is from shedding light on the nature of the atonement, however little of the spiritual light which he had himself he has imparted to us in an intellectual form which we can understand, and however startling, and incapable of acceptance according to their sound, are the expressions of which he makes choice in speaking of the relation to our sin, into which Christ came in working out our redemption: these things in him are very clear, viz. that he saw the Father in the Son, and therefore had confidence towards God, because of what he thus saw God to be; and that he saw Christ, and in Him all things pertaining to life and to godliness, as the gift of God to men, to all men, to every man:- so that he neither spoke of God as having come under an obligation to do certain things for an unknown some; nor as having put it in His own power righteously to extend mercy to all who would receive it on the ground on which it was offered; but as having already done the greatest thing for all men, and as calling upon all men to believe and enter upon the enjoyment of what He had done.

Yet while Luther's teaching has all the superiority which is implied in a truer conception of what is presented to our faith, as well as the advantage of a juster appreciation of the excellent nature of faith viewed in itself, it seems to me, as compared with the teaching of the Apostles, wanting in its setting forth of that to which the gospel calls man; a defect which, in reference to the two-fold revelation in Christ, the revelation of fatherliness, and of sonship, may be expressed by saying, that his preaching is more a setting forth of the fatherliness in which we are to trust, than of the sonship to which we are called. Luther keeps before the mind God as He is revealed to be trusted in - trusted in at this moment, by those who have never trusted in Him before; rather than the contemplated life of Christ in us, in the conscious experience of which we are to grow day by day in the assurance of faith and free life of sonship. I do not at all mean that Luther would deny the soundness of all such increase of freedom, assuming it to be indeed that which has now been spoken of, viz. increased trust in God, and in His Christ, through the experience of trusting; but that this he does not set forth or dwell on. Therefore, while the history of his own first peace in God is, most profitably for us, present in all his commending of the gospel and putting away of the law, there is still in his renewed urging of the difficulty of trusting in Christ in seasons of deep realisation of our sins, a contrast, and, to my mind, an instructive contrast, to the calm consciousness of being, living the new eternal life which breathes in such words as these, "We know that the Son of God is come, and hath given us an understanding, that we may know Him that is true, and we are in Him that is true, even in His Son Jesus Christ. This is the true God, and eternal life."

There is a state of mind in relation to the view now taken of the sonship quickened in us in faith, which it is right here to notice. The character of salvation as now represented, as what is accomplished in us by our being "brought out of darkness into God's marvellous light," it is felt difficult to harmonise with the greatness of change which has come to pass in those who are saved, both as respects the condition of their own being, and their relation to God. It is asked, "If God is the Father of our spirits antecedent to our faith in Christ, and that the gospel reveals Him as our Father, how does the Apostle say - 'In this are the children of God manifest, and the children of the devil?' And how, when the Jews said, 'God is our Father,' did the Lord seem to deny that it was so? - 'If God were your Father ye would love me... ye are of your father the devil'." The harmony between the abiding truth of our relation to God as we are all His offspring, and the oppositeness of the conditions of our being, which are by choice of our own will, according as we receive the light of Christ or believe the devil's lie, not being understood, it is felt that the expressions used in relation to those who are alive to God through faith in Christ cannot have their truth simply in the spiritual conformity of these individual men with a relation of all men to God, and a constitution of things in Christ which embraces all men; and therefore the gospel is received only as a revelation of a *willingness in God to become our Father*, and so a manifestation of the *highest benevolence*, but *not* the revelation of the *interest of the Father of our spirits in us as His offspring*.

In consistency with this conception of the gospel, it is held that in such discourses of our Lord as that recorded in the 5th, 6th, and 7th chapters of the Gospel of Matthew, the use of the name "Father" on which I have dwelt above as a part of our Lord's coming to men in His Father's name, is not to be understood as a claim made for God, and the setting forth of the conception of God with which men ought to approach Him, but as assuming faith and justification and adoption; so that to say, "When ye pray, say, Our Father," was not to teach men what they were to believe God *already* to be, but what He would *become if* they believed: so also that to say, "If ye then, being evil, know how to give good gifts unto your children, how much more will your heavenly Father give the Holy Spirit to them that ask Him?" was not intended by our Lord to be understood as the proclaiming of a will in God to impart His Spirit to all because He was the Father of the spirits of all flesh, but only of such a will as to those who had become His children by faith.

If it were only meant that our *acting* on such teaching implies faith, and that we only *truly* pray the Lord's prayer in the measure in which we receive the Son to reign in our hearts, there would be in this no more than a most needed warning - seeing the great self-deception connected with the use of that prayer in a way of more fleshly repetition of it, void of all life of sonship. But this is not what is meant; and so the parable of the prodigal son, on which so much weight has now been laid, is denied to be a preaching of the gospel, or a revelation of the interest with which God regards men - all men - while yet in their sins; its comfort being reduced to what, in consistency, can only be offered to men on the assumption that they have been adopted through faith, and are such as only need to be encouraged to return to their first love.

But while I notice this state of mind, and do so in much sympathy with the deep sense which it implies of the great issues involved in passing from death to life, I do not do so with the purpose of attempting to offer any help in relation to it that has not been presented already in these pages. To my mind the expression of which I have made so much use - "*My Son* was *dead*, and is *alive again*," both accords with the great change that faith implies, vindicating the strongest language in which its important results are ever expressed, and also fully recognises our original and abiding relation to God as the Father of our spirits.

But while some feel as if it were taking from the sense of salvation with which they themselves call God Father as believing in Christ, thus to regard Him as the Father of the spirits of all flesh, others can testify, that the perfect freedom of sonship has only been attained by them in seeing the heart of the heavenly Father towards all men, to be revealed in Christ, and the life of sonship manifested in Christ to be the fulfilment of the divine purpose in themselves, because it is the fulfilment of the divine purpose in man.

I have just noticed the increased freedom in living the life of sonship, and increased assurance of being in the light of God, which comes through the actual experience of a true and living Christianity. Now, while this is, in one view, *personal*, it is in another view only a deeper certainty of knowledge as to the will of God in relation *to all men*, and the "common salvation." It is the record that God has given *to us*, that is, *to men*, eternal life, and that this life is in His Son, which he that believeth *hath in himself*. Therefore is the Christian *a living Epistle of the grace of God*.

The progress of mind often experienced in relation to the gospel is very instructive. Some who have at one time contemplated the atonement as having reference to an elected number, and have then felt that their own personal hold of salvation would be weakened if Christ had died for all men, have afterwards come to see, that they could never have felt intelligently certain that Christ had died for them, excepting as that fact was included in the fact that He had died for all men; and the unsatisfactory shifts had recourse to, in the attempt to combine a free preaching of Christ with a limited atonement, have become very palpable to them, and they have wondered how, saying that, "though Christ had died only for some, He was freely offered to all," could ever have been received by them as an adequate foundation for an appropriating and personal faith.

And so, as to the results of the work of redemption - what we are called to apprehend as true *antecedent* to our faith - what the statement "that God *has given* to us eternal life, and that this life is in His Son" amounts to - mercy in God embracing them, such as Christ's death for their sins implies - a will in God to bestow benefits on them through Christ, who afterwards come to see, that a relation to them more internal to their own being is alike implied in the language of Scripture, and required by their need - if indeed they are to be alive to God through faith in Jesus Christ. They, therefore, welcome that fuller light of truth which at once reveals to them a gulf as left between them and Christ by the simple fact of an atonement external to their own being, and that gulf as done away with in the actual nearness of Christ to their spirits - His presence in them as their true life. For they now understand the teaching of the Father, and His drawing of us to the Son, as what is in the Spirit, and not in the Scriptures only, and as what directs us to Christ, as he is present in our inner being, there where the sap of the vine passes into the branch - a present life to be welcomed or rejected - the ingrafted, in-breathed word, which is able to save our souls.

To this presence of Christ in us is the testimony of God "that He has given to us eternal life, and that this life is in His Son," now known to refer. And as now the literal spiritual truth of the testimony that God has *given* this gift, and *brought it into the needed nearness* - and if He had not, how should we? - is apprehended, so now also the manner of the teaching of the Son, the manner of His shewing us the Father, is understood. For it is found that, according as we receive the testimony of the Father to the Son, and in obedience of faith, receive the Son as our true life, and in Him call God Father, the divine fatherliness becomes known by us as it can be known to sonship alone. For, as in respect of the natural relation which typifies the spiritual, where a father and his children are present together with others also not his offspring, the children alone, yea, the children who know that they look upon their father, see - with the eyes of the heart - see a father; so also in the higher region in which we now are the Son enables us, God's offspring, to see our heavenly Father, when, receiving Christ as our life, we in Him raise to the Father the eyes and the heart of true sonship.

In thus receiving and obeying the testimony of the Father to the Son, and, in consequence, knowing the Father as the Son knows Him, and gives us to know Him, is the deepest manner of experience of that word - "The secret of the Lord is with them that fear Him and He will shew them His covenant."

But let us be clear as to the elements of our consciousness when this is our conscious history. We have not by any movement of our own being caused this drawing of the Father; we have only yielded to it; - neither have we by any movement of our being brought the Son thus near to us. He was thus near to us even when we knew it not. Only under the teaching of God we have Christ revealed in us the hope of glory. The mystery hid from ages and generations is made known to us. Therefore, understanding the nature of the grace of which we find ourselves the objects, we recognise it as that gracious kingdom of God within us which the gospel proclaims. We find our feet in a large place - we are consciously in circumstances to receive and obey the word of Christ "Abide in me;" the personality of these circumstances in relation to us not being less, nor the importance of the issues that depend on the faith of them less either, because the grace in which we stand is the "common salvation." And, like the man who are one time felt that to believe that Christ had died for all would weaken His own conscious hold of salvation, but who has subsequently understood that unless Christ died for all there was no certainty that He had died for him; so, if we ever felt a distinctive and elective character in the divine drawing which draws to Christ, and a distinctive and elective character in Christ teaching us to call God Father, an element in our religious peace, we now find the stability and depth of that peace to consist in the unindividual, the universal character of that testimony of the Father to the Son, and of that testimony of the Son to the Father, in which we are rejoicing with an individual and personal hearing and obedience of faith. Surely that others refuse God's teaching no more affects my certainty that I am receiving the light of truth in welcoming that teaching, than that others are refusing Christ, for whom He died as truly as for me, affects my peace in trusting in His death for me. Nay, that the voice of the Eternal Wisdom to which I listen is "unto the sons of men," and to me individually, just as I am one of the sons of men, is one element in my certainty that it is the voice of God.

It is a remarkable and instructive fact, that the experience that the faith of a work of Christ without us, which left us without the knowledge of a presence and power of Christ within us, was inadequate to sustain the intelligent purpose of living the life of sonship - and that the recognition of a nearer relation to Christ was needed - has been to some the attraction of the doctrine of baptismal regeneration; the spiritual change in our inner being, so conceived of, seeming to supply that living link with Christ which has been felt to be necessary to our living by Him, and which the fact of the relation of Christ's work to all men did not provide. Yet the difference between a spiritual relation to Christ as our life, revealed in the preached gospel, and made known to us as a spiritual reality in our own inner being by the divine teaching (the drawing of us to the Son by the Father) and such a relation as coming into existence in connection with the ordinance of baptism and subsequently assumed in a way of faith in that ordinance, is one of the greatest possible amount and greatest possible importance.

Christian baptism is into "the name of God, the Father, and the Son, and the Holy Spirit." It relates to a gospel proclaiming that name. It is administered to those capable of intelligent apprehension of the gospel, as believing in that name as the true name of God, and that in the light of which they see their relations to Him. Its administration to infants is only understandable on the assumption that they are already interested in that name of God, and that parents and ministers of Christ know them to be so, and are justified in bringing them up in the faith of that name as the true name of God. But that we should find in our baptism *more than is in the name* into which we have been baptised, and *that* "more," that spiritual relation to Christ in the light of which we can alone hear and respond to the call to follow God as dear children; this is in effect, to believe about baptism that which would make it a contradiction of that name of God into which we are baptised. For to say that baptism brings us into the needed spiritual relation to Christ as our life is to say that we were not in it antecedently to baptism, that the grace which the gospel reveals to our faith has not amounted to this; that is to say, that we might know the name of God the Father, the Son, and the Holy Spirit, and yet not feel in possession of the light of life.

I would not have risked any distraction of thought by the notice of this subject here, were it not for the preciousness in my apprehension of that sense of the need of a personal relation to Christ with which to begin to live to God, which the doctrine of baptismal regeneration at once recognises and misdirects. As to the more usual objection to the doctrine of baptismal regeneration, viz. that it hinders the sense of the necessity of being personally alive to God as alone as condition of justifiable peace; I do not see how it is possible for any thoughtful mind to feel at rest in the contemplation of a fact of this kind, whatever it may be believed to have implied, *while* that fact has been *common to the history of all the baptised*, and has not hindered any subsequent manner or measure of evil. No man can believe that baptism has secured his salvation: at the utmost it can only be conceived of as placing the human spirit in a higher spiritual condition; which if it implies the capacity of higher good, implies also that of greater evil - a deeper fall. And so all who believe in baptismal regeneration, whether Romanists or Protestants, would speak of it.

2. What affects the conception we form of the sonship towards God to which the gospel calls us, must in a corresponding way affect our conception of that consciousness of brotherhood with man to which we are also called. The light of truth in which I see God as my Father is the light in which I see men as my brethren. If, on the other hand, the gospel does not reveal God to me as my Father, neither does it reveal men to me as my brethren.

I have considered above that fulfilment of the righteousness of law, which takes place in us when we walk not after the flesh, but after the spirit, and which the Apostle represents as the result which God contemplated when He sent His Son in the likeness of sinful flesh, and as a sacrifice for sin, and so condemned sin in the flesh; and I then illustrated its relation to sonship as the law of the spirit of the life that was in Christ, in which the power was found to make free from the law of sin and death. The righteousness of the law is to love men as well as to love God; and its fulfilment therefore implies love to men as well as love to God. But the life of love which we have in Christ, which is sonship towards God, is, in being so, brotherhood towards men; and as it is in being sonship that it fulfils the first commandment, so it is in being brotherhood that it fulfils the second commandment. Therefore, as it is true that until we know God as our Father we cannot love Him with all our heart, and mind, and soul, and strength; so is it also true that until we know men as our brethren we cannot love our neighbours as ourselves.

We know when the question was put to our Lord, by one willing to justify himself by the law, "Who is my neighbour?" how our Lord answered. Let us not under the gospel be found asking, "Who is my brother?" or coming to conclusions as to the answer of that question which will leave us in the position of finding that some are our neighbours who are not our brethren: for to find a neighbour who is not a brother, is to find a neighbour whom I cannot love as I love myself; for unless I can feel towards him as towards a brother, unless in the life of brotherhood given to me in Christ I can see him with the eyes of a brother, and love him with the heart of a brother, I cannot love him in spirit and in truth as I love myself.

It thus more and more appears that the question as to the nature of the atonement is in truth nothing else than the question, "What is Christianity?" It is so, as we have seen, as to the God-ward aspect of the eternal life given to us in Christ. It is so, we now see, as to the man-ward aspect of that life also. In contemplating the eternal life in Christ as taking the form of the atonement, the outcoming of love has been seen to be one and the same thing as sonship towards God and brotherhood towards man; and all that has been presented to our faith as entering into the work of Christ, has appeared to have been equally called for by love to God and by love to man - a *self-sacrifice* which was at once *devotedness to God* and *devotedness to man*. The eternal life being unchanging in its nature, it follows, as urged above, that what it was in Christ as an atonement, it will be in us as salvation. Therefore Christ, as the Lord of our spirits and our life, *devotes us to God* and *devotes us to men* in the *fellowship of His self-sacrifice*.

This He does in giving us to know God as our Father and men as our brethren. Seen in the light of God, our state of sin, and life of self, is solitary in all aspects of it. In it we are "orphans of the heart," brotherless as well as fatherless; for in it the life of true brotherhood is as unknown in relation to man as that of true sonship is in relation to God. "God setteth the solitary in families." This is accomplished for us spiritually in our passing from death unto life, "for by this we know that we have passed from death unto life, because we love the brethren. He that loveth not his brother abideth in death." Christ gives us to possess not God only, but men also as our riches, the unsearchable riches which we have in Him. But, I say, in doing so He is, at the same time, devoting us to God and to men, in the fellowship of His self-sacrifice. He thus calls us to poverty, in calling us to the true riches; calls us to have nothing, in calling us to possess all things; and thus the pearl of great price, which is given us without money and without price, while it is above all price, is yet that of which it is said, that a man must sell all that he has, that he may buy that pearl. If I am to be rich in the consciousness of having God as my Father, this must be in that entire devotion of my being to Him which is in loving the Lord my God, with all my heart, and mind, and soul, and strength. If I am to be rich in the consciousness of having men as my brethren, it must be in loving my neighbour as myself.

Here it may occur, that though to say that Christ gives me God as my Father has indeed a gospel sound, this is not felt equally as to the statement that He gives me men as my brethren. Yet are the gifts related, inseparably connected; their bond being the relation of the second commandment to the first. No doubt the difference, and more especially the immediate difference, between these gifts is very great in all views, but especially in this, that, by the latter, Christ lays a weight upon me, the burden of others; while, by the former, He lays my burden on God, enabling me to cast all my cares upon Him, knowing that He careth for me. Yet it is an obvious comfort here that the burden of others, which He lays upon me, being truly borne by me, becomes a part of that burden which He enables me to cast upon God.

But that we may see the whole transaction in both its parts, that which refers to our relation to men, as well as that which refers to our relation to God - as *one grace*, we must see it in the light of that word, "He that loveth not his brother whom he hath seen, how can he love God whom he hath not seen." In the life of love which we have in Christ, not only will God have His proper preciousness to us, but men also will have theirs - as was Christ's own case. Love will go out to men as well as to God, though its goings out may be, in the one case, with sorrow and anguish of spirit, while in the other, it is with peace and joy. Neither can we know the fellowship of our Lord's peace and joy, as what belong to the life which we have in Him in the one aspect of it, while we refuse to share with Him the sorrow and anguish which pertain to His life in the other aspect of it. *If we refuse to be in Christ the brothers of men, we cannot be in Christ the sons of God.* This is in another form of words our Lord's teaching, when He says, "If ye forgive not men their trespasses, neither will your Father forgive you your trespasses." We must die to self in the fellowship of the death of Christ, if we would live to God; and, so dying as to live to God, we shall live to each other also.

Self is essential and necessary solitude, with whatever society and show of social life it may encompass itself. In the inmost circle of our being we abide alone, until, in the death of self, the life of God is quickened. Then God becomes the centre which self was while yet we were as gods to ourselves, and then the harmony of the first and second commandment is known by us. We find that Christ, in reconciling us to God, has reconciled us to men; and though comfort, and peace, and joy alone come out of the former of these results of His love, and sorrow, and vexation of spirit, yea, fellowship in Christ's own sorrow, may come abundantly out of its latter result, yet, even as to this latter, the sorrow is not unmixed. If the afflictions of Christ abound in us, our consolation, even as respects men, shall also abound through Christ; and if men are a weight upon our spirits, and a deep and constant sorrow as they never were before, yet shall we know now, as we could not before, the fellowship of the joy that is in heaven over sinners that repent; and, in the communion of saints, shall know what man can be to man when met together in the pure light and life of the divine love. While as to the hope set before us we know, that united to men by the bond of that love in which Christ died for them, our fellowship in His death will prove the seed and earnest of fellowship in His joy in that ultimate result in which He shall see of the travail of His soul, and shall be satisfied.

Self is most unwilling to die, and can gather around it so many sweetenings of life in the form of social relations, which give a certain superficial sense of communion of heart and mind without touching its (self's) life at the core, that we need not marvel that the call to deny self, and take up the cross of Christ, is resisted so long as only the sacrifice required is realised, and not also the exceeding gain that is to come through that sacrifice; and of this gain nothing is, I think, less anticipated than what is found in the new aspect which our brother men will present to us, and the sense of eternal life that accompanies that new interest of love which they will have to us in the fellowship of Christ's love to them, and which will take the place of that self-reference with which they were formerly regarded; - though broken, it might be, by occasional outbursts of kindly and generous feeling - grapes, as it were, from the land of promise tasted in the wilderness, but yet their promise not believed.

Would that these outcomings of a better nature were traced up to their ultimate source in the depths of our being, and, instead of the passing comfort and satisfaction which in their present form is all they usually yield, were employed as threads to lead us back, through the labyrinth of our outward life, to meet and know Him within us - the Lord of our spirits - who came not to be ministered unto, but to minister, and give His life a ransom for many, and who would teach us the life of self-sacrifice, with all its peculiar and proper sorrows, doubtless, but also with all its peculiar and proper joys. Nay, have not the bitterest sorrows proper to that life a root of sweetness in them which renders them better, more to be chosen than other joys?

CHAPTER XVI

CONCLUSION

Having in this attempt to illustrate the nature of the atonement insisted so much on the application of the words, "In Him was life, and the life was the light of men," to the whole work of Christ in making His soul an offering for sin, I am anxious not to be misunderstood as to the aspect of the subject of the atonement, in which it has appeared to me reasonable to expect it to be light to us, and not darkness; and that, in closing this volume, the reader should carry away with him a distinct conception of the limits, which, in writing, I have realised, and kept in view.

I have not attempted to divest the subject of the atonement of all mystery. I have not cherished the hope, or in truth the desire, of doing so. The self-righteousness that takes the form of a submission of faith to mysteries, I, indeed, feel to be altogether a delusion. The assumed merit of a blind faith, in addition to the error implied in all idea of merit on our part in relation to God, involves the absurdity of expecting to please God by exalting one of His good gifts, to the depreciation of another gift, equally to be traced up to the grace of the Father of lights. Any manner of subordinating of reason to revelation must be wrong, in which it is forgotten that we honour God in assigning to reason its due place, as truly as we do in assigning to revelation its due place; for to be jealous for reason is to be jealous for God, as truly as to be jealous for revelation is to be jealous for God. If self comes in, and forgets that reason is a gift as well as revelation, and, claiming reason as its own, is puffed up on behalf of that which we have thus identified with ourselves, the temptation that thus arises to exalt reason and depreciate revelation is obvious, and the evil consequences to be anticipated great. But the remedy, the true and the only remedy, is, that we should hear the voice of God in reason as well as in revelation - that God in whose presence no flesh shall glory.

But as to mysteries, reason has its mysteries as well as revelation; and to shrink from mysteries, is to shrink from all deep thinking on any of the high problems of our existence. The practical question for us, as God's thinking, intelligent offspring, always is as to the limit of light and darkness; which practical question we are to entertain under the sense of this twofold responsibility; that, as it would be wrong to attempt to push beyond that limit, or to be impatient of its existence, so would it be also wrong to fix it more near to us than it is in the truth of things, or at least in relation to the dispensations of light vouchsafed to us by God. For would not this be to refuse to use a portion of the grace of God, to us, and be one form of folding in a napkin and hiding in the earth a talent of which an account must be rendered?

Therefore, under the sense of a responsibility of which the twofold aspect as appeared to me thus unquestionable, I have now considered the elements of the work of Christ as what His participation in humanity, and our participation in the divine nature through Him, seemed to place within the limit of the light of life that shines for us in Him; while I have simply recognised, abstaining from all attempt at explanation or elucidation, the underlying and deeper facts of the relation of man to God the Father, the Son, and the Holy Spirit, implied in the relation of the work of Christ to all men, and in the spiritual reality of that which is stated when it is said that "this is the testimony of God, that God has given to us eternal life, and that this life is in His Son." As to these deepest facts of our being and of our relation to God, I have not even attempted to determine the line that separates the darkness and the light *now*; or at all to say what its *eternal* and *necessary* place is; while neither am I to be understood as passing any judgment on attempts to do so, or on the going of others nearer to that awful line than I have done. But I am anxious that the reader should realise how much on the light side of that line I have kept, having determined to approach it no more nearly than an attempt to illustrate the nature of the atonement required me to do.

Reason has its mysteries as well as revelation, the mysteries of deepest interest to us being, indeed, common to them both; though, inasmuch as revelation carries us further into the region to which mystery pertains, the sense of mystery in occupation of mind with the discoveries of revelation is greater. But the aspect in which the atonement has now been contemplated does not belong to the proper region of mystery at all. That region, whether as respects reason or revelation, is the divine and the infinite; and the atonement has now been considered simply as a transaction in humanity, contemplating results in man, to be accomplished by the revelation of the elements of that transaction to the spirit of man, and in a way of participation in these elements on the part of man. It is not in this transaction, *viewed in itself*, that mystery was to be expected, or could exist, but in that relation of the Son of God to man which this transaction presupposes. This relation, whether we contemplate it as participation in our flesh, or as that relation to us in the spirit in respect of which Christ is our life, having power over all flesh to this end, is indeed a mystery as to its *nature* and *manner*, and to be known by us only in its *results*.

And this is true, whether we contemplate the personal work of Christ in making His soul an offering for sin, or His work in us in respect of which it is true, that when we live to God we must say, "Yet not we, but Christ liveth in us." The divine perfection of sonship in humanity, presented in Christ to our faith, is, in respect of its perfection, what leads us up to the mystery of the divinity of Christ as truly as His power to quicken and sustain sonship in spirit and in truth in us does. I can realise neither without feeling shut up to the faith of the divinity of the Saviour; while that faith so accords with the facts the contemplation of which thus leads directly to it, that, being received, it sheds light on them. For, believing in the divinity of Christ, we see how the atonement has that commensurateness with the infinite evil of sin, and infinite excellence of righteousness, which imparts to it its peace-giving power; we see how Christ is near to us in that nearness that accords with His being our life, and has that power in relation to us which justifies the confidence that through Christ strengthening us we can do all things.

But viewed in itself this faith has in it the deepest mystery; but it is mystery in the region in which we are prepared for mystery, being, first, in the manner of being of God, and then, where the line of meeting is between God and man. For here, also, we are prepared for mystery; and while we expect to understand what pertains to the *human* side of this line and to the divine nature *as in humanity*, we do not expect to understand what is on the divine side, and pertains to the acting of God as God. As to that ultimate mystery which our faith receives in believing in God the Father, the Son, and the Holy Spirit, while in itself eternal, and irrespective of all finite existence, *we* can only be called to the study of it *in its manifestation in connection with man.*

But even in this manifestation there remains a necessity for recognising the distinction now made. What the divine sonship is in its spiritual essence and consciousness, as presented to our faith in Christ, and as that to the fellowship of which we are ourselves called in Him, this the very nature of the divine purpose in relation to us prepares us to expect to understand. But the nature of the relation of the Son of God to humanity, whether we contemplate His own personal work in making His soul an offering for sin, making an end of sin, and bringing in everlasting righteousness, or His work in men as putting for the power in them which is implied in His being their life; - this belongs to the acting of God, as God, and to the divinity of the Son of God, in an aspect of the subject which all experience in thinking of our relation to God prepares us to find ourselves unable to understand.

Nor is the question of how this can be, or what the manner of the divine acting is which it implies, the only mystery here. The faith of the divinity of the Saviour, while in one view it affords light and explanation as to the facts which constitute the gospel, in truth *involves* and *deepens* all the *moral* and *spiritual mysteries of our existence*.

I believe, as I have said, that the faith of the atonement, and the faith that we have eternal life in Christ, is more easy to us when it rests on the faith of the divinity of Christ. Indeed, apart from that previous faith, the faith of what the gospel reveals Christ to be to us would be to me impossible. I cannot believe in one as my life, of whom I am not warranted to think as God; while, remembering that *in God* I live, and move, and have my being, I seem prepared to be told - I had almost said to understand - that the divine life of sonship is what I am to live *in* and *by the Son of God as my life*. The universal relation of men to the one Son of God, as He in whom they all have the life of sonship, accords as perfectly with the divinity of the Son of God, as it contradicts every lower conception of His being; and the Apostle, who preached to the Athenians, in relation to the unknown God whom they ignorantly worshipped, that "in Him they lived, and moved, and had their being," must be regarded as only presenting to our faith another part of the truth of man's mysterious relation to God, when he makes know the mystery hid from ages and generations - the mystery of "Christ in men the hope of glory."

Nay, how closely the one revelation is related to the other, we must see, if we connect the use which the Apostle makes of the recognition of man's relation to God by one of their own poets, "For we are also His offspring," with our relation to Christ in respect to that life of sonship in which alone men can call God Father in spirit and in truth. Surely the parallelism of these relationships to the Father and the Son is a help to our faith in the divinity of the Son, as it also explains the fact that this mystery of the divine existence is *made known to us*. But still, as I have said, this mystery, apart altogether from what men have felt of its intellectual difficulty, deepens the previous mysteries of reason with which all thoughtful minds have been exercised from the beginning.

Thus the great mystery of combined dependence and independence, as presented by our relation to God - the mystery implied in the fact that in God we live, and move, and have our being, and yet that we may be the opposite of what God wills us to be - this is not removed, but only deepened by all the thoughts of our relation to God which are connected with our relation to the Son of God.

If we think of the matter in the way of considering how in the nature of things the spiritual constitution of humanity can be a reality, there is no question that a manner of nearness to God and to goodness, is suggested by the statement that "God has given to us eternal life in His Son," - understood as implying an actual relation to our spirits to Christ as present in us, our true and proper life - which it is still more difficult to reconcile in our thoughts with the fact of sin than even our "living, and moving, and having our being in God" is.

If, again, we look at the subject in relation to the divine will as a will concerning us, the choice of God for men, in proportion as the gospel reveals the *love* in which the law has its root, and shews the demand *for love* to be the demand *of love*, the difficulty that exists in the fact of our being other than that love desires that we should be is increased, and reaches its maximum of difficulty when the love, which is seen seeking our well-being, is seen as the fatherliness that is in God, and its choice for us is seen as participation in the life of sonship, and the provision for the realisation of that choice is seen in the gift to us of this eternal life in the Son. Assuredly the mystery, the moral and spiritual mystery, is here increased in proportion as it is seen to be a mystery thus involving infinite love. But, though increased by all that magnifies God's unspeakable gift, let us not forget that it is not less truly the mystery of reason than the mystery of revelation.

Doubtless it is with a sense of mystery, often altogether oppressive, that we look upon human sin and degradation, and then pass upwards to the Father of the spirits in whom the sin and degradation present themselves and meditate on the thoughts of that Father in relation to them, and on all that our faith apprehends of what He has done, and is doing, to accomplish in them the good pleasure of His goodness. But though this mystery is greatest in the light of all those witnesses for His goodness towards men, without which God has never left Himself; and in respect of which the charge is just, that, in not being thankful, men were refusing to glorify God as God.

Some would cut this knot by saying that all contradiction between what God is, and what God wills, is but apparent; that nothing is, or can be, other than what God wills it to be; and that facts in the moral and spiritual region, even those that seem most contrary to the mind of God, are really related to Him just as physical facts are - hatred and love as much as cold and heat. *Hatred may believe* this, but *love cannot*. Self may believe that there is an end present to the divine mind which all moral events equally and necessarily subserve, and with reference to which it is that God wills them to be, and which it may call the divine glory. But love cannot believe that the divine glory is of this nature, or that that will, in respect of which God is love, and the manifestation of which must be His glory, can, in respect of moral beings, be fulfilled but in *their loving*.

The existence of a contradiction between what man is, and what God wills him to be, is indeed a mystery. The faith of the fact, however, is demanded by what is highest and deepest within us, which forbids our grasping at a seeming intellectual consistency of thought, at the expense of denying this contradiction, and accepting all the fearful moral and spiritual results which such denial involves. And even as to the intellectual relief sought, in denying that contradiction between man and God, which all ascription of goodness to God, and all hope of goodness for man alike imply, (for if evil be not contrary to the will of God, what hope of deliverance from it?) this seeming intellectual relief is but such in seeming; for it is but the removal of the contradiction, from where conscience recognises its existence, to place it *in God* Himself, by representing Him as what the Apostle so solemnly disclaims His being - a fountain giving forth at the same time sweet waters and bitter.

Nor can we be otherwise than thankful for the utter failure of all attempts made in this direction to solve this great moral and spiritual mystery; for its weight is nothing in comparison of what would be laid upon us by taking away the faith that God is love which involves that mystery, and representing the great First Cause as at the most only an intelligent fate. Nay, we may surely say, that what of mystery in relation to the actual facts of human existence, as it presents itself to us, the faith of love involves, the faith of love will itself enable us to submit to in the patience of hope.

But if the love of God to man presents deep mysteries, and mysteries that deepen to our apprehension as our faith that God is love is real, having also more claim on our attention in proportion as they are not intellectual, but moral and spiritual; and, more especially, if that spiritual constitution of the kingdom of God in relation to man, which the gospel reveals, be the deepening to the utmost of that mystery which the contradiction between what man is and what God wills him to be presents, how have I now attempted to illustrate the nature of the atonement, without entering upon the consideration, either of this moral and spiritual mystery, or of the intellectual mysteries to which the atonement is related? Because none of the mysteries which encompass the atonement are so related to it as that we must *first* solve them before we can understand it; a course the opposite of this is rather that to which we are called; and whether we would ascend upwards to questions connected with the name of God the Father, the Son, and the Holy Spirit, or meditate on the present or future of man, the due preparation for these regions of thought is the exercise of faith in the actual condition of things which the gospel reveals, and which, in the light of the kingdom of God within us, and in the measure in which we are taught of God, we know as the truth.

I have, therefore, felt at liberty to consider the nature of the atonement, without first considering the mysteries which encompass it. Nay, what I have just said implies that I must have begun with this subject, had my ultimate purpose been to consider these mysteries; so that even with regard to those questions in relation to God and man, which take us most to the verge of light, the inquiry which has now engaged us attaches to itself all the interest and importance which may be felt to belong to them.

But while I hope for good only from all holy and reverent meditation on any of the deeper subjects of thought to which I have now referred, my immediate purpose has not been to offer help towards such meditation, though I should be thankful to be found to have actually done so - as doubtless much of what has now been presented to the reader's consideration has been such help to myself - but my immediate object has been the urgent practical one of illustrating that spiritual constitution of things in which, in the grace of God, we have a place, and to which we must needs be conformed if we would partake in the great salvation. Such conformity, that amen of faith to the atonement which I have sought to illustrate, is that to which our Lord calls us when He says - "Seek ye first the kingdom of God and His righteousness," - adding, in order that we may be altogether free to give heed to the call, the assurance "and all other things will be added unto you." All inquiry as to what is truth is solemn, and the sense of responsibility that belongs to it, weighty. But, manifestly, that inquiry becomes more solemn, and that responsibility more weighty, in proportion as the answer to the question - "What am I to think? - What am I to believe?" - becomes one with the answer of the question - "*What am I called to be?*" And *this* is the solemnity, *this* the importance that belongs to the question of the nature of the atonement.

The reader who has accompanied me to the close of this volume, in the fair mind and with the patience of love, has, I trust, felt that throughout I have simply sought to awaken a response in his own inner being - whether in this I have succeeded or have not - and that I have written, not with the interest of theological controversy, but as a man communing with his brother man, and giving utterance to the deep convictions of his own heart as to the spiritual need of humanity, and the common salvation. For I have written as seeming to myself to hear, and as desiring to be used to help others to hear with personal and practical application, the Son of God saying to us "I am the way, and the truth, and the life; no man cometh unto the Father, but by me," the Father saying to us, "This is my beloved Son, in whom I am well pleased; hear ye Him."

NOTES

NOTE TO INTRODUCTORY CHAPTER

On the tendency to resolve religion into love of man to man

It has been said that the teaching of a religion which is not morality has led to the teaching of a morality which is not religion. Whatever causes have contributed to so evil a result, there is no doubt that our time is characterised by an ideal of the bond which connects man with man which is being raised higher, combined with a waning sense of the bond which connects man with God. Men seem as if they were awakening to the due feeling of the beauty and of the obligation of love to man our brother, but not as what is quickened by the faith that One is our Father, nor as a natural development of love to Him.

I say not how far it is possible to understand and obey the voice that bids us love one another, while that voice is not yet recognised as the voice of God who is love, and has made love - the law of His own being - the law of our being also. The light is shining in darkness - darkness which yields to it but gradually and perhaps we may say in no fixed order; so that some points it may illumine while others remain invisible. In the full clear light of life, the *first and great* commandment - love to God - is seen *as such*; and the second - love to man - which "is like unto it," is seen as a corollary to it, a necessary development of it. In that light also, it is seen that all intelligent peace in the discernment and choice of goodness implies the faith that God is, and that He is good, and that all goodness is of Him. Apart from this faith the vision of goodness would indeed be as the vision of a light, which, for all we knew, might at any time be extinguished in eternal darkness. In the light of goodness we feel its supreme excellence because of what it is in itself, and irrespective of all considerations exterior to itself: so that, were existence limited to a moment, we should prefer goodness as the life of that moment. But that any man contemplating goodness while not seeing it in God its fountain can do so peacefully, or can hopefully choose it as life while not discerning it to be eternal life, must, I believe, imply the working of a deep spiritual instinct which makes it impossible to feel goodness to be but a passing self originated phase of a perishing mind.

I know how plausibly, but most superficially, men have spoken of love of man to man as what has its purity and disinterestedness marred by a reference to the will of God in cherishing it. Such a reference as a mere sense of personal dependence, and of the importance to us in our weakness of the favour of the Almighty, may, viewed in itself, be thought to have this tendency, and, doubtless, cherished alone, would have this operation; though it cannot be otherwise than healthful to realise our dependence on God simply as dependence, and as a part of the truth of things. But reference to God's aspect towards us, when God is known as love, while He is felt to be the searcher of hearts who sees us just as we are, can have no other operation than to cherish and develop that life of love in us which we are knowing as the divine life.

But however great the value of the first and great commandment in its relation to the second, its importance in itself - that in its own nature because of which it is the first and great commandment - is its highest importance to us. It is not merely, or chiefly, because in order to our dwelling together as brethren it is necessary that we shall know God as our Father, that the knowledge of God as the Father of our spirits is the first and highest knowledge for man. "Behold what manner of love the Father hath bestowed on us that we should be called the sons of God." Could men attain to a perfect brotherhood in relation to each other, while putting from them their high birthright as God's offspring, what remained to them of the privilege of existence would be small indeed in comparison with that which was lost. Low conceptions of salvation, which have been possible only when man's root relation to God as the Father of spirits was left out of account, and God has been thought of only as a sovereign Lord and righteous Judge, have hindered occupation of men's spirits with the life of sonship which we have in Christ, as being the highest aspect of our existence. But, in proportion as faith in the incarnation strengthens, and the atonement in both its retrospective and prospective aspects is understood as the development of the incarnation, Christianity will be more and more seen as a life of sonship in the fellowship of the life of the Son of God.

This will be to return to what Christianity was at the beginning; and I believe the words which the Apostle addresses to us as individual Christians may be heard as addressed by our Lord to the church - "Hold the beginning of your confidence steadfast unto the end." Men still regard as a part of the ideal contemplated in the early Church, and in measure realised, that men should love one another, and dwell together as brethren: but not less unmistakeably, was it another and a higher part of that ideal, that men should love God and follow Him as dear children. Man's relation to God was as truly the practical interest of life as was man's relation to man: Christ as the Son of God was no less the example and pattern studied than Christ as the Brother of man.

If I say that the contrast between this latter aspect of Christianity, as presented to us in the early Church, and the ever lessening interest in the first and great commandment, and the merging of religion in obedience to the second, indicates a putting from us of the life of sonship towards God, that is, of our birthright as heirs of God and joint heirs with Jesus Christ, many readers knowing that they are not in their own thoughts Atheists or Pantheists, or in any form theoretically losing a personal God in the reign of law will feel as if my words did not touch them. Still less will they be felt to apply to themselves by those whose occupation with the duty man owes to man has a certain habitual reference to God as a moral Governor. I am not to be regarded as making no distinction among these classes of men. Nevertheless my conviction, even as to the latter, is that Christianity as a fellowship in the Sonship of the Son of God has still to be revealed in them.

Yet what I thus place in contrast with primitive Christianity is, I fear, the conscious position of some, and is regarded by them as differing from that taken by the first Christians only in being higher; the transference of the relationship of father and child to our relationship to God being looked on by them as only an anthropomorphic form of the religious instinct, to rise above which belongs to philosophy. But very few comparatively, recognising Christianity as a gift of God and the highest hitherto known, will thus regard philosophy, in this development of it, as a higher gift still - the latest and the best. Those few can speak of Christianity passing into a philosophy, but the multitude of those who believe in Christianity as of God, if they recognise at all the fact of the present absorption of practical religion in obedience to the second commandment, will see in it, not progress, but a fearful departure from the first principles of Christ. Our highest relation, that in which we stand to the Father of our spirits, can no more pass away in a philosophy, and from a life of love become a form of thought, than any other relation of which love is the essence.

NOTES TO CHAPTER II

Luther's teaching of justification by faith alone

I believe that I have truly expressed Luther's personal faith and consciousness in his contending for Justification by Faith; that which also was the secret of his power and the value of his work.

Faith is the right attitude of the human spirit towards God - the due response to His revelation of Himself to us, in rendering which our hearts are right towards God. "Justification by faith alone" means that in pronouncing us just God regards only and exclusively the attitude of our spirits towards Himself. What elements will be present in the response of faith must depend on the elements present in the revelation of God to which it is a response. As a preacher of Christ, Luther insists on a response to the revelation of God, in Jesus Christ. Of that revelation he conceives as necessarily inspiring confidence and love, entire reconciledness to God. These he expects to abound in the spirit of him that believes, in proportion to the simplicity and exclusiveness of the occupation of his spirit with that which his faith is apprehending. Therefore, he permits no division of trust. Such division is to him a hindrance to the soul's life in God's favour. Hence it is that we see him placing together in one category things so different as penances and good works; whereby he has exposed himself to much reproach; many, while rejecting the former as pertaining to superstition, being jealous for the latter as belonging to morality, and what to undervalue is Antinomianism.

But, if we would do justice to the great Reformer, we must read his pleadings for faith as we read St Paul's commendation of charity. The place which the

Apostle claims for charity, or love, accords exactly with the place which Luther claims for that faith which worketh by love. Good works are related to charity as its proper outward form. They are related to faith as its proper outward fruit. Being really good they mar not the purity of the love which they express, while they are an outgoing of its life, which tends to the developing and strengthening of that life. Being really good they mar not the simplicity of the faith of which they are the fruit; rather, as an experience of the Divine Power of faith, they strengthen faith, deepening, as by a special additional evidence, the confidence with which it is held. "He that believeth on the Son of God hath the witness in himself," viz., a witness "that God hath given to us eternal life," in addition to the witness of God which is presupposed, and which faith accepts. But good works of which the praise is not thus given to God, and which are contemplated, not as adding to our obligations to God, but as bringing Him under obligations to us, only hinder faith as they must also hinder charity.

To this light it is that we must take Luther's teaching if we would understand his including good works with penances in his denunciations. Even the more refined teaching "that faith to be accepted must be perfected by charity," he saw to be still a marring of the simplicity of faith - a distraction of the regard of the spirit from the object of faith. The faith whose power to inspire confidence towards God is suspended, waiting for the consciousness of a supplement of feeling, is not that faith of love which quickens love. Of this Luther had the clearest discernment in the light not of a severe logic, though it is consonant with the severest logic, but of a deep personal existence - the experience first, of the mental agony he endured while engaged in the anxious attempt to perfect faith in the use of all the discipline prescribed for that end; and then, of the happy emancipation of his spirit as soon as he had fixed his exclusive regards on the Cross of Christ:- an experience identical with that which Bunyan gives as that of his pilgrim when he came in sight of the Cross and the burden which he bore fell of itself from his back.

The Divine acceptance of faith has as its counterpart in him that believes peace with God and joy in God, a peace and joy proportioned to the simplicity and strength of the faith from which they spring. This aspect of Luther's teaching we must realise if we would understand its power. God as revealed in Christ asks our undivided trust. But may this be an assured personal trust? Luther's reply was Yes - a trust, the personal assurance and peace, and joy, of which has no limit in its object, but only in the clearness and steadfastness of the faith with which that object is regarded. Hence the attraction of his preaching. It drew men by the promise of perfect peace with God - a true and holy peace in harmony with the character of God. For, however much Luther's seeming depreciation of good works has been urged against him, I have no doubt that in reality his great power was that, like St Paul whose disciple he specially claimed to be, he commended himself to every man's conscience in the sight of God. The testimony of conscience was on his side in showing how empty of any real righteousness were men's endeavours by mortification and penances to commend themselves to

God. The testimony of conscience was also on his side in setting forth the true righteousness that is in faith, because faith gives His true glory to God.

The conception of faith working by love is exceedingly simple - love believed operating in him who believes effects according to its own nature; the measure of the result of good being the strength and steadfastness and purity of the faith. Self-consciousness is necessarily present and is an element in our understanding of the love revealed. It is love to us taking its form from what we are: "God commendeth His love toward us, in that, while we were yet sinners, Christ died for us." But our self-consciousness is simply that of recipients of love, helped to understand love by what they feel themselves to be, while all our feelings towards God are unmixedly what His love quickens. Any element of confidence or hope originating otherwise, originating in anything individual, anything because of which a man separates himself from others is a foreign admixture, hindering the purity of faith, and so weakening its power for good.

Here let us realise that the exclusiveness of the mind's regard as fixed on God's revelation of Himself in Christ being preserved, no measure of personal confidence towards God can be too great, and all jealousy of such confidence, as if it were inconsistent with humility is only possible when that which is so judged is not understood. We cannot be too jealous of foreign elements mingling with the confidence of faith, but this, and this alone, is here a legitimate jealousy. As, in the light of God in Christ, we cannot be uncertain whether it is the light of truth; so also, when we are yielding to that light the obedience of faith, we cannot be uncertain as to whether that is Eternal Life which that faith is quickening in us. And just as, being in the light of the Truth, we refuse the demand made in the name of the church that we should suspend our confidence that it is the truth, until the church has sealed it with her authority; so, in experiencing the power of the Truth to inspire confidence towards God, we refuse the corresponding demand that we should suspend our confidence in God's acceptance of us, until we have availed ourselves of the church's help and guidance for the perfecting of faith. "Where is there room for the grace of humility?" is the question urged, when our obedience to divine light is regarded as presumptuous confidence in our own judgment. This question is repeated, when our joy in that personal assurance of God's acceptance which accompanies the response of faith to the divine love is assumed to be an unwarranted self-complacency in our own conscious state before God. But, as it is true humility to believe, so is it true humility to rejoice in that which we believe. "My soul shall make her boast in the Lord: the humble shall hear thereof, and be glad."

I have said that, if we would do justice to the great Reformer, we must look at his commendation of faith as we do at St Paul's commendation of charity. Commendations of faith have not that ready response which commendations of charity, at least of charity as love to man, seem to command. I believe that this is so because we are more alive to what is wanting in the feelings of man to man, than to what is wanting in the feelings of man to God. It is not indeed in the pure light of the love due from man to man that men are speaking when they are able so readily and almost self-complacently to praise charity; for in the light of love the sense of short-coming and self-condemnation would be their prevailing feeling, yet there is no doubt that the obligation of love to man is more generally felt than the obligation to faith in God, or love to God either. But what I feel is that, as in the light of love, *i.e.* of love as love to God and love to man, we assuredly feel that St Paul's teaching in chapter xiii. of his first Epistle to the Corinthians is so full of self-evidencing light that we regard it as giving him a claim on our faith as far above that of the miracles which he wrought as he himself places charity above miracles, so also the true teaching of faith has upon it as unmistakeable a divine mark as the true teaching of love. The attitude of the spirit towards God in faith is so truly its right and most excellent attitude - the highest, purest, and most perfect consciousness of being in one possessing a derived being - that the demand for it is felt to be made in pure light, and he who makes it is felt to be holding forth the word of life. "God raised Christ from the dead and gave Him glory that our faith and hope might be in God;" and though charity be greater than faith or hope, being fellowship in what God is, for God is love, yet are faith and hope precious in themselves, as well as in their relation to the charity which they feed (and which doubtless feeds and strengthens them in return), and we can no more doubt that we are hearing the very truth of God when we are being taught faith in God and hope towards God, than when we are taught love to God.

I, therefore, feel Luther's teaching of faith to commend Luther as a true witness for God, as Saint Paul's teaching of charity is felt to commend him: which is indeed, to claim for St Paul, whose disciple Luther was, the same acceptance on account of his teaching of faith which we accord to him on account of his teaching of charity.

In considering the present reaction against the Reformation and movement towards Romanism, no conviction is more strongly impressed on my mind than that, if we would deal with it hopefully, we must revert to the Reformation controversy in its pure essence - I mean, the teaching of Justification by Faith truly understood. And we shall revert to it with the greater advantage if we have advanced in the true understanding of the faith to which the Gospel calls us. There is no doubt that the forensic character of the systematic theology of the Reformers is to be traced to inadequacy in their conception of the grace which the Gospel reveals; to their not understanding that the Son reveals the Father in order that the faith of the revelation may quicken in us the life of sonship; that the faith of Christ is subjectively the fellowship of Christ's own faith; that the footprints of Christ in which we are to tread are the footprints of His faith; and that it is thus that we are to understand the example which He has set before us that we should walk in His steps.

But here the words suggest themselves, "First cast out the beam out of thine own eye; and then shalt thou see clearly to cast out the mote out of thy brother's eye." If the church before the Reformation marred the doctrine of Justification by Faith by that teaching which contemplated the perfecting of faith by charity - practically sealing the fountain of love by demanding the consciousness of love as a prerequisite to opening it; the Protestant portion of the church since the Reformation has not less certainly hindered the true life and power of faith by demanding charity and other Christian graces as fruits of faith, the consciousness of which is made a prerequisite to the free breathing of the assured life of faith in its personal confidence towards God. The Schoolmen could not trust faith to produce charity: the Divines of the Reformation schools can trust it as little, though the form of system in which they have severally manifested their distrust be different.

Distrust in the power of faith to produce love is distrust in the power of God's revelation of Himself in Christ to renew us after His own image - distrust, therefore, in the spiritual process of which the Apostle speaks: "But we all, with open face, beholding as in a glass the glory of the Lord, are changed into the same image from glory to glory, even as by the Spirit of the Lord." Such distrust, however impossible to us while in the exercise of living faith, is nevertheless what we are constantly tempted to when objects of faith become forms of dogmatic thought, and when, further, the holding of dogmatic truth takes the shape of a religious duty, and steadfastness in so holding it and zeal in contending for it come to be to us as our great debt to the truth. Nothing is more marvellous than the practical powerlessness of truth so held, and I have often felt how one tear of Jesus traced by faith up to its fountain in the heart of God would have a power to inspire confidence towards God which the mere reception of the fullest doctrinal conceptions of His atoning sacrifice for sin has not.

The present wide spread awakenedness of mind on the subject of religion may ultimately result in men's reverting to the simplicity of faith; but this is not its immediate operation. The first effect of an increased sense of the importance of our relation to God is usually practical. That we are not enjoying peace with God - are not having as sure hold of His favour, suggests a doubt not as to our knowledge of God but as to the use we are making of that knowledge. We assume that we have faith, and we go on to add to it whatever we are taught is needed for the completeness of our character as Christians. The practical work thus engaged in can in no measure supply what is all the while really lacking in our faith. The best result that can arise from our activity will be the experience of disappointment, the finding that all our doings are not bringing us nearer to that peace with God the desire for which first moved us. How should they? Not what God is to us or feels to us has been occupying our mind, but what we are presenting to Him - our measure of response to the demands which we understand him to be making on us. If disappointment have the result of sending us back to reconsider what we can our faith, to look steadfastly at the great facts which the Gospel professes to reveal to us, and to examine ourselves as to our realisation of them, and of the light they shed on our relation to God, on his mind towards us and on the response to that mind due from us - if we thus come under the power of the love of God, we enter into the peace and joy of believing, and reach at once that rest in God, the pursuit of which by exertions of our own has been so vain; while at the same time we receive light and strength for a true devotedness to God and to goodness in the fellowship of the life of Christ. This or some measure of this result will be our true gain. Some measure, I say, for it is not always the case that the full and clear understanding of what has been wanting in our faith is the result of the honest endeavour to add to our assumed faith good works. Our awakening to the sense of our actual ignorance of mind of God towards us, and the dawning light of what that mind is, may be very partial and at broken intervals and pure trust in God and deliverance from self-righteousness may be but very gradually developing in us; but the measure of our gain will clearly be, not the measure in which we have accumulated acts of outward goodness, but the measure in which we have been attaining to a pure and childlike trust in the Father of our spirits.

But other results of the disappointment experienced in our blind attempts at building a superstructure of religion without a foundation of living faith may ensue; and we are not to be surprised if among these we meet on the one hand conversions from Protestantism to Romanism or on the other departures to infidelity. The question, "What is religion doing for you?" when the answer is not one that can satisfy, may either turn us for hope to all the appliances by which the older church has supplemented its dogmatism, promising from submission to its guidance the comfort and peace which all it has taught concerning Christ has not imparted; or it may lead us to question the truth of the creeds which, held so long without questioning, have done so little for our spirits.

And here I feel the importance of the original protest of the first Reformers against the "general and doubtsome faith," of the Church of Rome. I have said that the Divines of the Reformation have not proved more able than the Schoolmen to trust the native power of faith - that devices have been had recourse to, to secure that faith shall be of the right kind, which in effect hinder the simple exercise of faith as much as the Schoolmen's demand for a faith perfected by charity; while practically the general and doubtsome faith protested against prevails in Protestant as well as in Roman Catholic countries. Yet that protest is an important gain, and the system in which it has been a starting point has an immeasurable superiority over that which made a "general and doubtsome faith" not only permissible, but alone *logically* possible. I refer to the doctrine that the atonement had special reference to original sin, while satisfaction for personal sin remained to be made in the form of penance - personal sin calling for personal satisfaction in some form or other; for this doctrine precluded the possibility of peace with God as an immediate result of faith. Original sin usually is present to men's minds, if thought of at all, as a dogma, not as a consciousness. It is to actual personal sin that the rebukes of conscience and the feeling of the need of forgiveness refer. This remains true even when actual sin most reveals to the sinner the corruption which it indicates. And, therefore, all the interest of the desire for pardon and for peace with God is by this system diverted from Christ and the forgiveness preached through Him to the forms of personal satisfaction for personal sins which the church prescribes. That penances, or any other means of peacemaking prescribed, are represented as accepted for Christ's sake, and so have their virtue connected with the merits of His great sacrifice for sin, does not alter the case. Whatever has been done *for* him, the anxious awakened sinner's interest is absorbed in what remains to be done *by* him; and, as the strength of a chain is measured not by its strongest but by its weakest link, so here does the measure of actual peace turn, not on the faith of which Christ is the object, but on the personal satisfaction rendered, whatever its form.

I use the word "*logically*" because I wish to be understood as speaking of the system, and not as questioning the reality of pure faith in God and joy in Christ attained to by so many, the form of whose religion has been determined by that system, but the essence of whose religion has in truth contradicted it. An early member of the Society of Friends, writing to a brother who was a Roman Catholic says, "Your religion and my religion must be the same in so far as we have religion, for there is but one religion." This true and deep word we are gradually learning to understand.

NOTE TO CHAPTER VI

"Mediatorial Religion" - *National Review* for April 1856

Those of my readers who are acquainted with this able review of the first edition of this book will expect some notice of it in a new edition.

The reviewer quotes (p. 495) my words (p. 137 of this edition): "All the elements of a perfect repentance in humanity for all the sin of man - a perfect sorrow - a perfect contrition - all the elements of such a repentance and that in absolute perfection - all - *excepting the personal consciousness of sin*." He proceeds to add, "This exception however contains just the essential element of the whole." That which is thus excepted is indeed an element necessarily present in a personal repentance for conscious guilt; and had I represented what Christ felt and confessed to the Father as a *substitute* for repentance in us, offered to the Father to save us from the necessity of repenting, as Christ has been represented as bearing the punishment of our sins as a substitute to save us from punishment, the reviewer's question "Is vicarious contrition at all more conceivable than vicarious retribution?" would have been apposite, and a fatal objection to my whole conception of the atonement. But this is not my teaching; and all that I have represented as the atonement remains untouched by his question.

I will not repeat what I have stated so fully in the text as the elements of the atonement. Is what I have ascribed to Christ truly and justly so ascribed? And, if so, is what is thus truly and justly ascribed to Christ to be regarded as an atonement for the sin of man? Both questions may be answered affirmatively, or the former question may be answered in the affirmative and the latter in the negative, or both may be answered negatively, according as I have commended my own faith to my readers entirely, or partially, or not at all. But the objection of the reviewer is rather to my use, though guarded, of the word repentance, than to the view I have taken of the nature of the atonement. That word will have its full meaning in the personal experience of every one who accepts in faith the atonement (as now represented); for every such individual sinner will *add* the *"excepted"* element of *"personal consciousness of sin."* But, if the consciousness of such repentant sinner be analysed, it will be found that all that is morally true and spiritual and acceptable to God in his repentance is an amen to Christ's condemnation of his sin, and that all the hope towards God, because of which his repentance is free and pure and imbued with the spirit of sonship, is equally traceable to the revelation of the heart of the Father in His acceptance of the Son's confession and intercession on man's behalf.

In his next paragraph the reviewer goes on to say - "Further: it seems a paradox to say with our author, that true repentance is impossible to man, who alone needs it: and can be realised only by the Son of God, in whom there is no room for it. It would indeed be a hopeless realm to live in, which should annex to all sins both an imperative demand and an absolute disqualification for adequate contrition, and first open the fountain of availing tears in holy natures that have none to shed." I have said that a true and adequate realisation of sin and confession of its evil in perfect response to the Divine mind and in perfect accordance with the moral truth of things has existed in humanity only in the Divine mind itself, as the mind of the Son in humanity. I have *not* said that repentance, including the personal element which I have excepted, has been present in the mind of the sinless one or was possible to him. As to the other part of the paradox ascribed to me, I have not spoken of repentance as impossible to the sinner *absolutely*, but only *apart from Christ*. To man as related to Christ repentance is possible, just as holiness, and righteousness, and love are possible. "I am the way and the truth, and the life: no man cometh unto the Father, but by me." Surely in this living way repentance is a step - the first. The spirit of the Son is in the purpose "I will arise and go to my Father." To conceive it a hardship that repentance should only thus be possible is to conceive it a hardship to exist in a world in which it can be said, "There is none good but one, that is, God" - a hardship to exist where fellowship in the divine mind implies participation in the divine nature.

As my use of the word repentance, however guarded, has come to suggest a seeming objection to my conception of the atonement, which yet does not touch that conception at all, I may here give the history of my using it. It is about forty years since the moral and spiritual nature of the atonement first dawned on my mind. What was then prominent in my faith and in my teaching was the Universality of the Atonement, and the assured peace with God which is quickened by the faith of the forgiveness of sins revealed in the Gospel. But my attention was drawn to the nature of the atonement in tracing out the moral and spiritual power of faith in it, and in considering its immediate and direct object of bringing us to God. This element in my teaching, however, was not included when that teaching was called in question. But subsequently it more and more occupied my thoughts; gradually, through many years, taking the form which it presents in this book, viz. a moral and spiritual atonement, and which was such in itself - not simply accepted as such because of the moral excellence manifested in Christ in making it. St Bernard speaks of the merits of Christ's death being the mind in which He died; and recent Roman Catholic writers dwell on the merits of Christ's satisfaction and sacrifice for sin, speaking of the relation of the excellence that was in Him to us and our demerits in a way that, though free from the charge of legal fiction, has in it the essence of that imputation of righteousness with which they reproach the divines of the Reformation. I have not thus conceived of merit counter-balancing demerit, any more than of penal suffering substituted for punishment. That the self-sacrifice present in it has been the atoning virtue of Christ's sacrifice is a form of this conception of merit which commends itself to some; though perhaps rather as a part of the *man-ward* aspect of the atonement, than as its power to prevail with God. Love is the life in which the atonement was made, and self-sacrifice, which is of the essence of love (though "self-sacrifice" is not an adequate definition of love), is the form in which love is seen in the atonement. But the atonement is such, not because of the self-sacrificing love manifested in it, but as that love taking a form determined by our need as God's offspring alienated from Him by sin.

A continually deepening sense of the importance of the conclusions at which I had arrived on this great subject at last induced me to write on it. And as a preparation for this task, I thought it right to acquaint myself as much as possible with the state of mind on the subject of the atonement in which I might expect to find religious men. In the reading which had this object I was led to consider more closely than I had previously done that teaching of Luther, of the older Calvinists, and of the modern Calvinists, to the consideration of which I have devoted three chapters of this book.

My endeavour was to discern any element of truth present in what I read, and to separate it from the error with which it might be combined; and thus, the words of President Edwards, "either an equivalent punishment or an equivalent sorrow and repentance," suggested to me that that earnest and deep thinker had really been on the verge of that conception of a moral and spiritual atonement which was occupying my own thoughts. Hence the use I have made of the thought of the alternative of repentance as it passed before the mind of Edwards; not for a moment forgetting the absence of the sense of personal guilt in all that I ascribed to Christ, but seeing that this took not from the adequacy of the atonement which I conceived of Him as making; while the presence of such a consciousness, had it been possible, would have altogether changed the character of His work as a suffering, "the just for the unjust." I did not anticipate misconception. Both my positive statements as to the response of the divine mine in the Son to the divine mind in the Father in relation to our sins, and my distinct recognition of the absence of the element of personal consciousness of guilt, made it impossible for me to do so.

The reviewer regards me as, while rejecting legal fictions, myself introducing a moral fiction. Of this I certainly had no consciousness or suspicion; nor does the fairest weighing of what he has written of which I am capable enable me to see that to this I have made any approach. I can see no moral fiction in my conception of the divine mind in Christ in His response to the divine mind in the Father in relation to our sins, for it implies no fictitious consciousness in Christ, as if He were feeling our sin personally and literally His own. I can see no moral fiction in the response to the Son's confession of our sins and intercession for us which I have ascribed to the Father, as if, while so responding, He were not seeing the Son in His personal separation from sin, or were hearing His confession as the confession of personal guilt. Any such fictions, conceived of as in the mind of the Son or of the Father, would destroy my whole conception of the atonement. I can see no moral fiction in the consciousness of the believing recipient of the grace of God; for the "forgiveness that is with God that He may be feared" has come to him in the form of Divine light - a revelation of the Father by the Son, reconciling him to God by the power of what was in the Father's heart towards him while a sinner. The reviewer says (p. 497), in reference to personal repentance, "In proportion as the soul is pierced with a sharper contrition, and attains a deeper and clearer insight into her own unfaithful disorder, will the inherent impossibility of any foreign exchange of righteousness become apparent, and the desire to be shielded from punishment will pass away: nor is the conscience truly awakened which does not rather rush into the arms of its just anguish than start back and fly away." The reviewer will be prepared for my disclaiming the faith of "any foreign exchange for righteousness." As to the "passing away" of the "desire to be shielded from punishment," I seem to myself to enter into both the words, "I will bear the indignation of the Lord, because I have sinned against Him," and the words, "If Thou, Lord, shouldest mark iniquities, O Lord, who shall stand?" But if the "just anguish" of "the conscience truly awakened" be what the reviewer contemplates as the "punishment" from which to be "shielded," the repentant sinner, whose repentance is, in the language of ordinary religious speech, not legal but evangelical, assuredly does not "start back and fly away" from it, although he does not "rush into its arms," as if his hope, under the quickened sense of sin, were from the anguish of his repentance, and not from the forgiveness of sin in which he believes. Whatever quickening of conscience he may have attained antecedent to faith, it has been as nothing in comparison with what, in the light of redeeming love, he is now experiencing; light which at once reveals the evil of sin and gives strength to look steadfastly at it.

I should have been tempted to regret my noticing at all the idea of an alternative repentance, as it passed before the mind of Edwards, could I refer to my doing so any obscuring of the perception of my view of a moral and spiritual atonement for sin to so acute a mind as that of this reviewer, as I should also regret what I have said of Luther's teaching could I accept, as I cannot, the reviewer's theory of his so insisting on the use of the pronoun "*our*." But any inadequacy in his apprehension of my view of the atonement I refer to a condition of his own mind which makes the great measure of his understanding of what I have written surprising, as well as his patience in labouring to understand it what gives him a claim on my thanks. He says (p. 497) "we are firmly convinced that the doctrine of *mediation*, - in the strict sense implying transactions with God on behalf of men, as *well as* in the opposite direction - cannot be harmonized with the modern *individualism*." Understanding, as I do, what he thus designates as the modern individualism as a form of metaphysical or psychological thought on the subject of personality accepted by the reviewer, which precludes the possibility of a dealing with God on behalf of men by Christ, my endeavour to shed light on the atonement has been to him the attempt to illustrate and commend an impossibility. I do not know enough of the nature of the difficulty which his conception of individualism placed in the way of his receiving the full impression of what I have written to attempt to deal with that difficulty directly. In reading the latter part of this review, I have felt that the "individualism" and the "realism" of which he speaks have been to me a Scylla and a Charybdis, between which I have steered in the *dark*, unconsciously, while I trust safely. I have had no conception of an "individualism" which made my personality to cut me off from Christ that I could not, except by a moral or legal fiction, represent Him to myself as under the pressure of my sins, both confessing them before the Father, and pleading with the Father on my behalf. I had no conception of a "realism" which represented humanity as one whole in such a sense as would have lost to me my personality, or would have helped me to the faith of an atonement by justifying me in looking upon Christ, as "realism" appears to the reviewer to have led Luther to do, as *literally* "the one sinner," chargeable, therefore, with all the sins of all partakers in humanity.

The reviewer believes that, if I "follow out the natural tendencies and affinities of my faith, I must rest exclusively at last in the other half of the doctrine which exhibits the *dealing with man on behalf of God*." The other half of the doctrine has not to my mind that adequacy as a witnessing for God to man apart from the first half which it has to the reviewer's mind. In meditating on the perfection of humanity in Christ I have often felt as if that very perfection was a pleading, *even were it silent*, with God for all humanity - a manifestation of a capacity in humanity having infinite preciousness in the sight of God, and the purpose and desire to realise which would necessarily have been present in His heart, even had not that purpose and desire already existed and manifested itself in the incarnation of which that perfection was the result. But I have not conceived of this perfection as what *could* be silent. On the contrary, I have conceived of it as what must have moved Him in whom it was a consciousness to all that I have represented as the atonement. Were, however, individualism that cutting off of Christ because of His personality from us, the other partakers in humanity, of which the reviewer conceives, the holy fountain of tears, which the divine mind in Christ opened in His humanity, might still have flowed, a when He wept over Jerusalem, or at the grave of Lazarus; but His tears would have had no ascending form of intercessory prayer, reaching to the heart of the Father. His consciousness of individuality would have as to our sin imposed on Him silence towards God, forbidding Him to plead with God for men, though it might have left Him free to witness to men for God in His personal bearing towards men. But, in that case, even the witnessing to men for God must have been imperfect, must have left untold all that mind of God which Christ's making His soul an offering for sin, and the Father's accepting thereof, have brought into manifestation. As spirits, our spiritual cleansing can only be through the power of spiritual light, entering into us in faith: and whatever spiritual element in the blood that cleanses, or whatever ray of the light of the mind of God shining in the death of Christ for our sins is left out must take so much from the cleansing power of faith.

As to the "tendencies and affinities of my faith," I have no response to the impression expressed by the reviewer; while any development of my sense of personality into his conception of individualism would, I feel, take from me, not only all that is retrospective, but also all that is prospective in my faith in the atonement - my faith in Christ as my life as well as my faith in Christ as having died for me. He speaks (p. 498) of us as "breaking through the restraints of the modern individualism" when we "strive to enter into that literal identification of Christ with Christians which is so frequent with St Paul." In the words of St Paul, "I am crucified with Christ: nevertheless I live; yet not, I but Christ liveth in me: and the life which I now life in the flesh I live by the faith of the Son of God, who loved me, and gave Himself for me," the assumption of the relation of Christ to humanity along with a recognition of our personal individuality, presents to my mind no aspect of contradiction; while my sense of the redeeming love for which I am a debtor requires for its fulness, alike the personal consciousness of the words "Who loved *me* and gave Himself *for me*," and the faith of personal union with Christ of the words "I live, yet not I, but Christ liveth in me." All St Paul's representations of our relation to Christ are pervaded by the same element of what, in the light of modern individualism, would, it appears, be regarded as a contradiction; and this the reviewer seems to recognise as the fact.

It is a natural result of recent modifications of men's conception of inspiration that criticism is seen passing from the *words* of inspired writers to their *thoughts*. Whatever abuse may be connected with this change, it is not without some advantage; in as much as the words of the sacred writers now run less risk of being twisted or distorted. So long as we contend for the divine truth of the words, there is a temptation to force them to say what we are willing to believe, and resistance to light may take this form. But this temptation ceases if men feel at liberty to receive their natural meaning without being obliged to receive it as absolute truth. And this liberty those critics obviously reach who feel that an apostle may have meant what he seems to mean, but may have been mistaken because of the limits within which he thought. This new freedom in criticism removes questions of truth from the realm of philology to that of psychology and metaphysics. While we are detained in the former, our Lord's words, "I am the vine, ye are the branches: . . . . without me ye can do nothing," could be emptied of their literal meaning only by being read as what might express our obligations to our Lord as a teacher, and not our relation to Him as our life. But now the latter may be recognised as the meaning with which they were written, while still it may be refused as, if not implying an error in our Lord's own thinking, at least implying such an error in St John; whose conception of his Lord's teaching, it will be said, is all that remains to us, while that conception may have been affected by any such ignorance of the true nature of personality on the part of St John, as the realism ascribed to Luther. So also as to St Paul's saying, "When it pleased God, who separated me from my mother's womb, and called me by His grace, *to reveal His Son in me*," his words may be received as meaning what they seem to mean, while that meaning itself may be refused because in contradiction to modern individualism, and no presence of Christ in St Paul be conceived of but as men might speak of a presence of Socrates in Plato. With a due sense of our intellectual limits, a due reverence for conscience, and the faith that spiritual things are only spiritually discerned, I should have no fear of psychology or of metaphysical thought, even in its most difficult region of ontology, any more than I have of scientific investigation, so long as it is realised that, "through faith we know that the worlds were framed by the word of God." Science, venturing beyond its due limits, may seem to itself entitled to sweep away our faith in the supernatural, and so speculation in the region of mind, going beyond its due limit, may preclude faith in the atonement by the assumed impossibility of such a thing in consistency with the manner of our being as persons. But, as Science never can reveal the living God to us, nor by its analysis reach to anything, visible or invisible - a palpable material substance, or a force of which our senses can take no cognisance, and the existence of which is to us inferential - of which it can say, "This is God;" so neither can metaphysical thought reveal to us the manner of our own being as God's offspring, who live and move and have our being in Him, or the relations to us into which the Eternal Son has come that He might be in us the life of Sonship.

NOTE TO CHAPTER XIII

The Death of Christ

I have endeavoured in this chapter to express what I am able to see of light in Christ's tasting death - for our sins - in the eternal life.

The sinless dying for sin is that in the history of Christ's suffering, the just for the unjust, which most approaches the conception of the innocent being punished for the guilty. We feel also that *His tasting death, the wages of sin*, is that in the experience of Christ in His bearing of our sins which is most out of sight to us. In those elements of the atonement which were purely conditions of the mind of Christ, however much we must feel that we come infinitely short in our realisation of them *because* we come infinitely short of the mind that was in Him, yet, partaking in it all even in the smallest measure, we know as to its essence what that mind was:- just as when we say "God is love" we, if in any measure dwelling in love, use the words in true light, though the love of which we speak is infinite and passeth knowledge. But there was that in Christ's tasting death the wages of sin as to which we have not the same consciousness; while we understand how this was a perfecting of the divine response in humanity to the divine condemnation of sin.

Yet whatever remains dark to us as going beyond our consciousness, our attention is kept ever fixed on the death of Christ, as it is on His resurrection from the dead; the one in relation to the remission of sins, as the other in relation to the gift of eternal life.

I have ventured to speak of what the atonement might have been, had we been only spirits, and how Christ's bearing of our sins on His Spirit before the Father, confessing them, and making intercession for us according to the will of God, needed to be perfected in His death for our sins because of the manner of our being as partakers in flesh and blood. (Heb. ii. 14) Our redemption has two aspects - distinct, while inseparably related. It is the history of spirits, God's offspring, alienated from Him to whom the light of life has come in the revelation of their own evil state, and of the holy love of the Father in what that love has felt regarding them in their alienation; the knowledge of themselves and of their God shining to them in the mediation of the Son of God, and quickening in them the life of Sonship in raising them to that eternal life which is communion with the Father and the Son in the Spirit; - this, if we may venture to contemplate it apart, is the aspect of our redemption as *spirits*.

The other aspect of our redemption is that which it presents to us when we take into view the whole of our composite being, and the meaning in relation to it of the words "The wages of sin is death; but the gift of God is eternal life through Jesus Christ our Lord." "For since by man came death, by man came also the resurrection of the dead." This looking at the history of our redemption first as we are spirits, and then in the totality of our being as men, I feel to have some help in it in considering the death of Christ for our sins and our resurrection from the dead through Him, as also our present relation to Him as having died in Him and having our lives hid with Christ in God. We see on the one hand sin and death, on the other righteousness and resurrection from the dead. We see ourselves related to both; to what is on the one side in being sinners, to what is on the other side as partakers in redemption. We pass from the one to the other through the death and resurrection of Christ. Thus our individual existences and histories are not, so to speak, a number of parallel lines, each first in darkness - the darkness of sin and death, and then in light - the light of righteousness and the resurrection life; on the contrary the lines of our being converge in Christ's death and radiate from Christ's resurrection.

This is a very imperfect image, but may help us in conceiving our relation to Christ as distinguished from a manner of being in which we would be all separate individualities, each having its own history of first tasting sin, and sorrow, and death: and then righteousness, and a resurrection life. The distinction which I am trying to mark becomes more palpable if we contrast the idea of each individual man as passing through his successive stages of being in the isolation presented to us in the history of the insect which we see as a caterpillar, a chrysalis, and a butterfly, with that relation to Christ in which we exist - sin and death ours - righteousness and life His - and He coming into such relations to our sin and death as issue in our partaking in His righteousness and life. I know that the former conception has found more acceptance with some men in their speculative thinking on the subject of humanity. The latter, however, is what the Scriptures present to us. It is very clear as also very practical in the teaching of the first founders of the Church, and has continued to be the teaching of the Church all along, though presented in various aspects, and often representing our relation to Christ in a way that has been artificial and forensic - a mere arrangement, and not what affects the manner of our being to its inmost depths.

I have used an image for illustration, from which I expect some help, but which is indeed very imperfect. A part of its imperfection lies in this, that our relation to Christ does not *begin* in resurrection; for He who is in the resurrection and the life is present in us, our true and proper life from the first, and is to be known by us as our life now in the spirit; while the perfecting of our participation in Him waits for our resurrection from the dead in spiritual bodies like to His glorious body. Now we know Christ as our true life, as it is written "God hath given to us eternal life and this life is in His Son. He that hath the Son hath life," while our faith and hope embrace the perfecting of the gift of eternal life when this corruptible shall put on incorruption, and this mortal immortality.

We must be thankful that a deeper understanding of our relations to Christ, and conviction that the manner of our being can only be understood in their light, is taking the place of former superficial and merely forensic representations of these relations. This is a fruit of that change in our faith in the divinity of Christ which I have noticed above (Introduction), viz., the change of regarding the incarnation not so much as a mystery, the faith of which tests the humility of our reason, as rather light in which to exercise our reason in all our thinking regarding our relation to God and the manner of our being as His offspring. Approaching from this side the death and resurrection of the Lord Jesus, and the relation of His death to our sins and of His resurrection to our participation in His righteousness, we come to see these events in the development of the incarnation in our redemption as the first Christians saw them, and to understand the constant references to them which meet us in what we possess of the teaching of the Apostles, and the practical nature of these references, and the *immediate and direct power* which the faith of Christ's dying for their sins, and being raised again for their justification, have had in determining the manner of their religion, and causing it to be a fellowship in the mind of Christ. "Forasmuch then as Christ hath suffered for us in the flesh, arm yourselves likewise with the same mind." "For in that He died, He died unto sin once: but in that He liveth, He liveth unto God. Likewise reckon ye also yourselves to be dead unto sin, but alive unto God through Jesus Christ our Lord."

In tracing our Lord's life on to its close as the two threads of sonship towards God and brotherhood towards man, I have marked, as the last ray of its light as brotherhood to man, the prayer in death "Father forgive them for they know not what they do;" the light in this prayer being bright to us in proportion as we realise the shame of the Cross, and all He suffered at the hands of wicked men. In like manner, the eternal life in which He tasted death as it was sonship towards the Father is last visible to us in the prayer "Father into thy hands I commend my spirit." The trial through which the faith which these words express had borne the Son of God, in that tasting of death by which death has been abolished, rests in part to us under the "darkness which was over all the land" from "the sixth hour unto the ninth hour" while the intensity of that trial is indicated by the cry "my God my God, why has thou forsaken me?" I have gone (Chap. xii) to the Psalm from which these words are quoted for what light it may shed on this most solemn darkness; and I appear to myself to have found help in it. But even if my readers feel otherwise, and that my understanding of the Psalm has not commended itself to them, they may still feel that, whatever remaining darkness we may be conscious to, even when most light falls for us on the death of Christ for our sins, we must guard against the temerity that would put into that darkness what is not revealed to have been in it, and what is not in harmony with what we are enabled to see in it. With this temerity those, surely, are chargeable who have placed in that darkness an experience on the part of the Son of wrath from the Father either commensurate with or an equivalent for the everlasting torments regarded as the punishment of the wicked. Apart from other objections, we must feel that such an element in the cup given to Christ to drink would have overborne all other elements, and made the place given to these by the sacred writer inexplicable (Heb. xii. 1). But the expressions, Cross of Christ, blood of Christ, death of Christ, could never have been read as covering such a meaning were it not for the error of thinking of death the wages of sin as death temporal, spiritual and eternal. Let any one weigh the words "He tasted death for every man" and then ask himself "does death here mean death temporal, spiritual and eternal," and he will feel it impossible to give an affirmative answer.

Mr Oxenham says in reference to the teaching of the Reformers on the subject of the atonement (p. 119):* "It was but the natural and logical inference from this strange notion of vicarious substituted punishment, that Christ endured in His Passion the pains of Hell; and this blasphemous corollary is distinctly put forward by Quenstedt, Gerhard and Calvin, as a necessary part of the idea of satisfaction. Well might Bellarmine call it a new and unheard-of heresy!" New in this definite and repulsive form it may have been; yet the language used in connection with the idea of Christ's paying the debt we owe to the divine justice, and the earlier idea of His paying a ransom for us to Satan, may well have prepared the way for the conception thus denounced. Besides, men's occupation of mind with the recorded sufferings of Christ had been so much with their physical aspect and simply as sufferings, without the discernment of any higher nature in them in respect of which they were a sacrifice for sin, that there was no protection from any exaggerated form of thought on the subject of Christ's sufferings for our sins: while the difference of view between the church and the Reformers as to the relation of the atonement to sin - the former limiting that relation to original sin, the latter holding it "to be a sacrifice not only for original guilt, but also for the actual sins of men" - naturally tended to

---

* Henry N.Oxenham, *The Catholic Doctrine of the Atonement*, pp.119-120.

the extremest conception on the part of the Reformers of what was implied in Christ's paying the debt we owe to the justice of God.

The Reformers felt that a divided confidence, resting in part on the atonement, in part on what we did ourselves to obtain remission of our actual sins, could never be a true peace with God. For they felt that the part thus assigned to man himself was one as to which it was impossible to be assured that it was adequately performed; nay, as to which it was self-ignorance ever to hope for such an assurance, seeing that all increase of true self-knowledge deepened the conviction that we could bring nothing to God in this way worthy of His acceptance. Even the love to Christ which men's occupation with His sufferings for them was fitted to quicken they found to be hindered by the motive for cultivating it, viz. the perfecting their faith by charity (Note to chapter II). On the other hand they found that in looking for forgiveness of sin exclusively to Christ and His sacrifice for sin, they tasted at once the liberty of the faith of forgiven sin, and entered into a peace with God of which these were the elements, a sense of His infinite love and free grace, and of their own utter unworthiness.

A sense of the infinite love and free grace of God and of our own sin as what casts us altogether for hope on that grace, and a consequent exclusive trust in Christ - these were the living elements of the faith of the Reformers. And we cannot allow that faith or their work to be depreciated because in their conceptions of the sacrifice of Christ for sin they developed the idea of Christ paying the debt which we owed to divine justice in a form and repulsiveness of which we do not deny, or because the doctrine of merit in Christ compensating demerit in us was developed by them into that of imputation of righteousness.

I have said (Note to II) that a successful dealing with the present reaction in favour of Romanism can only be through our reverting to the Reformation question of justification by faith alone; and that it should be more easy for *us* to occupy that ground in proportion as we may have attained to a higher and truer conception of Salvation - of that grace of God in Christ which faith apprehends. A moral and spiritual atonement stands in direct relation to a moral and spiritual salvation, Christ's giving Himself for our sins to our having in Him the life of Sonship. This *directness* in the relation of the remission of sins to eternal life accords and *alone* accords with the language of scripture. The death of Christ has been "the opening of a way into the holiest." "The blood of Christ, who through the Eternal Spirit offered Himself without spot to God, purges the conscience from dead works to serve the living God." "We are brought nigh to God by the death of His Son." "Christ suffered the just for the unjust that He might bring us to God." This direct reference of the sacrifice of Christ to our participation in the divine life contrasts strikingly with the conception of that sacrifice as having as its first and immediate object the bearing as our substituted the punishment of our sins. And it is because of the judicial and forensic character of the question of peace with God as that question was regarded by the Reformers that I speak of faith in the grace of God as being now cherished in a purer light, rendering faith more truly what the Apostle contemplates when he says, "We all, with open face beholding as in a glass the glory of the Lord, are changed unto the same image from glory to glory, even as by the Spirit of the Lord." When I say *now*, of course I only mean a more perfect return to faith as it was at the beginning than the Reformers attained. We do not retrace their steps; for, still less if possible than they can we allow penances or mortifications or deeds of any kind, even deeds of charity, to be any element in our confidence towards God. To know Christ as our life and that life as the life of sonship more completely shuts out from our trust in Christ all foreign elements than any meaning of the expression "trust in Christ" short of this ever could.

I may here add that as a moral and spiritual atonement is directly related to a moral and spiritual salvation, so its value is proved only in the experience of such a salvation. It is in coming to the Father by the Son that we know Christ's preciousness as the way, and the truth, and the life. Hence it follows that the habit of turning to the thought of the atonement for comfort under the sense of distance from the Father when the comfort sought is, as I may say, rather judicial than filial is injurious and to be guarded against. Such comfort is always unhealthy and foreign to the life that lies in God's favour.

I hope that some help has been added for the understanding of the immediate relation of the atonement to the life of sonship, in what in the introduction to this edition I have said of religion as the occupying of our right place in the kingdom of God. Help to occupy that place aright, not solace in not occupying it, is the bread of life that came down from Heaven that a man might eat thereof and not die. Philosophy has been called a homesickness. Christianity places us in our true home. "Thou hast been our dwelling place in all generations." The knowledge that in God we live and move and have our being is the conscious peace of home to our spirits when we know God as revealed in Christ.

LIST OF BOOKS QUOTED, WITH THE EDITIONS
FROM WHICH THE QUOTATIONS ARE TAKEN
(as in the first edition)

Commentary on the Epistle to the Galatians. By Martin Luther. London: Printed for Mathews and Leigh, Strand; by S. Gosnell, Little Queen Street. 1810.

The Works of John Owen, D.D. Edited by the Rev. William H. Goold, Edinburgh. (Vol. X.) Johnstone and Hunter, London and Edinburgh. 1852.

The Works of President Edwards, in 4 Vols. A Reprint of the Worcester Edition, with valuable Additions, and a copious General Index. New York: Leavitt, Trow and Co. 194 Broadway: London: Wiley and Putnam. 1844.

Four Discourses on the Sacrifice and Priesthood of Jesus Christ, and the Atonement and Redemption thence accruing. By John Pye Smith, D.D. F.R.S. Third Edition. London: Jackson and Walford. 1847.

Lectures on Divine Sovereignty, Election, the Atonement, Justification, and Regeneration. By George Payne, LL.D. Exeter. Second Edition.* London: James Dinnis, 62 Paternoster-row. 1838.

On the Extent of the Atonement, in its Relation to God, and the Universe. By the Rev. Thomas W. Jenkyn. Second Edition. London: John Snow, 26 Paternoster-row. 1837.

Discourses on the Nature and Extent of the Atonement of Christ, By Ralph Wardlaw, D.D. Fourth Thousand. Glasgow: James MacLehose, 83 Buchanan St. 1844.

*A Treatise on the Physical Cause of the Sufferings** of Christ, and its Relation to the principles and practice of Christianity.* By William Stroud, M.D. London: Hamilton and Adams, 33 Paternoster-row. 1847.

Institutes of Theology. By the late Thomas Chalmers, D.D. LL.D. in 2 Vols. Vol. II. Published for Thomas Constable, by Sutherland and Knox, Edinburgh. Hamilton, Adams & Co., London. 1849.

The Atoning Work of Christ. By William Thomson, M.A. Oxford.

---

*   As the second edition is not easily available, the reference on page 86 is to the first edition of 1836.

**   The actual title is *A Treatise on the Physical Cause of the Death of Christ...*

TITLES ADDED (in this edition)

The Reasonableness and Extent of Religious Reverence: A Sermon, by John Gambold, in *Works*, second edition, with an introductory Essay by Thomas Erskine. Published by Chalmers and Collins, Glasgow 1823.

The Catholic Doctrine of the Atonement: An Historical Enquiry by Henry Nutcombe Oxenham (London 1865).

The Marrow of Modern Divinity, by Edward Fisher (1645); *The Sum of Saving Knowledge* (anon.); *Reminiscences and Reflections* of McLeod Campbell, edited by his son Donald (Macmillan, 1873) - all referred to in Prof. Torrance's Introduction.

Memorials of John McLeod Campbell DD, published in 2 vols. in 1877 by Macmillan, London - referred to in the preface.

INDEX OF NAMES AND TITLES

INDEX OF SCRIPTURE REFERENCES